The 100 Greatest [Train Journeys?] in the World

Katie Wood was born and educated in Edinburgh. After university she worked freelance in public relations and journalism. Having been born to a Belgian mother, and having spent a good part of her childhood commuting between Scotland and Europe, she developed an early love of trains and travel. This led to the decision that her ideal life would be to combine her two great loves: travel and writing. She spotted a gap in the market and convinced a publisher that a book on rail travel for young people would be a good idea, and consequently she took off on an eighteen-month trip round Europe to research the guide. The resulting book *Europe by Train* is today a classic guide in its tenth successful year.

Fourteen books later, and with fifty-seven countries behind her, she is now a highly respected full-time travel writer and journalist, contributing to the *Daily Telegraph* among many other publications. She has covered every aspect of the travel industry – from back-packing on £10 a day in far-flung dangerous lands, to round-the-world first-class tours. This book draws on the benefit of her wide travel experience. She also works on a consultancy basis for airlines, tourist boards and holiday programmes in this country and abroad.

Katie Wood is married with two young sons, and lives in Perth, Scotland.

By the same author

Europe by Train
The Round the World Air Guide
European City Breaks
The Best of British Country House Hotels
Holiday Ireland
Holiday Scotland
Winter Sun
Holiday Yugoslavia
Holiday Turkey
Holiday Coastal Spain
Holiday Portugal
Holiday Greece
The Good Tourist

The 100 Greatest Holidays in the World

KATIE WOOD

Sub-Editor and Adventure Holidays Researcher:
James Ogilvie
Cities, Classic Grand Tours and Great Journeys Researcher:
Donald Greig
Best Beaches and Great Journeys Researcher:
Tessa Williams
Great Events and Activity Holidays Researcher:
Elizabeth Archer
Adventure Holidays and Best Beaches Researcher:
Tim Page

Mandarin

*To my wonderfully supportive husband,
sons and mother*

A Mandarin Paperback
THE 100 GREATEST HOLIDAYS IN THE WORLD

First published in Great Britain 1991
by Mandarin Paperbacks
Michelin House, 81 Fulham Road, London SW3 6RB

Mandarin is an imprint of the Octopus Publishing Group

Copyright © 1991 by Katie Wood

A CIP catalogue record for this title
is available from the British Library

ISBN 0 7493 0681 5

Printed and bound in Great Britain
by Cox & Wyman Ltd, Reading

This book is sold subject to the condition
that it shall not, by way of trade or otherwise,
be lent, resold, hired out, or otherwise circulated
without the publisher's prior consent in any form
of binding or cover other than that in which
it is published and without a similar condition
including this condition being imposed
on the subsequent purchaser.

Contents

Map vii
Introduction ix

GREAT JOURNEYS 1
Train Journeys
The Venice Simplon Orient Express 4
The Queen of Scots 7
Malay–Siam Royal Mail Train 9
Rajasthan Express 11
Trans-Siberian Express 14
From the Rockies to the Pacific 17
South Africa's Blue Train 20
On the Tracks of Marco Polo 22
Great Britain and Europe Express 26
Railway Travel and Photography Rail Cruises 28

Flying
Round-the-World Air Tickets 31
Concorde Flights of Fantasy 34
The Jules Verne 37

Cruising
Hebridian Princess 40
QE2 to New York 43
Round-the-World Cruises 47
Caribbean Cruising 50
Ocean Cruise Lines 53
The *Sea Goddess* 55
Norwegian Cruise Line 57
Nile Cruising 60
Fjords Cruising 63
Luxury Barging 65
The *Canberra* 67

WORLD'S BEST BEACHES 71
Mauritius 73
The Seychelles 75
The Maldives 79
Thailand 81
Malaysia 84
French Polynesia 87
Kauai 90
Bermuda 93
The Bahamas 96
Antigua 99
Trinidad and Tobago 101
Jamaica 103
St Vincent and the Grenadines 106
Barbados 109
St Kitts and Nevis 113
The British Virgin Islands 116
Mombasa 119

CITIES 123
New York 126
London 129
Paris 133
Venice 137
Vienna 140
Hong Kong 143
Singapore 146
Leningrad 149
San Francisco 152

Sydney 155
Vancouver 159

CLASSIC GRAND TOURS 163
The Canadian Rockies 166
New England in the Fall 168
Art Towns of Tuscany 171
The Deep South: USA 174
British Country House Hotels 177
Italian Lakes 181
Châteaux of the Loire 184
Aeolian Islands 187
Amalfi Coast 190
European Battlefield Tours 193
American Civil War Battlefields Tours 196

ADVENTURE HOLIDAYS 199
Japan 202
China 205
Mexico 208
Eastern Europe 211
Venezuela 214
Indonesia 216
The USSR 219
Bhutan 222
India 225
Peru 229
Arctic Lands 232
Tibet 235
Morocco 238
Kashmir 240
Northern Canada 243
Safari in Kenya 246
Safari in Zimbabwe 250
Safari in Botswana 253
Safari in Zambia 256

GREAT EVENTS 259
Carnival in Rio 261
Bangkok at Songkran 264
The Holy Blood Procession in Bruges 266
St James's Day in Santiago de Compostela 269
Oberammergau Passion Play 271
The Edinburgh International Festival 273

ACTIVITY HOLIDAYS 277
By Steam across Southern Africa 279
Golfing in France 282
Outdoor Canada 284
Club Med Activity Holidays Par Excellence 286
Flotilla Sailing in the Aegean 289
Walking the Austrian Alps 292
Trail Blazing in the Wild West 295
Camel Safaris 297
Himalayan Trekking in Nepal 299
Diving in the Great Barrier Reef 303
An American Dream: Skiing in Colorado 305
Dragoman: Overland With a Difference 307

Appendix I: Tourist Board Addresses and travel details 311
Appendix II: Tour Operators 351
Appendix III: Hotels 361

100 Greatest Holidays

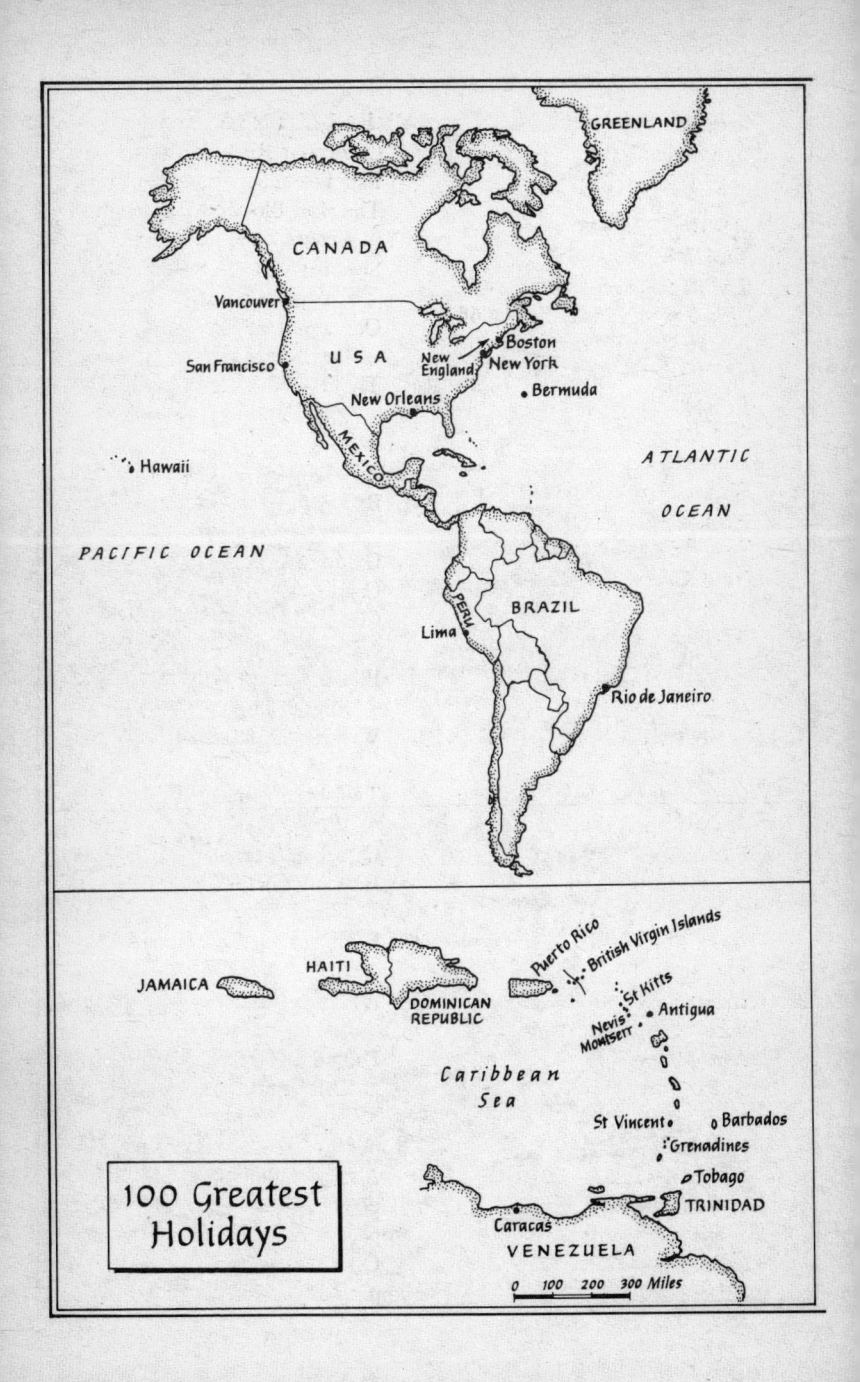

ICELAND
Leningrad
Moscow
U S S R
London
Paris
MOROCCO
Kashmir
CHINA
Beijing
JAPAN
Tokyo
Osaka
Nagasaki
PAKISTAN
TIBET
NEPAL
BHUTAN
Delhi
Calcutta
Bombay
INDIA
Hong Kong
PACIFIC
OCEAN
Arabian
Sea
Madras
THAILAND
Bangkok
Phuket
Penang
MALASIA
Singapore
Maldives
KENYA
Mombasa
Seychelles
INDONESIA
BOTSWANA
MADAGASCAR
Mauritius
Barrier Reef
Pretoria
SOUTH
AFRICA
Durban
Cape Town
INDIAN OCEAN
AUSTRALIA
Sydney

Bergen
NORWAY
Oslo
SWEDEN
Stockholm
Leningrad
Hebrides
Edinburgh
Moscow
DENMARK
IRELAND
UNITED
KINGDOM
North Sea
Copenhagen
U S S R
London
NETH.
Berlin
Warsaw
ATLANTIC
OCEAN
Bruges
BELG.
GERMANY
POLAND
Prague
Paris
CZECHOSLOVAKIA
R. Loire
Oberammagau
Vienna
Budapest
FRANCE
SWITZ.
AUSTRIA
HUNGARY
Lakes
ROMANIA
Bucharest
Santiago
de Compostela
Venice
YUGOSLAVIA
Belgrade
Black Sea
Florence
Siena
Sofia
BULGARIA
Istanbul
Lisbon
PORTUGAL
Madrid
SPAIN
ITALY
Rome
ALBANIA
Ankara
TURKEY
Amalfi
GREECE
Aeolian Is.
Mediterranean
Sicily
Sea
Athens

Introduction

The British travel industry is one of the most highly developed in the world. Not that this should come as a surprise, considering the Brits are among the keenest travellers in the world – over 60 per cent take at least one holiday a year, and a third of these are foreign trips. Most other European nationalities come nowhere near this, and compare it with the fact that only 9 per cent of US citizens own a passport, you can see that the British are way ahead in terms of globe-trotting.

Our travel industry can offer us travel to every corner of the globe at costs that make other nations green with envy. This is due to the proliferation of tour operators offering charter-flight deals and bargain rate accommodation. The infrastructure in our travel industry is second to none, and the last decade has seen even greater advances, especially in the long-haul, exotic holiday market. Trips which were once the dream (and savings) of a lifetime are now offered at such reasonable prices that they are affordable to most people.

The aim of this book is to bring you the very best from different categories of holidays. Many of the holidays covered here are one-man companies, never featured before. The size of their operation does not allow them to pay the hefty commission charges that it takes to get one's brochures into High Street travel agencies, so they are restricted to small ads in occasional travel supplements or word of mouth.

I have taken two years to research this guide, checking out many, many holidays in order to bring you this compendium of the best, the 'ultimate' in travel in the nineties. I hope everyone will find something they like.

Every continent is covered, for every continent is now accessible at prices unthought of just a decade ago. Complicated trips are now easy: all the hard work has been taken on by specialist companies, and the new inclusive tours are a million miles from the traditional package holiday image. Independent options are also covered so you can choose which type would suit you best.

Great Journeys starts the book, travel where the point of the holiday is the mode of transport or experience of the trip: classic train journeys; cruises; and more unconventional forms of transport, plying the great routes of yesteryear in a style no longer commonly found. Great Events covers travel where the point of the trip is to go for a specific happening – to witness one of the world's great spectacles! Activity Travel, as the name suggests, looks at travel with the purpose of pursuing a sport or activity in its very best location. Cities is aimed at the short city-break market – the world's great metropoli are detailed in this section: how and why to go, and what to see. Classic Grand Tours covers the time-honoured routes, the proven classics of the travel industry, areas which deserve slow, expertly-guided exploration. Adventure Tours are on a similar theme, but strictly for the adventurous and hardy. Perhaps more experiences than holidays, this is for seasoned travellers who will find delight in remote parts of dark continents. Sun worshippers have not been forgotten. The very cream of the world's beach resorts are here: some basic, far-flung and uncommercialised; some glamorous and ritzy – the very best places to catch a tan.

I hope this encourages you to try pastures new, and whatever you do, wherever you do it, may it be the ultimate holiday experience for you.

Katie Wood

Great Journeys

We all travel for different reasons. For some of us, travel is simply a means of getting from A to B. For others it is an experience which broadens the mind. And to others still, travel means a holiday, a rest, or even a chance to see the world. In former times, if you enjoyed travel for its own sake, it was only the privileged few who could afford any sort of style or luxury. Most travellers were forced to endure hardships, or at least discomfort. Today, technology has telescoped the world into a global village. More than ever before is it possible to travel quickly and reasonably efficiently to and from all points of the compass. But in the computerised scramble to process ever-increasing numbers of travellers, the travel industry has lost something precious. Travel for its own sake has become a concept on the decline, and 'old-fashioned' luxury has become conspicuous by its absence from most modern-day travelling. For the most part, gone are porters to carry your luggage, no longer are there chambermaids to tidy your room when it needs it, not just when it's on the rota, and luxurious, gracious methods of transport have become comparatively rare. However, bastions of old-fashioned luxury can still be found here and there, and ironically, although speedier means of transport are appreciated more, there is now an increasing demand to experience more leisurely and luxurious holidays. The luxury of high-class travel in days gone by is returning, but with all the added advantages of modern comforts and efficiency, and at a price that many find accessible.

It is not simply the pleasure of exploring a new country in style that has become more accessible: methods of travel have developed to the extent that your holiday may now consist of a journey in itself. Whether you fly in Concorde at twice the speed of sound, meander through Scotland in the stately grandeur of the Queen of Scots, or be pampered across the Pacific on board the *QE2*, travel for travel's sake is enough to justify your special chosen journey. Whether or not you discover the delights of foreign countries or the values of different cultures, the journeys detailed here combine the best of the old with the brightest of the new, creating a nineties holiday experience guaranteed to be unique.

Train Journeys

The Venice Simplon Orient Express

The 'Orient Express' is not just a name, but a concept of travel which has conjured up images of luxury and elegance for over a century. It is a concept which harks back to October 1883 when forty passengers set off from Paris, bound for Romania, on a journey that was to mark the beginning of a legend and the inauguration of a way of travel that has survived both world wars. In the century that has passed since then, the train has acquired a history that is comparable with no other means of transport still in use today and which has inspired six major cinema films, nineteen books and one musical composition. Despite fragmentation of the train in the sixties when old cars were detached, and new, less luxurious replacements were introduced, the Venice Simplon Orient Express is running again today. Complete with thirty-five historic coaches – restaurant cars, pullmans, sleepers, all of which have been restored to their former opulence – the Orient Express once again merits the 1890s description 'The Train of Kings, the King of Trains'.

Leaving London every Thursday and Sunday, the Orient Express itinerary remains true to tradition, carrying you to Venice by way of Paris, Zurich, St Anton and Innsbruck. During July and August, trips to Venice are alternated on a weekly basis with visits to Vienna. This journey follows the same route as far as Innsbruck but then heads northwards through Salzburg and up to Vienna. Both itineraries constitute the southbound Orient Express. For travellers already in Europe it is possible to join the train at any of its stopover points, to go south, or take the northbound journey for the return trip to London. On both trips Channel crossings are made between Boulogne and Folkestone by means of Sealink British Ferries, taking approximately two hours. During the crossing passengers can enjoy the facilities of the Orient Express lounge, reserved exclusively for their own comfort, though this is the least luxurious part of the journey.

From June 1991, it will be possible to travel to the Hungarian capital, Budapest. This is another step forward towards recreating the original route of the train and follows the same path as the Vienna train. Operating every other week, the service will depart on a Thursday; the return journey will depart on Saturday evening but will stop at Munich rather than either St Anton or Innsbruck.

Life on board the 'King of Trains' is in a class of its own. Extensive renovation and conversion of the carriages less than ten years ago has left the Orient Express resplendent in every detail. The nine vintage pullman cars which make up the English section stand out in their distinguished livery of cream and brown, complete with wood panelling and marquetry interiors. Once in France you are greeted by brass insignia shining brightly on a background of gleaming blue paintwork. This is the continental section of the Orient Express and, as stewards welcome you aboard, you will feel the genuine Orient Express journey getting under way.

Cabins function as private day rooms until their nightly transformation into bedrooms, when a top bunk swings down and the 'daytime sofa' is converted into a bed. Rooms are compact, indeed some would say small, with little space for two people changing at once, but they are also luxurious, decorated in polished wood with contrasting inlays. Hand basins are an integral part of your cabin; *en suite* facilities are not. The latter are communal and found at the end of each carriage. The three dining cars are magnificent in their twenties opulence, each separately appointed with individual trimmings and fittings. Although formal distinctions are made between first and second-class dining cars, this is not reflected in either the decoration or cuisine. In contrast with menus on many scheduled trains the choice of cuisine on the Orient Express changes in accordance with the seasons, ensuring that fresh ingredients are always used. Wines are carefully chosen to complement meals, and champagne (albeit at £35 a bottle) is always available. Dress is formal, although black tie is not obligatory.

The success of the Orient Express is due simply to the unique experience it offers in combining elegant surroundings, first-rate cuisine and quietly efficient service. The elements which make a trip on board this train so special are the beautiful changing scenery which is always outside your window and the historic towns and cities which make up the itinerary. On what other holiday would it be possible to enjoy fresh croissants at breakfast while skirting the lovely Boden See, lunch amidst the towering forests and peaks just beyond St Anton and tea and pastries while descending through the Dolomites to Verona? And if that is not enough the final touch is added with your arrival in Venice and the knowledge that you have as much time as you want to explore this romantic city. If you want to continue travelling on the Orient Express, you can always make it a round trip and spend another two days on the 'King of Trains' returning to London.

For passengers who want to make the most of their time spent on the Orient Express there are various options available for extending your holiday. Orient Express hotels are located, amongst other places, in all the major stopover points. Arrangements can be made to stay as long as you wish in any of these towns before continuing on your journey. The hotels are all luxurious, offering every amenity of a quality hotel. Details of inclusive arrangements are available with the standard Orient Express brochure and prices are based on twin-bedded rooms with private facilities. Breakfast is included each morning.

For the ultimate Orient Express holiday it is possible to make inclusive arrangements with the MV *Orient Express* cruise. The departure point for the cruise is Venice so this is a trip which can come at either end of a holiday – before you join the Venice Simplon Orient Express or after you have left it. The seven-day round cruise takes you between the vertical walls of the Corinth Canal, to Piraeus (Athens harbour) and the Parthenon, Istanbul and on to Kusadasi for the beaches of southern Turkey. The return to Venice is by way of the excavations at Ephesus, Patmos and Katakolon for Olympia. This cruise is available from 4 May to 27 October and, while prices vary depending on dates, the cost is roughly £1,800. This includes travel on the Orient Express from London to Venice (or vice versa), accommodation in Venice in a standard twin-bedded room, a shared two-berth de luxe cabin and all table d'hôte meals on board the MV *Orient Express*, with return transfers in Venice between the station, ship and hotel.

Prices for the Venice Simplon Orient Express train-only holidays are determined by how far you wish to travel and the starting point of your journey. Roughly speaking they range from £600–700 for overnight travel, and £140–350 for daytime travel, with supplements required for the usual extras such as a single cabin or a double cabin with single occupancy. Further details about travel on the Venice Simplon Orient Express are available from Venice Simplon Orient Express Ltd (see Appendix II for details).

The Queen of Scots

Imagine six days spent in a de luxe country house hotel with a different view outside your window every morning. Add to this some of the most spectacular countryside in the world, and what you come up with is one of the most memorable journeys ever taken, in the elegance and luxury of the Queen of Scots. Operated by the Scottish Highland Railway Company Limited, the Queen of Scots offers travellers a trip on which they immerse themselves in old-fashioned grace and enjoy the unobtrusive attention of skilled staff. Progress is stately as the train winds its way through the little-used lines of the Scottish Highlands, inviting a maximum of twenty-eight guests to observe from their privileged vantage point the unspoilt beauty and wilderness of the Scottish mountains and glens. Forget the myths about Scottish frugality: this is a trip which lavishes every luxury upon its guests and demands only their appreciation of its unique nature in return.

There is a choice of two tours aboard the Queen of Scots, and these two tours combined create a third option. This is a six-day 'full tour', covering the West Highland, the North and the East Highland Lines, which takes you as far north as the Strath of Kildonan (above Inverness), and right over to the Isle of Skye. Two shorter trips are simply incorporated into this and are classified as the 'western' and the 'northern' tours. The six-day tour departs from Edinburgh's Waverley Station on a Monday morning at about 11 a.m. and returns shortly before 6 p.m. on the following Saturday, from April to November. Shorter tours are run only at certain times with the western tour lasting three days, from Monday to Wednesday, and the northern tour lasting four days, from Wednesday to Saturday.

Itineraries for the tours certainly manage to include a wide variety of sights and places of interest, allowing the traveller to experience a characteristic sample of both traditional and modern Scottish life. Glide round the breathtaking curve of the 100-foot-high Glenfinnan Viaduct – the first concrete viaduct to be built in Britain – hear the Gaelic language and local clarsach (harp) music on the Isle of Skye; taste the renowned Cardhu whisky in a tour of its home distillery up at Keith, and return to Edinburgh across the spectacular Forth Rail Bridge (completed in 1890 and the greatest

8 Great Journeys

engineering feat of its time). Highlights of the tour are numerous, especially when you consider that as well as everything else there are trips to country houses, castles and beautiful gardens (most of which are not usually open to the public). At Dunrobin Castle, for instance, you alight at the only private railway station in Britain, and enjoy a tour of the castle and dinner with Lord Strathnaver, the present heir. All excursions are made with a qualified guide, who will keep you well informed about the places you visit.

Time spent on board the train could not be more enjoyable. The Queen of Scots is made up of a total of seven cars, so there is no need to worry about the usual lack of space. These carriages did, in fact, spend five years functioning as the Royal Scotsman, but have now been returned to private ownership. Their well-preserved interiors reflect the comfort and luxury of a bygone age, the character of which can never be reproduced by any modern counterpart. It is hardly surprising that the Queen of Scots is a member of the Classic Trains of the World association.

For those who simply want to admire the scenery there is an observation car, specially fitted with large picture windows, where you can also play cards or read. The historic dining car celebrated its centenary last year. During the First World War it was transported to France by the army, and was used as the mobile headquarters for the commander-in-chief, Field Marshal Earl Haig. If the history of trains (not to mention the history of Scotland) interests you, then you will certainly find the Queen of Scots fascinating. A further day car, the family saloon, was built in 1912 to be chartered privately by families travelling between their country estates and town houses. Today it is the only car in the Queen of Scots which is finished in varnished teak.

Sleeping cars on the Queen of Scots are a treat in themselves. All are state cabins (twins or singles are available), and all have opening windows, full-length wardrobes, call buttons, electric heating (often important for cool Scottish nights), and lower beds only. Cabins have *en suite* bathrooms with shower, basin and toilet. Storage space is ample in all cabins. With the added advantage that the train stops every night in a quiet siding or country station, passengers are guaranteed a comfortable night's sleep, leaving them fully refreshed to enjoy the next day.

An essential ingredient of any holiday is, of course, food. Like everything else aboard the Queen of Scots the standard of dining is first class. Fresh provisions are taken on daily ensuring a tasty selection of superb cuisine. A look through the menu reveals the emphasis on Scottish food: game, seafood, Scotch beef and traditional Scottish desserts. Wines are carefully chosen to complement dishes, and these, along with meals and all drinks, are included in the price of your ticket.

To add to the elegance of the tours, certain evenings are designated 'formal', when dress requirements should be noted: gentlemen in tuxedo or kilt; ladies in evening dress. For the rest of the time dress should be 'casual but smart', something in the style of a weekend away at a country house hotel.

Prices for the Queen of Scots tour start at £1,200 for the three-day western tour and go up to £3,000 per person for the six-day full tour of Scotland. These prices remain the same throughout the year with no variation for one season or another, and include everything provided on board the train or as part of the tour – all meals, drinks, excursions and accommodation.

Further information can be obtained from the Scottish Highland Railway Company Limited (see Appendix II for details).

Malay-Siam Royal Mail Train

There is perhaps nowhere in the world more mystical or alluring than the Far East. The cultures of countries such as Malaysia and Thailand are so far removed from what we are accustomed to, that to experience them is to have a real taste of the exotic. This is an area of the world that has not yet been completely compromised by modern tourism, although it does cater superbly for both adventurers and holiday-makers alike. Centres such as Bangkok, Kuala Lumpur and Singapore are well used to foreign visitors, but their attractions retain their exotic appeal. This is equally true, if not more so, of the more remote parts of the Far East, where dense tropical rainforests still flourish, and animals can be seen in their natural habitat. But to really appreciate the diversity of such places, you need to travel through them, viewing the scenes consecutively and in conjunction with each other.

Soon to be launched (mid 1992) by the same company which operates the world-famous Venice Simplon Orient Express, the Malay-Siam Royal Mail Train will give travellers the opportunity to journey through Thailand and Malaysia in a style that is unequalled. In all, 1,243 miles will be covered in about forty-two hours, with trains leaving Singapore at 8.30 p.m., and arriving in Bangkok at approximately 10.25 a.m., just over one-and-a-half days later. Included in the itinerary are Kuala

Lumpur; Butterworth on the west coast of Malaysia, opposite the island of Penang; Ipoh, and Hua Hin. In addition, a stop in northern Malaysia may be added, to give passengers the opportunity to visit rubber and oil-palm plantations. Should the political situation in surrounding areas become more settled, it is hoped to extend the itinerary into Cambodia, Laos, Vietnam and Myanma – countries that have been virtually closed to all but official visitors for some time.

As the Venice Simplon Orient Express is in Europe, the Straits Bangkok Royal Mail will be a highlight of a visit to the Far East. Thirty-one rail cars have been purchased, all of which were built twenty-nine years ago for the Silver Fern Train in New Zealand. Following mechanical restoration, the interiors have been totally refurbished in Singapore. The Royal Mail will comprise twenty to twenty-five cars, including three restaurant cars, bar/casino cars, sleeping cars, baggage cars, and an observation car.

Interior refurbishment of the Royal Mail has been executed under the expert guidance of Parisian designer, Gerard Gallet, who was also responsible for recreating the luxury and elegance of the Orient Express carriages. Traditional wood carvings, silks and batiks blend together in a style that underlines the exotic nature of the tour. Double cabins, including suites and de luxe cabins, are available, and every sleeping compartment has its own washing and lavatory facilities. In each sleeping car there are also several shower rooms. The entire train is air-conditioned, and equipped with 'state of the art' on-board communications.

Entertainment, like the decor, is drawn from local culture. Local musicians play in the restaurant cars, while calligraphy writers demonstrate their craft, and fortune tellers predict your future. Hostesses on board talk to passengers about the culture and traditions of Singapore, Malaysia and Thailand, as well as acting as guides on the sightseeing excursions which are an integral part of the trip. Alternatively, you can relax in the bar, to the accompaniment of live piano music, or if you prefer a gamble, there is always the casino car – a feature incidentally not included on the Orient Express. Passengers should note that the casino will only be in operation for the section of the journey between Singapore and the border of Malaysia and Thailand. For total peace away from the heart of the train, passengers can retire to the observation car. Situated at the rear of the train, this is a standard rail car which has been cut away to leave an open roofed terrace, giving passengers a superb panoramic view.

Train Journeys **11**

Other facilities on board include a bureau de change, a shop selling local souvenirs, and the Collection Venice Simplon Orient Express. Renowned for its fine quality leather goods, this collection includes accessories such as silk scarves, and ladies' and gentlemen's watches. It is hoped that a leading Paris fashion house will be commissioned to create a special collection of designer clothes and accessories with a Far Eastern flavour, to be sold on board.

The standard of cuisine on the Royal Mail is, of course, first class. With three dining cars there is certainly no lack of choice either. A nice touch is that while French cuisine is featured in one car, in the other two the finest dishes from Singapore, Malaysia and Thailand are served. Like the Orient Express, the Royal Mail is an unforgettable gastronomic experience. In addition, stewards provide twenty-four-hour room service to cater for any little extras you might want.

Final mention should be given to the possibility of combining a trip on the Royal Mail with various stopovers of your choice along the way. Both Malaysia and Thailand are home to some of the world's most beautiful and unspoilt beaches, not to mention the variety of fishing villages and market towns dotted across these countries. Passengers should look into the possibility of spending a few extra days at selected places, exploring the countryside, or relaxing on a beach, before rejoining the train. For example, from Butterworth in the north-west of Malaysia, it is possible to spend a few days on the island of Penang, just off the west coast. Alternatively, you could travel across to the east coast and see the giant turtles as they come in from the sea. There is such a range of things to do and places to see in these countries that it is advisable to make sure you know how to make the most of your time, and what options are available for extending your holiday. This is especially true if you are travelling in a group, since the Royal Mail is also available for private chartering.

Prices and dates for the Straits Bangkok Royal Mail have not yet been finalised. However, further information is available from Press Office, Orient Express Hotels Limited (see Appendix III for details).

Rajasthan Express

Maharajas' palaces, richly coloured howdahs and the smell of spice on a warm breeze are all part of India's five thousand-year-old history and culture. Britain's old 'Jewel in the Crown' is a sub-continent of twenty-five states, each with its own highlights and attractions, from the snow-capped peaks of the Himalayas to the unspoilt, sun-drenched beaches of Goa. If you've got the time and patience, then independent travel in India is extremely rewarding, given the enormous diversity of customs, creeds, and caste. But exploration of a country this size could extend to months. So one of the best ways to discover the delights of India, especially for the first-time visitor, is to concentrate on a single state, either as part of a wider-reaching itinerary, or as a holiday in itself. One of the best ways to do this is on the Rajasthan Express.

The Rajasthan Express, or as it is otherwise known, the 'palace on wheels', is a unique collection of rail coaches, once built for maharajas, but now elegantly and luxuriously restored for modern travel, while retaining its Edwardian opulence. The oldest coach was built in 1898, the newest in 1937, and each displays the Royal coat of arms that proclaims its noble antecedents. In all, some twenty coaches constitute the palace on wheels, including two dining cars, bar, observation car, and fully equipped first aid centre. Each accommodation car consists of saloon, four sleeping compartments with upper and lower berths, bathroom, shower, toilet, and small kitchen. The kitchen is there for any snacks you might want to make yourself, although room service is available at all times and the separate dining cars offer an excellent choice of either Indian or European cuisine. Unfortunately, there is no air-conditioning on the train, although this is compensated for by the series of ceiling fans installed in each carriage. Haulage is principally by diesel, but sometimes by steam. In general, it would be fair to say that the standards on board the Rajasthan Express render it a genuine Eastern counterpart to the Venice Simplon Orient Express: this is reflected also in the gleaming ivory paintwork of the exterior, and the plush furniture, velvet upholstery and brass fittings inside.

Leaving New Delhi every Wednesday between October and March, the Rajasthan Express follows an itinerary which gives passengers an excellent insight into Indian life in general (even though it is orientated almost exclusively around the north-western state of Rajasthan), as well as taking in the main monuments and landmarks which are so much a part of Indian culture. The package on offer from Cox and Kings extends to twelve days altogether, and this includes a couple of days in Delhi at the beginning and at the end of your holiday as well as seven days spent on board the train. During their first two days in Delhi, passengers are given a gentle introduction to the city, thus allowing them to recover from any jet-lag. Excursions on day two are organised around New Delhi, the capital city built by the British, followed on day three by a visit to the sights of Old Delhi. These include the historic Red Fort, the Jama Masjid, India's largest mosque, and the colourful, hectic Chandni Chowk bazaar. Your time in Delhi at the end of your trip is left completely free for any last-minute sightseeing or shopping, or simply to relax before your flight home. Your hotel is one of the traditional palace hotels – the Taj Palace Hotel, considered to be the best in India – and it certainly offers every amenity that could be wished for.

Your time on board the Rajasthan Express starts on day four of your overall holiday, when you join the train in time for dinner, at the start of its journey in New Delhi. Cabin attendants – who remain with you throughout your trip – see you to your teak-panelled quarters, where traditional carpets and painted ceilings all contribute to the predominant air of old-fashioned luxury. Dinner is a leisurely affair, allowing guests ample time to settle in before the train leaves.

Heading south overnight, you arrive the next morning in time for breakfast in Jaipur, the 'Pink City'. Excursions are organised to the City Palace and observatory, the Palace of the Winds with its delicate honeycombed windows, and Amber, the state capital. Amber is reached by coach from Jaipur, and once there you ride by elephant up to the ancient citadel. Lunch is taken at the Ram Bagh palace hotel, the former home and original palace of the maharajas of Jaipur. In the evening there is a cultural show and dinner at Nahargarh Fort.

After your second night travelling, breakfast is followed by a brief visit to Chittaurgarh Fort, before returning to the train for the connection to Udaipur, the City of Shimmering Lakes. Lunch at the spectacular Lake Palace Hotel is followed by a range of excursions, as well as afternoon tea at Nehru Park Island. Since the train actually remains in Udaipur overnight, there is also time for shopping before departing the next day.

These first couple of days give a good indication of the type of trip passengers can expect to enjoy while travelling on the Rajasthan Express. As the train continues you will visit Jaisalmer, last, loneliest, and some say loveliest of India's westernmost cities; Jodhpur, one of Rajasthan's legendary desert cities, and Agra, home of the Taj Mahal. Excursions over these days include a camel ride, Jaswant Thada, the marble cenotaph in Jodhpur, Bharatpur Bird Sanctuary, where more than 350 species of birds have been sighted, the deserted city of Fatehpur Sikri, built by Akbar, and Agra Fort. The contrasts between one stop and the next are quite stunning, drawing passengers into the history and culture of this beautiful land in a manner that is unforgettable.

Overall, travel on the Rajasthan Express is certainly to be recommended, either as a holiday in itself or as part of a longer holiday. The trip organised by Cox and Kings is just one of many packages which feature the train, and prospective passengers should look into options on offer from other companies. Alternatively, if travelling independently, it is possible to contact the main office of the Rajasthan Express, whose address is in Appendix II.

The price for the Cox and Kings Rajasthan Express holiday is roughly £1,900, based on full board while on the train, but room only while in your Delhi hotel. From London, this price includes economy class return air travel, 44 lbs or 20 kg luggage allowance, transfers between the appropriate overseas airports/stations/hotels according to your itinerary, twin-sharing accommodation with private bath or shower and toilet in each room where available, accommodation on the Rajasthan Express in four-berth compartments, excursions and tours as detailed, and the services of a tour leader. Departure dates from London are every Sunday between November and April.

Similar offers are also available from Jetset Worldwide and Speedbird Worldwide. Between the three operators there is little difference in price or inclusions. Itineraries are virtually identical, although optional extensions – to Goa or Nepal for example – do vary.

Further information is available from Cox and Kings Ltd, Jetset and Speedbird (see Appendix II for details). If you want you can contact the Rajasthan Express main Indian office (see Appendix II for details).

Trans-Siberian Express

There are few railways which, since their completion, have inspired so much interest as the Trans-Siberian. Built between 1890 and 1900 by the Tsars, it served in its early years as a vital, rapid link for Westerners, especially diplomats, to reach the capitals of China and Japan. Today it is one of the most culturally interesting and exciting ways of taking a passage from Europe to Japan or Hong Kong, and one of the most inexpensive ways of returning from the Orient to Europe.

As an engineering feat the Trans-Siberian railway is quite astounding: almost 10,000 km, or 5,778 miles, of track linking the capital, Moscow, in the west, with Khabarovsk, a Far-Eastern industrial and cultural centre on the banks of the Amur River, about 600 miles north of Vladivostok. Travelling west to east, the line takes passengers through European Russia; across the River Volga at Yaroslavl; across the Urals, the borderline between Europe and Asia; into the west-Siberian lowland and the level expanse of steppe to Novosibirsk; across the Rivers Ob and Yenesei to Irkutsk; through the mountainous Baikal region (including Lake Baikal), and finally through the Buryat Region and across the Amur River to Khabarovsk. It is a journey which takes almost a week from start to finish; approximately 130 hours of ever-changing countryside and scenery. It is probably the best way to see a true cross-section of Soviet life.

Travel on the Trans-Siberian, or, as it is known in the USSR, the 'Rossia' Express, is arranged through the Russian tourist agency, Intourist. Rather than simply offering the week-long journey on board the train, they have put together two fourteen-night packages, incorporating flights from the UK to Moscow, some travel on board the Trans-Siberian Express, and various organised tours and excursions in the cities of the greatest interest. Departure in the UK is from Gatwick, but itineraries for the two trips differ slightly once in the USSR. Places visited remain the same (with the exception of Novosibirsk, which is not included in the second tour), but the point at which they are featured in your itinerary varies.

For the Trans-Siberian Express section of the trip, passengers embark on one of the most spectacular portions of its journey between the Pacific and Europe. Two nights are spent on the train and during that time you cross two mountain ranges – the Khekhtsir and the Yablonovy – skirt the fringes of the Gobi Desert, cross the rivers and lakes of the upland forests, and curve around the edge of Lake Baikal, the deepest lake in the world, where there are unique flora and fauna.

This takes you as far as Irkutsk, where three nights are spent among the hills on the banks of the River Angara. Irkutsk is one of Siberia's oldest cities and has a history that goes back more than three centuries. Known as the 'Pearl of Siberia', it is an important trading post for fur, timber, gold and diamonds, and home to Siberia's only planetarium.

From Irkutsk, passengers are flown to Bratsk, slightly to the north. Intourist cater for one night spent in this town which, while it may qualify as one of the twentieth century's pioneering towns, seems to have little to offer in the way of sightseeing. Situated some distance away from the line of the Rossia, it is famous as the site of a hydro-electric dam which, when it was completed in 1964, was the largest in the world.

Leningrad is also featured in the trip. On both tours, two nights are spent in this fascinating city, the cradle of the great October Revolution.

The trip affords the casual observer a relatively interesting view of carefully chosen sections of Soviet life. For serious travellers though, keen on traversing the continent by train, it will simply be a brief taste of the varying styles and moods of this massive country, and they will be left wanting more. Although the price (which ranges from roughly £780–900) covers all air transport, rail transport with three meals a day, twin-bedded rooms with private facilities and half-board, airport charges, transfers, porterage, and a sightseeing programme in each city, in a country which is so vast fourteen nights are hardly sufficient for full, comprehensive coverage. It does, however, please most first-time travellers, though those going who expect Orient Express-type comfort will certainly be disappointed. Food and conditions are comparatively spartan.

In order to make the most of a trip to the USSR, combined with good use of the Trans-Siberian Express, it is advisable to consider taking the train right across the continent in either direction, incorporating a sequence of two- or three-night stopovers along the way. Intourist's package deal offers a two-day sample of the Trans-Siberian Express, but only skims the surface of this mammoth journey. Travelling towards the west there is still much to see after Irkutsk, especially if you are unfamiliar with the extremely varied nature of the Soviet and Siberian landscapes. Stops are made at Krasnoyarsk (which means both 'red' and 'beautiful'); Novosibirsk, (Siberia's biggest centre even though the city is less than a century old); Omsk on the Irtysh River; Sverdlovsk, an important Urals city; and Kirov. Excursions can be arranged in all of these places and all of them are certainly worth a visit.

Another trip to consider is from Bales World Wide Tours, who offer an eighteen-day escorted holiday by rail, from Moscow to Beijing (Peking). Flying from Heathrow, three nights are spent in Moscow before joining the Trans-Siberian Express for the three-night trip as far as Irkutsk. Passengers leave the train here for another three-night stay, during which excursions are arranged. Another overnight train journey takes you into Mongolia for a further three-night stopover at Ulan Bator, the remote capital of this country, once the stronghold of Genghis Khan. Following this, you take your final train, arriving in Beijing the next afternoon. Excursions during your two days in Beijing take in the Imperial Palace and the Great Wall of China. Departure is on day seventeen, arriving at Heathrow in the early morning of day eighteen. While this trip does not provide totally comprehensive coverage of the Trans-Siberian Railway, it does cater for the more serious traveller who is seeking further insight into the history and culture of two of the greatest nations on earth.

Prices for the Bales tour range from roughly £1,660–1,870, depending on when you travel. Included are economy-class return flights from London, transfer between airport and hotel, accommodation in twin-bedded rooms with private facilities where available (single accommodation is not available on this trip), full board throughout, excursions as detailed, and the services of a tour manager throughout. Departure dates are every month from May to September (inclusive), with two trips in June in 1991.

Further information is available from Bales Tours Ltd and Intourist Moscow Ltd (see Appendix II for details).

From the Rockies to the Pacific

Of all the areas in the world renowned for their natural beauty, the Canadian Rockies are one of the most stunning. Snow-capped mountains, cascading waterfalls and raging rivers are thrown together with dense forests of pine and fir, narrow canyons, broad valleys and abundant animal life. Yet only a short distance away lies Vancouver, Canada's gateway to the Pacific ocean, and 'laid-back' San Francisco, further south. The contrasts between such sights in close proximity to each other is really quite astounding.

As part of their 'Escorted Journeys', Thomas Cook, in association with Voyages Jules Verne, have put together a holiday which treats travellers to seventeen days (with various optional extensions) of the best of this breathtaking part of the world. Known simply as 'From the Rockies to the Pacific', this is a journey which combines travel by air, road, rail, and boat, from London to Calgary, and then on down to San Francisco, with the possibility of taking in Los Angeles or Hawaii as well. Three nights are spent in San Francisco; two each in Banff, Vancouver, and Seattle, and one each in Kamloops, Olympia, Newport, Gold Beach, Eureka, and Calgary. In each place there are organised excursions (all included in the price of the trip), as well as your own leisure time to relax or enjoy the many attractions.

One of the main highlights of this trip is the continually changing surroundings in which you find yourself. Your first taste of North America is in Banff, having transferred there after your arrival in Calgary. Here you have a full day free to relax, or explore the famous Banff National Park. Continuing south towards the coast you travel to Vancouver, which, set on delightful English Bay and overlooked by Grouse Mountain, is one of North America's most attractive cities. Excursions take you to such places as Stanley Park, False Creek, Gastown, and Chinatown, to name but a few. Seattle comes next, followed by one of the great attractions of the Pacific north-west, Mount Rainier, which is 14,410 feet high.

At this point in the trip you will have already seen an impressive range of towns, cities and countryside in general, yet you have only reached day eight of the overall tour, and still have nine days to come. Further high points are the opportunity to view sealions in their natural habitat at Sea Lion Caves, Newport; a visit to Redwood National Park where some of the ancient trees reach a staggering 100 metres; a trip through the Sonoma Valley, one of the wine-producing areas of California; and of course three days in San Francisco. Excursions in San Francisco are numerous, and take in the Civic Centre, Opera House, Golden Gate Bridge, Fisherman's Wharf, and Pier 39. Guests have a full day free, when optional tours are run for those who are perhaps at a loss for where to start in this city, known as the 'Paris of the America West'. A full-day tour to California wine country is available, with visits to two wineries and various wine-tasting sessions. Alternatively, you could join the visit to the island of Alcatraz. There are so many options open to travellers that they all should be looked into thoroughly if you want to make the most of your time here.

San Francisco, however, is not your last stopover of the tour: a final night is spent in Calgary before returning to London. Here, in this boomtown which straddles the Canadian Prairies and the foothills of North America's greatest mountain range, you can do any last-minute shopping and have breakfast in Calgary Tower. Your return flight to London is not until late afternoon, so there is also time for any final sightseeing.

Such is the basic Rockies to Pacific tour, but it need not end so soon. If you want to spend longer in San Francisco, arrangements can be made for you to continue in the same hotel for as many nights as you wish (watch out for additional charges though, including your departure transfer). Also on offer are extensions to Los Angeles or Hawaii. These take effect on day fifteen, when, while everyone else is flying to Calgary, you transfer to Oakland to board an Amtrak train to Los Angeles, or catch the plane to Hawaii. The Los Angeles option is for three nights, while the Hawaii tour lasts for four (with the possibility of 'extending your extension'!). Excursions on both tours are not included, with the exception of a half-day tour of the Arizona Memorial to Pearl Harbor in Hawaii. Travellers should also note that extensions are not escorted.

Rail travel in Canada is with VIA rail. Carriages are spacious and comfortable, and service efficient. On each train there is a restaurant carriage which serves full meals or light snacks; a 'dome' or observation carriage, and overnight sleeping carriages. All accommodation is in double cabins, based on two people sharing.

Prices for the basic 'From the Rockies to the Pacific' escorted journey depend on the time of year you choose to travel. In 1990 departure dates were scheduled for 18 May, 15 June, 20 July, 10 and 24 August, 14 and 28 September. Prices range from roughly £1,400–1,500, rising as the year progresses. Included in the price are return economy-class flights with Air Canada; morning tour of Banff; two full-day scenic journeys from Banff to Vancouver (via Kamloops); half-day sightseeing tour of Vancouver with lunch at Capilano Canyon; full-day tour to Victoria; full-day tour to Mount Rainier National Park; full-day tour to Redwood National Park; half-day tour of San Francisco; breakfast visit to Calgary Tower, with short sightseeing tour of Calgary; American visa; American departure tax; Canadian departure tax; services of a Thomas Cook tour manager throughout; porterage of one item of luggage, and either a first-class return rail ticket to a mainline London station, for Heathrow, or car parking near your departure airport for the duration of your holiday. These last two inclusions are particularly helpful.

A couple of things to watch for when booking are exactly what meals are included in the price. These are specified, and there is a non-refundable deposit of £100.

Final mention should be given to the travel seminars which are organised in association with Voyages Jules Verne, and are held at a country house hotel overlooking Windrush Valley in the Cotswolds. For a nominal charge, anyone who books a holiday with Thomas Cook can attend these seminars, which usually include two lectures and discussions, as well as access to a well-stocked travel and film library. Seminars are run throughout the year, and feature all countries dealt with by Thomas Cook. Check in the brochure exactly what is happening each month, but note that this offer is subject to availability, on a first-come-first-served basis.

For further information on the Rockies to the Pacific escorted journey, and travel seminars, contact the Thomas Cook Group Ltd (see Appendix II for details).

South Africa's Blue Train

South Africa is a country about which people often base their knowledge on media reports. Despite the troubles and the iniquitous system, tourism in this beautiful country is still as strong as ever, and a holiday there need not be inextricably linked with apartheid or the troubles associated with racial tension. In terms of land area, South Africa is five times the size of Britain, and is made up of four provinces: Cape Province in the south; Natal in the east; Orange Free State in the centre, and Transvaal to the north. Three capitals are acknowledged: Pretoria, the administrative capital; Cape Town, the legislative capital, and Bloemfontein, South Africa's judicial capital. English and Afrikaans are the two official languages spoken by a population which now numbers twenty-nine million. The time difference between South Africa and Britain is small: in summertime South Africa is just one hour ahead of Britain, and two hours ahead in winter. The climate is pleasant the whole year round, with temperatures ranging between 21–28°C in the summer (October to April), and winters comparing favourably with British summers. Humidity is low, except along the Natal coast.

So much for the facts about South Africa, but still to be mentioned are the many different attractions which make this country so fascinating to foreign visitors. Safaris, beaches, gold mines, and wineries all form part of South Africa's tourist attractions, although in a country so large, it is difficult to see everything in a short space of time. One of the most effective ways of combatting this problem is to travel down from Pretoria in the north to Cape Town on the south coast on the most famous means of transport in South Africa – the Blue Train.

Taking its name from the colour of the original dining car, built around 1937 for the so-called 'Union Limited' which pioneered the line from Johannesburg to Cape Town, the Blue Train carries 107 passengers the length of the country, in a style that is on a par with the Venice Simplon Orient Express or the Queen of Scots. Travelling a distance of roughly 1,600 km in some twenty-six hours, the Blue Train's itinerary takes in Pretoria, Johannesburg, Potchefstroom, Klerksdorp, Kimberley (headquarters of the famous diamond group De Beers), Beaufort West, Paarl (home of KWV, whose vast wine cellars are the largest in the world), and Cape Town. There are in fact two Blue Trains, both of which consist of sixteen carriages, all of which were built in 1972.

Accommodation on board is split into four categories. Type A is classed as luxury accommodation and offers passengers an exclusive three-roomed suite, comprising double-bedded sleeper, elegant drawing-room, and private bathroom and toilet facilities. Type B is made up of compartments and coupés, each with their own facilities. Type C is similar, but with a shower instead of a bath, and minor differences in room size. Type D offers compartments and coupés again, but with shared facilities. Accommodation, along with the rest of the train, is carpeted and air-conditioned throughout, and all suites and compartments have wardrobes, full-length mirrors, and shoe-cleaning lockers. Each bathroom is equipped with a shaving point, and an iced water tap as well as hot and cold running water.

Meals are taken in two leisurely sessions and your seat, once chosen, is reserved for you throughout the course of the journey. All meals are freshly prepared on board the train, and all fruit is hand-picked. The menu is usually typically South African, and delicacies such as crayfish (South African rock lobster) are often served. Alternatively you may enjoy dishes such as Karoo lamb, duckling Maltaise, or a simple fillet of pork. Any special dietary needs are accommodated where possible, providing enough notice is given. Wines are mainly South African, although a small selection of imported wines and spirits is also available. Drinks are served in both the dining car and the luxuriously furnished observation car.

A useful facility of the Blue Train is its ability to transport passengers' cars, although loading ramps are only available at Johannesburg and Cape Town. Nevertheless, this does allow holiday-makers the opportunity to save both time and money, if they can retain the same car for the duration of their trip. While most passenger cars can be accommodated, there are certain restrictions on ground clearance. Reservations for car space should be made at the same time as booking your cabins.

Overall, South Africa's Blue Train offers travellers a luxurious and unhurried opportunity to observe a large part of this beautiful country. From the comfort of your rolling hotel you can relax and watch the magnificent scenery pass by, and enjoy the attentive service, excellent cuisine and well-chosen wines which help make a holiday in this country so unique.

Prices for the Blue Train itself range from £160–320, depending on your date of travel, and your choice of accommodation. This includes meals and accommodation, but not drinks. Departure from both Pretoria and Cape Town is on Monday, Wednesday and Friday throughout the year, with occasional minor alterations. Travellers should note that there are no package deals to South Africa which include flights and a trip on the Blue Train. The price quoted above is for your time on the train only.

Further information is available from the South African Tourist Board (see Appendix I for details).

On the Tracks of Marco Polo

In the thirteenth century it took Marco Polo approximately four years to travel from Venice (his birth-place) to Shang-tu (the Mongolian summer capital) where he presented Kublai Khan with papal letters and sacred oil from Jerusalem. Four years of toil, anxiety and difficult journeying across unknown terrain. Little was he to realise that almost seven hundred years later modern travellers would deliberately follow his journey, crossing countries that still remain mysterious, in an effort to discover the glittering mosaic which constitutes the Far East and the Orient. No longer are European and Far-Eastern civilisations cut off from each other by a formidable wedge of Muslim nations. For those of us who are intrepid enough, there is now the possibility of following 'On the tracks of Marco Polo' and enjoying the twentieth-century version of what has become a classic journey.

Thomas Cook, in association with Voyages Jules Verne, are the agents for this tour and, while they have named it after Marco Polo, it functions also as a commemoration of 2,100 years of the Silk Road. Traditionally this was the ancient trade route that linked China with the West, carrying goods and ideas between the two great civilisations of China and Rome. Silk came west while wools, gold and silver went east. With the gradual loss of Roman territory in Asia, and the rise of Arabian power in the Levant, the Silk Road became increasingly unsafe and untravelled. However, during the thirteenth and fourteenth centuries, the route was revived under the Mongols and, at that time, Marco Polo used it to travel to Cathay. Today the road partially exists in the form of a paved highway connecting Pakistan and Sinkiang Uighur Autonomous Region, China. The old road has inspired a United Nations plan for a trans-Asian highway.

The itinerary offered by Thomas Cook creates a route loosely based on a combination of Marco Polo's travels and the traditional Silk Road. It is also partly inspired by the original Orient Express whose path is followed for the first twelve days of the journey as far as Istanbul. Departure is from Charing Cross, London, and the final destination is Hong Kong – a journey of over 7,000 miles which takes forty-seven days (not bad when you consider it took Marco Polo four years!). Travel is mainly overland and mainly by train (some steam-hauled), with boat crossings of the Black Sea and the Caspian Sea. Some road travel is also involved during the first few days in China, while the final leg of the journey, Xian (Chang'an) to Hong Kong, is made by chartered plane.

All in all around twenty cities, towns and villages are visited along the way, with a variety of organised excursions and tours. Generally stops of two nights and one day are made in each place, with arrivals usually scheduled for early evening (in time for dinner) and departures timetabled roughly thirty-six hours later, straight after breakfast. Notable exceptions to this are Vienna, Istanbul, and, once in China, Turfan and Lanzhou. A slightly longer period is spent in all of these places, due to either a larger number of features of interest or to time dedicated to independent sightseeing. It should be noted that a total of ten nights are spent travelling between cities on board chartered trains. Consequently travellers miss out on some of the breathtaking scenery – Paris to Salzburg for instance or the trip across the Gobi Desert – although this is certainly compensated for in action-packed daytime agendas. The Black Sea crossing is also made overnight, but this is to the traveller's advantage since the sight of dawn breaking over the Bosporus, together with the unique spectacle of early morning in Istanbul (old Constantinople), is a scene never to be forgotten.

As you can probably guess, the tour as a whole tends to adopt a fairly fast pace, although it does offer a combination of maximum sightseeing time with the minimum number of hours spent actually travelling. Nevertheless, due to the huge distances to be covered, passengers should be prepared on one or two occasions to spend quite considerable stretches of time on board trains or, towards the end, travelling by road. For instance the itinerary of day twenty-five illustrates exactly the type of demands made on travellers in terms of numbers of hours spent consistently 'on the go'. At this point in the journey (roughly the half-way mark as far as days are concerned), twelve hours spent crossing the Caspian Sea after an early morning start are followed by an overnight trip on a train to Ashkahabad. This mammoth twenty-four hour connection between cities is equalled later on in the trip by crossing the Sino-Soviet border on day thirty-four and the subsequent journey to Yining. Since the railway has not yet reached this far into China the connection is made by road over a distance of 390 km from Alma Ata to Yining. Thomas Cook admit in their brochure that this is 'a long day', (including a morning tour in Alma Ata), although they do add that it is 'rewarding'. Given the fact that this is a border crossing point between the Soviet Union and China which until 1985 had been closed to virtually everyone, it is fair to say that to Westerners this part of the journey is unique. As well as the novelty of a rare border crossing there is the spectacular scenery of the Heavenly Mountains and, once at Yining, the magnificent blue of Sayram Lake. From a historical point of view this area of China is filled with strands of the ancient Silk Road, including, at the oasis of Turfan, ruins of large city states and the tombs of Tang dignitaries. Due to the recent extension of the railway to Shihezi, travel by train has once again been resumed and continues as far as Xian, the penultimate stopover.

This brief glimpse of the final stages of the trip reflects fairly accurately the type of travel involved in this dynamic overland tour. The intensity with which Thomas Cook/Voyages Jules Verne have condensed Marco Polo's four-year sojourn (not forgetting the sixteen or seventeen years he actually spent in China) into a forty-seven-day tour, indicates quite reasonably that this is an adventure (as opposed to a luxurious experience) for the 'serious' traveller. This is also implied in the tour price of £4,300, although this does represent good travelling value for money. Included in this price is accommodation on trains (twin sharing), twin-sharing accommodation in hotels, with *en suite* facilities, full board throughout, a comprehensive sightseeing programme, porterage for one item of luggage, services of the tour manager, visa fees, and administration. Potential travellers should note there is also a non-refundable £300 deposit.

'On the Tracks of Marco Polo' only takes place once a year, leaving on or around 3 September and returning forty-seven days later. While Thomas Cook do leave the final day free for you to explore Hong Kong independently, they realise that some travellers may wish to make the most of a visit to the Far East and offer a variety of 'Different Ways Home'. These include an extended stay in Hong Kong and a 4–5 day trip to Japan for about £690. You should check when booking exactly what options are available. Remember also to check vaccination requirements.

Another option available to travellers is the chance to join the Voyages Jules Verne Travellers Club 'for the benefit of the serious traveller'. Membership of this club entitles you to a complimentary two- or three-night travel seminar at a country house hotel in the Cotswolds, where you are given the chance to meet other travellers, as well as attend lectures and talks about the trip you are going to take. The seminars are held several weeks prior to departure, throughout the year.

The creation of 'On the Tracks of Marco Polo' by Thomas Cook and Voyages Jules Verne reflects a type of holiday that is becoming increasingly popular: an exciting journey across continents and seas augmented by well organised tours and excursions. The price is higher than you would expect to pay for an average holiday. It is well justified, however, for giving you almost seven weeks of stimulating travel and relatively comfortable accommodation. Experienced travellers might find the pace somewhat tiring though. While stopovers are designed to allow time for relaxation, the intensity of the journey does demand a healthy amount of stamina. Frequent changes in time zone can often take their toll and a certain amount of disorientation is to be expected. Nevertheless, this is a journey so packed with interest and so closely linked with history, tradition and legend, that its value in today's travel market is extremely high.

Further information on the trip can be obtained from the Thomas Cook Group Ltd and Voyages Jules Verne (see Appendix II for details).

Great Britain and Europe Express

Launched in 1989 by Abercrombie and Kent, the Great Britain and Europe Express is the ultimate way to travel Europe by train. This is the ideal opportunity to travel to any of nine countries under the expert care of a knowledgeable guide, on a tour that combines luxury and elegance with genuine value-for-money accommodation and cuisine. Of particular significance is the emphasis on problem-free rail travel and the concept of the 'travelling Bell Boy'. On every tour there is a seldom seen, but appreciated, efficient young man who transports luggage between hotels, relieving guests of all responsibility save the actual packing of their personal belongings. No more getting up at the crack of dawn to place your bags outside your room; no more in-transit fussing over lost luggage, and no more tedious waiting for fresh clothes once you reach the next hotel. The travelling Bell Boy picks up your suitcases from your rooms once you have left, and deposits them in your new rooms at the next stop, even before you have arrived. This luxury reinstates the high standards of personal service of days gone by, and complements the excellent level of comfort and courtesy maintained throughout the tours.

Tours encompassed by the Great Britain and Europe Express cover England and Scotland (run as one tour), Wales, France, Germany, Spain and Switzerland. In addition to these, 1990 saw the introduction of the Great Italy Express, the Great Scandinavian Express and the Great Austria Express. The duration of these holidays varies from five days spent in Wales to eleven days spent in France. Features included in the price of all tours are a cocktail party held at the hotel on the first evening (except in Burgundy, where there is a wine-tasting session at Dijon's celebrated Academy of Wine), and a farewell dinner. In every itinerary there are also at least two two-night stays at the same de luxe hotel, allowing for a more leisurely pace. Rail travel is always in the comfort of first class and motor-coaches are only used on occasion for hotel transfers and local sightseeing.

Factors which have influenced the choice of hotels on the tours are the degree of comfort weighed against actual cost, location and style. In the medieval village of Rocamadour in western France for example, there is no de luxe hotel. This is more than adequately compensated for by the charm of the clean, comfortable and well appointed Hotel Beau-Site. The hotel in Granada is chosen for its location since it actually stands in the grounds of the Alhambra itself. Naturally, though, where more luxurious accommodation is available, Abercrombie and Kent make sure they secure their guests the best deal possible. On top of that, where they have been able to secure a guarantee from the hotel for special accommodation at a reasonable cost, you will find that attention has been paid to providing rooms which overlook a lake or gardens in an effort to make your stay more enjoyable.

Throughout the tours the flexible approach to meal times is one which allows guests maximum independence, but which also provides the opportunity to sample as many delights as possible. The individual demands of the itinerary, the desirability of independence, particularly at lunchtime but also on at least one evening per trip, and the importance of sampling attractive local restaurants are all taken into account when planning the tours. The variety of venues and types of cuisine on each trip is impressive. Specialities that are included are lunch at a famous château in France's wine district of the Medoc and dinner at Dalmeny House, the stately home of the Earl and Countess of Rosebery, just outside Edinburgh. These are all incorporated in the price of the trip, as is breakfast every morning and wine with certain meals.

The carefully thought-out itineraries of these rail tours provide a sure foundation on which to build a first-class holiday. Guests are offered the opportunity to enjoy everything from the Military Tattoo at Edinburgh's International Festival to gambling in Monte Carlo. Alternatively, you could be at a lively and colourful flamenco performance in Granada or visiting a baroque Benedictine Abbey in Germany. If spectacular scenery is a priority for your holiday then choose Snowdonia National Park in Wales or the otherwise inaccessible villages of the Switzerland between St Moritz and Zermatt, crossed by means of the unique Glacier Express. The introduction of three new tours in 1990 means that travellers can now go further afield in the same style, taking in Pisa, Venice and Florence in Italy; Norway; Stockholm in Sweden; Denmark; Vienna, the Danube,

Salzburg and the mountains of the Tyrol in Austria. The concise nature of the tours solves any problems of limited travelling time, but in a manner that concentrates on leisure rather than speed.

Tour prices for the Great Britain and Europe Express range from £700–1,650, based on double occupancy with private facilities where specified. Breakfast and evening meals are included. For those who have purchased a first-class rail pass for more extensive travel in Europe, prices are slightly lower. On the whole, Abercrombie and Kent make sure that everything is provided with value for money as well as the invaluable advice of the professional guide who always accompanies the tours. Remember though that airport transfers, beverages, excess baggage fees and gratuities (which are not included in the price) can soon mount up, especially when moving relatively quickly between towns and cities. Travellers from Britain should note that if booking for any of the European tours, economy-class airfares to the starting points of the trips are included in the overall price, as well as two nights' accommodation for the one night immediately preceding and following the basic tour.

Further information on the Great Britain and Europe Express can be obtained from Abercrombie and Kent Limited (see Appendix II for details).

Railway Travel and Photography Rail Cruises

The idea behind Railway Travel and Photography's (RT&P) concept of 'Rail Cruising' stems from the days when tourist travel was leisurely and sedate and journeys were undertaken for the pleasure they afforded. The pleasure, that is, of the personal discovery of new sights and sounds, augmented by a comfortable and enjoyable means of transport. These are not holidays which combine a hurried train journey with a supplementary cruise (as the official title may suggest): rather they are the product of an efficiently organised company which has managed to create well-planned, short-break train holidays whose pace is akin to a luxury cruise. Destinations seem almost immaterial as you soak up the passing countryside. Gourmet meals and well-chosen wines complete the picture in a style that is quite simply first class.

Railway Travel and Photography offer their Rail Cruises in a variety of countries: Canada, India, China and, most recently, New Zealand. These all cover a minimum period of sixteen days which for many people might in fact exceed the definition of a 'short' break. Closer to home are the European options of France, Germany and Switzerland which extend to a maximum of eleven days, and price-wise are certainly more accessible than their Transatlantic or Far-Eastern equivalents. Of the three European countries to choose from France lasts the longest at eleven days, while the German and Swiss trips take eight days. If your time is limited, this really is the way to see Europe.

Itineraries for the holidays are carefully thought out to offer an interesting mixture of national characteristics and local specialities. In France you are taken from Paris, through Amboise in the Loire Valley, down to Aurillac in the Dordogne, then further south to Carcassonne, before coming up again to Nimes, along the Mediterranean coast to Provence and then back to Paris via Tain l'Hermitage on the Rhone. All transfers between towns are made by train, and the final leg of the journey is made by the fastest train in the world – the TGV (Train Grand Vitesse) – to Paris. Some coach transport is necessary for excursions, although travel by road is kept to a minimum and offers little, if any, inconvenience.

Excursions on this trip are designed to let you experience and observe a cross-section of French life: everything from lunch at a sixteenth-century château to a fascinating trip by steam train. Excursions are included in the overall price of around £650, so there is no extra cost and no dilemma about how to make the most of your time in France. Also included are your Air France flights to and from Gatwick or Manchester, half-board accommodation (except in Provence where it is full-board) in rooms with private facilities (watch out for any minor qualifications to this), a first-class 'France Vacances' pass for unlimited free travel on French Railways, all detailed excursions plus specified meals, baggage transfers between hotels and a RT&P tour escort throughout. There is, in fact, little that RT&P do not take care of. Luggage transfers are particularly helpful, contributing to the relaxed atmosphere and generally unhurried pace. Departures for this trip are usually twice a year, one towards the end of May and the other around mid-September.

Switzerland provides the setting for the second European Rail Cruise and it is here that you will find some of the most spectacular scenery in the world. There is a choice of two Swiss tours: the 'Swiss Winter Wonderland' trip in mid-February, and the 'Swiss Scenic Rail Cruise' in both June and August. Arrivals and departures for both trips are to and from Zurich. On the 'Swiss

Scenic Rail Cruise' two nights are spent in Interlaken, two nights in Weggis, two nights in Lugano, and two nights in Montreux. Excursions are made on most days, allowing you to structure your holiday with leisure cruises and trips into the beautiful Swiss mountains. Plenty of time is left to explore the villages and towns for yourself, and the RT&P escort will ensure that you are informed of all the features of interest within the vicinity.

The price of this Rail Cruise is roughly £675. Included are scheduled flights by Swissair from London, Birmingham or Manchester to Zurich, accommodation with half-board throughout the tour, rooms with private bath or shower and toilet, a first-class Swiss pass for unlimited free travel on most railways, lake steamers and post buses for the duration of the tour, a cruise on Lake Luzern with lunch on board, welcome drink before dinner on the first evening, transfer of luggage from Zurich airport to your hotel, between resorts and from your last hotel to your UK airport, and RT&P's own tour escort. Departure dates are twice a year, in June and August.

The 'Swiss Winter Wonderland' tour follows a similar format, but over a different route. Your itinerary includes four nights in Interlaken and three nights in Chur, in the area known as the Grisons. Excursions run throughout the week; guests have the opportunity to travel into the massive mountain range of the Jungfrau – which includes such famous peaks as the Eiger and the Monch, take a train to the Jungfraujoch, at 11,340 feet the 'Roof of Europe' – spend a day in Luzern and St Moritz, travel over the spirals and tunnels of the Albula Pass, and sample the narrow-gauge Apenzellerbahn at St Gallen. Several days are reserved for your own leisure: the RT&P escort can direct you to places of interest.

The price of the 'Swiss Winter Wonderland' tour is roughly £520. This includes scheduled flights by Swissair to Zurich, accommodation with half-board throughout the tour, rooms with private bath or shower and toilet, a first-class Swiss pass for unlimited free travel on most railways, lake steamers and post buses, transfer of luggage from airport to hotel, between Interlaken and Chur, and from Chur to your destination airport in the UK, and the usual RT&P tour escort. Departure is mid-February.

The final European option from RT&P is slightly different. Classified as a 'Steam Tour', it is an eight-day trip to Eastern Germany, aimed primarily at the dedicated steam enthusiast. Departure is from London Heathrow to West Berlin, from where you transfer to Karl-Marx-Stadt. Three nights are spent here, followed by five nights in Dresden, with visits to Crottendorf, Zittau, Aue, Meinersdorf and Zwickau. Excursions are organised for each day (apart from your final day in Dresden), and are orientated around Eastern Germany's rail and steam network. Trains featured are a class 38 4-6-0, a class 86 tank, a class 41, the older type 2-10-2T's, an 0-8-0T, and Saxon-Meyer 0-4-4-0T's, to name a few. Obviously this is a tour for those who know their trains. However, it should be pointed out that steam in Eastern Germany is now reaching its end, and this tour may well offer a final chance to see some of the classes that this country still has to offer.

The price for the 'Steam Tour' is roughly £670. Included are flights from London to Berlin, and transfer to Karl-Marx-Stadt, steam tours as detailed (with locomotives to be confirmed nearer the time), all transportation, half-board accommodation with private facilities wherever possible, local and railway guides, permits and visas, and the services of an RT&P tour courier. Departure is around mid-May.

Overall impressions of the European Rail Cruises are that they provide a relaxed short break which is ideal as a holiday in itself or which can be easily incorporated into a wider itinerary. With your own tour escort and specially chartered train carriages, trips become more personal and you certainly get to parts of the country that conventional tours do not reach.

Prospective travellers may be interested to learn that 1991 sees the introduction of two new tours covering Spain and Austria, both of which will follow a similar format to those in France and Switzerland. Also of note, if you're interested in travelling further afield, and have the time, is a new mammoth tour of China, with four departures a year from the UK. Prices are in the region of £2,000–2,500.

Further information is available from Railway Travel and Photography (see Appendix II for details).

Flying
Round-the-World Air Tickets

Although travellers have been attempting to circumnavigate the globe for many years, the concept of an air ticket which permits you to fly between continents, just as you might take a bus around town, is relatively new. Travelling around the world is neither as expensive nor as time-consuming as you might at first think. Admittedly there are ways of circling the globe which are both costly and demanding in time, but with a round-the-world air-ticket these problems can be eliminated. Restrictions and conditions of travel are being continually eased, and 'flexibility of flight' has become the order of the day. The rest of the world is, literally, only a flight away.

There are several factors to be considered when planning a trip round the world. Most of these depend on personal preference, but others are dictated by factors such as your choice of itinerary, departure point, or the time of year. Airlines are generally fairly helpful although there is a limit to what they can do in assisting every passenger who wants a round-the-world ticket. Theoretically, the combinations of countries you choose to visit should be endless, but in reality the situation is somewhat different.

The most important aspect of a round-the-world ticket, and one which influences almost all aspects of your trip, is your choice of itinerary. Usually, passengers must fly continually in an eastward or westward direction, with no back-tracking at all. Thus, if you wish to visit Hong Kong and Australia, it is not possible to return by way of Japan. Occasionally, a minimum stay – usually fourteen days – is stipulated for each destination, but more significant is the maximum stay of either 180 days or a year from the date of purchase of your ticket, which must not be exceeded. Also to be remembered is that all tickets follow prearranged routes, including either destinations solely in the northern or solely in the southern hemisphere, or in a combination of both. Northern routes, if departure is from the UK or the US, mean that you will have less overall flying time to reach your destinations. An attractive offer comes from British Airways in conjunction with United Airlines, whose northern hemisphere trip takes in London, Rome, Bahrain, Bombay, Hong Kong, Tokyo, Honolulu, and at least one major city in North America. Northern routes also allow you to avoid the excesses of tropical temperatures, but still enjoy many warm destinations.

Southern routes are most suited to those who wish to visit the less common holiday destinations. The main southern stopovers include South America, Australasia, and most of Malaysia and Singapore. Ideally, though, your route should include a combination of destinations in both hemispheres, since these will afford greater variety of both culture and climate.

Once an itinerary has been decided, the next step is to find the combination of airlines which most closely matches your plans. For example, if you wish to visit New Zealand, together with Australia, Singapore and perhaps somewhere in the Caribbean, there are only a limited number of airlines which will meet your requirements. All in all there are a possible fifty-eight combinations of airlines which offer round-the-world tickets, all of which have their own conditions concerning stopover restrictions, validity of ticket (time-wise), discounts, cancellation fees, and optional extras.

Personal financial considerations must, inevitably, be taken into account, since travelling around the world could cost you £2,000–3,500. The main factor which affects this price is your choice of class, ie: Economy, Business or First Class: most round-the-world tickets are, in fact, Economy Class.

One of the most comprehensive selections of round-the-world tickets is offered by British Airways, in conjunction with United Airlines, Qantas and Air New Zealand. Fares range from roughly £1,300–3,900. All routes carry optional extras such as crossing the Atlantic on Concorde, or additional stopovers for a small surcharge. If travelling first class, some stopovers are included free of charge, such as the North American and Hawaiian option on one southern hemisphere route (British Airways/United Airlines), or the New Zealand option on another (British Airways/Qantas/United Airlines). British Airways will also arrange car rental in each of your destinations.

Pan Am, America's leading airline, was the first major international carrier to pioneer round-the-world tickets. Their offers today are in conjunction with Cathay Pacific, United Airlines, Qantas and Air Pacific. Fares from London start at £1,150 – for routes via the North Atlantic and North Pacific – and go up to £3,400 for first-class travel via the North Atlantic and South Pacific. Excursions are available for both routes, and include Trinidad, Barbados, the Virgin Islands and Alaska, for anything from roughly £350–600, depending on class of travel.

If the standard of in-flight service is an influencing factor in your choice of airlines or routes, then potential round-the-world travellers should try and include South African Airways as one of their carriers. This national airline is one of the largest operating from a southern hemisphere base, and offers a wide range of long-haul routes between South Africa and Europe, Israel and Brazil. In-flight catering is outstanding, and even in 'Silver Class' (economy), there is more space to stretch out than on most other airlines. Considering one of their most popular routes is the daily, twelve-hour, non-stop haul between London and Johannesburg, this comparatively greater leg-room is a definite asset.

A final option for serious round-the-world travellers is the 'do-it-yourself' ticket, which opens up countless combinations of routes and stopovers. This ticket is most suited to travellers who wish to include more unusual destinations in their journey. Entirely original itineraries can be made up from either standard scheduled or discounted flights, although they may be more expensive than the usual round-the-world ticket. Two airlines to consider in particular are Wardair, which offers very competitive seats to Canada and further afield in its global routings, and Virgin Atlantic, one of the cheapest airlines crossing to the USA. In general, a DIY ticket will be more expensive, more time-consuming and more problematic in preparatory stages, but it does offer unlimited freedom of where to visit, and how long to stay in each destination.

The main international airlines dealing with round-the-world tickets are Air Canada, Air New Zealand, British Airways, Canadian Pacific Airlines, Cathay Pacific, Chinese Airlines, Japanese Air Lines, KLM Royal Dutch Airlines, Malaysian Airline System, North-West Orient, Pan Am, Qantas, Singapore Airlines, South African Airways, Swissair, and United Airlines. It should be noted that any round-the-world ticket will deal with at least two airlines, and possibly as many as four.

Further details of round-the-world air tickets should be available from your local travel agent, but if not, then it would be advisable to contact direct any of the above named airlines. Comprehensive coverage of both round-the-world tickets and air travel in general can be found in the British Airways-recommended *The Round the World Air Guide* by Katie Wood and George McDonald, published by Fontana Paperbacks.

Concorde Flights of Fantasy

Since its maiden flight just over twenty years ago Concorde has become a household name. Flying at twice the speed of sound at over ten miles high it is now the world's most prestigious aircraft, but there is more to Concorde than its speed and excitement.

For jetsetting businessmen it may be the quickest way of flitting between countries, but for devoted travellers the possibilities are almost endless. The sky is literally the limit!

Amongst a number of companies, Goodwood Travel have developed a series of Concorde Charters since their inaugural flight to the Monaco Grand Prix in 1983, and are now offering a total of thirty-four destinations which make up their 'flights of fantasy'. These journeys are designed to offer the ultimate in modern holidays, and even day-trips to places such as Cairo are featured. What better way to treat yourself or a relative to an experience they will remember for the rest of their lives!

The various destinations to choose from range from Amman to Yeovilton, although not all are available at all times of the year. The most popular trip is a visit to Cairo. This is offered as a day-trip, a weekend tour, or a three-day tour and is available on specific dates only. The attention paid on all three trips to ensuring full value for money cannot be doubted, and is evident from the moment you take off and are served a champagne breakfast. This is a feature which is encountered on most flights of fantasy, on all of which the quality of service can definitely be classed as 'champagne'. On arrival at your destination you will be met by prearranged transport, sometimes in the form of coaches or alternatively limousines (if you are going to see *The Phantom of the Opera* in New York) or horse-drawn carriage (if you are on the three-day Cairo tour).

Other favourites with 'flights of fantasy' followers are the various Christmas and New Year trips. In particular, 'Christmas Concorde to Lapland' offers a meeting with Santa in and around Rovaniemi, the capital of northern Finland. As well as the trip on Christmas Day itself there are three others in the lead up to Christmas. During the flight you are treated to the usual champagne breakfast while witnessing the unique phenomenon of the sun setting in the east and then rising again shortly afterwards. Also included in this festive sojourn are a meeting with a Lapp family in traditional costume (accompanied of course by their reindeer), the opportunity to drive reindeer sleighs through the snow, a fifty-dish banquet and a parting gift from Santa himself. All in all, this is a trip which would make a most original Christmas present, although at £1,195 you might expect your stay in the Artic Circle to be longer than eight hours.

Vienna is the destination for Concorde's last trip of the year where you can toast the New Year in at the Imperial Ball at

Hofburg Palace. The advantage of this trip is that it extends over four days, from your departure on 29 December to your return on 1 January. The city provides the perfect setting for a time of year when good living, fine music and celebration are particularly welcomed and appreciated. Your itinerary takes you on vintage tram-cars, a tour to the Schonbrunn Palace, dinner with unlimited wine and musical entertainment at the Altes Presshaus in Grinzing, and a trip in a horse-drawn carriage to the ball itself.

One of the delights of this tour is that not all your time is taken up with organised excursions and you are actually given a day to explore Vienna for yourself. Accommodation and breakfast at a five-star hotel are all included in the price of £1,545, as is your ticket to the Imperial Ball and the Gala Banquet served during the evening. You will need to arrange accommodation in London though, before you leave and once you return. While the initial check-in is held at a Heathrow hotel (with a champagne reception) no accommodation is actually provided at this hotel for the night before you leave, and check-in time *is* 9.00 a.m. Remember also that if you live any distance from Heathrow Airport, arriving in this country on New Year's Day may prove awkward for the final leg of your journey. Despite this, a New Year Vienna visit by Concorde is a real once-in-a-lifetime trip.

If theatre-going interests you, why not make it a memorable night out and see *The Phantom of the Opera* on Broadway! For around £2,100 you can fly to New York (arriving only five minutes after you leave) and spend two nights and three days in the largest city in the USA. No time is wasted on this trip and you are whisked straight from the plane to an exclusively chartered yacht which will take you past the fantastic Manhattan skyline, along the Hudson River to the Statue of Liberty and back again. While on board, cocktails and canapés are served and you are free to enjoy the musical entertainment. What a welcome to the 'Big Apple'! Other highlights on this trip come in the form of luxury limousine transfers, a helicopter sightseeing tour and, if you go at New Year, the New Year's Eve Ball at your Broadway hotel after *The Phantom of the Opera* performance. Even if you do not go at New Year there is still a Concorde gala dinner to be enjoyed on each trip, as well as the pre-theatre cocktail party. Once you are at the theatre there is no need to worry about missing half the show because of awkward seating arrangements, since your top-price tickets (included in the overall price) guarantee some of the best seats in the house.

Excursions are also included and these offer more excitement than the usual coach and sightseeing tours. If you want time to yourself outside the busy itinerary, you are still left with two free afternoons to browse around the shops, visit museums or simply relax and absorb the atmosphere of this vibrant city.

This is just a small selection of the Concorde 'flights of fantasy' now on offer. Other trips include a three-day tour to the Soviet Union – 'Moscow and the Bolshoi Ballet', a two-day visit to 'Leningrad, the Hermitage and the Kirov Ballet', or alternatively, a four-day trip to Jordan in the footsteps of Lawrence of Arabia through some of the world's most incredible ancient monuments. For many of these journeys the term 'luxury' seems inadequate. They really are the ultimate in modern travel.

More information is available from Goodwood Travel Limited (see Appendix II for details).

The Jules Verne

Intrepid travellers and pioneering adventurers have been with us either in fiction or as fact, for many hundreds of years, discovering new continents, unearthing ancient tribes or conquering terrain that has previously proved unmanageable. Although it may seem as if there is little left for any of us to discover, it is possible to make your own personal exploration of the world in a style that would have left Phileas Fogg astounded, and rendered the function of his valet, Passepartout, somewhat redundant. Thomas Cook, in association with Voyages Jules Verne, have come up with perhaps the most luxurious, and certainly the most enjoyable way of travelling across countries, in a circumnavigation of the world which, quite appropriately, is known simply as 'The Jules Verne'. London to Luxor, the Seychelles to Sydney and Bangkok to Barbados all form part of this trip with a host of countries, towns and cities carefully selected as part of the itinerary. If you want to really see and experience the world, this is probably the best way to do it.

Travel on the trip is primarily by air, but, while this may have proved a novelty for Phileas Fogg, Thomas Cook and Voyages Jules Verne realise how monotonous this can be and have therefore devised a number of features to provide variation. For a start they have planned the itinerary in such a way that whenever flying is necessary you never have longer than six hours in a plane at one time. All connections are relatively short since the distances involved between stopover points are kept to a minimum. On top of that you also have the added advantage of flying by privately chartered plane, thus eliminating the usual series of tedious flight changes which are often involved when travelling on scheduled services from one country to another.

Other attractive highlights include a three-night cruise down the Nile on the *Presidential Nile Cruiser* (or similar) as far as Aswan on the northern shores of Lake Nasser; a rail trip in India from New Delhi to Jaipur in Rajasthan, on to Agra and then back to Delhi again; and a cruise down the Chao Phraya River in Thailand. Generally, though, the emphasis is on flight as a means of transport and this is clearly reflected in the fact that day-time excursions are often made by air. Whilst in the Seychelles for example, even though you are situated on the principal island of Mahé, there are a further eighty-five enchanting islands which make up this archipelago and which are easily reached by plane. The options offered by Thomas Cook come in the form of excursions to Praslin, the second-largest island, to Bird Island, home to a wide variety of birds, or to pretty la Digue, where transportation is by ox-cart or bicycle. All of these are certainly worth a visit and all are made accessible with the help of an organised flight.

The itinerary of the trip as a whole follows a southerly trail, starting in London, heading towards the Far East, Australia and New Zealand, and returning by way of Easter Island, Peru and Barbados. Total travelling time amounts to thirty-five days, in the course of which approximately twenty-two stopover points are scheduled. This gives a fairly good indication of the pace adopted for the trip and the sort of 'sightseeing intensity' which travellers will experience. Throughout the tour, days of busy cultural activity are alternated with periods of ease and leisurely contemplation, ensuring that the trip remains enjoyable and saturation point is avoided. There are excursions from virtually every city, village or island that you visit, some of which are included in the price; others are optional.

These excursions are well organised and efficiently planned, allowing travellers to experience as many different cultures and ways of life as possible, without becoming repetitive or over-ambitious. In Egypt attention is focussed on the tombs, pyramids and temples, while in Old Delhi it is the Red Fort and the memorial of Raj Ghat, Ghandi's burial place, which occupy much of your time. Bangkok finds you visiting a floating market and only twenty-four hours later, once in Penang, you will be driving through the spice and rubber plantations which contribute so much to the Malaysian economy. In Australia there is a trip to the famous Ayers Rock in the Olgas; on Easter Island your excursion takes in the Rararanaku Volcano, and in Peru you can spend a day in the 'Lost City' of Machu Picchu. Before returning to London, there are three nights and two days spent in Barbados, where you can relax and sunbathe on the beach, or travel round to the west coast and go snorkelling and deep-sea diving. The Jules Verne certainly offers something for everyone, circling the globe in style and comfort to create a truly unique holiday.

The cost of the Jules Verne, 'A Circumnavigation of the World by Private Aeroplane, River Boat and Train' is roughly £10,500. Included in this is accommodation in hotels (twin-sharing) with *en suite* facilities, twin-sharing accommodation on trains, transportation on chartered plane and other scheduled transportation in the itinerary, all specified sightseeing tours, porterage for one item of luggage, services of a tour manager, occasional guest lecturers and local taxes. Board arrangements are half-board throughout the tour, with lunch included when actually travelling at lunchtime. Other factors to take in to account are the £500 deposit, and supplement of £995 if you want a single room. This price compares favourably with a round-the-world ticket and obviously the convenience of having your hotels, trips and guides pre-organised is worth a lot to the traveller.

The 1991 departure date for the Jules Verne is 25 February, returning on 31 March. The journey is undertaken using a Boeing 767 and the same crew remains with you for the duration of the tour.

Also on offer from Voyages Jules Verne is membership of their exclusive Travellers Club. This is automatically granted to anyone who makes a booking with them to the value of £850 per person. As a club member you are entitled to attend a two- or three-night travel seminar at a country house hotel in the Cotswolds, going to lectures by guest speakers on your prospective journey and enjoying the facilities of the hotel. These seminars are run over a period of five months and are a source of invaluable advice and information for any serious traveller. They also provide the perfect opportunity to meet your future travelling companions, as well as learning from other members what else is on offer from the company.

Full information on the Travellers Club seminars and the

Jules Verne tour are available from Voyages Jules Verne and the Thomas Cook Group Ltd (see Appendix II for details).

Cruising

Imagine for a moment the experience of a touring holiday without the inconvenience and upheaval of living out of a suitcase. Imagine travelling to some of the world's most beautiful and glamorous destinations with just one luxury base. Imagine a holiday during which you may cover thousands of miles but never suffer jet-lag. A cruising holiday offers all this and more.

Gone is the old idea that luxury cruising is the preserve of retired millionaires. Many elderly people do still tour the world by cruise liner because it is something they have always longed to do, but increasingly it has become the choice for young singles, romantic couples, and families. Parents can take advantage of the excellent facilities provided for keeping children amused on board ship, to steal a little time on their own. Once on board, most things are included in the price, and there is not the inconvenience of settling large bills as you go along. The highest prices on the cruise market are for liners carrying small numbers of passengers and with the atmosphere of private yachts.

Today's luxury liners are equipped with an impressive range of things to do and pride themselves on their high standards of service, entertainment and cuisine. Passengers are often surprised to find how easy it is to make friends and to fill their days on board with as much or as little activity as they choose.

The list of fine cruise ships and fabulous destinations is long, but here are just some of the most beautiful and exciting cruises available today.

Hebridean Princess

Relaunched in April 1989 after a £1.5 million refit, the *Hebridean Princess* brings to the waterways of the Scottish Highlands and Islands the same grace, elegance and opportunity for de luxe travel that the Queen of Scots bestows on Scotland's railways. Accommodation, cuisine and entertainment on board this luxury miniliner are of the very finest quality, drawing all who sail on her into the spirit and splendour of this beautiful part of Britain. To all intents and purposes you are staying in a country house hotel, although this is a floating hotel which can transport you to a new destination every day. From the security and luxury of a five-star base you can enjoy the most remote and isolated places in the British Isles; the Outer Hebrides, the Flannan Isles, and St Kilda – owned by the National Trust and otherwise very inaccessible. With a crew of twenty-two to look after a maximum of forty-six guests you can be assured that your every need will be attended to and always in the most unobtrusive but efficient manner possible.

There are five different itineraries available, with departures between May and October. The duration of trips runs to a maximum of seven nights, with the possibility on a couple of tours of splitting this time into three- or four-night options. End-of-season cruises around the islands of the Firth of Clyde and up to Argyll are run as separate holidays of three or four nights. Ports of call and places of significance can be roughly categorised under: the islands of the Inner and Outer Hebrides; St Kilda and the Small Isles; Loch Torridon; Mull of Kintyre and the Clyde; the Firth of Clyde islands, and the Highland scenery of Argyll.

Accommodation on board is split into seven different categories consisting of Staterooms A-F and the Yachtsman's Cabin (grade G). Unlike many luxury liners your choice of accommodation has no bearing at all on access to the facilities you may use. The public rooms are for the enjoyment of all passengers and the only factor determined by the price of the holiday is, in fact, your accommodation.

Entertainment while you are cruising is varied and if you are not absorbed by the superb views or engrossed in spotting the many different kinds of seabirds (oystercatchers, dunlin, and puffins to name but a few), there is still plenty to amuse you. For those with sporting interests, sailing, private fishing trips and clay pigeon shooting are all included in the price of the holiday, while those who favour more leisurely pursuits can make full use of the lounge and areas such as the Princess Foyer or the library. Plenty of open deck space is supplemented by the sheltered Promenade Deck which, with its comfortable lounging chairs, offers relaxation and fresh air away from the heart of the ship.

The Columba Restaurant, with its large fitted windows, provides an extremely pleasant setting for meals on the *Hebridean Princess*. Fresh produce is taken on board at each port of call, thus ensuring a selection of the best of traditional Scottish specialities along with the usual nouvelle cuisine. Vegetarian and special dietary needs can be accommodated as long as the chef is given reasonable notice, and every effort is made to provide a first-class standard of cuisine. All main meals are served in the Columba Restaurant and all passengers can be seated comfortably at one sitting. Given appropriate weather conditions, barbecues are also held on deck.

One of the advantages of the new-look *Hebridean Princess* is the garage space that has been incorporated into the design of the vessel and, for an extra charge, passengers are able to take their own cars on board. Essentially this means that whenever the boat is actually in dock, guests have access to their own means of transport for the day and are free to go wherever they choose. It should be pointed out though that many places which the ship visits do not have suitable docking facilities. Passengers are therefore transported to shore in the quick launch and recovery tenders on board.

Highlights of the various tours are numerous and not a day goes by without a visit to one or two places of interest. The remote Kinloch Castle on the Isle of Rhum (owned by the Nature Conservancy Council) is undoubtedly one of the most interesting places in Scotland to visit. Intact for the last century, this eccentric millionaire's shooting lodge captures all the romance of Highland Scotland. Other historic sights such as the spectacular Eilean Donan Castle at Kyle of Lochalsh feature on this trip. While on the Isle of Skye the opportunity exists to visit the MacDonald Centre which, in its well kept, picturesque garden setting, portrays the history of the 'Lords of the Isles'. A visit to the remote archipelago of St Kilda is certainly one of the high points of the tours. Set 110 miles out in the Atlantic Ocean this group of four islands and five towering rock stacks was designated by UNESCO in 1986 as Scotland's first World Heritage Centre. The main island, Hirta, is known to have been inhabited by man for up to 2,000 years before the last thirty-six residents were evacuated at their own request on 29 August 1930. The islands of St Kilda were bequeathed to the National Trust for Scotland in 1957 and have since been declared a National Nature Reserve. Trips to the islands are made by the *Hebridean Princess* with the permission of the National Trust and are subject to the sea and prevailing weather conditions.

These are just some of the features of a cruise on board the *Hebridean Princess*. Comments from guests indicate that the main attractions of this ship are the large amount of space, the comfort and quality of cuisine on board, and views of the magnificent scenery of the Western Highlands and Islands. Also commented on is the ability of the ship to anchor at a different location each night, plus the ability to take guests ashore at least twice each day to make visits to castles, gardens, distilleries and all the other places which are so much a part of Scottish history and tradition. Perhaps the most telling point to bear in mind is the fact that this is a ship which used to carry 600 passengers as a ferry, but now, in its new luxury status, carries around thirty-five guests on an average cruise.

Full-board prices for a seven-night cruise range from £450–1,400 per person, according to accommodation chosen. Yachtsman's Cabins come in at a lower price, starting at £260 per person. Prices include all excursions and full use of all the luxury facilities of the ship.

Further information can be obtained from Hebridean Island Cruises Ltd (see Appendix II for details).

QE2 to New York

While cruises to America remain as popular as ever, the range of companies and impressive choice of boats which sail these waters has declined rapidly since the 1960s. Today, the only passenger liner which continues to cross the Atlantic is Cunard's famous flagship, the *Queen Elizabeth 2*. Trips from Southampton to New York are made in a style that guarantees nothing less than the best. The options open to travellers give you a choice of the number of days per holiday and the chance to combine your cruise with perhaps the most sophisticated way of air travel: a flight on Concorde. The flexibility of these holidays caters superbly for today's traveller, in a manner which unites traditional luxury with present-day efficiency.

Ever since her launch in 1967 the *QE2* has stood out as perhaps the single most luxurious liner afloat. At 963 feet long, weighing 67,139 tons and standing thirteen storeys high, she is certainly the largest passenger ship you are ever likely to sail in. With that size comes a stability, comfort and safety which all contribute to your general enjoyment of a stay aboard this floating five-star hotel. And of course there is plenty of space in which to indulge whatever pastime may take your fancy. There is very little in fact which the *QE2* does not offer. With one crew member for every two passengers, service is unquestionably efficient and, just as the brochure boasts, 'courteous stewards and stewardesses can organise anything from breakfast in bed to a private cocktail party in your stateroom.'

Entertainment between ports of call caters for all tastes, with novel possibilities such as the computer learning centre or more traditional pursuits such as shuffleboard or deck tennis. In addition there are four swimming pools, a health club, a 500-seat theatre, lavish entertainment lounges and a shopping mall with exclusive names such as Gucci, Christian Dior and a branch of Harrods. In the evening there is no lack of entertainment either and, what's more, there are no laws about closing times or drinking after hours! The choice extends to seven different bars, dancing in the Queen's Room, disco in the Club Lido and cabaret in the Grand Lounge. For those who enjoy a flutter there is also the casino with its blackjack tables, roulette and a bank of slot machines.

The class of your accommodation determines which of the four restaurants you are given access to. However, all the restaurants have a five-star rating, (though the Mauretania and Columbia are more like three–four star), and both the Queen's Grill and the Princess Grill carry a Fielding 'Five-Star Plus' award, the highest accolade awarded to a cruise ship dining room. For all passengers it is necessary to make a dining room request, indicating on a reservation form your preferred table-size and whether smoking or non-smoking. In the case of the Mauretania Restaurant, passengers also have the choice of later or earlier sittings for meals if the cruise is heavily booked. While this is an added convenience for those who are allocated the sitting of their choice (for example a 9.00 a.m. breakfast might be preferable to the earlier 8.00 a.m. sitting), it can also be somewhat irritating to find yourself being ushered out of a leisurely 6.30 p.m. dinner to make way for 8.00 p.m. guests. On the whole though, this system works well and causes little inconvenience, with restaurant managers making every effort to comply with all requests.

Accommodation is essentially what cruising is all about, since the ship becomes your world and your room becomes your only area of truly private space. There is certainly no shortage of choice where rooms are concerned, since the *QE2* has twenty-two categories within two basic classes: First Class and Transatlantic Class. All cabins are air-conditioned, have generous storage space and their own private facilities. Following recent refurbishments there are now eight new luxury suites on Signal Deck, each with its own private veranda. Telephones in the rooms can be used to dial anywhere in the world and televisions feature satellite transmissions (weather conditions and position of *QE2* permitting) as well as video films, documentaries, and news programmes. In top-grade staterooms there are also complete entertainment centres with video cassette player, colour TV and radio. An extensive selection of video films can be found in the general library.

Such are the standards on board the *QE2*. But time spent cruising is only half the holiday, and once the ship has docked there is still plenty of excitement to come. Sailing to New York has the added advantage of the thrill of discovering one of the world's most exciting cities and Cunard have put together a variety of packages which show you this city in their own unique style. New York is the US's capital city for theatre, the arts, sport and finance.

The *QE2* trips which deal exclusively with New York can be split into three categories: ten-, twelve- or fifteen-day options, all of which offer a total of eight days cruising, with the number of nights actually spent in New York being the variable factor. The ten-day cruise is little more than a glorified shopping-trip, with little time actually spent in New York. Fares are not exactly cheap, at around £1,200. However, given the nature of *QE2*'s excellent service, along with an organised morning tour and a buffet lunch at the Waldorf Astoria Hotel, it is fair to say that you will certainly get your money's worth.

For just £40 more you can enjoy the standard *QE2* cruise as well as two nights at the famous Waldorf Astoria Hotel, situated on fashionable Park Avenue in the heart of Manhattan. Alternatively, you can remain on board and spend two days cruising Long Island Sound for what Cunard call a 'Party at Sea'. Included in the price of both of these trips is, for Waldorf Astoria guests, a comprehensive sightseeing tour of Manhattan, and for Long Island Party-Time Cruisers, a short morning tour of Manhattan highlights, followed by a buffet lunch at the Waldorf. Transport is, of course, provided.

Finally the fifteen-day cruise provides a perfect balance between time spent cruising and time spent in the city. The usual sightseeing tour is included in the price of £1,365, but apart from that your time is basically your own. Staying at the Waldorf places any New York tourist in a prime position for getting out and seeing the city. Attractions such as the Metropolitan Museum, Central Park, Empire State Building and Rockefeller Centre are all close by, not to mention the excellent selection of stores such as Macy's and Bloomingdales. This cruise is only run once a year, usually around September/October time, so it's likely to be fairly busy.

For all cruises the fare covers the following items: all meals, entertainment and accommodation on board the *QE2*, sightseeing tours and hotel accommodation in New York, and first-class return rail travel between the nearest British mainland station and, either the main London rail termini, or Southampton Central Station. Watch when booking to see exactly which meals are included during your stay in New York since these are not always clearly specified.

Variations on the above holidays are also available. For example '*QE2* Skyscraper Holidays' which offers a cruise to New York, a three-night stay at the Sheraton Centre Hotel and a scheduled overnight return flight to London. The fare for this holiday is usually £875, although after the end of August it does start to get cheaper, reaching £755 by the end of November.

Flying features in the final variation which comes in the form of Concorde Holidays. These give you the opportunity to combine a flight on British Airways Concorde, either out to New York or returning to London, with a cruise on board the *QE2* (in whichever direction you do not fly). Time spent in New York can be classed as anything from a one-day sightseeing fly/cruise to a four-night experience at Manhattan's Waldorf Astoria. Alternative accommodation is offered, if preferred, at the New York Hilton, also situated in Manhattan. Prices range from £1,135–1,765 and include the usual accommodation arrangements, sightseeing tours, etc. Not included in the price however, and this applies to a selection of cruises (check with your travel agent before leaving), are port taxes of £51 per person, insurance, drinks, meals in destination cities, gratuities and US Airport Departure Tax of £2 per person. Some of these may seem minor but they can soon all add up. If you are intending to take advantage of offers which go further afield than New York, then you should also check up on vaccination requirements.

Dress on board the *QE2* is fairly relaxed and informal, but remember to take any sports gear that you might need for deck games and keep-fit classes. Lightweight sweaters or jackets are also advisable due to the ship's air-conditioning. Dress for the evening is sometimes formal, in which case it is black tie for gentlemen and evening dresses for the ladies, and when informal, a jacket and tie for gentlemen and cocktail or dinner attire for the ladies – generally, keep in style with the often elegant surroundings in which you will be travelling.

Further informations can be obtained from Cunard (see Appendix II for details).

Round-the-World Cruises

A round-the-world cruise is the sort of holiday which many people dream about, without actually realising how accessible, both financially and time-wise, such a trip can be. If you want to see the world, there are several advantages in cruising which merit spending a bit extra. First of all, cruising is definitely one of the most leisurely and pleasurable ways to travel; while on board there is no queuing; no fastening seat-belts or turbulence; no baggage restrictions; no jet-lag; no searching for hotels and restaurants and no baggage-laden airport dashes. Instead, you can establish yourself in your cabin – your home for the duration of the cruise – spend your days in the sun, look forward to the next port of call, and simply enjoy the novelty of not having to worry about the responsibilities of 'life on land'. Add to this your enjoyment of the many facilities which all the world cruise liners have on board and the attentive and efficient English-speaking staff, and what you have is one of the easiest ways to see the world. A cruise is a holiday in itself; days at sea exist solely for your entertainment and pleasure. If you're interested in different cultures, then it is simply an added bonus that you are crossing from one side of the globe to the other, and back again, in the luxury of your floating hotel.

Most round-the-world cruises follow a westerly trail from their starting point, and feature a number of standard ports of call which never lose their interest. Central America, Mexico and the South Pacific are always popular, with the Panama Canal providing the essential link between places such as Montego Bay, Balboa and Acapulco. The itinerary across the South Pacific varies between companies, although two or three islands at least are usually included. Nuku 'Hiva (Marquesas Islands) is a common port of call, combined perhaps with Tahiti in the Society Islands. New Zealand is sometimes featured, although Australia provides an abundance of alternative ports, giving a good taste of the Antipodes, as well as the ports of Papua New Guinea. Heading into South Asia, two ports included on virtually every world itinerary are Hong Kong and Singapore. Penang, just off the west coast of Malaysia, is frequently featured, as well as either Phuket or Pattaya in Thailand. Bombay serves as an introduction to India, followed by a tour of the Middle East, featuring ports such as Aqaba (Jordan) and Safaga (Egypt), before transitting the Suez Canal. The final days of most world cruises are spent in the Mediterranean, for which there is not really any set pattern. This is an area about which companies seem to have their own preferences regarding ports of call; suffice to say that comprehensive coverage is normally given.

Such is the standard itinerary for the majority of world cruises. But within that itinerary there are significant differences between separate cruise companies. At the end of the day, these will probably be the deciding factors in your choice of cruise. P&O's world cruise is on board their luxury liner *Canberra*, and their itinerary combines most of the standard ports with a selection of alternative islands and cities. The cruise departs from Southampton (usually in January) and lasts about eighty-five nights. Your first port of call is Madeira, where a day is spent allowing you to relax at the very start of the cruise. North and South America come next, where one of the highlights comes in the form of Bonaire, a little-known island paradise at the tip of South America. Here you can explore the fish markets, laze on the pink sand beaches, go snorkelling or watch the flamingoes on Lake Goto, prior to your transit of the Panama Canal. Rather than heading straight across the Pacific, *Canberra* takes you north again for a visit to San Francisco. This is a definite bonus, and one which is featured by relatively few companies. Another city included in *Canberra's* itinerary is Auckland. If you want to visit New Zealand, you have a full day to explore this city, which has been described as being 'more English than England'! Another day is spent in the thriving port of Keelung in Taiwan. Here you are given the opportunity to visit the capital, Taipei, the fastest-growing city in Asia. Temples and memorials stand next to offices and tower-blocks in this fascinating city. Following almost a month's tour of the Middle and Far East, you emerge from the Suez Canal to spend time in the Mediterranean. Athens and Naples are both featured, where you have the opportunity to see the Acropolis or Parthenon, followed by visits to Mount Vesuvius and Pompeii. You arrive back in Southampton at the beginning of April.

Sagafjord and *Vistafjord* are Cunard's round-the-world liners, both of which depart from the USA – Fort Lauderdale (Florida) and New York respectively – in January. Highlights of *Sagafjord's* itinerary are numerous; Papeete in Tahiti is followed by Moorea in the Society Islands, as well as Bali in

Indonesia and Bandar Seri Begawan in Brunei. Heading towards the Middle East, visits are made to Karachi and Muscat, both relatively uncommon ports to find in a world itinerary. Muscat is especially worthwhile since tourism is relatively scarce here. You will be surprised by the rugged beauty and ancient history of Oman, a state more commonly associated with oil rather than its tourist value. Transit the Suez and you are in a different world altogether. Haifa (Israel), Kusadasi and Istanbul (Turkey), Yalta (Russia) and Varna (Bulgaria) are all featured. Again, it is unusual to find all these ports included, although they are all equally worth visiting. Around the Mediterranean, Catania (Sicily), Villefranche (France) and Malaga are there for your enjoyment before *Sagafjord* makes the transatlantic crossing back to Fort Lauderdale around the middle of April.

Vistafjord's itinerary is almost completely different from her sister ship's, and includes places such as Cartagena (Colombia), Los Angeles, Tarawa (Gilbert Islands), Guadalcanal (Solomon Islands) and the island of Male in the Maldives. The main difference occurs shortly after Male when, following stops at Goa and Bombay, *Vistafjord* does not transit the Suez Canal, but heads south again towards the Seychelles, Kenya, South Africa and Brazil. Mombasa, Durban, Cape Town and Rio de Janeiro precede calls at Salvador de Bahia and Belem in Brazil. If you're interested in this part of the world, this has to be one of the most relaxing ways not only of reaching it, but also of spending time there. A final day is spent in Barbados before *Vistafjord* returns to Fort Lauderdale (not New York) towards the end of April. All in all you will have enjoyed 108 days at sea.

CTC are another company who offer world cruises, on board the *Azerbaydzhan*. Departing from Tilbury in January, you can look forward to thirty-six ports in twenty-three different countries, covered in just over three months. Ponta Delgada (Azores), Guadeloupe (Leeward Islands) and Santo Domingo (Dominican Republic) are just three of CTC's alternative ports. Also worth mention are Santiago de Cuba (Cuba) and Montego Bay (Jamaica), both of which are outstanding in their features of natural beauty. In Australia, Whitsunday Isle is a highlight in itself. The Isle is one of the great uninhabited national parks that form the core of the amazing 2,000 km-long Great Barrier Reef. Semarang in Indonesia and Colombo in Sri Lanka (formerly Ceylon) are both ports worthy of inclusion as is Aden in South Yemen. Aden used to be featured more frequently in the range of world cruises available to travellers, but companies today seem to be opting for other Middle Eastern ports. This is an ideal opportunity for you to re-familiarise yourself with one of the world's great harbours. Before returning to Tilbury, you visit the Mediterranean ports of Genoa and Lisbon. Long associated with voyages and the sea, both ports provide a fitting conclusion to any world cruise.

Great distances have to be covered on a world cruise, and consequently, the majority of your holiday is actually spent at sea. Companies have to make sure that passengers are provided with all that they might need, and it is fair to say that facilities on board all the liners mentioned are more than adequate. Dining rooms which serve excellent cuisine, bars, discos, libraries, casinos, cinemas, swimming pools, gymnasiums and nightclubs with first-class entertainment are more or less all standard features. Accommodation is usually split into three or four categories, ranging from the grandest of staterooms and suites to compact but comfortable two-berth cabins. In fact, you have at your fingertips all the amenities which you enjoy on land, simply transferred to your floating hotel.

Prices for world cruises range from £4,700–58,000, depending on your choice of accommodation. All passengers have access to every type of facility, and all meals, entertainment and accommodation on board, as well as some shore excursions and flights where applicable (check both when booking) are included in the price.

Further information about round-the-world cruises can be obtained from Canberra Cruises, run by P&O, Cunard and CTC Lines (see Appendix II for details).

Caribbean Cruising

Cruising around the islands of the Caribbean is definitely one of the most relaxing and leisurely ways of spending a holiday. Several days, or even weeks, spent aboard a floating five-star hotel in an area of the world renowned for its climate, beautiful beaches and stunning sunsets, has to be one of the world's greatest travel experiences. Not only are you offered the opportunity to enjoy the delights of the waters south of Florida and north of Trinidad, but you also have a wide choice of ships which, between them, cover a good range of ports of call. Choose an itinerary, find the liner to carry you, and leave the rest to the efficiency and excellence of the staff who cater for your every need. This has been the playground of the wealthy US market for many decades, but is now opening up to UK holidaymakers, with flights to Miami at giveaway prices keeping costs down.

The main ports around the Caribbean, and those which are frequented most by cruise liners, offer you a great variety of sights and attractions to fill your days. Snorkel over coral gardens off St Thomas, a US Virgin Island; play tennis or golf on St Maarten; see the architectural treasures and the great Gothic cathedral of San Juan, or climb the 600-foot-high Dunn's River Falls on the Jamaican island of Ocho Rios. Alternatively, visit St Pierre (once the Paris of the West Indies) on Martinique, or stroll around 'Tall' Basse-Terre and its 74,000-acre national park on Guadeloupe. And of course there is always colonial, yet cosmopolitan Barbados, or the splendid paradise of Bermuda (Mark Twain once said 'Americans on their way to heaven call at Bermuda and think they've arrived'). There are so many different bays, beaches and hidden corners around the Caribbean that you could quite easily spend six months trailing at leisure from one sun-drenched spot to another. But such decadent luxury is not always possible, so to make the most of the time you have, all you need do is select the cruise which offers those islands you want to visit and decide when you want to go.

One of the main companies dealing with the Caribbean is Royal Caribbean Cruise Line. Their six liners cover seventeen ports of call in total, and offer a selection of three-, four-, nine-, ten- and twelve-day cruises. With ships ranging from 23,000 tons to a massive 74,000 tons, there is ample space on board for the sort of facilities which help make a cruise so unique. Saunas, gymnasiums, shops, casinos, discos, restaurants, lounges and cinemas are all there, complementing the excellent standard of accommodation. Royal Caribbean offers a variety of cabins, from de luxe staterooms with a view, to inside doubles, all with their own private facilities. There are three price categories for different times of the year.

St Thomas, St Maarten and San Juan are the islands frequented most by Royal Caribbean, with Barbados, Antigua and Martinique included on several itineraries. Other ports covered are Ocho Rios, St Lucia, Guadeloupe and St Barts, to name but a few. The shortest cruises are the three- and four-day options, which can be combined with a Florida holiday if desired, although the basic price – anything between £300–850 – is for the cruise only, including full-board (based on double occupancy) and port taxes. This is on board the MS *Nordic Empress*.

Nine-day fly/cruises are offered around both the eastern and western Caribbean, on board the MS *Sovereign of the Seas* and MS *Song of America* respectively. As with shorter cruises, the departure point for both these trips is Miami. Prices range from £850–2,000 for the eastern cruise, and are slightly lower for the western. You should, however, take note of the 'Early Bird' booking offer which could entitle you to reduced fares. Also worth noting is the ten-day eastern cruise on board the MS *Nordic Prince*. For just a little extra, passengers can enjoy another day at sea, as well as an alternative (and larger) selection of eastern Caribbean Islands. Prices for these, and the rest of the longer cruises, include return flight, full-board accommodation, transfers and accommodation in Miami.

There are three twelve-day fly/cruises: The Antilles (MS *Nordic Prince*), and two southern Caribbean options on either MS *Sun Viking* or MS *Song of Norway* (southern cruises depart from San Juan and not Miami). Antilles cruisers spend ten nights sailing, combined with time in Miami, while those on the southern trips have seven nights cruising and four nights in a San Juan hotel. San Juan is the capital of Puerto Rico – the third largest island in the Caribbean – and offers visitors an exciting mixture of old forts, late-Gothic churches and Spanish-style plazas, complemented by sparkling white beaches, bustling streets and lively nightlife. Also on offer are para-sailing, golf, windsurfing, and an abundance of other sunshine and sea activities. Prices for the three twelve-day cruises range from £1,200–2,200, and include the same features as above (accommodation in San Juan instead of Miami, where applicable).

Royal Caribbean's cruise seasons vary from trip to trip. The nine-day eastern and western cruises, and the *Song of Norway* twelve-day southern are available throughout the year, while the ten-day eastern, twelve-day Antilles and *Sun Viking* twelve-day southern are only on offer from January to April (inclusive) and in November and December. Three- and four-day cruises run from May through to December.

Overall, it is fair to say that if you want to cruise the Caribbean, then Royal Caribbean Cruise Line is one of the best companies to travel with. There is very little that they do not organise or cater for, and with the added bonus of having flights pre-arranged (with free UK connecting flights to Heathrow thrown in!), your holiday plans require almost no effort at all. Flights, itineraries and hotels are all detailed clearly, and all you have to do is choose when and where.

Anyone considering a holiday with RCCL should look further into the many different combinations of cruises available. If you want to incorporate a cruise within your own itinerary for example, this is also feasible, and optional extras such as car hire or extended stays are offered as well. All in all, the permutations and combinations of cruise-orientated holidays are almost endless.

Further information is available from Royal Caribbean Cruises (see Appendix II for details).

Ocean Cruise Lines

Pearl Cruises are part of the UK-based luxury Ocean Cruise Lines. The *Ocean Pearl* is their Far-Eastern-based liner, and is generally considered to be among the finest of her kind. Certainly cruising in the exotic locations of the Far East is a rare treat, and to have the opportunity to visit countries such as China and Indonesia, which are not known for their creature comforts for travellers, while based on a luxurious floating hotel with 'guaranteed no tummy upsets', has a great appeal. As the ship accommodates only 400 guests, you will find pre-booking well in advance is essential. Word-of-mouth recommendations and repeat passengers keep her running at high occupancy rates all year round.

Being a small ship ensures a friendly, intimate atmosphere. By the end of the first week you will have encountered most of your fellow passengers, many of whom are well-travelled Americans and Europeans. This is a ship for the sophisticated, mature market. It's not a first-time cruiser's ideal: the entertainment is not in any way the main feature; the accent is more on fine dining, spacious cabins, excellent service, and a proper appreciation of the exotic ports you will call at.

Cabins range from inside basic to outside suites. The fact that 200 are outside, and that there is a ratio of 230 staff to around 400 passengers should tell you a lot about the high-quality appeal of this ship. All cabins are *en suite*, with showers or baths, and on board is a casino, fitness centre, indoor and outdoor swimming pools, beauty and hair salons, library and boutique. The nightlife is mainly musical, with dancing and performances after dinner. A nice touch is that when the opportunity allows, performers from the host country come on board and give traditional entertainment: Thai dancers, boxers and musicians, for example. Between this, the good programme of excursions offered, and the port lectures on your destinations, no one can accuse Pearl Cruises of suffering from the 'you could be anywhere' syndrome as so many cruise lines do. Never for a moment will you doubt your location.

The dinners are splendid five-course affairs. There are two sittings: 6.30 and 8.00 p.m. and food is of a high standard. Buffet breakfasts and lunches are available in the Raffles Cafe, as well as sit-down restaurant alternatives, and if so inclined it is possible to eat at virtually any hour of the day: breakfast, elevenses, lunch, afternoon tea, canapés, dinner and midnight feast! The crew are Filipino, the officers British, and nowhere in the world will you find a more efficient and friendly complement than on board the *Ocean Pearl*.

Following the Captain's first-night party, expect three 'formal' evenings, when cocktail dresses and black tie are in order. The remainder of the time is split between 'informal' – tie and jacket, and dresses – and 'casual', when anything goes.

Of the five cruises offered, the Spice Islands stands out as one of the most interesting and exotic. All cruises feature two- or three-day stays in the major cities of Asia, to start or end your cruise, but great city visits apart, what makes the *Ocean Pearl* so unique is that it goes to places where few travellers get to, let alone cruise liners. You will not at any time feel trapped in the herded cattle syndrome, a fact which makes it popular with people who are not great cruising buffs, and who would not even consider a Caribbean cruise.

The twenty-day Spice Island Tour takes in the lesser-known and better-known islands of Indonesia, and also Thailand's showpiece Phuket, and Malaysia's Penang. Sailing in the Andaman Sea, Indian Ocean and Java Sea you come to some fabulous islands, and will have some quite unusual experiences. There is a two-day visit to Bali, and this cruise begins with some time in Singapore. This is *the* trip for keen sightseers, or those looking for a taste of adventure. The island of Nias is as exotic as one could want: off the west coast of Sumatra, far off the beaten tourist track, this lush island is home to the Nias Batak tribe. One good reason why few tourists would venture this far in recent years is that this tribe were notable headhunters until just two generations ago. Today the only heads you see are carved in stone and for sale as souvenirs. The word souvenir perhaps conjures up the wrong image of this magical place though. The handicrafts are all made on the island and peddled in the streets by the children and the men of the tribe. To witness a primitive culture, complete with open sewers, large extended families, animals sharing living quarters with humans, and subsistence farming, while still enjoying all the air-conditioned luxury of twentieth-century living on the ship, has to be one of the great ironies of our disparate and divided world.

While on Nias the tribe will perform their colourful (and terrifying) war and welcome dances, and the youths will perform their traditional stone-jumping, where they clear seven-foot-high stones with great ease. You reach their hill-top village by open truck, and a tender takes you back to the ship, where all the modern luxuries await.

Other stops of memorable importance are on Bali, Phuket, and Penang. Bukittinggi, reached from Padang on Sumatra, is the centre of a matriarchal Minangkbau culture, and an attractive hill-top town, where the stiflingly hot humidity is replaced by refreshing breezes and temperatures more attuned to European bodies. Sailing from Padang towards the bustling city of Jakarta you pass the haunting island of Krakatowa, scene of the world's most violent volcano, which in 1895 claimed 35,000 lives.

Overland tours are a further unique feature of this cruise. Two are available, and on both you leave the ship for two to three days and travel overland into Indonesia. One is to Lake Toba; the other to Jogjakarta to see the Sultan's Palace and the temple complex of Borobudur, where you dine with a local artist and, in *Ocean Pearl* tradition, are further immersed in the cultural aspects of this fascinating land.

The price of cruising on *Ocean Pearl* is not low. It tends to attract the professional, wealthy, older market, and US visitors outnumber Europeans and other nationalities as a rule. The cost of all holidays on *Ocean Pearl* includes air fares from London, all meals, room service and entertainment on board. Excursions, gratuities and alcoholic drinks are extras. The basic cost of the Spice Islands cruise in a middle-range cabin is around £2,900 per person.

For further information contact Ocean Cruise Lines (see Appendix II for details).

The *Sea Goddess*

A trip on one of the twin *Sea Goddess* ships has to be one of the ultimate cruising experiences. Spacious and stylish, with a crew and staff of eighty, and never more than 116 passengers on board, your cruise will have the feel of a private yacht, calling at exclusive ports worldwide.

The facilities and quality of service on board the *Sea Goddess I* and *II* are matchless. Accommodation is in suite-size cabins, complete with roomy wardrobes, a television, video, sound system, combination wall safe, and a bar stocked with whatever drinks you request on embarkation, all on a complimentary basis. Each bathroom is a revelation, with its piles of magnificently fluffy towels and designer toiletries, while guests enjoy the luxury of attentive room service day and night.

Dinner is the main event of the day, and the mood is formal. The nouvelle cuisine, fine wines, and first-class service are immensely impressive: guests are encouraged to dine whenever they like between the hours of 8 p.m. and 10 p.m. and are offered the option of a private candlelit dinner served in their cabin. Breakfast and lunch are usually served *al fresco* in the cafeteria.

Diversions are plentiful on board the *Sea Goddess* ships, but there are no lists of organised activities – it is always assumed that guests will have their own ideas about how to spend their time. The atmosphere on board is sociable, and the small number of passengers means that people usually get to know one another quickly: the emphasis is on fun, sophistication and relaxation. Athletic opportunities are numerous: there is a health spa with jacuzzi, gymnasium and sauna, a swimming pool on deck, and – when the ships are anchored – a retractable mooring at the stern which acts as a launch for all kinds of watersports: windsurfing, water-skiing, snorkelling, and jet-skiing. For those who prefer the quieter life, there is a wide choice of reading and viewing material available in the well-stocked book and video libraries. On the top deck you will find a spacious sun-lounge. For evening entertainment, there is a smart casino, dancing takes place every night in the marble-floored Main Salon, and an occasional cabaret is also staged.

On *Sea Goddess* cruises, the ports of call match the sophistication of the vessel. The ship's small size and shallow fourteen-foot draft means that it can reach the parts (or the ports) other cruise lines cannot: exclusive marinas, tiny inlets in and around the Caribbean, and secluded bays. *Sea Goddess I* and *II* have a comfortable cruising speed of 17.5 knots, and usually travel early in the morning to allow guests to spend as much time on shore as possible – up to a day at most ports of call. The hours spent ashore exploring ancient and picturesque villages, or sampling the nightlife and meeting friends, is as organised as individual guests want it to be. Ships' staff are happy to order taxis or cars, book restaurants, or arrange temporary membership of the many exclusive golf and tennis clubs which open their doors to *Sea Goddess* guests.

Throughout the year these ships ply some of the world's most desirable routes and visit some of its most exclusive destinations. Mediterranean cruises highlight famous towns and cities – Lisbon, Athens, Marseilles, Barcelona, Rome, Venice, St Tropez, Monte Carlo (the list goes on and on) interspersed with lesser-known harbours. Transatlantic cruises, with as many as six consecutive days spent at sea, are only for those who really relish life on the ocean wave. Caribbean cruises are popular, calling at the quietest, most exclusive islands, among them Virgin Gorda, Mustique, Tobago Cays, and Gustavia on St Barts. Alternatively, you can take in the Panama Canal in style, from Barbados to Acapulco, or explore the Far East: Singapore, Goa, Bombay, Bali and the clear waters and coral islands of Sri Lanka. Perhaps the most outstanding *Sea Goddess* cruise of all is from Barbados to Manaus. This 1000-mile journey takes you through the Caribbean and up the Amazon, right into the heart of the Brazilian interior.

Everything on a *Sea Goddess* cruise from cocktails to water sports is included within the price. The exact figure varies according to the timing and length of the cruise, but it is never cheap. For example, the fabulous eleven-day cruise from Barbados to Manaus which departs mid-February costs £4,355 per person sharing a suite-room. A seven-day cruise during August, taking in Venice, Mykonos and Athens among its ports of call, costs £2,250 per person. For passengers who want to fly to their point of departure, Cunard has arranged an air/transfer package, costing extra for London using First or Club Class scheduled airline travel, together with the necessary transfers from airport to ship and vice versa.

For enquiries and bookings contact Sea Goddess Cruises at Cunard (see Appendix II for details).

Norwegian Cruise Line

One of the ideal ways to experience the magical beauty of the Caribbean is island-hopping with a luxury cruise ship as your base. Few cruise lines offer a wider selection of luxury Caribbean cruises than Norwegian Cruise Line. This company operates a fleet of six ships, with itineraries ranging from three-night cruises to the Bahamas and the west coast of America, to seven-night sailings throughout the Caribbean and Mexico.

Norwegian Cruise line's flagship is the MS *Norway*, converted in 1979 to one of the Caribbean's most splendid liners. There is room for more than 1,750 passengers on this gracious vessel, and accommodation ranges from comfortable and spacious cabins to lavish suites complete with TV, refrigerator and balcony. Room service is swift and attentive. Like the *Norway*, the *Seaward* – Norwegian Cruise Line's newest addition, built in 1988 – offers all the diversions and facilities you would expect from a luxury liner: numerous lounges and restaurants, swimming pools, shops and a casino. For a more intimate atmosphere there are four smaller ships in the NCL fleet, each with room for 700 passengers.

Norwegian Cruise Line is renowned for the high standards of entertainment on board its fleet. The company's proud boast is that for several years in succession it has won the World Ocean and Cruise Liner Society's award for best entertainment afloat. The *Norway* has its own 800-seat auditorium and the *Seaward* has a smaller cabaret-style theatre in which musicals and revue shows are frequently performed. Opportunities for nightclubbing and ballroom dancing are also plentiful. During the day, passengers can take part in a number of sporting activities on board, from clay-pigeon shooting to golf – players drive the golf balls from the deck as far as they can into the Caribbean sea. There are swimming pools on all six ships, and aerobics classes and gymnasiums for the really energetic. NCL's annual programme of events includes several popular theme cruises, special sailings focussing on particular interests which range from jazz to baseball; from fitness to beauty.

The facilities for children on board the NCL fleet are good, though the company does not offer as comprehensive a babysitting and entertainment service as some other cruise lines. Staff are available to amuse and take care of children aged between six and twelve all year round on the *Norway* and the *Seaward*, and during the summer and Christmas sailings for the smaller vessels. Children have their own film shows, story-telling sessions and parties while parents can enjoy a little time to themselves.

The key attraction of NCL cruises is the Caribbean itself. On a typical seven-day cruise there are four or five different ports of call and, as you hop from island to island, you get a taste of the individuality of each stopover. There is Antigua with its 365 beautiful powder-white beaches, sophisticated hotels and cafés and long English colonial history; the French chic, and the black sands of Martinique; the stunning (if sadly over-commercialised) beauty of Dunn's River Falls in Jamaica and the pleasures of afternoon tea served in the shade of a palm tree in Barbados. There is not time on the cruises to explore each island in depth and in order to see the key sights many opt for the lightning organised tours arranged by the company. Others, keen to branch out on their own, hire scooters, jeeps and sometimes even light aircraft to tour the islands. Watersports enthusiasts and sun worshippers on the other hand find it hard to drag themselves away from the coast where the scuba diving, snorkelling, surfing and water-skiing conditions and beaches are some of the best and most beautiful in the world.

Most NCL cruises combine ports of call in the Caribbean with stopovers in west America and Mexico: Catalina, Curaçao, Cozumel, San Diego and Miami. If you are sailing on the *Norway*, the *Seaward* or a smaller ship called the *Sunward II* you will visit NCL's private island in the Bahamas, Great Stirrup Cay, a little palm-fringed hideaway surrounded by coral reefs and white sands. Temperatures are tropical all year round in the Caribbean but for the driest weather the best (and most expensive) time to go is between November and April – the high season.

Caribbean cruising, though not cheap, is no longer the preserve of the super-rich, and the low cost of flights from the UK brings it within easy reach of many British holiday-makers. The atmosphere on board the ships is probably best described as smart but informal. During the day casual clothes and swimwear are fine and after 6 p.m. evening wear is the norm. Almost everything is conveniently included in one price – the transatlantic return flight, all transfers, all accommodation, meals and entertainment. As an example, the price of a nine-night fly-cruise aboard the *Norway*, calling at Miami, St Maarten, St John and Great Stirrup Cay during peak season in a luxury cabin is £1,400 per person. Aboard the *Starward* on a cruise around Barbados, St Thomas and San Juan, the cost for similar accommodation is also around £1,400 per person. Alternatively, a three-day cruise leaving from Miami and visiting Nassau and Great Stirrup Cay costing from £180-449, full-board, can be incorporated into a wider itinerary.

For more information on cruising in the Caribbean with Norwegian Line Cruise ships contact Norwegian Cruise Line (see Appendix II for details).

Nile Cruising

The Nile is flanked by some of the most awe-inspiring wonders of the ancient world, and cruise ships of all kinds ply the famous route between Aswan and Luxor, some sailing as far as Beni Hassan and Cairo. Sightseeing in Egypt can be a hot and exhausting experience and cruise tours have become highly popular with holiday-makers who want to explore the country's glorious monuments from a comfortable base and with trouble-free travel arrangements.

Most Nile cruises begin or end with a stay in the extraordinary city of Cairo. Many find the high-speed chaos and deafening noise of Cairo repellent; nevertheless, it is an Egyptian experience not to be missed. When you first arrive, all of Cairo looks much the same: a brown mass of densely-packed buildings huddled together with desert on all sides. As the city becomes more familiar though, you will find it's divided into several quite distinct areas. The first and least historic is downtown Cairo, a cramped collection of Western-style buildings which lies on two islands connected to the banks of the river by several bridges. Here you will find the Museum of Egyptian Antiquities, the world's greatest collection of Pharaonic art, highlights of which include the astounding treasures of Tutankhamun's tomb. Old Cairo is the name given to the Christian quarter of the city, which dates back to Roman days. Its relative peace and quiet, intriguing narrow alleyways, and steep flights of stairs which lead to ancient places of worship, make it a pleasant diversion from the noise and bustle of the modern city. You can only explore the medieval Islamic quarter properly by foot. Set inside city walls, it is a maze of narrow streets, dotted with many Islamic mosques and shrines, some ornate and lavishly decorated, others austere and imposing. Here also is the site of Khan el-Khalili, Cairo's renowned bazaar.

In the suburbs of Cairo are the magnificent pyramids of Giza, and, adjacent to these, the mysterious Sphinx. First impressions of these ancient wonders may be marred by the sprawling suburbs which have crept right to their very feet: however, the scale on which they are built is still, close up, one of the most awe-inspiring sights in the world.

Luxor, the site of ancient Thebes, and Egypt's capital for fifteen dynasties, is the next port of call on most Nile cruises – all but the longest journeys bypass Beni Hassan and other northerly destinations along the river. Modern Luxor is dependent on the tourists who come here in droves to visit the two fabulous Pharaonic Temples and the west-bank necropolis, yet the pace here is slower and more relaxed than in Cairo. Luxor's temple, built between 1,400 and 1,250 BC, grand though it is, pales beside the Great Temple of Amun at Karak, two miles north. The most imposing part of this colossal building is the Hypostyle Hall where the temple walls and columns are covered with hieroglyphs. In the evening a *son et lumière* show displays the Great Temple at its most impressive, beautifully reflected in the sacred lake. Across the river from Luxor, the Theban necropolis, City of the Dead, is undoubtedly the highlight of a cruise on the Nile. Set in arid hills, the necropolis is divided into three groups of tombs – the Valley of the Kings, the Valley of the Queens, and the Tombs of the Nobles. The most spectacular sights are in the Valley of the Kings. Around sixty Pharaohs lie in rock-hewn sepulchres in this barren valley – on most tours you will visit just two or three. Many of the interiors of the tombs are decorated with fascinating detail: instructions for the journey to the afterlife, sacred animals, and colourful deities.

Between Luxor and the next major stop, Aswan, cruises usually call at three Pharaonic temples dating from the Ptolemaic era. In the little town of Esna is a delightful temple dedicated to the ram-god, Khuum. Edfu's temple, dedicated to Horus, the falcon-headed god, is well-preserved, and the temple at Kom Ombo boasts a beautiful view overlooking the Nile. Dedicated to the crocodile god, Sobek, it has in a small stone store a macabre pile of mummified crocodiles.

Aswan is less notable for its antiquities than its peaceful riverside setting. It is a growing city, but the part you are most likely to visit as a tourist still has the feel of a sleepy village, and in the evening the breeze wafts the scent of exotic perfumed flowers over the water. Aswan's most famous sight is modern: completed in 1972, the High Dam holds the flood waters back from the Nile Valley, and from the top of this great feat of modern engineering you can see Lake Nasser stretching southwards through Nubia towards the Sudan. One of the best outings available during the stay at Aswan is a felucca ride to some of the nearby islands. This basic sailing craft has served the Nile Egyptians for centuries, and in one you can take a leisurely journey to Elephantine Island or Kitchener's Island, the site of a fine botanical garden.

A cruise on the Nile is not just about ancient temples and monuments. Most of the excursions take place very early in the morning in order to miss the hottest part of the day, and there is plenty of time to sunbathe on deck, relax in the shade and take in the sights and sounds of Egypt as you slip past the shores of the Nile.

Nile cruises come in all forms but undoubtedly among the finest are those offered by Bales Tours, Thomas Cook, and Twickers World. In 1869 Thomas Cook himself took a party of Victorian travellers to see the sights along the Nile. Cook's were the first to introduce the concept of Nile cruising, and have maintained high standards of excellence on their cruise boats, having developed a wide range of Egyptian itineraries.

Twickers World offer an impressive range of holidays to Egypt with an emphasis on adventure. They provide tailor-made itineraries to suit individual customers, which are excellent value. Twickers' brand new and most luxurious cruise ship is called MS *Spring*, and prices for a four-night Nile cruise begin at around £736. The most comprehensive and adventurous Twickers Nile tour is called 'The Nile and Beyond'. Most of the time on this holiday is spent on land, but you are also offered a chance to experience life on the waters of the Nile, sailing for three days on a felucca, and spending three nights camping ashore. The cost of the Twickers 'The Nile and Beyond' cruise (ten nights) begins at around £785.

For value for money, though, it is hard to beat Bales Tours. Their sightseeing on land and Nile cruise combinations are exceptionally good, and the quality of their tour leaders and hotels used is hard to surpass. Bales' programme to Egypt ranges from the basic £400 package to de luxe tours at three times that. They bring a very personal touch to their operations; use good hotels, middle of the range boats (authentic Agatha Christie types), and offer extremely good value for money.

Over fifteen different tour operators offer cruises of all kinds on the Nile. For more information on Nile cruising and the sights

Fjords Cruising

The scenic splendours of the Norwegian coastline quite literally take your breath away. In the west, where fjords reach like long fingers hundreds of kilometres inland, the combination of dark mountains, snow-capped summits and deep blue water is awe-inspiring. Travel north and you come to the land of the midnight sun where sheltered fjords, thousands of islets, and majestic mountains are bathed in light, night and day, from April until November.

The best way to explore this magnificent coastline is by boat, and many cruise ships ply the western fjords, some venturing to cross the Arctic Circle into the realms of the midnight sun. Most cruises begin in Bergen on the magnificent Hjeltefjord, the gateway to fjord country which nestles among wooded hills. From the city centre you can take a funicular railway to the summit of Mount Fløyen and marvel at the panoramic view of the city and the fjord below. From here you have a bird's-eye view of Bergen's famous Grieghallen, the concert hall built in the shape of a grand piano.

Just west of Bergen is the Hardangerfjord. The gentle slopes of Hardanger, lined with fruit trees, are often called Norway's largest orchard and are at their most beautiful when the fruit trees are in blossom. North of Bergen runs the longest fjord in Norway, the majestic Søgnefjord and further north again is Geiranger, the most stunning of all. As you sail down this beautiful waterway you will pass a myriad of waterfalls tumbling thousands of feet down spectacular, sheer cliffs.

After crossing the Vestfjord, you sail to the beautiful Lofoten Islands. Viewed from a distance, their ghostly outlines form the awe-inspiring Lofoten Wall. Towering needle-shaped peaks rise vertically from the sea, and at their feet, houses and farms cling to the rocky shores. Artists come from far and wide to these islands in search of tranquillity and inspiration from their scenic beauty. In these waters, if you are lucky, you may catch a glimpse of the smooth back of a whale. After the Lofoten Islands many cruise ships detour to the spectacular Trollfjord. On each side of this 2-km-long fjord precipitous cliffs plunge vertically into the dark waves. It is an atmospheric and mysterious place.

Those exploring the coastline of this beautiful country will soon discover Norway's erratic climate. The weather constantly takes visitors by surprise. Bergen, for instance, has the reputation of being one of the wettest cities in Europe, though during summer it can be delightfully warm. The western fjords always look beautiful: in the mist and rain, the mountains loom and the landscape is threatening and mysterious, and in the sunshine, waves sparkle and the sky turns an incredible blue. As you travel north up the coast into the Arctic there can be times when the famous midnight sun is covered with thick cloud, but, when its golden rays break through the twilight it is a sight never to be forgotten. In order to find the warmest weather and the longest hours of daylight, it is best to travel in mid-summer. Northern Norway in the winter is a cold, twilight zone.

All cruise ships which sail the waters of the Norwegian coast offer high standards of service and comfort. Perhaps the most luxurious are Ocean Line's *Ocean Princess* and Cunard's *Vistafjord*. Both are equipped with all creature comforts and offer passengers the luxury and convenience of a five-star base. However, beautiful though these liners are, they are sometimes too large and formal to be the best way of seeing Norway's staggering natural phenomena. Color Line are the specialists in informal fjord cruising. On board CL's small, sturdy steamers you feel that you are part of the Norwegian way of life. These are working ships and provide a vital lifeline to the outside world for many isolated settlements nestling along the great fjords of western Norway, delivering passengers and goods all along the route. Color Line's Coastal Voyage is eleven nights long and has thirty-five ports of call, steaming through stunningly beautiful, ever-changing scenery. Sometimes the shipping lane is broad and spacious, at other times it is just a narrow corridor with high, overhanging mountains. Color Line does not pretend to its customers that their voyages are luxury cruises – the coastal steamers were built more functionally than luxuriously, to carry mail, freight and passengers from port to port along Norway's long coastline. Accommodation on board is compact but comfortable and, though time on land for shore excursions is limited, the views from land as well as on board are always absorbing.

Color Line cruises sail between April and September. For an eight-day Nordfjord Round Voyage the cost is around £360 per person, depending on the standard of cabin you choose. Generous meals, mostly traditional Norwegian fare, shore excursions and entertainment on board is all included in the price. The cost of the eleven-night Coastal Voyage is around £1,110 per person.

For more information on cruise tours in Norway contact the Norwegian Tourist Board (see Appendix I), or Cunard and Color Line direct (see Appendix II for details).

Luxury Barging

Luxury barging has become a popular way of touring at leisure through rural England and France. The market now offers a choice of barge hotels and exclusive charter vessels with their own crews, pre-planned itineraries, and gourmet cuisine, or the less expensive, less luxurious, more flexible option of chartering an unskippered craft, planning your own course, and catering for yourself. Throughout the range, the barges are maintained to a high standard, and there are many beautiful English and French routes from which to choose.

Abercrombie and Kent offer an unrivalled selection of luxurious hotel barges and smaller exclusive charter craft with itineraries in Bordeaux, the Loire, Alsace, and the Thames Valley. The cruises – for which all accommodation, the services of the crew, high-quality food and wines, excursions, and return flights are included – last between four and seven days. Optional daily trips by minibus combine cultural and historic interest with scenic beauty, taking you to châteaux, cathedrals and rural churches, gardens and famous vineyards. The climate and topography make Burgundy and the Loire ideal places for ballooning, and on most of the French cruises it is also possible (at extra cost) to take a once-in-a-lifetime balloon ride over some of the most beautiful rural landscape in Europe.

The chefs on board Abercrombie and Kent barges aim to match the high quality, and create the regional delicacies, of the many fine restaurants within the different cruise areas. Guests are offered continental or full breakfasts, and lunch varies from a four-course buffet to a canal or riverside picnic. Dinner is sumptuous and served with wines from the region.

Accommodation on board is spacious, well-designed and elegantly furnished. The hotel barges carry around twenty passengers, while the charter vessels have room for between six and twelve guests. The crew to passenger ratio is high: there are one or more crew members to every two passengers.

Flagship of the Abercrombie and Kent fleet, and one of the

most luxurious charter barges in the world is the *Fleur de Lys*. A choice of four-, seven-, or ten-day cruises takes you through the waterways of the Loire, famous for its châteaux and fine wines, and the little-known region of La Puisayne between Montargis and Briare – a fertile area of forests, fields and lakes. If passengers wish to see the famous castles of Chambord or Chenonceau, a helicopter excursion can be arranged. However, the highlight of a holiday on board the *Fleur de Lys* could well be the boat herself. The same size as a spacious hotel barge, it is built to take just six or seven passengers, and has a salon, sun deck, heated swimming pool, dining room and three sumptuous staterooms with *en suite* bathrooms. Exceptional service is provided, with as many staff on board as guests.

La Litote, one of the three barge hotels available from Abercrombie and Kent, was purpose-built in 1975 for travelling the Burgundy Canal, adjacent to the Côte-d'Or – an area of magnificent wines, castles, vineyards, and many art treasures. Here, the Pouilly Tunnel, built by English prisoners during the Napoleonic Wars, connects the Auxois countryside to southern regions of Burgundy. Excursions on this cruise include a visit to Semur-en-Auxois – the medieval walled town overlooking the River Armançon – and a walking tour of Beaune and of old Dijon, and there is also a chance for a glimpse into the past with a visit to the seventeenth-century moated Château Commarin. Accommodation on *La Litote* is on upper and lower decks, and is comfortable and compact.

Less up-market perhaps, but lots of fun (and more hard work) – and all the more authentic for it – are the barge holidays offered by Bridgewater Canal Boats. This Berkhamsted-based company have a fleet of eleven colourful, traditional-style barges which they charter for long and short periods of time. Depending on size, the boats have living and sleeping accommodation on board for between four to eight people, and all are well equipped and maintained. The barges all start out at Berkhamsted, and from there skippers chart their own course, depending on factors such as their boathandling skills and the length of their holiday. A long weekend could take you to Bulbourne and through the nature reserve at Tring to Marsworth and the market town of Aylesbury. On a longer holiday, you could cruise to London through Gade Valley, passing Bourne End Farm, Kings Langley, and Croxley, until you eventually find yourself gliding through the heart of London Zoo, Regent's Park and Little Venice.

Other popular destinations on Bridgewater Barges are Oxford, Cambridge, Windsor, Hampton Court and Runnymede.

Holidays on small charter barges are suited to people who relish an element of hard work involved in their fun. They seem particularly appealing to families with school-age children. The initial cost of hiring a boat is relatively low – for instance, *Macavity*, a six-berth boat, would cost £650 to hire for a week at peak season during July and August – but added to this is the price of gas and diesel (a nominal charge of £25), a damage waiver fee and damage deposit, and the cost of self-catering.

Luxury barging of the kind offered by Abercrombie and Kent is an expensive alternative, and since it has none of the hard work that independent charters involve, it is ideal for those who just want to relax in luxurious surroundings and watch the passing scene. The all-inclusive cost of a seven-day cruise on the top-of-range *Fleur de Lys* is £2,353 during the peak season.

For more information and booking details, contact Bridgewater Boats and Abercrombie and Kent (see Appendix II for details).

The *Canberra*

Despite a variety of ports of call worldwide, cruising on board the *Canberra* is a quintessentially British affair. *Canberra* is the only British cruise ship, and her 1,600 British passengers enjoy food, entertainment, and service designed to remind them of the very best at home. The atmosphere is congenial and relaxing, and diversions are plentiful. Guests find that they make friends on board very quickly.

Launched in 1960, *Canberra* has travelled millions of miles, and won particular fame for her role as hospital ship during the Falklands conflict in 1982. *Canberra's* great size means that there is room for an impressively wide range of facilities, while the crew to passenger ratio – roughly one crew member to every two passengers – ensures a quality standard of service. She has fifteen public rooms, two restaurants and nine bars, all luxuriously decorated and furnished. There are over 700 passenger cabins, the most expensive of which are spacious and elegant.

Food served on the *Canberra* is unmistakably British, and of a consistently high standard. Sea breezes are said to sharpen the appetite, and there is enough food available from early morning until late at night, included in the price of a cruise, to satisfy the keenest appetite. Vegetables and fruit are freshly bought at ports of call, but all other foodstuffs are shipped from the UK, ensuring that holiday-makers are spared stomach upset, unfortunately a feature of so many holidays abroad. Drinks are not included in the price of the cruise, but are available from the bars and the wine cellar at duty-free prices.

Diversions abound on board *Canberra* and details of the day's activities are printed in the ship's daily newspaper – *Canberra Today*. The size of the ship means that it can accommodate a wide range of sporting facilities: three swimming pools, a children's pool, a gymnasium, golf-driving nets, a jogging track and a games deck, with facilities for tennis, cricket and football. If you want to acquire a new skill or brush up on a neglected one, *Canberra* offers classes in subjects ranging from ballroom dancing and windsurfing to glass-engraving and flower-arranging. *Canberra* also presents several theme cruises accompanied by experienced professionals: among these are the Ballroom and Latin Dance Festival, golf and tennis at some of Europe's top clubs, and a bridge-playing congress. There are also ample facilities for those who want to just sit back and relax: a well-stocked library, sun deck and games room. Entertainment on board is outstanding (what other cruise ship has its own repertory theatre company?) and there is a wide choice available each evening to suit a range of tastes and moods: cinema, theatre, musicals, classical recitals, cabaret, comedy and dancing. The entertainments crew on the *Canberra* are impressively talented and professional.

High standards of facilities and activities for children on board mean that *Cranberra* cruises have a special appeal for families. The Junior Club is open from 9 a.m. until 8 p.m. Children join their parents for breakfast and lunch, but a special children's tea is laid on at 5 p.m., so that parents are free to dine alone or with friends later on. The Club has its own magician, and a range of toys, books and drawing materials that will keep children happy for hours. It also organises theme parties, supervised swimming, games and video showings, details of which are given every day in the children's news-sheet. In addition, there is a supervised night nursery for young children, open until the small hours. A word of warning, though, to parents with small babies and toddlers: care facilities are not available for children under two, and the on-board arrangements are not suitable for toddlers.

Canberra plys the oceans of the world all year round, calling at exciting and glamorous destinations. Early in the year she begins her famous three-month world cruise. It is possible to sail from

Southampton, round Europe, to the Near East, Africa, the Far East, through the Pacific, round North and South America, and right back to where you started from. Alternatively, for a shorter break, you can choose only part of the cruise and fly either there or back. During the summer and autumn there are shorter round trips, lasting from nine to twenty-six nights, to destinations like east-coast America, the Iberian Peninsula, the Canaries, the Mediterranean, the Near East, the French Riviera and Italy, Scandinavia, the Caribbean, and a special Christmas cruise from Southampton to Freetown, via Vigo, Gibraltar, Madeira, and Tenerife. Organised tours at ports of call take passengers to the most famous sights, but independent exploring is a possible option. Either way, time ashore is limited and the pace of sightseeing often hectic. At times passengers may feel that the short time at each stopping place means they miss local cuisine, traditions and customs.

The cost of a *Canberra* cruise is middle-range and aimed at the middle-aged, middle-class market. The cost of the three-month World Cruise with a court cabin (two lower berths and shower room) is around £12,240 per person. A nine-day summer cruise in similar accommodation to the Iberian Isles, Lisbon and Vigo would cost £1,215 per person. For more details contact Canberra Cruises at P&O (see Appendix II for details).

World's Best Beaches

Sunset on a palm-fringed beach, mile after mile of deserted white sand, warm turquoise water, lush greenery and bright tropical flowers. This is paradise, but, outside our dreams, does it exist? The answer is yes: in just a few very special corners of the world.

For the great escape holiday you need more than just a beautiful beach. The most cherished of the world's resorts are blessed with calm waters, a range of holiday accommodation to suit most tastes (and budgets), and diversions inland which will make a day trip away from sun-lounger or surfboard more than just a duty.

Those who think that beach holidays are all the same could not be further from the truth. There is the chic sophistication of islands like Bermuda and Jamaica, the exciting oriental culture of Thailand and the peace and scenic perfection of the islands of the South Pacific. From a luxurious over-water bungalow on a blue lagoon in the South Pacific to a simple beach-side hut on the shores of a Thai resort island there are many different ways of staying at the world's best beaches.

Of course it is impossible to make out a definitive list of the best beaches in the world, but here are just a few of those which come closest to earning the name of paradise.

Mauritius

Mauritius lies in splendid isolation 1,110 miles off the east coast of Africa. The leading tourist attraction of this beautiful island is its superb sheltered coastline. However, diversions away from the beach are numerous. The island is a cultural melting-pot, home to people from diverse communities and religions. Mosques, temples and pagodas stand side by side and the restaurants and markets offer an exotic mix of Chinese, Indian and Creole cuisine. A long history of French and British colonial rule has also left its mark. Mauritius was once a possession of the French but it was captured by the British in 1810. The wide boulevards and elegant French architecture of its capital, Port Louis, serve as a reminder of those distant days of French rule.

Sheltered by a semi-circle of mountains, Port Louis is the main harbour in Mauritius. Off the town's main square – the palm-lined Place d'Armes – there are many fine French colonial buildings, in particular Government House and the Municipal Theatre, both built at the height of French power on the island in the eighteenth century. In marked contrast to this French architecture are the magnificent Jumnh Mosque in Royal Street and the beautiful pagoda in the Chinese quarter of Port Louis. The most famous of all Mauritian inhabitants is, of course, the extinct Dodo. You can see stuffed specimens of this long-lamented bird at the Natural History Museum in the centre of the town.

One of the island's most spectacular natural attractions is Trou aux Cerfs, an extinct crater, 280 feet deep and more than 600 feet wide. Those who climb to its rim have a view of almost all the island. At Rochester Falls, near Souillac in the south, water cascades over spectacular volcanic rock formations. In Paplemousses Gardens, known to naturalists all over the world for their rare and beautiful collection of plants, 100-year-old tortoises roam the undergrowth and visitors marvel at the talipot palm said to flower only once each century.

Mauritian beaches lie like a string of pearls around the island's coastline. All have fabulous locations and excellent conditions for watersports, particularly windsurfing and scuba-diving. The most beautiful beaches are at Belle Mare and Blue Bay in the southeast. The Belle Mare coastline has wide sweeping sands and it stretches out to the picturesque seaside village of Grand Port. Blue Bay is fringed filao and is renowned as the best bathing spot on the island. Here watersports enthusiasts are in their element and the deep, clear blue water is a swimmer's delight. In contrast, the ocean swell at Tamarin in the southwest, under the shadow of the River Noire mountains, attracts surfing enthusiasts from far and wide.

The northern coastline beyond Baie du Tombeau has a beautiful string of beaches: Pois aux Piments, famed for breathtaking underwater scenery, and Trou aux Biches, fringed by casuarina and coconut palms and the site of a splendid Hindu temple. Further up the coast, Choisy is one of the most popular resorts, offering marvellous opportunities for swimming. Finally the coastline curves gently into the Grand Baie itself, the sailing and watersports centre of the island.

The island's warm climate is one of its chief attractions. The heat of high season is tempered by cooling sea breezes especially on the east coast. Tropical storms are likely in monsoon season, which runs from December to March, and the best time to visit is early summer when the weather is warm and dry.

Accomodation: The standard of accomodation on Mauritius is high, and the atmosphere in the hotels and around the beach resorts is generally informal. The most prestigious hotel on the island, and reputed to be one of the most beautiful in the world, is Saint Geran on Belle Mare Beach. It lies on a peninsula flanked by the ocean and a shimmering lagoon, and is set in a beautiful tropical garden. Le Touessrok on the east coast of the island is a quiet romantic hotel in a unusual setting. The 130 guestrooms are isolated from the main building on an islet accessible only by a footbridge across the lagoon. La Pirogue is south of Port Louis. Accommodation here is in thatched cottages leading onto gardens and beautiful uncrowded beaches.

How To Get There: Mauritius is an increasingly popular destination with tour operators. Among the best inclusive tours are those offered by Abercrombie and Kent, Silk Cut, Twickers World, Kuoni and Thomas Cook. Many operators offer two-centre holidays combining Mauritius with the Seychelles, Kenya, or Madagascar. Abercrombie and Kent offer a wide range of up-market resorts with an emphasis on luxury and informality. The cost of a twelve-night stay at the Saint Geran hotel with Abercrombie and Kent during the peak season – mid-September to April – is about £1,840 per person.

Independent travel to Mauritius is easily arranged but is generally more expensive than booking an inclusive tour. Air Mauritius operate a regular service from London to the international airport southeast of Port Louis. Internal transport is well-run, with bus services to all parts of the island and there are numerous car hire firms. If you are travelling independently it is advisable to book accommodation well in advance during the months from May to September. Independent hotel bookings can be made direct.

A full list of addresses and prices is available from the Mauritius Government Tourist Office (see Appendix I for details).

The Seychelles

The Seychelles is a fascinating group of nearly a hundred islands lying far out in the Indian Ocean, a thousand miles east of the African coast. They are made up of a mixture of spectacular tips of massive undersea granite mountains and largely unpopulated coral islands. Despite being a British colony into the 1970s, French influences predominate. The result is an intriguing blend of French, British, African, Indian, and Chinese cultures which has created a unique, friendly and hospitable creole atmosphere.

The government of the Seychelles has limited tourism in order to preserve the unspoilt nature of this beautiful archipelago. These lush, tropical islands are quiet, uncrowded, and unhurried, making a perfect location for a relaxing beach holiday, where you will find colourful coral reefs for diving, isolated beaches, and fantastic natural reserves. In fact a larger percentage of the Seychelles is set aside for nature reserves than in any other country because of its unusual animal and plant life which has evolved in geographic isolation.

The mountainous island of Mahé is seventeen miles long by four miles wide, the largest of the group, and contains 90 per cent of the population, yet it revels in the fact that it also contains the world's smallest capital – the sleepy town of Victoria. Mahé is surrounded by the vivid colours of coral reefs and about seventy fine white sandy beaches, while inland there are granite mountains covered in dense green jungle and graceful plantations of coconut palms, cinnamon, vanilla and tea. Victoria has wonderful Creole restaurants and lively markets where you can buy delicious mangoes and passion fruits and see the Seychellois parading in their best finery on Saturday mornings. The National Museum describes their potpourri of folklore and history. Nightlife in the Seychelles is relaxing (as is everything here), with local *camtolet* music and *sega* dancing, and small friendly bars. From Victoria you can take an enchanting trip in a glass-bottomed boat or subsee viewer – like a combination of a boat and submarine – to the wonderful reefs of the nearby Marine National Park. Here you can see an explosion of colour as some of the Seychelles' 900 species of fish swim amongst the 100 species of coral. From the lush slopes of Morne Seychellois, at almost 3000 feet the highest peak, you can see a beautiful panorama of many different islands. Most beach resorts reside on Mahé, and the most popular is at Beau Vallon Bay which lies beneath the soaring misty mountains of the interior. Here you can fish, windsurf, canoe, waterski, sail, or go para-gliding. The quieter and more isolated beaches of Anse Takamaka and Anse Forbans lie amongst swaying tropical trees.

Praslin, the quiet, second largest island has prehistoric forests and sandy beaches. The towering palm trees and waterfalls of the nature reserve of Vallée de Mai were believed by General Gordon to be the original Garden of Eden. In this ancient forest, rare black parrots live amongst the unique coco-de-mer (sea coconut), whose huge erotically shaped seeds gave rise to many legends when they washed ashore in Africa. The beach at Anse Volbert is beautiful with two charming islets just off shore, while Anse Lazio is an even more peaceful and undisturbed place in which you can relax.

The island of La Digue has some of the best beaches in the world. The main method of transport on this unspoilt little island is by ox-cart through the overgrown tropical vegetation and past the brightly painted buildings and old plantation houses to its beautiful beaches. Small sandy coves lie carved into great granite boulders to form secluded beaches. The beach at Anse Union has a clear, shallow lagoon, and the best swimming beaches are Grand Anse and Petite Anse. Snorkelling off nearby Cocos Island reveals a myriad of colourful tropical fish amongst the coral.

Bird Island is a nature-lover's dream with its great migration of two million Sooty Terns between April and October. This peaceful coral atoll has quiet thatched cottages which you can use as a base for watching wildlife – including the 150-year-old tortoise Esmeralda – snorkelling, or deep-sea fishing for marlin and dogtooth tuna.

There are many other captivating places for 'island-hopping' in the Seychelles. Silhoutte has mist-clad mountains, empty beaches, fine examples of wooden Seychellois architecture, and a tiny population amongst whom it is rumoured Lord Lucan lives. Frégate is the peaceful home of rare magpie robins and a beautiful plantation house hotel. Cousin was bought in 1968 by the International Council for Bird Protection and Aride boasts the largest colony of seabirds in the Seychelles. Denis is a sandy coral atoll with great facilities for watersports, especially coral diving.

While the other islands are near Mahé, the huge atoll of Aldabra lies 700 miles to the southwest and encloses the largest lagoon in the world. Populating this low-lying coral atoll are a mere twelve people, together with an estimated 180,000 giant tortoises. The islands of the Seychelles are a unique collection of beautiful locations and suit those looking for a beach holiday with a difference.

How To Get There: At least thirty-five UK operators currently run trips to the sun of the Seychelles. Select Holidays, the market leader to this destination, offer many exciting holidays in these beautiful islands, such as a self-catering apartment for a week on Mahé for £750 per person, a week in half-board accommodation on the exclusive island of La Digue for £850 and a week on full-board at the scenic Plantation House on the small island Frégate for £930. They also offer a number of fascinating multi-centre 'island-hopping' holidays including a fifteen-day, half-board visit to Mahé, Denis, and Praslin for £1,200 and a similar trip to Mahé, Bird Island, and Praslin for £1,100. Speedbird offer eleven days in Mahé and three days in an elegant plantation house on Frégate on half-board for £1,200. Silk Cut offer a thrilling holiday which includes a week on Mahé and a week cruising between the islands on a fifty-foot catamaran for £2,150; half-board on Mahé, full-board on the boat. Tradewinds combine the friendly island of Mauritius with Mahé and Bird Island, fifteen days on half-board for £1,700. Twickers offer a luxury nineteen-day cruise, through the islands of the Seychelles, west past the isolated Aldabra Atoll, to Kenya where five of the days are spent on safari; full-board on the cruise, half-board elsewhere for £4,300–7,255. Other experienced operators to the Seychelles are Abercrombie & Kent, Cox & Kings, Kuoni, Eco Safaris and Thomas Cook. All prices quoted include return travel from the UK.

Independent travel to the Seychelles is possible but expensive because the government allows no charter flights in order to avoid mass tourism. Once there, there are regular flights between the major islands as well as government-run ferries. Accommodation is usually not cheap and ranges from modern luxury hotels to self-catering apartments to charming old guest houses, which are often the best value, and local-style thatched-roof beach cottages. All these buildings blend into the scenery since by law hotels must be lower than the height of palm trees. Somerset Maugham stayed in a quiet guest house and used the Seychelles as his haven of peace, while writing. Hotels are often full so pre-booking is usually necessary, especially during the high season, mid-December to mid-January and August, but those without accommodation can try their luck at the Information Booth at Mahé Airport.

A number of airlines fly to the Seychelles, including the national airline, Air Seychelles (via Frankfurt, Rome, or Zurich), British Airways (via Bahrain), Kenya Airways (via Nairobi), and

Air France (via Paris). Information can be obtained from the Seychelles Tourist Office (see Appendix I for details).

The Maldives

The Maldives are a string of thousands of beautiful, unspoilt coral islands – described by the explorer Thor Heyerdahl as a 'few innocent pepper grains on an ordinary map' – tucked away in the turquoise vastness of the Indian Ocean, four hundred miles southwest of India. Each of these small tranquil islands is ringed with isolated beaches and palm trees, and surrounded by fantastic coral reefs. More than fifty resorts have grown up in this idyllic location, which is fast becoming a popular destination for 'get away from it all' holidays.

The archipelago is grouped into nineteen atolls, rough circles of islands surrounding a large, crystal-clear lagoon. Each resort is a self-contained community alone on a small island, and every one has beautiful, lonely white sandy beaches and superb facilities for snorkelling, windsurfing, and night-fishing. Most have scuba-diving, water-skiing, and island-hopping trips in a traditional Maldivian *dhoni* – an elegant sloped-sail fishing boat, handbuilt of coconut timber. The only concession to the predominance of Islam is a minimum dress requirement. Women must keep their shoulders, arms and legs covered and men must not wear shorts when visiting a mosque.

Underwater diving in the Maldives is among the best in the world, for every island has amazing reefs which teem with exotic, rainbow-coloured fish and turtles. Many islands have a diving school which caters for both the total beginner and budding Jacques Cousteau. These resorts are not the last word in luxury, but simple and friendly places to play Robinson Crusoe for a while.

Most resorts are in the North Male' Atoll near to the capital island of Male' and the airport island Hulule'. Bandos is a beautiful, small coral island only five miles across the lagoon from the airport. Its 140-room hotel sits near the beach (in fact everywhere in the Maldives is near the beach!). Watersports and relaxing are the main pastimes, with a fully accredited diving school and facilities for windsurfing, water-skiing, and catamaran sailing. Next to Bandos is Baros, a mere 500 yards long and 200 yards wide. It is ideal for watersports; one side of the island is covered with exotic coral, creating a small lagoon for snorkelling, while the other is open beach, good for swimming and water-skiing. The half-mile-square island of Kurumba, two minutes from the airport, has 150 cottages and a newly designed conference centre which blend into the palm trees. Kanifinolhu is an exclusive castaways' paradise set in thick vegetation, with para-sailing, and diving to explore wrecks and meet friendly moray eels!

Dhigufinolhu in South Male' Atoll is a lively little desert island on which you can live out your fantasies. Embudhu is yet another beautiful, unspoilt island to relax on and experience the unsophisticated tranquillity of the Maldives. West of Male' in the Alif Atoll is Kuramathi, which has excellent diving and where you can see hammer-head sharks. Nearby is a small, ancient Maldivian fishing village. The fun island of Bodufinolhu is a small and scenic island set in a massive lagoon with superb beaches and is connected to two small islets reachable at low tide.

Many resorts run day trips to the only city, the capital Male', which is one of the few places to meet the local people. It is here one realises that the Maldives is a Muslim country with the gold-domed Grand Friday Mosque which can hold 5,000 worshippers (2.5 per cent of the population of the Maldives). The lively vegetable, fruit, and fish markets give you a flavour, literally, of local life. The National Museum demonstrates the roots of the present Islamic society.

Most of the Maldivian people live in small, isolated fishing villages, cut off completely from tourists, living a quiet and basic traditional way of life. This side of the Maldives is difficult to find, but it is possible on village visits and *dhoni* safaris, where you might also catch a glimpse of the crumbling remains of Buddhist and Hindu temples built of coral on tiny lonely islands, ignored since Islam was accepted in the Maldives in 1153. These islands make an unusual and secluded place to relax and forget the rest of the world altogether.

Accommodation: There is a lack of accommodation in the Maldives. Male' has only three hotels, thirty-four guest houses, and some rooms in private houses. There is precious little other accommodation to speak of besides the numerous resort communities. Accommodation in these resorts ranges from the luxurious to the simple, and usually means thatched-roof beach houses. Those without accommodation can book through the Airport Tourist Information Centre once they have arrived, although pre-booking is strongly advised. The cost of provisions, which are nearly all imported, also makes independent travel expensive.

How To Get There: Many tour operators have now added the Maldives to their destinations and nearly thirty UK operators journey there. Holiday Islands, in association with Maldive Travel, offer custom-made holidays to fifteen different islands at about £800 per person for a week on half-board, including flights, and can include *dhoni* safaris. Thomson offers a week's half-board accommodation on the 'fun island' of Bodufinolhu for £850 per person including flights. Hayes & Jarvis offer the tiny island of Kurumba for a week on half-board for £900. Kuoni provides a number of packages, including a week at the exclusive island of Kanifinolhu for roughly the same price, as well as two-island holidays with a choice of islands, fourteen days on half-board for about £1,600. Speedbird offer a seventeen-day, half-board trip combining the stunning beauty of Sri Lanka's relics with a week on the small island of Bandos for £950. Ingham's 'Golden Triangle and the Maldives' journeys to the beautiful sights of Delhi, Jaipur, and Agra in India with a week on the beaches of Embudhu; fifteen days on half-board for £1,450. Other operators to the Maldives include Club Med and India Dream Holidays.

Once in the Maldives, independent travel is difficult because of the lack of internal travel routes (Maldivians travel little), although it is possible to hire a *dhoni* or speedboat, and there are some helicopter services. A number of airlines currently connect Europe and the Maldives, including Monarch, Emirates Air via Dubai, Air Lanka via Sri Lanka, and Singapore Airlines via Amsterdam, Brussels or Zurich.

Information on the Maldives can be obtained from the official UK tourist representative, Toni de Laroque (the 'Maldive Lady' who has a number of cocktails named after her!) at Maldive Travel (see Appendix II for details).

Thailand

Thailand is difficult to sum up because it is so many things all at once. Thai people are some of the most polite, charming and graceful in the world. Their country is scenically fabulous: in the countryside orchids grow in profusion, and before harvest-time the paddyfields of the central plains are like seas of vivid green. In the hot, teeming city of Bangkok, crossroads of southeast

Asia, both old and new, Orient and Occident converge in heady confusion. Nothing could be in sharper contrast to all this than the lotus-eating lifestyle of Thailand's beautiful beach resorts. From glitzy Pattaya to secluded Koh Samui, each has a character all of its own. What they have in common are white sands, lines of coconut palms, coral reefs, and exclusive hotels.

The most famous of all Thai coastal resorts is Pattaya. Hotels, beautiful beaches, good watersports facilities, and pulsating nightspots are plentiful here. Sadly though, over-commercialisation of this once-tiny fishing village has made it brash and unattractive to many holiday-makers.

The pace of life is quieter and slower in Phuket, largest of a cluster of islands washed by the Andaman Sea off the western coast of Thailand's snake-like peninsula. From November to May the climate is idyllic in Phuket while it is best to avoid the June-to-October monsoon season if you can. Some sixty minutes' flying time from Bangkok, Phuket also has its share of commercial development. In Patong Beach, the most built-up area, large hotels line the crescent-shaped shoreline, and still more are being built. However, there are many quieter beaches still left in the resort: Nai Yang, Kata, Relax Bay, Thavorn Bay and the most secluded of them all, Freedom Beach. The coral reefs off Phuket's sandy shores are a snorkeller's paradise, and watersports are plentiful. Swimmers must be warned though: swimming off some of Phuket's western beaches can be dangerous, especially during the monsoon season.

Conventional sightseeing on the island is limited. Visitors spend most of their time exploring the coastline and the beautiful inland scenery. There are also many excursions to surrounding reefs, pearl farms and coral islands. These are well-advertised, and are easily arranged through hotels. Among the most exciting of these excursions is Phi Phi Island. On a calm day, the long journey past shoals of flying fish is idyllic. Phi Phi is actually two islands. Phi Phi Don, the larger of the two, is one of Thailand's most beautiful sights – a shining isthmus covered in palms and surrounded by white sand and amazingly blue sea. Other popular excursions include the trip to Phang-Nga: here strange limestone pillars rise from an eerie green sea, and the boat glides past prehistoric-looking mangrove swamps. The most famous attraction, however, is what has come to be known as 'James Bond Island', that famed location shot for *The Man with the Golden Gun*.

Koh Samui is the largest in a collection of eighty islands which form the Samui Archipelago off the south-east coast of central Thailand. Famed for its seclusion, it has become one of the tour operators' most popular destinations. If not quite the Robinson Crusoe hideaway the travel agents want to make out, its charms are undeniable: more informal and relaxed than Phuket, it boasts empty white beaches, fringed with literally thousands of coconut palms, blue, blue water, little traffic, and a choice of accommodation to rival any other Thai resort. As with all Thailand visits, holiday timing is crucial. The months between October and January are the monsoon season and best avoided.

On Koh Samui sunning, swimming, watersports, and beachcombing are the most popular pastimes. Alternatively, you can rent a jeep and explore the interior, passing a landscape of bamboo groves and coconut plantations dotted with friendly villages and Buddhist shrines. It is also possible to charter a fishing boat and explore Koh Samui's tiny, secluded neighbouring islands. Another popular excursion is to the beautiful Anthong Marine National Park.

Accommodation: In comparison with other exotic locations, Thailand offers very good value. Sumptuous Western-style hotels are available at a price, but, for the budget-conscious, bungalow accommodation is cheap and plentiful at the beach resorts. Thailand is famous as a shopper's paradise. Designer fakes abound, and if you are prepared to argue over the price of things, you will come home with some fabulous bargains. Beach resort shopping is nothing in comparison with the selection on offer in the cities. For really exciting shopping you will have to go to Bangkok, or Chiang Mai, in the north, home of some of the best crafts in Thailand. Places to stay are numerous in Thailand's larger beach resorts. The most stylist holiday complexes in Pattaya are to be found on the higher ridges of the resort. Royal Cliff Beach and the more modestly-priced Orchid Lodge are particularly noted for their high standard of service. A double room during the peak season at the Royal Cliff Beach costs around £150 a night.

In Phuket most of the best accommodation is near the beaches. There is a chance to escape from it all in style at Amanpuri (Thai for place of peace). This forty-suite hotel is set in twenty acres of coconut grove above a sandy cove, a wooded enclave of miniature Thai temples with sweeping rooflines and ornate decorations. The price per night for a double room at this exclusive destination is around £150. Other recommended hotels include the expensive international Pearl Village, and the more modestly-priced Kakata Inn. In Koh Samui one of the most recommended hotels is the secluded Tong Sai Bay. In addition, there are hundreds of small inexpensive bungalows to suit the younger independent traveller.

How To Get There: Thailand's popularity as a holiday destination has increased dramatically during the last few years, and now over fifty UK tour operators offer inclusive holidays to a wide variety of their destinations. Tour operators offering the best selection of beach resort holidays are Kuoni, Asian Affair, Thomas Cook, and Speedbird. All offer the chance to combine a beach holiday with sightseeing in Bangkok or the rural areas of the north, but Kuoni have the most outstanding range of Thai holidays. Asian Affair and Kuoni probably offer the best value, offering charter flights and so keeping prices down.

The independent travel option is a popular one among visitors to Thailand. Large hotels are generally much cheaper when booked with a tour operator in the UK, but many travellers prefer the freedom to choose their own tour itinerary. Independent air travel to and from Thailand poses little difficulty: Bangkok is a classic bucket-shop destination, and so the price of flights varies a great deal, depending on the comfort, length and convenience of your journey. Scheduled non-stop flights by Thai International and British Airways take about twelve hours from London. Internal transport is simple to arrange. There are regular, inexpensive flights from Bangkok to Phuket, all of which are easily booked through hotels. To reach Koh Samui passengers fly to Surat Thani, then take a taxi and a boat. Pattaya is accessible by road or rail. Hotel accommodation is probably best booked before you go. You can book direct or through several UK agents, and addresses and telephone numbers are available from the London office of the Tourism Authority of Thailand (see Appendix I for details).

Malaysia

Besides cosmopolitan cities, historic towns, teeming national parks, and picturesque fishing villages, Malaysia has some of the most beautiful beaches in the world. You can combine sightseeing in Kuala Lumpur and the highlands with beachcombing, sunbathing and watersports on the uncrowded white sands of the east coast or the tropical island hideaways in the west. Malaysia is divided in two by the South China Sea. Sabah and Sarawak in the north of Borneo make up East Malaysia, and across the water is Peninsular Malaysia where you will find most of the tourist attractions and the best coastal resorts.

The island of Penang, often described as the 'Pearl of the Orient', lies just off the northwest coast of Peninsular Malaysia. It is accessible by a spectacular new bridge – the longest in South-East Asia and the third longest in the world. Penang is the epitome of tropical beauty, with lush green scenery and a white sandy coastline, washed by the warm waters of the Indian Ocean, excellent for a wide range of watersports. The most attractive and popular stretch of coastline is Batu Feringgi in the north, where many resort hotels have sprung up under the shade of the casuarina trees.

People call Penang 'Malaysia in miniature'. In Georgetown, the capital, you will find a combination of Eastern and Western influences that is typically Malaysian. Its inhabitants are a mix of Malay, Chinese and Indian, and the influence of many years of British colonial rule can still be seen. Churches, mosques, and Buddhist temples stand side by side and many are worth a visit. The Kapitan Kling mosque in Pitt Street is one of the largest in Malaysia. Buddhist temples to visit include the lavishly decorated Kek Lok Si, set in its own beautiful gardens, the Band Hood Pagoda of Ten Thousand Buddhas and the ornate Khoo Jongse – or Clan House – in Cannon Square. On a visit to the waterfront you can see the Chinese Clan Piers, traditional houses supported on stilts above the water. Shopping opportunities in the town are numerous – there is a lively night-time market called the Pasar Malam, and a whole street of antique shops along Rope Walk. The Chinatown district is filled with restaurants, hawkers, stalls and duty-free shops. Outside Georgetown, one of the most unusual sights on the island is the Temple of the Azure Cloud – more commonly known as the Snake Temple – not an attraction for the faint-hearted: the temple swarms with venomous snakes. The reason visitors are able to pluck up the courage to enter is that the snakes are heavily drugged with incense. Less nerve-wracking is an outing to Penang Hill in the centre of the island. You can reach the 2,300-foot summit by funicular railway and enjoy beautiful views and leisurely walks.

Malaysia's climate is tropical all year round. Rainfall differs on the east and west coast according to the prevailing monsoon winds, but the main rainy season to avoid in the east runs between November and February, while August is the wettest month on the west coast.

Accommodation: Penang is now Malaysia's main beach resort and the recent expansion in tourist facilities has resulted in a wide choice of holiday accommodation. The best hotel in Penang is Rasa Sayang on Batu Feringgi beach. Its fine reputation and beautiful setting have attracted many British visitors over the years. Rasa Sayang's sister hotel, Golden Sands, is also highly recommended. The quality of service in both is high.

Around 150 miles south of Penang is Pangkor Island. Pangkor has recently gained popularity with holiday-makers as a result of two international hotel developments, but the island, accessible only by boat from mainland Lamut, has retained an air of seclusion. Hundreds of picturesque bays, beautiful uncrowded beaches and plenty of opportunities for watersports are Pangkor Island's chief attractions. The best beaches for swimming and snorkelling are on the west coast, and between May and July turtles come to lay their eggs on Telok Ketapand beach. The most recommended hotel on the island is the 161-room international Pan Pacific, set on the edge of a crescent-shaped sandy beach on the west coast. Accommodation is spacious and watersports equipment is available.

The finest Malaysian beaches are without a doubt on the unspoilt east coast. Mile after mile of white sand washed by the clean waters of the South China Sea unfold along this coastline with a backdrop of dense green jungle. There are also dozens of offshore islands fringed by coral and surrounded by aquamarine waters. The capital, Kuantan, is fast gaining popularity as a beach resort and the surrounding region is also well known for traditional crafts – weaving, woodcarving and batik. The leading hotel in the area is Kuantan Hyatt; spacious and well-appointed in traditional style, the Kuantan Hyatt offers a choice of restaurants and a range of watersports facilities.

How To Get There: Many tour operators have realised the growing popularity of Malaysia's beach resorts and offer a wide selection of holidays to coastal and island destinations. Hayes and Jarvis, Silk Cut, Kuoni, Thomas Cook, Speedbird and Abercrombie & Kent all offer a range of holidays to up-market beach resorts and include the option of combining a beach holiday with sightseeing in Kuala Lumpur and the Malaysian highlands. With Abercrombie & Kent and Silk Cut it is also possible to venture to the states of East Malaysia, Sabah and Sarawak. Asian Affair offer an exceptional range of tour itineraries in Malaysia, each one combining a beach resort with sightseeing in Kuala Lumpur and Singapore. There is also a separate programme for budget-conscious travellers who are looking for an inexpensive way to see Malaysia. A thirteen-night tour of Singapore, Kuala Lumpur, and Pangkor Island with accommodation in de luxe hotels costs £929 per person during peak season. An Asian Affair budget seventeen-night tour to Singapore, Malacca, Kuala Lumpur, the Cameron Highlands, Pangkor and Penang in moderate accommodation (meals not included) costs £859 per person.

Independent travel to Malaysia is a possible alternative to booking through a tour operator, though costs involved can be higher. Malaysia Airline operate regular flights from London to Kuala Lumpur, while internal flights serving over twenty commercial airports in Peninsular Malaysia and East Malaysia are run by Malaysian Airline System and Malaysian Airline Charter. For accommodation in popular destinations, notably Penang and the highlands, it is necessary to book well in advance, especially at Easter, midsummer, and Christmas.

A full list of holiday accommodation and booking details can be obtained from the Tourist Development Corporation of Malaysia (see Appendix I for details).

French Polynesia

Tahiti has become a byword for tropical beauty and remote tranquillity, but it is only the most famous of 130 high volcanic outcrops and low coral atolls scattered over a vast stretch of the South Pacific, collectively known as French Polynesia. The islands divide into five archipelagoes, the most densely populated and frequently visited being that group known as the Society Islands. Visitors may have different ideas on how to divide their time on these islands, but most would agree on the highlights – white coral beaches, blue lagoons, magnificent sunsets, graceful people, and the towering mountains of Moorea and Bora Bora.

Fact and fiction about the island of Tahiti have become confused. Sadly, much of it is not the unspoilt paradise that permeates so many dreams. The capital, Papeete, like any other modern commercial centre, is crammed with cars and motorbikes, and many of the old buildings, including Quinn's, the most famous haunt of seafarers in the South Pacific, have been torn down to make way for high-rise shopping centres and blocks of flats. However, outside Papeete, there is still beauty and tranquillity in abundance. One of the most favoured spots on the island is Point Venus – reputedly this is where the first Europeans set foot on the island. Here the large black-sand beach has marvellous swimming, and stunning views of green-peaked mountains. A leisurely drive around Tahiti reveals more scenic beauty: rivers, waterfalls, bright flowers, coconut plantations, and picturesque Polynesian thatched houses known as *fares*. Perhaps the most fabulous sight of all is at sunset on the waterfront at Papeete, where, from one of the pavement cafés, you can watch the sun sink behind the beautiful island of Moorea, twelve miles across the bay.

It is little wonder that Tahiti's sister island, Moorea, is the best loved of the Society Islands. Its peaks and spires swathed in cloud, are an awe-inspiring sight. Spectacular twin bays, Cook's and Opunolul, deeply indent the coastline, and coral reefs protect the lagoon from pounding surf. The blue waters are warm and calm, and most of the island's hotels are situated on white sand beaches. Beautiful beaches and fabulous swimming and diving conditions mean that most people's time is spent on or near the shore. However, the breathtaking scenery is not to be missed, and many of the hotels arrange guided tours. Alternatively, visitors can hire bikes or cars and drive round the thirty-seven-mile coastline and up into the valley of Opunohin, passing coffee plantations and pineapple fields on the way. No tour guide will fail to point out the needle-shaped mountain of Mou'aroa, more familiar as the mythical Bali H'ai in the film *South Pacific*.

Around 140 miles northwest of Tahiti, fifty-five minutes by air from Papeete, is Bora Bora. People who have seen this tiny island wax eloquent about its beauty, its majestic mountain peaks ringed with coral beaches, clear lagoons, and colourful coral gardens. Off shore are numerous islets – each one like a tiny desert island – called *motus*, where visitors can spend time swimming, snorkelling and picnicking. Tour Bora Bora by car, bicycle, or motorbike, and you will inevitably pass ancient temples, called *maraes*, and charming villages.

Maupiti is 232 miles west of Bora Bora. This beautiful, small island, sheltered by a barrier reef and fringed with *motus*, is one of the Society Islands' best-kept secrets. The only remnants of a once-powerful civilisation here are scattered ruins of *marae* temples. There are no large hotels, and visitors can enjoy the white sands and excellent snorkelling waters in perfect peace and quiet. There are more beautiful beaches on the island owned by Marlon Brando, Tetiaroa, a seventeen-minute flight from Tahiti. Accommodation here is in fourteen bungalows or a scattering of A-framed beach-side rooms built of coconut palms, and there is little to do but drink in the delights of beautiful beaches, deserted *motus*, and a stunning land-locked lagoon. For those who have dreamed of perfect peace and quiet and glorious beach locations, a visit to the Society Islands is the holiday of a lifetime. Those more interested in culture, sightseeing, or nightlife, however, should look to beach resorts elsewhere.

Accommodation: For those travelling from the UK, the price of getting to paradise, and island-hopping is expensive: budget travellers are likely to find the costs prohibitive. Holiday accommodation, however, ranges in price: moderate tariffs are available on almost every island, and de luxe hotels are also plentiful on the larger islands. The most idiosyncratic, charming and expensive holiday accommodation on the islands are overwater *fares*, or thatched bungalows built on promontories over the edge of a lagoon. Most of the luxury hotels have several *fares* to offer their guests. Dining out is expensive in the Society Islands, and the price of things in general on the more remote islands tends to be higher than in Tahiti. On Tahiti, hotel buildings are more conventional than on the other islands. The best and most expensive are Hotel Sofitel, Maeva Beach, Taharasa and the Tahiti Beachcomber. The latter boasts the most scenic location: on the west coast of the island, four miles from Papeete, it looks out to Moorea, and has several overwater *fares*, as well as conventional accommodation. Neighbouring Moorea has the widest choice of accommodation of the outer islands. The best of all its resorts is the 146-room Sofitel Tiare, opened in 1987. The choicest rooms are in fifty overwater *fares* with fine views, and ladders leading to the lagoon. Bora Bora boasts the most expensive hotel in the South Pacific: the beautifully situated Moana Beach. Rates here go up to £263 per night for a double room. Hotel Bora Bora is less expensive and situated in fifteen acres of tropical gardens, bordered by a long sugar-fine white beach and some of the best snorkelling waters in the world.

How To Get There: Travel agents dealing in holidays to French

Polynesia are few and far between. For up-market luxury locations try Elegant Resorts. They offer a wide range of holidays in the South Pacific including several in the Society Islands. There are destinations in Bora Bora, Moorea, Tahiti and Rangiroa, in high-class beach-side bungalow complexes, and also the option of an idyllic sailing trip on the luxury cruiser *Windsong*, stopping at Huahine, Raitea, Bora Bora, and Moorea. The cost of a seven-night inclusive tour to the Sofitel Kia Ora on Moorea with Elegant Resorts between January and March, the peak season, begins at £1,795 per person. The price per person sharing a twin cabin on the *Windsong* cruise including flights to and from Heathrow is £2,820 between November and December. South Pacific is the only specialist British tour operator to the South Pacific, and offers a wide range of destinations in the Society Islands.

Independent travel is a possible but expensive alternative to booking through a tour operator. French Polynesia is served by UTA for international flights, and the approximate flying time from London to Papeete is twenty hours. Regular reliable domestic flights run by Air Polynesia connect Tahiti with neighbouring islands. For more information and independent hotel booking details contact: Syndicat d'Initiative de la Polynesia Français, the Office de Promotion et d'Animation Touristiques de Tahiti et ses Iles, or the French Government Tourist Office (see Appendix I for details).

Kauai

Hawaii is a collection of stunning islands, part Polynesian, part American, and part Eastern, which have caught the imagination of many over the years, including the not easily impressed Mark Twain, who remarked, 'they remain my idea of the perfect thing in the matter of tropical islands . . . No alien land in all the world has any deep, strong charm for me, but that one; no other land could so longingly and beseechingly haunt my sleeping and waking, through half a lifetime, as that one has done'.

Kauai is roughly circular and the fourth largest of Hawaii's seven main islands. The centre is dominated by the lofty volcano, Mt Waialeale – the wettest place on earth and known for its innumerable rainbows – and the great Alakai Swamp, a near-impenetrable area thick with bright red poinsettias and rare animals, such as the exotic *'o'o'a'a* bird. Kauai is a huge, brightly coloured garden and the most lush of Hawaii's islands.

You will find the pace of life slow, the people friendly, and, unlike neighbouring Maui or Oahu, the island has not been overcome with tourism. This breathtaking 'garden island' comprises densely forested valleys, dramatic cliffs, waterfalls, and ninety miles of coastline with beautiful beaches and colourful reefs. Legend has it that Kauai is the home of the *Menehune* – a Hawaiian version of leprechauns – who are credited with the building of many ancient walls which puzzled the early Polynesians, whose overgrown ancient *heiau*, or temples, are still visible.

Magnificent, unspoilt, white-sand beaches ring the island. Poipu on the sunny south shore is one of the largest resort areas and has a beautiful coastline ideal for swimming and coral diving alongside friendly sea turtles and strikingly coloured fish. Just up the coast is the spectacular Spouting Horn, which is a series of lava tubes through which waves crash and are fired high into the air like a geyser. Captain Cook's famous landing on the south coast in 1778 is re-enacted every February during the Captain Cook Festival. The east coast also has fine palm-fringed beaches with accompanying resorts. Kalapaki Beach on Ndwiliwili Bay and Coconut Plantation are a bit windier and therefore good for surfing, the sport of ancient Hawaiian kings. The huge Princeville resort in the northeast has elegant hotels set on superb tropical beaches.

The north coast is dramatic and secluded, with mountains stretching right down to the shore. Just beyond the small town of Hanalei, which is buried in a huge valley, is the most famous of Kauai's many beaches, Lumahai. Set against steep cliffs, tropical trees, and rocks of black lava, the golden sand of Lumahai was the setting for the film *South Pacific*. West of the beautiful Ke'e Beach stretch thirteen miles of the amazing Na Pali coast, where emerald cliffs soar 4,000 feet above completely isolated beaches accessible only by boat. You can best view this amazing sight on a thrilling helicopter or boat ride. Some of Hawaii's best deep-sea fishing is just off these cliffs where large schools of marlin and tuna are found. At the cliffs' end are the pristine beaches of the Polihale State Park, and further down the west coast are Kekaha beaches which you can have completely to yourself.

The land between the volcano and the coast is carved with spectacular canyons and valleys and rolling hills covered with sugar cane. The old plantation town of Lihue – the government centre of the island – contains graceful reminders of nineteenth-century history in old plantation houses and missions, as well as the Kauai Museum which describes the island's art and history. To the north, the River Wailua flows through Fern Grotto, a memorable lava cave covered in gigantic Maidenhair ferns, before forming a majestic waterfall. In the south you should visit the impressive Pacific Tropical Gardens in Lawai, 186 acres covered with brightly coloured exotic flowers and plants. The Russian Fort tells of a strange period in Kauai's history in the early nineteenth century when Russia tried to gain a foothold on the islands. Anton Scheffer organised the building of this star-shaped fort in traditional Kauai stonework, before being thrown out by the Kauai's leader Kaumualii, who only a few years before had finally recognised the sovereignty of the great unifying King Kamehameha of Oahu.

In the west is the mighty Waimea Canyon, called 'The Grand Canyon of the Pacific' by Mark Twain. This enormous, half-mile deep canyon extends for ten miles, its bright rainbow of colours changing throughout the day. At the end of it is the dense green wilderness of Kokee State Park where you can fish for rainbow trout. Between Kokee and the Na Pali Coast is the vast 'hidden valley' of Kalalau, an area inhabited only by mountain goats and covered with thick forest, waterfalls and the crumbling houses of ancient hermits. Kauai is the perfect place for you to experience a lush South Seas island with beautiful natural sights and beaches, and also enjoy a high level of comfort in your accommodation.

How To Get There: A large number of UK tour operators now travel to Hawaii. American Dream Holidays offer a week at the exclusive Westin Kauai hotel for £600 (accommodation and internal transport only) and an exciting eight-day cruise journeying to Kauai and six other Hawaiian islands (£625 from Oahu, all-inclusive), and will even create a personal itinerary for you. Air Tours offer a week on the beaches of Honolulu and a week on Kauai at Coconut Plantation, for £800 including accommodation, all flights to and in Hawaii, and a car in Kauai. Page & Moy offer a week at Poipu for £320 (accommodation and internal Hawaiian transport only). Hawaiian Magic offers an exciting fifteen-day trip to the jetset beaches of Oahu, the volcanic wilderness of Hawaii, the undeveloped beauty of Molokai, and the scenic Maui as well as Kauai for £1,600 (accommodation and all flights to and in Hawaii). Thomson offer a three-destination fifteen-day holiday which includes San Francisco, Oahu, and a week in Kauai for £1,000–1,200 (accommodation and all flights). Other experienced operators to Kauai are Exotic Islands, Mason International, Silk Cut, and Unijet.

Most of the hotel rooms on Kauai are in de luxe beach hotel resorts, such as at Princeville, Poipu Beach, and Coconut Plantation, but there are some more modest hotels and simple cabins in the woods. Hotel prices usually do not include food. As hotel occupancy is higher in Kauai than New York City, pre-booking through a tour operator is usually necessary. Nightlife is still undeveloped in Kauai and is centred around the large hotels, and often involves *luaus*, Hawaiian feasts. Independent travel in Kauai is expensive because of the limited availability of accommodation, and in Hawaii generally because of the very high cost of living, in particular, food. There are fifty-four flights a day from Honolulu (Oahu) to Lihue on Aloha, Hawaiian Airways, and Mid Pacific for about £57 return (flight-time about 20 minutes). Princeville Airways fly to Hanalei Airport.

American Airlines, Continental, Delta, Northwest, Pan Am, TWA, Air New Zealand and British Airways (in association with United Airlines which flies direct to Kauai from Los Angeles) all fly from the UK to Honolulu via the US mainland, where stopovers can often be made. Soon Virgin Atlantic will also be flying there in association with Hawaiian Airways. Sample fares are Delta £559 return low-season. Northwest £641 mid-week, including a week's car rental, and British Airways/United Airlines £893 high-season. Long-haul charter flights to Hawaii are becoming more popular: Air Tours has led the way with a £399 return fare. Information can be obtained from the Hawaii Visitor's Bureau (see Appendix I for details).

Bermuda

Bermuda is a tiny smattering of islands and outcrops in the middle of the Atlantic. Its turquoise waters are warmed by the Gulf Stream, and temperatures average around 70°F, rising in the summer months to the high 80s and cooling down to the low 60s during the winter. With an impressive range of up-market accommodation, and a friendly welcome guaranteed, Bermuda is, for many, the perfect island retreat.

Sheltered coral-pink and white beaches, all immaculate, are Bermuda's pride and joy. Most of the best hotels have their own private stretch of sand, pink or white, depending on the location. The island's most famous beaches lie along the southern coastline – generally considered to be one of the most beautiful is Horseshoe Bay. Here the smooth pink sand is edged with dramatic grey rocks, and however busy the island, the beach never seems to be crowded.

On and off shore there are excellent opportunities for sports enthusiasts in Bermuda. The conditions for snorkelling and scuba-diving are good, with visibility underwater often as far as 200 feet. Experienced scuba-divers have the chance to tour the fascinating wrecks sunk on the treacherous Bermudan reefs. Here is some of the world's finest deep-sea and light-tackle fishing, and you will find equipment easy to hire. Sailing is also a highly popular sport in Bermuda. The world-famous blue-water classic – the Newport to Bermuda Ocean Yacht Race – takes place in June every other year, and is followed by week-long festivities at the Royal Bermuda Yacht Club. There are 100 tennis courts on Bermuda, most of them owned by the larger hotels, and the island has more golf courses per square mile than any other country in the world. Cricket plays such an important part in Bermudan life that there is even a two-day public holiday at annual Cup Match time, when the rival clubs of St George and Somerset vie for the prized Championship Cup.

Tourists are forbidden to hire or bring their own cars to Bermuda, so the best way to explore on your own is by renting a moped, or arranging with a taxi driver to become your tour guide for the day. The Bermudan capital – Hamilton – is situated at the end of Great Sound. Here you can browse through numerous fashionable shops – the Harrods equivalent is Trimmingham's – or relax in one of the many cafés or bars. Ferries regularly tour around Hamilton Harbour, and there are longer cruises to Great Sound and Somerset village.

The old capital of Bermuda is St George. Here the winding streets, many of them more than 300 years old, have a very English feel to them. Look for quaint street names like Featherbed Alley, Needle and Thread Lane, and Slippery Hill. Appropriately for somewhere with such an English atmosphere, St George is renowned for its excellent pubs. For a glimpse of Bermuda's long seafaring history visit Ireland Island where a Maritime Museum displays an array of treasures from sunken ships. For a spectacular view of all Bermuda climb to Gibb's Hill Lighthouse, one of the oldest in the world.

Accommodation: From the modest guest house to the de luxe hotel, holiday accommodation is of an impressively high standard on Bermuda. Prices are high throughout the range although rates are often quite substantially reduced during the rendezvous or low season. Three-quarters of visitors to Bermuda are from the United States, and the larger hotels tend to be geared to the American market. Among the smartest of the island's resort hotels is the Southampton Princess. Perched high on a ridge overlooking the Atlantic Ocean, this luxury complex has 600 rooms, a beautiful private beach, pools, shops, restaurants, bars and an eighteen-hole golf course. The price per person per night on half-board is around £80. The island's all-inclusive hotel is the Harmony Club where everything from afternoon tea to scooter hire is included in the price. The hotel, a pink and white manor house, is situated further from the beach than most Bermudan properties, and has lush garden surroundings. Only couples are welcome. The all-inclusive price for a couple per night is around £100.

As an alternative to hotel accommodation, several high-class apartments have banded together to call themselves Bermuda's Exclusive Small Properties. They are divided into three categories: Standard, Superior, and Deluxe. Almost all have kitchen facilities, and the best have private swimming pools and stunning views. The price per person at Marley Beach Cottage, a Deluxe property, is £44 per week. Cottage colonies are a Bermudan innovation offering an ideal, somewhere between the comfort and convenience of a hotel, and the privacy and flexibility of a holiday apartment. They are usually set in landscaped grounds, with a clubhouse, their own pool and a private beach. Horizon's Cottage Colony costs around £71 per night on half-board.

How To Get There: Tour operators offer a wide range of destinations on Bermuda, from luxury resorts to modest self-catering apartments. Kuoni offers a selection of holidays in Bermuda's top hotels, including the all-inclusive Harmony Club. Tradewinds has all these and a range of exclusive small properties. Thomas Cook sells holidays to Newstead (a bastion of tradition opened in 1923), the Harmony Club and Elbow Beach resort. A two-week stay for one person on half-board at the Southampton Princess resort with Kuoni costs £1,229 in peak season. Other tour operators who travel to Bermuda include Cadogan Travel, Bermuda Bermuda and Caribbean Connection.

Those interested in the freedom and flexibility of independent travel will find that the price of independent bookings are far higher than those which tour operators can afford to set. However, prices drop during the cooler winter months, when temperatures fall into the low 60s. British Airways operate four flights weekly to and from London. Independent travellers will find that the Bermudan Department of Tourism booklet, *Where to Stay in Bermuda* has a useful list of holiday accommodation. Contact Bermuda Tourism BCB Ltd (see Appendix I for details).

The Bahamas

The Bahamas comprise 700 beautiful low-lying islands and cays stretching hundreds of miles from the Florida coast to Cuba. It is an intriguing combination of the glitter, bright lights and excitement of its two main islands, and the tranquil, unspoilt charm of its outer islands, where diving, fishing, sailing, and simple relaxation on the sumptuous deserted beaches and cays is the order of the day. The jetset congregate in New Providence and Grand Bahama, where fast living and casinos are *de rigeur*. The people – largely of African descent – are some of the friendliest and most polite anywhere in the world (you can meet volunteer families with shared interests through the 'People-to-People Programme'). British influence has been strong since the seventeenth century when the people drove off the dastardly likes of Blackbeard. Christopher Columbus first came ashore in the New World on San Salvador Island in the Bahamas, and said 'This country exceeds all others as far as the day surpasses the night in splendour'.

Life in the Bahamas revolves around the island of New Providence, which, although only twenty-one miles by seven miles, contains a lively capital city of Nassau where half of the Bahamas' 250,000 people live. Set on a scenic harbour, Nassau is a blend of old and new, the colonial splendour of Parliament Square contrasting with ultra-modern casinos. You can buy delicious conch and other fresh seafood at the exciting Potter's Cay Market and intricately weaved goods at the Straw Market. On the outskirts, overlooking the harbour, is the British Fort Montague and Blackbeard's Watchtower, and the brand-new Coral World, which is a fascinating underwater observatory in which you can see an explosion of colours and undersea life. The streets come alive with the colourful parades of the Junkanoo Festival on Boxing Day and New Year. The Goombay Festival combines music and dance and runs all summer. Paradise Island, across the harbour from Nassau, is a beautiful resort with a huge casino and wonderful beaches including Pirate's Cove and Love Beach. Along the coast from Nassau is the sophisticated modern resort of Cable Beach, with yet another casino. The rest of New Providence is ringed with mile after mile of empty beaches.

Grand Bahama also has wild casino and glamorous nightlife at Freeport and Lucaya. In fact gambling is a way of life here. Freeport is a cosmopolitan city where you can find intriguing winding pathways in the International Bazaar, ancient artefacts of the Lucaya Indians at the Grand Bahama Museum and the enchanting Garden of the Groves bursts with beautiful tropical flowers. Five miles to the east, Lucaya has wide white sandy beaches. West End is the oldest settlement on the island and is now a secluded 'get away from it all' resort set on beautiful tropical beaches.

All the other outer islands of the Bahamas are known as the Family Islands; they are out of the way and peaceful with very low-key nightlife. Eleuthera is a beautiful, long and thin island (at one point only the width of a car!) of pink sandy beaches and dramatic cliffs, where there is little else to do but swim and sunbathe. Harbour Island, off the north coast, is one of the prettiest places in all the islands, with its largely unchanged seventeenth-century Dunmore Town and lush tropical vegetation. Windermere Island off the south coast is a stylish resort.

Bimini lies just off the Florida coast and is a world centre for big game fishing, as Ernest Hemingway knew only too well when he lived there in the 1930s and immortalised Alice Town in his novel *Islands in the Stream*. Diving is also excellent here, and you can explore the enormous underwater stones claimed by some to be the lost continent of Atlantis.

The Abacos are a boomerang shaped chain of islands north of New Providence. New Plymouth on Green Turtle Cay is a typical New England village built by loyalists fleeing the American Revolution. The sailing between these islands is some of the best in the world, and is centred at Marsh Harbour and the luxury beach resort of Treasure Cay. On Man O' War Cay shipbuilders practise their art as they have been doing for hundreds of years.

Andros is the largest and least changed island. Its interior is an unexplored and unspoilt wilderness of dense pine forests and rivers. Less than a mile off its east coast is the huge Barrier Reef, one of the world's largest, which is a riot of exotic fish, bright colours, and ancient shipwrecks.

There are many other fascinating islands for you to visit. The Exumas offer great sailing throughout its 365 mostly uninhabited islands and spectacular diving at the National Land and Sea Park. Cat Island hosts a world-famous regatta in August. Acklins Island is very quiet and has golden beaches. Near Cuba is Inagua, whose Lake Windsor Wildlife Preserve has a colony of 40,000 flamingoes. What's so nice about the Bahamas is that you can experience life in the fast lane in the casinos and nightclubs, or simply forget it all and relax on a deserted cay.

How To Get There: Around fifty UK operators currently travel to the Bahamas, including Tradewinds who offer a week on half-board at a Nassau resort from £848–1,058 for a shared double room and a two-week holiday combining Nassau with Orlando, Florida from £869–1,152 (for room-only accommodation, flights not included). Pegasus offers ten nights in Nassau from £425–475. Hayes & Jarvis offer a week on beautiful Harbour Island for £714–947. Jetset offer a week at the exclusive Green Turtle Club in the Abacos for £944–1,098. Speedbird offer a great fourteen-day package combining the nightlife of Nassau with the peace of Exuma from £881–1,382. Kuoni combine the Bahamas with the rich culture and wonderful beaches of Jamaica, fourteen days on half-board from £1,281–1,869. Other experienced operators are Thomson, Unijet and Thompson.

There is a very wide selection of accommodation, ranging from small guest houses and cottages to large luxury hotels. The Bahamas are a popular tourist destination, especially for Americans, and so accommodation should be booked beforehand. Prices are much higher during the high season – mid-December to mid-April – and so the best time to go is during the 'Goombay Summer' when prices are lower and the festival is on. Temperatures, which generally hover around 80°F, earned the Bahamas the title of 'Islands of Perpetual June' from George Washington. Prices are relatively high, for tourists and natives alike, due to the high standard of living and cost of imported food.

The national airline Bahamasair and six smaller charter airlines link Nassau and Freeport with the Family Islands, which are all less than an hour from Nassau. Piedmont Airlines offer a Bahamas Air Pass from the US. British Airways fly direct to Nassau from London for £449 return in the low season and £543 in the high season. Virgin Atlantic, Continental, and Pan Am fly via Miami or Orlando.

Information can be obtained from the Bahamas Tourist Office (see Appendix I for details).

Antigua

Antigua has some of the finest stretches of soft white sand in the Caribbean. Its clear, calm waters attract watersports enthusiasts and yachtsmen from around the world. The island boasts an impressive range of excellent holiday accommodation and is an increasingly popular destination with both American and British visitors.

The Antiguans claim that their island has a different beach for every day of the year. Whether or not this is true, the beach-lover is certainly spoilt for choice. Most of the exclusive hotels offer guests the use of a private beach, and many now include a full range of watersports in their price. Scuba-divers and snorkellers will be in their element off Antiguan shores. The waters are strewn with fascinating wrecks and spectacular reefs which experienced divers can explore at length.

The island has long been regarded as a place of shelter and safety for weary travellers, and there is evidence of its fascinating sea-faring history right round the coast. Nelson's Dockyard in English Harbour, twenty-five minutes by road from St John's, has the reputation of being one of the world's safest land-locked harbours. It is here that the fashionable yachting set of Antigua now congregate and where, in more turbulent days, Nelson sheltered the British fleet. Tourists can visit the museum in Nelson's house and see the neighbouring Copper and Lumber Store, now restored as a hotel. Overlooking the harbour is Clarence House, once the home of William IV, now the Governor-General's summer residence and open to visitors for part of the year. To the east is the ruined eighteenth-century fortress at Shirley Heights. There is little left of the original fort, but you can enjoy a memorable view right over the harbour.

Scenically Antigua is not as impressive as neighbouring St Kitt's or Nevis, and the generally poor state of roads on the island makes inland exploration difficult. There is, however, an accessible and picturesque route along Fig Tree Drive which takes you in a circle through lush banana palms and mango trees and past the pretty fishing villages of the southwest coast.

In the cheerful capital of St John's itself, you can visit the nineteenth-century cathedral which looms over the town's brightly painted wooden houses, or simply wander round the colourful town, at its liveliest on Saturday mornings.

Accommodation: Whether you are hoping to enjoy de luxe-style hospitality at an exclusive Antiguan resort, more modest comfort at one of the island's less expensive hotels, or the option of self-catering apartments, you are likely to encounter a friendly welcome and a generally high standard of service. Low-budget travellers, though, will find Antigua out of their price range. There is no campsite on the island, sleeping on beaches is strictly prohibited, and the cost of living is high.

Tourism tends to be concentrated at Dickenson Bay, but more isolated resorts have sprung up right round the coast wherever there are beautiful and accessible beaches. Antiguan hoteliers have made the most of their coastline's natural assets. Hotels are almost always sited on, or right next to, a beach, and opportunities for marvellous swimming, the full range of watersports, tennis and ocean-side golf are always close at hand.

Arguably the best hotel on the island is Curtain Bluff on the south coast. This luxury American-style complex has two beaches and offers guests a wide range of watersports. The public rooms are light and stylish and the private accommodation, spacious and luxurious. In peak season, the price, per night, for a couple sharing a twin room on full-board ranges from £287–429. Also secluded and luxurious with a mile-long crescent-shaped beach and plenty of watersporting facilities is the Half Moon Bay Hotel on the southeast coast of Antigua. Added attractions of Half Moon Bay are a nine-hole golf course and five tennis courts. You can expect to pay from £175–206 per night here at peak season for a double room on half-board. Self-catering options on Antigua include the Barrymore Beach resort, located at Runaway Bay, near St John's. Most of the twenty apartments have two bedrooms and each has a kitchenette for self-catering. Two people sharing a one-bedroom apartment at Barrymore would pay from £64–129 a day at peak season.

How To Get There: There are a score of reliable travel operators now offering inclusive tours to Antigua. At the most exclusive end of the market, offering high-quality flights and accommodation is Elegant Resorts. Their most de luxe holiday at the Curtain Bluff complex costs around £2,895 per person for two weeks at peak season on full-board. Tradewinds' Tropical Elegance also aims at the top end of the market, but offers a smaller range of exclusive destinations on Antigua. Among tour operators who include the more modest option of self-catering apartments, as well as medium-priced and luxury accommodation, are Sovereign, Speedbird and Thomas Cook. The Thomas Cook price for two in a self-catering apartment at Barrymore Beach in peak season is around £1,446 for two weeks.

Antigua makes a good base for 'island-hopping', and tour operators are now eager to offer holidays which combine Antigua with one or more Caribbean destinations. Unspoilt Barbuda, famous for its huge beach of white sand at Cocoa Point, is only fifteen minutes by plane from Antigua. Nevis, Montserrat and Guadeloupe are all less than thirty minutes flying time away, and Barbados, St Martin and Anguilla are also easily accessible. Tour operators who offer the 'island-hopping' option include Silk Cut, Elegant Resorts, Tradewinds, Speedbird, Thomas Cook and Kuoni. Silk Cut, for instance, combine holidays to Antigua with Barbados, St Lucia, Nevis and Guadeloupe, but they are also able to arrange other island combinations to suit individual customers. Elegant Resorts and Tradewinds also provide this kind of 'tailor-made' service.

Independent travel to Antigua is a possible alternative to the inclusive tour, though the independent holiday-maker will find the costs involved are usually higher. For the budget-conscious it is worth remembering that hotel rates – and often air fares – drop quite considerably during the summer months when sudden downpours are frequent. Whenever you are planning your visit you will need to book flights and accommodation well in advance, especially for the winter season between November and March, when temperatures in the 80s are tempered by light winds. British Airways and BWIA travel direct from London to Antigua. For independent hotel reservations, it is possible to book direct by telephone or letter.

A full list of hotels, guesthouses, and self-catering apartments is available from the Antigua and Barbuda Tourist Office (see Appendix I for details).

Trinidad and Tobago

Though they form one nation, Trinidad and Tobago are worlds apart. Trinidad – the wealthy, cosmopolitan home of steel band and carnival – perfectly complements its tranquil neighbour,

Tobago, with its calm waters and vast white beaches. Tobago is only twelve minutes away by plane from Trinidad, and together they make a great Caribbean combination. The heat of the tropical day on Trinidad and Tobago is tempered by cool trade winds, and daytime temperatures average around 84°F. The peak tourist season lasts from December to April, avoiding the rainy months from May to November.

Most of what is quintessential to Trinidad you will find in Port of Spain. Architecturally, the city is a haphazard mixture of neo-Renaissance styles, ornate Victoriana and high-rise developments, while diverse cultures bring an exciting cosmopolitan feel to the streets. Fredrick Street is the lively crowded shopping area in Port of Spain, and well worth a visit. Nearby, but set apart from the bustle of shops and stalls, are the Royal Botanic Gardens, seventy acres of what was once sugar plantation, now an extravagant show of tropical flowers. A popular day-trip from Port of Spain is to Maracas Beach, enclosed by mountains and fringed with coconut palms, while nearer to the city, Blue Basin provides an idyllic swimming spot with waterfalls filling a deep cold lake. Trinidad's 1,500-foot summit at Fort George, ten miles outside Port of Spain, affords a spectacular view of the Boca Grande and the Venezuelan mountains.

Tobago's capital – Scarborough – is quiet and slow-moving in comparison with Port of Spain, and the island as a whole offers little for sightseers. However, Tobago is the beach-lover's paradise. Pigeon Point on the southwest coast is one of the most renowned stretches of sand in the Caribbean, and a mile offshore is Bucco Reef, the coral habitat of a stunning array of tropical fish. Glass-bottomed boats leave the beach for the reef at regular intervals, while the teeming, shallow waters are a snorkeller's haven. At the opposite end of the island is Man O'War Bay, a fine natural harbour with a long sandy beach on its southern shore. Nearby is the picturesque fishing village of Charlotteville, with Pigeon Peak, Tobago's highest mountain, rising behind it.

The fine cuisine of Trinidad and Tobago reflects the islands' cosmopolitan population: a British influence is identifiable in the tradition of afternoon tea, served with ceremony in the hotels, but the dominant culinary influences are African and Bengali.

Accommodation: Trinidad is not strictly a holiday island, and though there are several high-class hotels round the Port of Spain, they are all a good distance from the beaches at Maracas Bay and the north coast. However, establishments like the Trinidad Hilton and the Holiday Inn are convenient for sightseeing and shopping in the bustling capital. The Trinidad Hilton has a hill-top location, and is known as the Upside-Down Hilton because the entrance is on the top floor.

The hotel industry on Tobago is nowhere near as developed or sophisticated as on Antigua, Barbados or the Bahamas. Most accommodation is simple, but the welcome which visitors receive is relaxed and friendly. De luxe hotels include the fabulous Mount Irvine Bay Hotel, fifteen minutes from Scarborough, and made popular with golfers by the superior course on site. The hotel restaurant is a converted sugarmill and there is a freshwater pool, two floodlit tennis courts and a private beach. Arnos Vale Hotel is small and secluded, with a beach: its clear waters are ideal for snorkelling.

How To Get There: Fewer tour operators offer holidays to Trinidad and Tobago than to other Caribbean destinations, and those who do are restricted by the relatively small range of good hotels available, particularly on Tobago. However, Caribtours, Speedbird and Thomson all offer popular holidays to Tobago, and travelling with Wings, holiday-makers have the opportunity of combining Tobago with St Kitts or Nevis. A one-week stay per person sharing a double room at Turtle Beach during the winter season costs £895 with Caribtours.

The price of independent travel and accommodation will probably be higher than an inclusive tour, though it might be worth remembering that air fare and hotel prices fall considerably during the summer months when the weather is less reliable. Out-of-season travellers will also find the beaches, hotels and places of interest far less crowded. BWIA International operates regular direct scheduled flights from London to Port of Spain. British Airways operates the same route with BWIA connections to Tobago.

You can book accommodation direct: a full list of telephone numbers and addresses is available from the Trinidad and Tobago Tourism Development Authority (see Appendix I for details).

Jamaica

Jamaica offers what must be the ideal Caribbean combination: sweeping beaches of white sand, breathtaking inland scenery, vibrant bustling towns and friendly welcoming people.

Martinique may be more sophisticated, Grenada more stunning scenically, but Jamaica comes closest to having all of the ingredients for a perfect Caribbean sojourn.

The island's most beautiful beach resorts are on the north coast. Negril, in the west, has seven miles of golden sand, cut short at the island's westernmost tip by cliffs and rocky bays. Here, at Rick's Café you can watch a classic sunset over miles of blue water and fine sand. The atmosphere of relaxed *joie de vivre* at Negril has made it a mecca for pleasure-seekers.

Along the coast is Montego Bay, the tourist capital of Jamaica. Mo' Bay (as it is known) is less of a beauty spot than a convenient base for sightseeing. However, there are several fine beaches to choose from, including Doctor's Cave Beach, where the clear water is fed by mineral springs, and the standard of holiday accommodation in the surrounding area is high.

To the west are Falmouth, Runaway Bay, and Ocho Rios. Ocho Rios itself is little more than a high-rise tourist centre with a busy cruise ship harbour. Outside the town, though, are some of the finest hotels in Jamaica, and, nearby, the famous attractions of Dunn's River Falls, Carinosa Gardens and Firefly. At Dunn's River Falls water cascades down steep stone steps to join the sea, and, for a small charge, there is a guided 600-foot climb to the top. Its natural beauty has sadly made the spot a crowded tourist trap, but it is still something no visitor to Jamaica should miss. The Carinosa Gardens are also an unforgettable sight. Here, in a natural gorge, are fourteen waterfalls, a little forest brimming with exotic plants and flowers, a hillside garden, and an amazing aviary of curious, colourful birds. Along the North Shore Road, between Oracacessa and Port Maria, take a right turning to find Firefly, Noel Coward's diminutive hill-top home. Beautifully simple and filled with mementoes, Firefly is just as Coward left it in 1973. The view is staggering. Also near to Ocho Rios is Fern Gully, a four-mile road winding along an ancient riverbed lined with giant ferns. Still more natural wonders are in store at the Shaw Park Gardens, high on a hill-top overlooking the city.

A long scenic drive away from Ocho Rios is Port Antonio where the Blue Mountains meet the sea. This peaceful picturesque bay offers a relaxing alternative to the bustling streets and pulsating nightlife of commercial centres like Ocho Rios and Montego Bay. Scenic splendour sets Port Antonio apart from other Jamaican resort areas. Against the constant backdrop of the Blue Mountains you can swim or water-ski in the Blue Lagoon, one of the finest coves in the whole Caribbean, visit the San San Beach and Monkey Island, and sample Jamaican 'jerk pork' at Boston Bay. Alternatively, like Errol Flynn before you, you can enjoy the tranquillity of rafting on the Rio Grande – a quintessentially Jamaican experience. The journey begins high up in the hills at Berrydale. Rafters pass wide sandy beaches and rocky gorges, towering trees and banana and sugar plantations, stopping halfway for a swim in the cool, peaceful river.

Evening entertainment on Jamaica all too often resembles what is fed to tourists on so many of the Caribbean islands: the stock torch-lit-steel-band-limbo-dancing extravaganza. For something less commercial, more genuinely Jamaican, visitors can take part in what are called Boonoonoonoos – meaning 'delight' in local patois. These are weekly parties with a uniquely Jamaican flavour. Each area has its own kind of celebration: in Montego Bay, for instance, the evening begins with a torch-lit canoe ride and ends with drinks, dinner, and dancing: and at Ocho Rios there is a feast followed by music and dancing at Dunn's River Falls. They're great fun, far more entertaining than the tourist nights, and can easily be arranged through hotels.

Jamaica offers a wide variety of sporting opportunities. Surfing is best on the north coast, east of Port Antonio, where long lines of breakers crash into Boston Bay. Many places along the north coast are scuba-diving and snorkelling havens, with a multitude of different corals and tropical fish accessible within 100 yards of the beach. Further out, experienced divers can explore caves, shipwrecks, and giant forests of sponge. For watersports enthusiasts there are numerous opportunities for windsurfing, water-skiing and sailing, while Jamaica also has some of the most beautiful and challenging golf courses in the Caribbean. The Montego Bay area alone has four courses.

Temperatures outside Kingston during the winter range from high 70s to mid-80s, but the heat is tempered by the prevailing northeast tradewinds. Showers, usually brief, are most frequent during May and early June, and again during October and early November.

Accommodation: Jamaica offers a range of high-class hotels to match any other in the Caribbean. Many have beautiful settings, but few are inexpensive. Throughout the island there is a vogue for 'all-inclusive' hotels where one price covers everything from cocktails to scuba-diving; holiday-makers have warmed quickly to this idea. Among the companies offering one-price resort holidays are Sandals Resorts, who own hotels in Montego Bay, Negril, and Ocho Rios. Exclusively for couples, and with every creature comfort provided in one price, they aim at the young professional market and their holidays are now on offer from the UK as well as the US.

Three of Jamaica's finest hotels are all situated just outside Ocho Rios. The refined and expensive Plantation Inn, 'the' place to be seen having afternoon tea, has a formal, English atmosphere. Jamaica Inn has equal charm. The nightly half-board rate at the Plantation Inn in peak season starts at around £56. The Sans Souci is another of Jamaica's all-inclusive hotels. Accommodation is elegant, and there is the added attraction of a spring-fed mineral pool and a wide sandy beach. Prices for a three-night stay per person during peak season start at £260. Ten minutes from Port Antonio is the small resort of Trident Villas. Trident is a little enclave of cottages set in a tropical garden right on the edge of a craggy coastline. During peak season, the cost per night at this intimate hideaway is from £40–90.

How To Get There: A large number of reliable tour operators deal in holidays to Jamaica including Elegant Resorts, Kuoni, Sandals Resorts, Silk Cut, Meon Villa Holidays and Thomas Cook. For example, the price per person travelling with Elegant Resorts during the winter season for a fourteen-night stay on half-board at the Trident Hotel is £1,766.

Independent travellers will find the Jamaican Tourist Board helpful in providing lists of accommodation which can be booked direct (see Appendix I for details). For those who are free to travel during the summer months, it is worth remembering that accommodation prices fall quite considerably during the low season, and the island will be quieter and less crowded. Generally, independent travel to Jamaica will be more expensive than going with a tour operator. In addition, you will need to book flights and accommodation well in advance, particularly for a holiday taken during the winter season. Air Jamaica, British Airways, BWIA and Lufthansa all fly direct from London.

St Vincent and the Grenadines

Life on St Vincent and the Grenadines is simple, informal and relaxing. The islands boast some of the most secluded and exclusive resorts in the Caribbean, and are the renowned hideaways for the world's rich and famous. The Grenadines and St Vincent also have a wide range of moderately-priced accommodation and reputedly the finest sailing grounds in the world.

The Grenadines form an archipelago of over a hundred beautiful islands and cays which stretch southwards from St Vincent. Among them are picturesque Bequia – accessible only by boat – Canouan, secluded Tobago Cays, gem-like Mustique, Palm, Union and Petit St Vincent. All have stunning white beaches and clear blue water. The St Vincent coastline has a quite unique and varied beauty. Its sandy western shores are washed gently by the calm waters of the Caribbean, while Atlantic breakers pound the steep rocky cliffs off the eastern coast. In the north, beaches of black volcanic sand edge the shore, and in the south – where most of the resorts are situated – the sand is golden coral.

Life on the islands for both residents and visitors revolves chiefly around the sea – locals make a living when they can from boatbuilding and fishing. Hotels usually have beach locations, and apart from swimming and sunbathing, sailing and scuba-diving are the most popular pastimes. Sailors especially will be in their element. Many hotels give their guests the use of dinghies, and yachts – either bareboat or with crews – are available in St Vincent. Scuba-diving conditions are particularly good around India Bay (on the southern end of St Vincent) and in the waters surrounding Tobago Cays, Palm and Young Island.

Conventional sightseeing on St Vincent is limited. However, in the lively capital of Kingstown you can take a walk along the waterfront, a hive of activity, where schooners and freighters load and unload their cargo. Overlooking Kingstown, in the north, is Fort Charlotte. From here there is a memorable view of the rest of St Vincent and the Grenadines beyond. From this vantage point you will also be able to spot the Botanic Gardens, said to be the oldest of their kind in the western hemisphere. For those who want to explore the island there are several magnificent scenic routes. The first is the Leeward Highway which runs north from Kingstown. It climbs a range of steep hills with marvellous sea views before dropping close to the shore. Pass the Aqueduct Golf Course and you will come to Layou, where you can see a series of cave drawings made by Carib Indians over thirteen centuries ago. Along the Atlantic coastline of the island runs the Windward Side Highway. On one side are rolling hills and green plantations, on the other, rocky shores and foaming surf. In Marriaqua Valley (also called Mesopotamia Valley) you can get a flavour of the lush fertile inland landscape of St Vincent. The route begins at Vigie Highway, east of Arnos Vale Airport, and continues to the town of Mesopotamia, passing terraced farms, winding rivers and dark forests. Heading north, you will eventually come to Montreal Gardens, a picturesque stopping place, with a restaurant, swimming pool and natural mineral springs. The Queen's Drive begins at Sion Hill, southeast of Kingstown and climbs Dorsetshire Hill and Millers Ridge, with breathtaking views over all of Kingstown and the Grenadine islands along the way.

Each of the beautiful Grenadines has its own special diversions. Bequia (pronounced Beck-wee), the largest of the Grenadines, has a coastline of golden sands dotted with picturesque coves. On the waterfront in the main town of Port Elizabeth you can watch boats being built by hand. At the southern end of the island, you can see Moon Hole, an amazing community of private homes built into the cliffs. South from Bequia is Mustique, famed as the winter retreat of celebrities like Princess Margaret and Mick Jagger. This exclusive destination with its gently rolling landscape and fabulous beaches is only around six square miles. Canouan has some of the best beaches in the Caribbean, long ribbons of powder-white sand with warm shallows and beautiful coral. Barely visible on the map are the Tobago Cays. Swim, snorkel and sunbathe here in seclusion: they are only accessible by private or charter yacht.

The peak season on the islands is from November to April when prices are at their highest. However, temperatures are in the high 70s all year round, tempered by gentle breezes and brief downpours which happen almost daily.

Accommodation: The Grenadines and Young Island, off the coast of St Vincent, are the locations for some fabulous resorts, available to those who can afford fabulous prices. However, some moderately-priced holiday accommodation is there too, and for the budget-conscious it is worth remembering that prices on the island generally drop by about 30 per cent during the summer months (May to October). Located 200 yards off the south shore of St Vincent is Young Island. This private island resort has twenty-nine secluded cottages spaced out on the lush hillsides and beaches. There is an elegant clubhouse, a swimming pool, and tennis court. The less expensive Cobblestone Inn is a converted 200-year-old sugar warehouse in the centre of Kingstown.

One of the attractions of its location is a stunning view from the rooftop cocktail lounge. The most exclusive resort hotel in the Grenadines is the Cotton House on Mustique. The main house is a beautifully converted eighteenth-century plantation manor, and the twenty-two private rooms are situated in secluded villas. The famous Frangipani Hotel on Bequia has eleven private rooms located in hillside cottages. For one person sharing a double room during the winter season, expect to pay from £26–53 per night. The Palm Island Beach Club on Palm Island is relaxed and luxurious, while still more elegant and informal is the private resort island of Petit St Vincent. Accommodation here is in twenty-two hillside and beach bungalows, and at high season a double room with full-board will cost around £380 per night.

How To Get There: Tour operators tend to concentrate on top-of-the-range accommodation in St Vincent and the Grenadines. Among the most popular resorts with the tour operators are the Cotton House, Young Island, and Petit St Vincent. Companies with these and similar destinations are Abercrombie & Kent, Caribbean Connection, Elegant Resorts, Kuoni, Silk Cut, Speedbird and Tradewinds. Travelling with Tradewinds, one week at Young Island Resort on full-board would cost around £1,648 per person during peak season.

With so many beautiful small islands all so close together, opportunities for 'island-hopping' are of course numerous on St Vincent and the Grenadines. In addition, Barbados is only fifty minutes flying time away. Most of the tour operators offer the island-hopping option, but independent travellers can island-hop without being tied to only two or three resorts. However, the price of independent hotel bookings is high, and because so many of the best hotels have so few rooms, early booking is advisable.

A full list of accommodation prices and addresses is available from the St Vincent and the Grenadines Tourist Board (see Appendix I for details). There are regular British Airways and BWIA flights to Barbados. From here there is a LIAT service to St Vincent. Some of the Grenadines have their own airstrips, but many are only accessible by boat.

Barbados

Barbados has, for many years, been known as 'Little England' due to the strength of British traditions which date back over 350 years. This is seen in the national obsession of Barbados – cricket – but is also evident in the legal system and the abundance of British place names. Fortunately for those seeking a sun-drenched beach holiday, this is where the similarities end, for Barbados' beautiful beaches and warm climate have made it the premier holiday destination in the Caribbean. As it is the most easterly of the Caribbean islands, rough Atlantic surf crashes into spectacular cliffs on the east coast, while gentle Caribbean waters wash up on the golden beaches of the west. Tourists from Britain and elsewhere have long been attracted to this relaxed and civilised island, yet it has not been overcommercialised and still remains a very friendly and absorbing place to visit.

The west coast – the 'lee' side of the island – is a developed area with elegant resorts overlooking palm-fringed beaches and a warm gentle sea, good for watersports. The water here is among the purest in the world as it is all naturally filtered by the coral reefs. The Heywoods Barbados Resort in the north is a beautiful complex situated on over a mile of beach. Nearby Speightstown is a friendly West Indian village with picturesque wooden houses. Further to the south is the world-famous Platinum Coast – a sophisticated millionaires' playground of luxury hotels on fine sandy beaches which stretch down to Payne's Bay, where you find the beautiful Treasure Beach Resort. Holetown, the centre of the Platinum Coast, is also the oldest settlement on the island, dating from 1627, and this fact is celebrated in the annual Holetown Festival held in February. Nearby is the spectacular Folkestone Underwater Park, a marine reserve where you can see colourful reefs and fish, and explore the wreck of the old steamer *Stavronikita*.

In the southwest lies the capital, Bridgetown, a place with a decidedly English character reflected in its St Michael's Cathedral and its own Trafalgar Square, complete with a Nelson statue which predates its London counterpart. Bridgetown is a major stop for cruise liners and so its duty-free shops along Broad Street can get very busy. The Careenage (old harbour) is the haunt of many colourful fishing boats and here you can experience the best of real Bajan cuisine (especially flying fish) at the hectic Fairchild Market. The biggest event of the year in Bridgetown and all over the island is the summer Crop Over Festival, when street fairs and concerts abound. Just outside is the Barbados Museum which has beautiful Indian artefacts, arts and crafts, and tells the story of Barbados' long parliamentary history. Beach resorts continue all along the south coast in the southern-sounding towns of Hastings and Worthing to Oistins Bay.

The eastern Atlantic coast is very different. Trade winds and rough surf pound this rugged and undeveloped coastline of isolated beaches and coves. The surf is often too rough to swim in but is great for surfing – this is where Barbadians like to take their holidays. Sam Lord's Castle is a refined mansion (now a hotel), built by a privateer who is supposed to have made his fortune by luring ships onto the treacherous rocks. Crane Beach in the southeast is a remote beach lying underneath a cliff, from which you get a dramatic view of the stunning coast. Bathsheba is a small town of colourful houses on chalk cliffs with a wonderful beach. You can escape at the Atlantis Hotel, which is frequented as much by locals as by tourists. Nearby are the brilliant colours of exotic tropical plants at the beautiful Andromeda Gardens. The East Coast Road continues north from Bathsheba past the breathtaking coastline up to the highlands of Scotland District in St Andrews Parish.

The centre of the island consists of rolling hills of sugarcane – often with wonderful views to both coasts. Welchman Hall Gully is a lush valley of citrus trees, rare tropical plants, and wild monkeys. A spectacular one-mile train ride runs through the nearby Harrison's Caves with an unbelievable panorama of stalactites, stalagmites, underground pools, and a waterfall. The Farley Hill National Park is in the grounds of an old ruined plantation house overgrown with flowers, and has a marvellous view to the Atlantic coast.

Barbados does not have the most dramatic scenery in the Caribbean as it is relatively flat, but it still continues to grow in popularity because of the great rapport between local people and tourists, and because of its two contrasting coastlines and ways of life – gentle and relaxed or rugged and isolated. Here you can enjoy a sophisticated nightlife and first-class hotels and still get to beautiful, isolated retreats.

Accommodation: Barbados has a very wide selection of accommodation, ranging from the top luxury hotels to guest houses and a huge number of self-catering apartments. Most of the hotels are along the west coast, and self-catering apartments and guest houses predominate along the south coast. Winter rates (high season) range from £45–400 per night for a double room in a hotel – the average is about £85; £25–130 per night for a single bedroom apartment – average about £60, and £10–60 per night for a double room in a guest house.

Two of the best hotels featured by Elegant Resorts in their programme are Sandy Lane in St James and Cobblers Cove in St Peter's. Prices drop dramatically in the low season and are usually at least one-third lower, sometimes as much as two thirds! The lower prices and the Crop Over Festival make summer the best time to visit, when the temperature remains in the 80°F and it rarely rains. You can book rooms in Bajan hotels from the UK through William Galley and Associates, tel: 081-935-5828, and Utell International, tel: 071-995-8211. The cost of living is lower in Barbados than many other tourist islands as it is nearly self-sufficient in many respects – food costs are roughly comparable to the UK.

How To Get There: Caribbean beaches were once only within reach of the jetset, but lower prices have increased interest and now at least thirty-five UK operators travel to Barbados, including the up-market specialist Elegant Resorts who provide a comprehensive programme with lots of choice, such as a week on the Platinum Coast for £750–990 per person for a shared double room (meals not included). Elegant Resorts also offer a sixteen-day holiday combining a weeks' stay in Barbados with an eight-day cruise on the Cunard *Sea Goddess*, visiting the Grenadines, Antigua, the British Virgin Islands, St Barts, and the US Virgin Islands, from £3,135-3,850. They also arrange personalised itineraries in the Caribbean and their selection of hotels on the island is unbeatable, making them my personal choice for Barbados. Meon Villa Holidays offer a week at the elegant Springhead Plantation from £1,180–1,715. Airtours offer a much cheaper option with two weeks in a self-catering apartment costing as little as £500. Speedbird offer many different packages, including a seventeen-day trip to Antigua and St Lucia as well as Barbados for £987–1,735. Thomas Cook offer a weeks' full-board on Barbados for £945–1,364. Tradewinds offer two-centre holidays linking Barbados with Grenada, Tobago, Antigua, or St Lucia. Cruise lines to Barbados include Royal Caribbean Cruises, Paquet Cruises, CTC Lines and Cunard, who offer a twenty-one-day cruise on the *QE2* to New York, Philadelphia, St Maarten, Barbados, and the US Virgin Islands, starting at £2,330 (an extra £1,550 if you fly Concorde). Other experienced operators are Abercrombie & Kent, Hayes & Jarvis, and Silk Cut.

The roads around Barbados are good, and taxis, buses, and rented cars are the main forms of transport. BWIA, LIAT, Tropicair, Aero Services, and Air Martinique all fly from Grantley Adams International Airport, which is the hub of the Caribbean, to all of the neighbouring islands. British Airways fly direct to Barbados from London and Manchester for £497 in the low season and £584 in the high. BWIA also connect Britain and Barbados and offer a good service.

Information can be obtained from the Barbados Board of Tourism (see Appendix I for details).

St Kitts and Nevis

The volcanic sister islands of St Kitts and Nevis lie just two miles apart in the eastern Caribbean. Despite occupying the crossroads of the 'Mediterranean of the Americas', St Kitts and Nevis have not yet suffered from tourist invasions and are both still quiet and easy-going places off the beaten track. Nevis in particular is the exclusive resort it was in the eighteenth-century, when it was known as the 'Queen of the Caribbean', while an unknown seventeenth-century traveller called St Kitts the 'first and best earth that ever was inhabited by Englishmen in America'. Both St Kitts and Nevis offer some of the most dramatic scenery in the West Indies as both revolve around large central volcanoes clad in dense lush jungle. Gentle hills rolling down from the mountains are covered with the brilliant green of vast sugarcane fields and a scattering of grand plantation houses, some now only crumbling remains, others elegant hotels. Although St Kitts and Nevis do not have as wide a selection of beaches as Antigua, there are good coastlines with facilities for watersports, and the islands' scenery and history more than compensate for the comparatively small number of beaches.

St Kitts – officially called St Christopher – is the larger of the two islands at sixty-five square miles. Wrapped around the volcanic cone of Mt Liamuiga, which rises to almost 4,000 feet, are deep ravines, thick virgin rainforest with tropical flowers and monkeys, and green foothills of sugarcane and woodland which continue down to the beautiful palm-fringed beaches of the coast. Frigate Bay is the best beach resort area, with its fine white sandy beaches on both the Caribbean and Atlantic sides. The beaches at Sandy Point, Conaree, and Friar's Bay are also superb and are mostly a vivid black colour. Those near the small fishing village of Dieppe Bay are the best for you to windsurf from, and to snorkel and scuba-dive amongst the rainbow coral.

The capital of both islands, Basseterre, still retains an atmosphere of the colonial period of both French and British occupation, with refined Georgian buildings grouped around attractive squares and the beautiful St George's Church. Along the south coast from Basseterre is the impressive Brimstone Hill Fortress built on volcanic stone, the so-called 'Gibraltar of the West Indies'. From its commanding position on an 800-foot hill you can see for many miles across the turquoise Caribbean to numerous other islands. Enclosed in the fortress is a museum describing the turbulent history of these islands with exhibits on the eighteenth-century wars between the French, British and original inhabitants, the Carib Indians.

Two miles to the south is the smaller, circular Nevis, a quiet and exclusive island with a relaxed atmosphere and friendly people. The near-perfect cone of its extinct volcano Mt Nevis rises out of the middle of the island. Nevis's beaches are beautiful and isolated; to the north is the best and longest, the silver sands of Pinney's Beach backed by the palms of a coconut forest, while further to the north is a black sandy beach. The beach next to Nisbet Plantation is also well worth visiting. Colourful coral reefs lie off the north and west coasts and can be seen from hire boats.

Charlestown – the capital of Nevis and its only real town – is made up of old, brightly-painted pretty wooden buildings. Its market gives you a good flavour of local life. The élite once came in droves to the mineral springs of Nevis, some of which are still open beside the ruins of the old Bath Hotel on a hill above Charlestown. Nelson Museum recalls the Admiral's marriage here in 1787 to a local girl, Fanny Nisbet. The most exciting time on both islands is during Carnival between Christmas and New Year, with colourful street dancing, calypso music and masquerades, in which visitors are encouraged to join. Nevis also has a cultural festival in late July and early August. These two islands make for comfortable and exciting beach holidays beneath scenic mountains.

Accommodation: There are about twenty hotels in total on both islands, most of them on St Kitts. These comprise grand converted plantation houses such as Rawlins Plantation on St Kitts and Nisbet Plantation on Nevis, modern resorts, small informal hotels, self-catering villas, and a small number of inexpensive guest houses. As there are so few hotels on the islands, most of which deal directly with tour operators, it's difficult to arrange accommodation independently once you arrive, especially during the high season (mid-December to mid-April) when prices are more expensive. If you're going independently, it is possible to book accommodation while still in the UK through the Caribbean Reservation Service (see Appendix II) and Hotels of Distinction (see Appendix III). The cost of living is not as high as in the Bahamas or Barbados, but is still reasonably expensive, since most goods are imported.

How To Get There: St Kitts and Nevis are becoming increasingly popular with UK operators, including Elegant Resorts which offers a week at either of two exclusive plantation houses on Nevis for £1,000–1,250 per person depending on the season. This is for half-board and flights are included. Hayes & Jarvis offer a week at an all-inclusive resort on St Kitts for £870–1,200. Thomson offer a cheaper alternative, with a week's self-catering on St Kitts for as little as £640. Tradewinds provide two-centre holidays to Nevis and the wonderful beaches of Antigua. Fifteen days on half-board costs from £1,300–2,000. Caribtours and Speedbird are other experienced operators to St Kitts and Nevis (see Appendix II for details of tour operators).

The local airline, Leeward Islands Air Transport (LIAT), flies five times a day between St Kitts and Nevis, also connecting them with many other Caribbean destinations, as does Caribbean Airways. LIAT's Explorer Fare, at approximately £220, allows for thirty days of travel on all of their routes – they serve about twenty-four destinations including Puerto Rico, Caracas, Barbados, Grenada, St Lucia, and Trinidad and Tobago. There is also a regular ferry between Basseterre and Charlestown which takes about forty minutes. British Airways fly to Antigua for £483–560 depending on the season, as does British West Indian Airways via Barbados for £464 return in the low season, and £545 in high season. And from Antigua LIAT fly to St Kitts and Nevis for £59 return. You can also fly Air France via St Maarten or Guadeloupe.

Further information can be obtained from the St Kitts and Nevis Tourist Board (see Appendix I for details).

The British Virgin Islands

The British Virgin Islands were the haunt of innumerable pirates and buccaneers in the seventeenth century, and some say they were the inspiration behind Robert Louis Stevenson's *Treasure Island*. Today, ancient mariners have been superceded by yachtsmen more concerned with sailing than pillaging. The waters around these islands afford some of the world's best sailing, through Sir Francis Drake Channel to isolated islands and cays with names like Dead Chest, Great Dogs, and the Invisibles. These fifty or so islands in the eastern Caribbean are quiet and untouched, and the tourism which has developed has been low-key and upmarket, unlike its larger and more frenetic neighbour, the American Virgin Islands. Isolated coves surround mountainous interiors, and there are miles of unspoilt beaches: this is a quiet and relaxing place, where you can sail in the calm tradewinds, or simply lie on a beach.

The people here are friendly and courteous. Three-quarters of the BVI's 12,000 population live on the largest island of Tortola, whose northern coast has many beautiful beaches, whose centre has hilly green ridges, and whose south coast is home to a large number of marinas. The north coast faces the Atlantic and is carved by many near-deserted sandy bays where seabirds outnumber people. Smuggler's Cove is tranquil, while Long Bay, large and dramatic, is dominated by a ruined fort. Behind the beautiful palm-fringed Cane Garden Bay is an old Rum distillery with an ancient giant still, where you can buy the real thing for a third of the UK price. You can reach the isolated Brewer's Bay only by boat.

Rising to 1,780 feet in the island's interior, Mt Sage is cloaked in dense rainforest and gives you a superb view of the coast and surrounding islands. Sitting on a huge bay on the south coast lies Road Town, the BVI's capital and the only place even approaching a town. Here you can charter almost any type of boat, from a small sailboat to an enormous luxury yacht. Along Main Street are well preserved colonial and colourful West Indian-style buildings. The old Prison and Drake's Channel Museum reflect its piratical past. Tortola comes alive during the Spring Regatta in April and Carnival in August, but the rest of the time the nightlife on all the islands is very low-key, and based around the hotels. Along the coast is the beautiful Sea Cows Bay, near the colourful Prospect Reef. The only other two towns are at West End where a ferry leaves for St John (US Virgin Islands) and East End which is connected by a bridge to Beef Island, the only land flat enough for a runway.

The island of Virgin Gorda is to the east, and is now a stylish resort, although cars only arrived here in the 1960s and electricity in the 1970s, and many places are still reachable only by boat or on foot. From the observation tower on Gorda Peak, 1,370 feet high, in the mountainous north, you can see many smaller islands, including those in the peaceful North Sound, where you can take a submarine ride to meet amazing colourful fish face to face. There are sixteen beaches spread around this beautiful island, mostly in the southern plain where most of the hotels are located and its 1,000 people live. The beaches at Little Dix Bay and Biras Creek have been developed but The Bitter End and Savana Bay remain quiet. The Baths are an amazing rock formation of huge boulders which form spectacular caves and grottoes where you can swim. Spanish Town is the only settlement but is very small. A sixteenth-century Spanish Copper Mine lies in ruins just south of the airport.

Anegada lies to the northeast and is the only island which was not formed by volcanoes, for it is a low-lying island of coral and limestone – a Pacific atoll seemingly out of place in the Caribbean. It is surrounded by thirteen miles of spectacular and treacherous reefs, which have been a graveyard to some 300 ships over the centuries, making it a great place for scuba diving. Many world deep-sea fishing records have been set in these waters, especially in catching Blue Marlin. As there is only one hotel and only one small settlement (called The Settlement!) you have the miles of beaches, lagoons and marshes all to yourself.

The small mountainous island of Jost Van Dyke, northwest of Tortola, has two small resorts and no cars, and is a popular spot to anchor, especially near the beautiful beach at White Bay. A whole string of splendid islands lie south of Tortola across Drake Channel, including Norman Island, which was named after a pirate, where you can take a boat ride into caves supposedly full of pirate treasure. Peter Island is a private de luxe resort with magnificent beaches, especially at Dead Man's Bay. Salt Island is home to 200 goats and nine people, who still harvest salt from ponds and send a bag of it to the Queen as rent! The Royal Mail

Steamer *Rhone* sank off Salt Island in a hurricane in 1867, and is now the 'best dive' in the islands as it is covered in coral and lies only thirty feet below the sea. The tiny island of Fallen Jerusalem is a National Park and you can rent the whole of Necker Island (owned by another famous Virgin, Richard Branson) with its mansion for a mere £3,500 a day.

Accommodation: The BVI continues to be a small exclusive resort area and so rooms are few and expensive and must be booked well in advance. If you are going independently you could try booking through the Caribbean Reservation Service (see Appendix II), or Hotels of Distinction (see Appendix III). Hotel rates in Tortola are generally room only and about £80 a night for a double, and on outer islands are full-board for about £150 a night for a double. Hotel prices are reduced by as much as half during the low season, mid-April to mid-December, when the temperature remains in the high 70s and low 80s °F and there is still little rain. There are a few less expensive guest houses in Road Town for about £16 a night and some self-catering villas and campsites. About two-thirds of visitors actually stay on yachts or, as they are called, 'floating hotels'. Food is imported and therefore expensive, but at least the rum's cheap.

How To Get There: The British Virgin Islands are becoming more popular with UK tour operators, including Thomas Cook who offer a week in the exclusive Sugar Mill Estate on Tortola for £900–1,250 depending on the season, meals not included, and two weeks on the beautiful beaches of the BVI and Antigua for £1,780, meals not included in the BVIs and half-board in Antigua. Hayes & Jarvis offer a week on full-board at the Peter Island Hotel and Yacht Club for £1,350–1,650. Elegant Resorts offer a week on full-board at Little Dix Bay on Virgin Gorda for £1,420–1,880. Sunsail International, in association with Stevens Yachts, offer a week of exciting yachting between all of the BVI's islands for £775–2,300 depending on the season and size of yachts (this does not include flights to BVI). Other experienced operators are Exotic Islands and Speedbird.

The national airline Air BVI connects Tortola (actually Beef Island) with Virgin Gorda, Anegada, the US Virgin Islands and surrounding islands, as does Virgin Island Seaplane Shuttle from West End. You can also charter a plane for island-hopping. The 'Bomba Charger' hydrofoil connects West End, Virgin Gorda, and

St Thomas for about £15 return. British Airways flies to Antigua for £483 return in the low season and £560 in the high season, as does British West Indian Airways via Barbados for £464 return, low season, and £545 high season. From Antigua Air BVI fly on to the BVI for £82 return.

You can obtain information from the British Virgin Islands Tourist Board (see Appendix I for details).

Mombasa

Kenya has long been associated with magnificent scenery, wildlife, and safari holidays. A trip to Kenya is often considered to be something for those with a more adventurous spirit, journeying across plains, attempting to scale at least some of Mount Kenya, and camping under the stars at night. But there are other, less strenuous attractions to be found in this beautiful country, and you don't have to be one of life's more intrepid travellers to appreciate them. Kenya's Indian Ocean coastline stretches for over 200 miles and is home to some of the most beautiful and unspoilt beaches in the world. A holiday at any one of these beaches is all about relaxing in the sun, exploring the local towns and enjoying a sense of the exotic. If you want a taste of safari as well, it's easy enough to combine the two and spend a few days observing animals in their natural habitat. This combination is very popular since it allows you an enjoyable mixture of real 'leisure' time, along with the opportunity to experience the type of country often only seen second-hand on stylised films.

The main tourist city on the Kenyan coast is Mombasa. Some say Mombasa should have been Kenya's capital, but when Africa was divided in the 1880s, Arab and Indian traders had a stronghold on the city, then the most commercial port in East Africa. Kenya's capital, Nairobi, only came into existence – as a shanty town at that time – when the British built the Mombasa–Lake Victoria railway line, linking the coast with Uganda. Much of Mombasa's long history has been centred on Fort Jesus, built in 1593. This Fort was built by the Portuguese, and has been the focal point of many battles, changing hands several times. Today it houses a museum, and is one of the city's most impressive historical monuments.

Mombasa is actually built on an island, connected to the mainland by a bridge on one side, and a ferry on the other. As well as the more modern harbour, there's a medieval waterfront, where you can take a dhow cruise. With its network of alleyways, Mombasa's Old Town, in the south-eastern part of the island, is home to many of the city's museums. Elsewhere on the island, numerous bazaars and open markets sell an excellent selection of silks, jewellery, spices and carvings.

The coastline around Mombasa is split into four areas. To the south, Diani beach is one of the quieter corners, simply because it's only accessible from the city by ferry. Across the bridge, the north coast is where most of Mombasa's hotels are found, as well as its nightclubs, discos and restaurants. On both stretches it is possible to hire from among a variety of boats and explore the surrounding waters. One of the best ideas is to take a glass-bottomed boat and see the splendid coral reefs around the island.

In the north you will find Watamu and Malindi, with more beautiful white-sand beaches and high-quality hotels. Along with Mombasa, Malindi is known as the gateway to the Kenyan coast. Slightly further north lies the Lamu archipelago, where the old Arab town of Lamu dates back to the tenth century. Veiled women wandering the narrow streets conjure up images of Zanzibar as it might have appeared a century ago, an effect enhanced by the fact that cars are banned from the island.

Many visitors to this part of Kenya do not take Mombasa itself as their base, but one of the nearby beach-hotels, away from the bustle of city life. All hotels offer a selection of activities such as snorkelling, scuba-diving, windsurfing and para-sailing, as well as swimming pools (most of these are fresh-water, although some hotels offer sea-water pools as well). One of the most noticeable things about Mombasa and its environs is the interesting mixture of old and new. Top Kenyan hotels such as Nyali Beach Hotel tend to be very luxurious, and in many you will find surviving traditions of colonial days, such as roast beef for Sunday lunch! Thankfully, in most hotels, modern and traditional have been blended together to offer the best of both worlds.

Kenyan cuisine caters for an immense variety of tastes, so there should always be something to suit everyone. Naturally, seafood is superb – lobster and king crab are easy to come by here – while a complete range of dishes, from African and Asian to European, is also commonplace.

Excursions to places of scenic, cultural and historical interest are numerous. In Jadini Forest, on the way to Diani beach, you can see monkeys and brilliant birds and butterflies, while in Shimba Hills Game Reserve – the closest wildlife park to Mombasa – there are sable antelope, elephant, lion and leopard. If the shops are of interest, there is an abundance of stores and markets, not only in Mombasa itself, but also around the hotels. Best buys in Kenya include gold, silver and brassware, basketwork, 'Zanzibar' chests and wood carvings, as well as the many articles made from reptile skins (these need export licences, and it is illegal to import them to the UK, so, irrespective of what the traders tell you, don't buy them). As in many countries, it is probably best to ignore curio shops which tend to sell low-quality mass-production goods.

How To Get There: There is a wide range of tour operators offering Kenyan holidays from this country, including a company called Grass Roots Travel, who offer a good range of combined safari and beach holidays. Time watching the animals is followed by a relaxing week lazing in the sun. Prices start at roughly £1,200 for a two-week safari, all-inclusive, and from £230 for another week in Mombasa.

Abercrombie & Kent have been organising holidays to East Africa for almost thirty years now, and offer an excellent range of beach and/or safari holidays, in everything from five-star hotels to traditional tents. Prices start at around £900, and include return flights, accommodation, transfers, and meals where specified.

Kenya Airtours' brochure is equally comprehensive, as are offers from Speedbird, Sovereign, Thomson, Kuoni, Bales Tours, and Guerba Expeditions.

Further information is available from the Kenya Tourist Office (see Appendix I for details).

Cities

Cities: places bustling with activity, usually with some sort of town square or city focal point, and steeped in history and culture. The 'Classic City' is essentially a European phenomenon, and one which we all too often take for granted. Many of the world's great cities are in Europe: consequently over half the cities in this section are located in this continent, while the others have been chosen because they represent the best of the new-world city phenomenon.

Cities can often be seen at their best during the winter months, when the tourist trade is at an ebb and sights are not packed with jostling crowds. The exception to the rule of crowds is, of course, Vienna, where Christmas time is one of its busiest seasons. But even then, the city is enhanced by the diverse range of people who gather for the Ball Season, and by the transformation of its fabulous architecture into weird and wonderful snow-covered shapes and forms.

Short city breaks to Europe have been popular for some time. Hopping on a plane to Paris or Venice is something which many have become accustomed to. A metropolis may be a metropolis wherever you are, but different traditions, languages, highlights and attractions provide the distinction needed to make each place unique. Vancouver's backdrop of the Canadian Rockies gives the city an incomparable setting; Sydney's magnificent harbour, complete with the 'sails' of the Opera House, cannot be rivalled by any other bay area in the world, and Hong Kong's shops will provide you with a wider selection of goods than you're ever likely to find in such a small area again. These are the things which help make a city holiday so enjoyable.

A visit to a city is all about immersing yourself in its life, so that you come away with a greater understanding of its culture and history: spending as long as you wish in galleries and museums, dining out in anything from a five-star restaurant to a local market café, exploring the streets and alleys, rubbing shoulders with the locals, and staying in a choice of accommodation best suited to your pocket. It is also about pampering yourself, and receiving the sort of treatment and service that only come your way on special occasions. And perhaps more than anything else, city holidays are meant for living your life in the fast lane for a few days. Their very nature makes them the perfect way to enjoy life to the full, for as long or short a time as you wish.

New York

There are few sights more well-known than the Manhattan skyline set against the pale glow of the evening sun. New York – spectacular in its diversity of cultures, sleek in its towering skyscrapers, and sleazy in its downtown bars and clubs – welcomes its visitors to the cosmopolitan bustle of daily life, offering them the opportunity to enjoy one of the most exciting cities in the world. There is little than cannot be seen or done in this sensational major centre, and a holiday here can be anything from lazy and relaxing to hectic and stimulating. Central Park, Chinatown, Broadway, the Rockefeller Center are all within easy reach, and that's only on Manhattan. New York is made up of five boroughs; Queens, Brooklyn, the Bronx and Staten Island are also to be explored, all of which contribute to the many contrasts and contradictions so unique to this city. Towering wealth stands next to shattered tenements, Monday to Friday wheeling and dealing gives way to weekend shopping and touring, and twenty-four hours a day 'the Big Apple' buzzes, always awake and ever-changing.

As New York is the third largest city in the world, and the largest city in the US, knowing where to start can pose a bit of a problem. Taking to the water is a fairly good idea, since the city is situated at the mouth of the Hudson River, and the metropolitan area is surrounded by fifty-five miles of beach. The Staten Island Ferry takes you through lower harbour and New York Bay, passing the Statue of Liberty along the way. If you've been feeling slightly disorientated by the New York experience, this is a good way to get your bearings back and see the city from the outside before tackling the inside.

Finding your way around Manhattan is relatively easy since streets and avenues are numbered consecutively and laid out in a straightforward grid. Even if you do happen to lose your way, with over seven million inhabitants in the city, there will always be someone who can help. The renowned subway system operates throughout the city, although if possible this should be avoided during morning and evening rush-hours. There is also a comprehensive bus network, and taxis can be hailed on the streets (although again, in the rush-hours, this may prove difficult, as well as costly, since meters run oblivious to traffic jams). By far the best way to negotiate Manhattan is on foot. Distances can be covered fairly quickly, and you can make as many detours and stops as you wish along the way.

How you fill your days obviously depends on personal preference, although there are a few attractions which deserve mention. If you have a head for heights, then don't miss the World Trade Center. This is now the tallest double skyscraper in the world, and, as you admire the view from the 110th floor, you'll certainly be able to believe it. A quick walk down Avenue of the Americas (6th Avenue) brings you to Soho, where the buildings inside and out bear testament to the bohemian, artistic life of this area. Quaint stores and boutiques give way to a spate of off-Broadway theatres, nightclubs and bookstores, leading you just around the corner, and into Greenwich Village. For many years this was the city's 'artistic' quarter, rivalling the Latin Quarter and Montmartre in Paris. If you're a theatre lover, then you not only have a chance to see all the major shows on Broadway, but can explore 'behind the scenes' and visit the Lincoln Center for the Performing Arts. This immense complex of white marble is home to the city's principal cultural groups, and is surrounded by the New York State Theatre (home of the New York City Opera and Ballet companies) and the Metropolitan Opera House, to name just two famous theatrical groups. Free tours take place daily from the Avery Fisher Hall. Alternatively, if you prefer something quieter, stroll around Bronx Zoo or the spectacular Metropolitan Museum of Art, or watch the open-air performers in Madison Square Garden or Central Park.

Shops and restaurants in New York cater for every taste, at every price. If you're there at Christmas you will see some of the most spectacular window-displays in the world. There are also roughly 10,000 restaurants in the city, with dishes from every corner of the world. Shops are open from 9.30 a.m. to 5.00 p.m. Monday to Sunday, so there's ample opportunity to buy souvenirs. Watch out for banking hours though, since during the week banks are open from 9.00 a.m. to any time between 2.00–5.30 p.m., but are closed at weekends.

New York really is a city worth exploring: there's no substitute for experiencing it yourself. It doesn't matter how long you are there for, or how many times you've visited before, there's always something new to be discovered. In terms of climate, the city is probably at its best in the autumn, since in summer you can expect short, sharp periods of heat and humidity (average temperature 24°C), while in winter it can become extremely cold (average temperature 2°C).

Accommodation: Like everything else in New York, accommodation is extremely varied. Financially, prices range from $20 a night at the YMCA to $300 at the Astoria, but reductions are offered almost everywhere at weekends. All the main hotels are situated centrally, and offer the range and type of amenities you would expect from international names. The Waldorf Astoria and the Westbury are two of the most distinguished hotels, but equally worth mention are United Nations Plaza and Sheraton Center and Towers (although the latter could be criticised for its impersonality). The Westin Plaza has long been a synonym for New York glamour and sophistication, and as one of the US's most historic hotels, it has an added appeal. Situated at the junction of Central Park South and Fifth Avenue, it is one of the most popular hotels in the city. Time has not altered the standards of gracious living still maintained here, and guests can enjoy tea in the Palm Court accompanied, as ever, by violins, before spending the evening mingling with New York high society in the Oak Room.

How To Get There: The three best tour operators specialising in New York are American Express, Jetsave, and Virgin Holidays. Virgin Holidays offer some of the most exciting New York holidays that are available at the moment. 'Broadway Breaks', 'Manhattan Shopping Breaks' and 'Business Executive Specials' provide travellers with the opportunity to enjoy a more personalised holiday in this huge city. Tickets for the theatre, well-organised shopping trips (perfect for Christmas) and executive suites in a first-class hotel can all be arranged, leaving you to enjoy your time in New York without the usual bother of finding your way around the city before getting to grips with it. With an excellent selection of seven hotels to choose from (all on Manhattan of course), you can't really go wrong.

Main airlines to New York are American, British Airways, Continental, Delta, Pan Am, TransAm, US Air and Virgin. A return ticket will cost you from £250–500.

Further information about New York in general can be obtained from United States Travel and Tourism Administration or the State of New York Division of Tourism (see Appendix I for details).

London

As the capital of Great Britain, London is a city that no traveller should miss. It is the heart of one of the world's greatest historic empires, and offers visitors enough excitement to fill more time than they can probably afford. The 'City' is London's financial nerve centre; Westminster is its political and religious centre, and the West End is the home of British theatre and cinema, along with smart shops and clubs. These three areas, in conjunction with over 1,000 years of history, make London the stimulating city that it is. Buckingham Palace, Covent Garden and the Houses of Parliament are among the most famous landmarks, but beyond these there exists a diverse range of sights and sounds unique to this city alone. At any time of year, London is a thriving tourist centre: museums and shops are followed by afternoon tea; then out to dinner, a concert and later a nightclub. London enjoys itself and plays the perfect host to all its visitors.

London is served by three airports. The main one is Heathrow, which is the world's busiest international airport. Situated approximately fifteen miles west of London, Heathrow has four terminals to cope with its annual twenty-seven million passengers. Transfers into the city are made either by bus or the underground, both of which operate frequently. Taxis are also available but cost considerably more. The second airport is Gatwick, fourth busiest in the world. It lies twenty-seven miles from London, and passengers can transfer to the city by bus, train or taxi. Inter-airport transfers also operate. Both airports have a range of hotels situated close by, offering convenient accommodation if required. The third airport is Stolport – London City Airport – built on reclaimed dockland. Its location is a bonus to travellers, since anywhere in the city can be reached fairly easily. Stolport handles 1.2 million passengers annually, and is aimed primarily at the short-haul business traveller from Europe. Eurocity Express and Bryman Airways operate European and domestic flights from Stolport.

Public transport in London carries visitors to any corner of the city. The London Underground (known as the 'Tube') is by far the quickest and easiest means of transport. However, during morning and evening rush-hours it is also one of the busiest, and is therefore best avoided during these times. London buses run a comprehensive network of routes, carrying passengers throughout the city. Taxis can usually be hailed on the streets, and while car hire is always an option, it is not to be recommended. The only way you're likely to see the city from the privacy of your own car is while you're searching for a parking space.

London has grown significantly over the past twenty to thirty years, to become one of the most exciting and diverse conurbations you can visit. Its separate areas are very different in character, so it's worth trying to travel around the capital and see more than the obvious centres. But time does not always cater for the luxury of exploring everywhere. A visit to London might be more satisfying if you target one or two specific points on the map each time you are there, perhaps just spending one weekend in the city at a time. Covent Garden is a must for any market-lover, as is Petticoat Lane. Trendy shops abound on Camden High Street, and Carnaby Street, with its colourful mosaic pavement, offers shoppers a wide range of goods, especially clothing. For some of the biggest shops, take a trip down Oxford Street and then on to Regent Street. Here you'll find all the traditional British names offering traditional British goods. But for the best of everything, get on a tube to Knightsbridge and go to Harrods – the shop that can literally sell you anything. Of equal merit, both Fortnum and Mason on Piccadilly and Liberty's on Regent Street are worth seeking out, especially for that great British institution, 'Afternoon Tea'.

The highlights of London are so numerous that to see them all in one visit is practically impossible. You can escape from the city bustle for a relaxed stroll in Hyde Park, or alternatively, feed the pigeons in Trafalgar Square. Famous sights such as Eros, Piccadilly Circus, Nelson's Column, Tower Bridge (Tower Hill) and Big Ben in Westminster can all be seen. Why not lose yourself in the maze in the gardens at Hampton Court Palace, or enjoy the peace of the botanical gardens at Kew – they are quite magnificent. St Paul's, London's beautiful Renaissance cathedral, stands as proud as ever. If you've a head for figures, you could spend some time at the Stock Exchange watching the intricacies of international wheeling and dealing. And no visit to London would be complete without a trip to Madame Tussaud's near Regent's Park. Here the famous are immortalised in wax in a style that leaves you wondering what's real and what isn't. It's worth a visit for the chamber of horrors alone!

Other museums around London display every conceivable type of object that history has left us. In fact, the city has so many museums that you're not likely to make it round them all in one go. Try to be selective and don't aim to see too many in one day. The British Museum (Russell Square) is one of the largest and most important historical museums in the world, and really needs at least a whole day to be appreciated. At Greenwich, the National Maritime Museum is excellent for its comprehensive coverage of nautical history, while the Imperial War Museum at Lambeth North has a huge collection of documents and artefacts relating to the Commonwealth during the two World Wars. If you want to know more about London, the Museum of London is dedicated to the long history of the capital. It can be found in the Barbican Centre. The Natural History Museum in South Kensington is also worth a visit for its excellent exhibitions relating to man's evolution.

Art galleries are equally abundant. The best to visit are the National Gallery (Charing Cross/Leicester Square), the National Portrait Gallery (Piccadilly Circus), and for modern and contemporary art, the Tate Gallery (Pimlico). Also of distinction is the Victoria and Albert Museum in South Kensington. Although called a 'museum', its exhibitions are of fine and applied arts from all around the world.

There is very little that cannot be done or seen in London. The city is hectic, fast and chaotic, but in its quiet parks and luxurious hotels it is also relaxing and peaceful. During the day it is the businessman's workplace, the shopper's paradise and the tourist's haven. At night a spectacular transformation takes place: bright lights, theatre crowds, Soho, and every type of cuisine from gourmet to fast-food. Piccadilly Circus glows with neon signs and all around the West End the sophisticated and chic mingle with the sleazy and laid-back. A trip to London is a memorable experience.

There is no best time to visit London. It is at its busiest during the peak months of July and August, and at its quietest (although you'd hardly notice the difference) in February. It is the perfect place, and one of the most popular, for long-weekend breaks, either as part of a package deal or under independent arrangements. Dipping in to the city life-style for forty-eight hours can be very rewarding. With not enough time to get tired, you'll always be left wanting more.

Accommodation: London's accommodation is no longer the most expensive in the world, although it is still pricey. The city is busy the whole year round, so advance thought and early booking are always advisable. All the international hotel chains offer accommodation in London, but an attractive alternative is to opt for a small selection of exclusive establishments, run as part of the individual and independent 'Prestige Hotels'. Duke's Hotel in St James's, The Fenja in Sloane Square, and Inn on the Park on Park Lane are three of the very best hotels in London. Guests would be hard pushed to find higher standards of comfort, cuisine and service elsewhere. Inn on the Park is the largest of the three, while Duke's offers something more personal with only thirty-six rooms and twenty-six suites. The small Fenja was once a grand, private residence, and has been beautifully restored to offer guests the elegant ambience of an Edwardian town house. All three hotels have excellent situations, convenient for the town, and offer guests only the best of all that is traditional and British. Prices start at around £190 a night for a double or twin room.

For slightly cheaper, though still comfortable accommodation, you could consider Lowndes Thistle Hotel, Hospitality Inn, and Norfolk Hotel. All three are of commendable quality and provide guests with every amenity they could wish for. More modestly-priced hotels are easy to find, not to mention a range of guest houses and B&B's (bed and breakfast). Visitors are advised to contact the London Tourist Board to be sure of making the right choice about where to stay (see Appendix I, United Kingdom for details).

How To Get There: British Travel offer a comprehensive range of tours, dealing with roughly three dozen hotels. American Express is one of the best tour operators, along with British Airways' 'London for You' programme, which offers accommodation in seven different hotels. Trusthouse Forte Hotels offer a range of package deals, in modest-budget to luxury accommodation. Rail, coach and flight-inclusive breaks are featured in their programme, between April and October. Mount Charlotte Hotels also offer city breaks, at a price which many may find more accessible; weekends are available for as little as £25 per person, per night and while their range of hotels is limited, they do allow children under sixteen to travel and stay completely free of charge, assuming they can share with two adults, and provided the child to adult ratio is one to one. Also worth consideration are offers from British Rail and Gold Star.

British Airways is the main airline serving London. For domestic flights within the UK, British Airways and British Midland are the main carriers.

For further information on Prestige Hotels (see Appendix III. For further information about London generally, contact the London Tourist Board or the London Tourist Centre (see Appendix I for details).

Paris

There are few cities in the world more exciting than Paris. Every facility, amenity, and type of entertainment associated with a great cultural centre can be found here in the French capital. What makes Paris different though, is its immense variety of features of interest – possibly more than in any other European city – and the style in which those features can be enjoyed. *Haute couture* was born in Paris and, over the years, it has become one of, if not *the*, main trademark of the city: architectural feats such as the Eiffel Tower, the sophistication of 'Prêt-à-Porter' spring fashions, and the charm of the Champs Elysées all bear testimony to this in their unique style and unfailing originality. Paris is a must for any traveller, and with the added bonus of its accessible location, visitors from the UK can be there within a matter of hours, and at a price that doesn't break the bank. Needless to say, this city is now the top weekend break destination for British holiday-makers. And come the completion of the Channel Tunnel, even rail travel from capital to capital will only take about three hours.

Charles de Gaulle Airport is situated roughly twenty miles from the city centre. Bus and rail connections into town run frequently, as well as bus transfer to Orly Airport, which handles mainly charter flights. The inter-airport journey takes about seventy-five minutes. Getting around town is easiest on the Metro rail system – equivalent to London's Tube – although a comprehensive bus network also operates to all parts of the city. *Carnets* of ten tickets will save you time and money, and can be used on both Metro and bus routes. Taxis can be hailed on the street or found at ranks but are more costly.

Paris is a popular holiday spot throughout the year, either as a short-break destination, or for more extended periods. It is at its best though, in the spring, when all those romantic clichés can easily come true! If you don't mind a slight nip in the air, late February and early March are extremely rewarding times to see the city – high season hasn't quite started, and attractions aren't obliterated by crowds.

Palaces, churches, museums and galleries abound in Paris, scattered throughout the city in what seems to be such a haphazard manner that it is difficult to know which way to turn next. A trip down the Seine can be a good starting point, since it highlights certain attractions on both sides of the river, and gives you some idea of how the city is laid out. Generally speaking, there is enough around the centre of Paris – and the historic Place de la Concorde – to keep you occupied for weeks. But of course, there are a host of different features of interest further afield. The Left Bank has long been considered the bohemian 'student' area of Paris, full of cheap(er) cafés and bars, continually buzzing with activity, and home to intense Gauloise-smoking latter-day Brigitte Bardots. Wander up Boulevard St Germain and into the heart of the Latin Quarter, and you'll be surrounded by some of the last bastions of French academia. Alternatively, go a bit further down river and you'll come to Paris' most famous landmark, the Eiffel Tower. Built for the World Fair in 1889, the tower would have been pulled down had it not been for its invaluable service to radio transmission. Today the top is still adorned by aerials and satellite dishes. The Tower – almost 1,000 feet high – can be seen from virtually anywhere in the city. From all levels (there are three in total) there are wonderful views, and at night in particular, floodlit from all sides, it makes an impressive sight.

Several historic bridges cross the Seine: Pont Neuf is the oldest, having been completed in 1603 on the direct orders of Henry IV. This bridge crosses the Seine via Île de la Cité, the original island on which Paris first took shape. Here you can see Notre Dame Cathedral, with its magnificent twin towers and stained glass rose windows. Building began in 1160 but was not completed until the end of the thirteenth century. The massive cathedral organ has recently been restored and now produces an even more impressive sound than ever. If you're there on a Sunday afternoon, there are regular concerts and services to be enjoyed.

Attractions on the Right Bank are numerous. La Place de la Concorde, where the guillotine stood during the Revolution, is a huge square (84,000 square metres to be precise) steeped in history. Louis XVI was executed here in 1793, and Marie

Antoinette in October of the same year. The obelisk in the middle of the square came from Egypt in 1836, when it was given to Louis Philippe by Mohamad Ali. It is now the most ancient monument in Paris, dating from the twelfth century BC. The historic buildings flanking the edge of the square are an attraction in themselves. The French Admiralty Office and Assemblée Nationale are both here, as well as the beautiful Hôtel de Crillon. Today the Crillon is the only remaining French-owned palace hotel in Paris.

To one side of the Place de la Concorde is the Champs Elysées, running straight up to the Arc de Triomphe. On the opposite side there are the Tuileries Gardens, stretching along the Seine to the Louvre Art Gallery. The Louvre is one of the largest galleries in the world, and could easily occupy you for a full week, if not longer. Other museums of note not too far from here, include the Musée d'Orsay, which has an outstanding collection of paintings from the nineteenth century, and the Musée Rodin, which is dedicated to the life and work of this famous sculptor.

The controversial Pompidou Centre is one of the most remarkable buildings in the world: escalators, stairwells, electrical and plumbing pipes are all on the outside of the building. Inside, amongst other attractions, is the National Museum of Modern Art. A short walk from the Pompidou Centre will find you in Montmartre, the Soho of Paris. Cabaret, bars and discos can all be found here, including the renowned Moulin Rouge and Lido.

Directly behind (and above) Montmartre is the beautiful Sacre Coeur, a Romano-Byzantine church which overlooks the city. The interior of the church is quite breathtaking, especially when seen in the evening, lit by candles. At this time of day also, you'll get an especially romantic view of the city laid out at your feet – in itself worth the walk up the hill.

These are the highlights of Paris, features which make this city one of the most diverse in the world. There are few places where the old and the new mingle with such ease or in such style, and with such eventual appeal and success. If you attempted to compare Paris with anywhere else, your description would probably include London, New York and Vienna, all rolled into one. Even then there would still be much more to be said, for the Paris experience is one of the most exciting in the world.

Accommodation: Paris hotels offer accommodation for every budget. Hôtel de Crillon is arguably France's finest hotel, and offers some of the best *haute cuisine* in Paris in its beautifully restored Les Ambassadeurs restaurant. The hotel was built as a royal palace (Marie Antoinette lived here) and its standards today can quite easily be described as 'regal'. Alternatively, both the Meurice and Bristol offer luxurious accommodation with a double room for over 1,000 f per night. Slightly cheaper are the Mayfair and Marriott Prince de Gaulles with double rooms around 550 f per night, while Regyn's Montmartre, Hôtel Notre Dame, and L'Aigon offer comfortable accommodation at more modest prices (3–400 f for a double room). In general, hotel prices are comparable to those in London.

How To Get There: There are a vast range of companies who operate tours to Paris. One of the best is Kirker Travel Ltd, whose personalised service takes care of every detail and problem, even before you have left the country. Kirker also offer a wide range of hotels, and a wide range of prices. One of their main advantages is that they deal with regional airports, and can cut London out of your journey if you wish to leave from elsewhere.

Alternatively, Paris Travel Service offers a comprehensive range of packages. This specialist tour operator has been dealing with Paris for almost forty years, and can now offer almost every imaginable type of holiday to the city, at prices to suit any budget. Most regional airports are dealt with, and rail and coach connections from London are also available if required. Paris Travel Service's choice of hotels is extremely wide-ranging, and optional extras, such as a trip on the Orient Express, are also offered. Quo Vadis is another company offering a wide range of hotels and prices. Their 'Bonjour Paris' brochure covers everything from Concorde flights and the Orient Express to scheduled regional departures, all at very competitive prices (see Appendix II for details).

If travelling independently, booking your Paris hotel can often be done through hotel group offices in London. Reservations for Hotel de Crillon and Hotel Le Bristol can be made through the sales office of Leading Hotels of the World. Hotel Meurice reservations can be made through the sales office of Ciga Hotels (see Appendix III).

The main airlines to Paris are Air France and British Airways. Brymon Airways also offer flights from London's City Airport.

Information about France and Paris in general can be obtained from the French Tourist Board (see Appendix I).

Venice

La Serenissima – the serene republic – was the name given to Venice during the Middle Ages. Today, Venetians still use this Italian term to refer to their magical city; there is something about it which captures perfectly the spirit of gondolas, bridges and fabulous artwork and architecture. Built on an archipelago of islands, with canals for streets and bridges for footpaths, it is a city that no traveller should miss. Eighteenth-century Canalettos and fifteenth-century Carpaccios alike portrayed Venice as it was then, and as it still is today, an association of all that is aesthetically pleasing. Buildings blend with their surroundings, music serenades the ear, and cuisine tempts the palate. Immerse yourself in the wealth of culture that is so much a part of the city's history, and indulge in a few peaceful moments of reflection. Venice, the home of Marco Polo; Venice, master of the seas since its victory over Genoa in 1571, and Venice the twentieth-century city that has prospered through tourism, but at the cost of some of its most ancient monuments. For years, pollution has caused a process of erosion that sadly threatens the city's future. The sinking of this city is no longer a topic of speculation: eventually the unthinkable will happen, and Venice will be removed from the map.

From the UK, Venice is only a couple of hours by plane. This makes it an attractive holiday spot throughout the year, although late spring or early autumn are the seasons for seeing the city at its best: temperatures are unlikely to go above 21°C and the bulk of the summer visitors are either yet to come or are long gone. During the winter Venice gets colder (sometimes dropping to freezing), and the city is often enveloped by a thick blanket of fog. As a result, sightseeing is virtually impossible.

Special events worth making an effort to reach are the pre-Lent carnival in February or March; the international Festival of Drama in June; August's International Film Festival; the Historic Regatta in September, and the Feast of the Madonna della Salute in November.

Arrival in Venice by plane is at Marco Polo di Tessera Airport, approximately eight miles north of the city centre. Connecting buses run throughout the day, taking you into modern Venice.

From there you can reach your hotel by vaporetto (motor boat) or waterbuses. These are the main means of transport in Venice, along with the distinctive, but expensive, gondolas. If your travel plans can accommodate more time, then an attractive alternative to flying to this city comes in the form of the Orient Express. Treating yourself to a couple of days of sumptuous opulence on board this famous train is the perfect prologue to a city renowned for its luxury and refinement.

As Venice is one of the world's most beautiful cities, sightseeing can be a wonderful experience. History has left Venice with an astounding number of palaces (something like 200), built between the twelfth century and the late Renaissance period. As an introduction to some of these, and other glories of Venice, you can take a waterbus down the Grand Canal, which is effectively the city's main thoroughfare. Piazza San Marco (St Mark's Square), one of the most magnificent squares in the world, is at one end of the Grand Canal, and here stands the magnificent Basilica di San Marco, Venice's main cathedral. Also at St Mark's Square is the Doge's Palace, the seat of Venice's wealthy republican government for almost ten centuries, until the abdication of the last doge (duke) in 1797. Inside this grand building you can see the largest oil painting in the world – Tintoretto's *Paradise* – which covers one entire wall. The Bridge of Sighs is the most famous of all Venice's bridges (there are almost 450). It leads from the Doge's Palace to the prison cells. The bridge's name stems from the morbid sounds that could be heard from prisoners who crossed it on their way to execution.

Museums and galleries seem to number almost as many as Venice's palaces. For sculpture the best place to go is the Accademia delle Belle Arti which provides a comprehensive introduction to classical Venetian work. Decorative arts can be viewed at the Rezzonico Palace on the left bank of the Grand Canal, while the Fortuny Museum has an interesting display of fashion items and rare furnishings by the designer Fortuny. The Venier dei Leoni Palace (also on the left bank) houses the Guggenheim display of modern art, and at the Maritime Museum at the Arsenale you can see the beautiful scale-models of Venice's historical boats. All of these, and more, are there to be discovered by the discerning tourist. Just wander the streets, explore the maze of canals, and see how much Venice has to offer.

Crowds and inflated prices can be part and parcel of a trip to Venice, although they can also be avoided, depending on when you go and where you stay. The luxury of spending time in a city with no cars, only boats, and no modern buildings, is an experience that should be enjoyed by all. Venice is a wonderful place, and offers visitors more than 'an average holiday' in 'just another city'. With 117 islets and 150 canals to choose from, few visitors could fail to be enthralled by Venice.

Accommodation: In Venice accommodation is provided in a wide range of hotels. The city's most luxurious (and expensive) hotel is the Cipriani; with its large outdoor pool and tennis courts, guests can enjoy the service of what is easily one of the best hotels in the world. The Venice Excelsior and Gritti Palace also qualify as 'first-class' hotels, as does the Danieli, Riva degli Schiavoni. At slightly less expensive prices there are also the Carlton Executive and Pullman Park.

Hotels are all very well if you're content to enjoy tourist status only in Venice. However there is one option which enables visitors to really live, and appreciate, the genuine 'Venetian Experience'. Venetian Apartments is a small company aimed exclusively at allowing visitors to become integrated into the city and living for a period as Venetians do. As its name suggests, Venetian Apartments deals solely with self-catering lets, but of a very high standard. It's a wonderful way to see Venice. Self-catering is virtually unheard of here, and in the UK market this company is unique. Venetian Apartments also handle additional properties in Venice, as well as Florence, Rome and all parts of Italy on request. Apartments range from the simple, but elegant, to the opulent and de luxe, and sleep anything from two to seven people. Prices range from roughly £180–600 per week, and are worth every penny. Shop at the market, mix with the locals, and see Venice through the eyes of the people that make the city what it is. Try out your Italian, get to grips with your lira, and become one of Venice's 90,000 inhabitants. You'll enjoy the unique lifestyle that ordinary tourists never really experience. For further details about Venetian Apartments see Appendix II.

Perhaps the ultimate Venetian experience would be to travel to Venice on the Venice Simplon Orient Express train, and then stay in one of Venetian Apartments' opulent flats which overlook the Grand Canal.

How To Get There: Alternatively, there are also a range of 'city-break' specialists who offer attractive tours and short trips to Venice. The main tour operators are Cresta Holidays, Kirker Travel, Osprey Holidays, Pegasus, Thomson, and Travelscene Ltd.

British Airways and Alitalia are the main airlines flying to Venice. Britannia also offers limited services. A return ticket will cost from £120–150.

Further information about Venice in general can be obtained from the Italian State Tourist Office (ENT) (see Appendix I for details).

Vienna

Whatever time of year you are there, Vienna is a magical place. But at Christmas, when the city's gilded domes are transformed into snow-capped peaks, Vienna becomes the winter wonderland you dreamed of as a child, and the winter playground for Austrian high society. As the festive season gets underway, the streets are filled with crowds jostling for their gingerbread hearts, jellied apples, marzipan bonbons and chestnuts for roasting. Come New Year the city is alive with music as the Vienna Philharmonic and the Vienna Symphony Orchestras give their annual concerts of Strauss and Beethoven, broadcast throughout the city and in all hotels. And of course the Vienna Boys Choir will be there, singing Christmas Mass on Christmas Day and Mass again a week later at New Year. To celebrate Christmas in Vienna is to be caught in the middle of the most festive city in the world. Vienna in season is a unique experience. Days are spent surrounded by sophistication and culture, while nights give way to the grace and elegance of palace balls.

Arrival at Vienna's international Schwechat Airport finds you approximately eleven miles east of the city centre. Transfers into town take the form of the 'Schnellbahn' (fast railway), and a regular coach service which takes about half an hour. Taxis are also available at the airport, but be prepared for pretty steep fares. Once in town the public transport system is swift and frequent, so getting about is no problem at all. Buses run throughout the city, as does the underground. The most popular means of transport are the distinctive red and white trams, with their recorded mechanical voices detailing the stops and points of interest. Maps detailing bus, train and tram routes are available from the city information office and most stations.

Vienna is the type of city that compels you to get involved

with everything that goes on. Although the main language is German, English is widely used and understood, so there's no danger of missing out on anything. As you wander about the streets you'll become increasingly aware of the exciting, and often turbulent history that made Vienna the home of the vast, powerful Habsburg Empire and the captivating place it is today. The city's first 'Golden Age' began in the fifteenth century, and recurred between a series of brutal wars for four hundred years. Leopold I led Vienna into the Baroque era, and of course much of this is still in evidence today. The strong Catholic influence which has been felt for many centuries is manifest in the striking Stephansdom – one of the largest cathedrals ever built. Nearby, the more modest Figarohaus will invite you to trace the career of Mozart. The composer lived here for three years, and the building has been turned into a museum dedicated to his life and work. A short distance away is the Cemetery of St Marx, Mozart's burial place.

Palaces abound in Vienna, but none are so great as the magnificent Hofburg. Since the thirteenth century this has been home to the country's ruling family, and its age is reflected in the variety of architectural styles which can be seen. Leave plenty of time if you want to explore the Hofburg fully, as its many chambers, chapels and state rooms demand more than just a quick glance. Liechtenstein Palace, another of Vienna's grandest buildings, houses one of the country's principal modern art galleries, the Museum of Modern Art. If you prefer something a bit more traditional, then take a trip to the Museum of Fine Arts. Antiques of every sort can be viewed here, as well as displays of Egyptian and Oriental art. The choice is almost endless. To list all sixty of Vienna's museums and galleries would not do each the justice that it deserves.

But this is Vienna at Christmas, and while it's all too easy to immerse yourself in the fabulous range of collections and valuable artefacts, the festive spirit is infectious. Of all the cities in the world, Vienna is probably the one that knows best how to celebrate this time of year with the most grandeur and sophistication. The air of quiet opulence which normally gives Vienna its dignified, civilised character, gains an extra dimension at Christmas. Preparations for the annual New Year's Day performance of *Die Fledermaus* have been underway for some time. Decorations, bright lights, colourful costumes and only the most choice food and wines, create an atmosphere that proclaims the start of the famous Ball season. Each major hotel hosts its own New Year's Ball: all of them are as glamorous as you could imagine. If you're really lucky you will have managed to get tickets for the Kaiser Ball at the Hofburg Palace. But such luxury only comes from good planning, and you'll have to book months in advance. The Kaiser Ball is the grandest in Vienna, and the perfect way to toast the New Year. For a really memorable evening, you might also look into the special Concorde trip which is run from the UK (Goodwood Travel).

Vienna at Christmas really does have to be experienced to be appreciated. The wealth of cultural and festive activities that take place at this time of year is quite astounding, not to mention the prevailing seasonal spirit enjoyed by all. There are few opportunities available to today's traveller which recreate with such finesse the elegance, style and sophistication of a bygone age.

Accommodation: With everything else that goes on in Vienna at this time of year, arrangements such as accommodation might seem too trivial to worry about – once you're there that is. Predictably, hotels do some of their best business during this period, so make plans well in advance to be sure of getting your first choice. International chains such as the Inter-Continental and Marriott both have hotels in Vienna, as well as the Wien Hilton International. Palais Schwarzenberg is one of the city's most beautiful hotels, although it is also one of the most expensive (over £150 a night for a double room). Equally worth mentioning is the Plaza Wien which was only opened in 1988. Less expensive but just as comfortable are the Astoria, Austrotel and Kaiserin Elisabeth, all of which have good central locations. And of course there is an excellent range of Pensiones and guest houses at more modest prices, starting at around £10 a night.

How To Get There: Main tour operators serving Vienna are American Express, Austrian Holidays, Cresta Holidays, Goodwood Travel, Kirker Travel, the Venice Simplon Orient Express, Osprey Holidays and Thomson (see Appendix II).

Main airlines flying to Vienna are Austrian Airlines and British Airways. An APEX return ticket will cost between roughly £100–140.

For further information on Austria in general, and details of the 'Ball Season' and availability of tickets, contact the Austrian National Tourist Office (see Appendix I).

Hong Kong

Imagine the clattering of mah-jong, the click of chopsticks, the smell of spice on a warm breeze. This is Hong Kong – exotic, dynamic, a shopper's paradise, always awake, always alive. From the moment you step off the plane at Kai-Tak airport until you reluctantly depart, you will be captivated by the sheer exuberance of this vibrant, pulsating city. Whether you're on mainland Kowloon, out in the countryside of the New Territories, or right in the centre of Victoria – Hong Kong's capital on Hong Kong Island – you'll be enthralled by the life that encompasses everything from a replica 1,000-year-old village to one of the world's most advanced planetaria and space museums.

Situated at the south-eastern tip of China, Hong Kong provides the perfect setting for open-air markets, air-conditioned department stores, bargains and bartering. Porcelain, jade, gold, silk, leather, hand-made jewellery, tailor-made clothes and designer fashions: these are just some of the attractions which make Hong Kong's duty-free shopping so special. Even the impending take-over of 1997 has not dampened the indomitable spirit of Hong Kong's thriving businesses, and all around you people are as busy as ever producing the kind of goods which can be hard to come by in this country, but sell for tuppence a piece in Hong Kong. The infinite variety and range is astonishing. Wander down the famous Nathan Road or cross the harbour to Hong Kong Island and explore the alleys, or head for the stalls of Stanley Market. It doesn't matter what you're looking for, Hong Kong caters for all tastes, and in a style that is irresistible and fascinating. Convenient shopping hours also add to the pleasure. In Central on Hong Kong Island shops are open from 10 a.m. to 6 p.m., while everywhere else they stay open until 10 p.m. Most are open seven days a week and most accept traveller's cheques and international credit cards.

Communicating with shopkeepers and the locals is no problem either. Hong Kong's two official languages are Chinese and English, so non-Cantonese speakers shouldn't experience too much difficulty. As for negotiating the various public transport systems, there is little that is not self-explanatory or easy to work out. A comprehensive bus system runs virtually all over the colony, and the Mass Transit Railway (MTR, Hong Kong's equivalent of the underground) provides more than adequate coverage of most places you might want to visit. With such a fabulous harbour to enjoy, there are also the regular, dirt-cheap and renowned Star ferry services to carry you from Kowloon to Hong Kong Island and back again, in a style so romantic it's straight out of the movies.

Shopping is only part of Hong Kong's appeal. The other, surprising, side of this extraordinary outpost is often unrealised. Travel north-west on the Kowloon–Canton railway, out of the bustle of city life, and you'll find the quiet tranquility of the New Territories countryside. Terraced farms, ancient temples and monasteries, and tree-lined bays reflect the undisturbed village life of the Hakka people and other indigenous communities. Experiencing the unhurried pace of traditional Chinese life, so far removed from the international atmosphere of the city, is like being in a different country. Alternatively, with 235 outlying islands also under her jurisdiction, Hong Kong's waters provide more than enough places to visit. There are regular ferry services to most of the main islands, as well as organised day-trips to some of the nearer islands.

The largest island in Hong Kong is Lantau. Although it is twice the size of Hong Kong Island, it has only 20,000 inhabitants, as opposed to Hong Kong's overall population of 5.3 million. Here, and on other islands like Lamma and Cheung Chau, there are small fishing villages, an abundance of seafood restaurants and beautiful beaches (although with winter temperatures sometimes dropping below 15°C, don't expect to be able to sunbathe the whole year round). Tours are operated to all the main islands, as well as to the Portuguese colony of Macau. Known primarily for its casinos, this is the oldest European settlement in China.

Hong Kong's hotels all serve a wide variety of Western food, as well as offering the delights of genuine oriental cuisine. Thousands of restaurants are at your disposal, catering for all nationalities and always with excellent service. Whether you're enjoying fresh lobster at a cordon bleu restaurant, or trying the traditional Dim Sum at an open-air market café, you'll find a feast of specialities to be savoured.

There isn't really a single best time of the year to visit Hong Kong. In terms of public holidays and festivals, Chinese New Year (end-January to beginning February) can provide a good insight into traditional customs. Since the main religion is Buddhism, Western holidays like Christmas and New Year are not really celebrated to any great extent. In terms of weather, Hong Kong enjoys a warm climate throughout the year (the summer average is 28°C), although winter temperatures can fall quite considerably. However, humidity is the real factor to consider; even in winter it only drops to 75 per cent, while in spring it stands at 84 per cent. The other main thing to watch for once you're there are exchange rates offered by money changers. These are usually worse than in the banks (which open 9 a.m. to 3 p.m.), and you should look around to find the best deal. Always ensure that quotes are net.

Otherwise, Hong Kong is everything its reputation says it is. 'Racy' is perhaps the best word to sum it up, since it's certainly one of the liveliest cities in the world.

Accommodation: The choice of accommodation in Hong Kong is comprehensive. The recent increase in top-quality hotels has allowed Hong Kong to become one of the most luxurious cities in the world. Kowloon and Central are hosts to all the major international hotels, and for many of them their Hong Kong branch is their flagship property. The Hilton, Holiday Inn, Hyatt Regency, the Regent and the Sheraton are all there, with prices ranging from HK$700 for single and double rooms to HK$9,000 for luxury suites. Worth special mention is the Mandarin Oriental; only twenty-seven years old, this hotel is acknowledged to be one of the best hotels in the world. With its magnificent harbour-front location, and over 1,200 staff for 545 rooms, the Mandarin is the epitome of gracious service and charm.

As an alternative, you might consider the Peninsula on Kowloon. Here the elegance of the old colonial days lingers on, combined with all the sophistication afforded by modern refinements. Slightly cheaper, but equally worth considering, are the Furama Inter-Continental and Excelsior on Hong Kong Island (the latter is at Causeway Bay and overlooks this pleasant harbour), and the Shangri-La on the Kowloon waterfront. There is also a superb range of comfortable guest houses at more modest prices. The YMCA has prices ranging from HK$140–350 (HK$140 is approximately £14). As with everything else in Hong Kong, you'll certainly find value for money in your choice of hotel.

How To Get There: The best tour operators dealing with Hong Kong are Asian Affair, Abercrombie and Kent, Bales Tours, China Travel Service, Kuoni, Magic of the Orient, Silk Cut,

Speedbird, Thomas Cook, and Virgin Holidays (see Appendix II).

Main airlines serving Hong Kong are British Airways, Singapore Airlines and Cathay Pacific. A return ticket will cost roughly £600–800, depending on when you travel.

For further information contact the Hong Kong Tourist Association (see Appendix I).

Singapore

Singapore! All the mystery of the Orient, the allure of an island and the excitement of a modern-day city. Small she may be, twenty-five by fourteen miles, but she is home to approximately 2.5 million people, and hostess to thousands of visitors each year. Singapore is the tradition of a Gin Sling at the stately Raffles Hotel, the brightness of the Temple of 1,000 Lights and the excitement of the ancient sport of crocodile wrestling. Since 1965 this has been an independent republic, with a history stretching back to the seventh century AD, when, known as Temasek – 'Sea Town' – Singapore was a trading centre of Sumatra's ancient Srivijaya Empire. The name derives from Singa Pura – in Sanskrit 'Lion City' – which, according to legend, was the choice of the Prince of Palembang. When he landed there in the thirteenth century, he encountered a 'very swift and beautiful animal, its body bright red, its head jet black'. The Prince mistook it for a lion – although it was probably a native tiger – and from then on the island was known as Singa Pura. Such exotic creatures still exist in Singapore. Rare breeds such as Sumatran Tigers and Komodo Dragons can be seen in Singapore's Zoological Gardens, itself just one of the many attractions so unique to the island.

Arrival at Singapore's Changi airport finds you roughly twenty-five kilometres (sixteen miles) east of the city. If you've had a long flight, it's a good idea to pre-arrange transport to make life easier, although taxis are always available and a regular bus runs every ten minutes. Preliminaries over and done with, head straight for your hotel, settle in, find your bearings, and relax.

Shopping in Singapore is everything it's made out to be, a staggering range of goods at an incredible range of prices. Basic shopping hours are 10 a.m. to 7 p.m. Monday to Saturday, although in tourist areas many shops stay open later, as well as on Sundays. Singapore is a duty-free port and, as such, is able to sell goods at lower prices than elsewhere.

Asian handicrafts, European *haute couture*, luxury leather goods and the latest electronic equipment are all available at bargain prices. Also to be found in abundance are Chinese carpets and a wide range of fabrics, many with colourful batik designs. As well as the modern air-conditioned department stores and shopping complexes, you will also find long strings of open-air markets, complete with traditional fruit and vegetable stalls and local specialities. A few words of warning should be heeded though. Always shop around and compare prices; check for correct voltages on electrical equipment; make sure you have an International Warranty Card for cameras, watches and electronic goods (and a receipt also), and obtain written confirmation of any instructions given to shops to post packages on. Although some of these may seem time-consuming, they're far less bother than chasing up shops after you've left, or sorting out unwanted problems before you leave.

Also to be watched out for are money changers. Most large department stores have their own, but there are a large number scattered around the streets. Be sure to look for their licensing sign and check commission rates before changing cash. If in any doubt, try the banks instead. These are open from 10 a.m. to 3 p.m. Monday to Friday, and 9.30 a.m. to 11.30 a.m. on Saturdays.

Once you have exhausted the shops (or, more likely, the shops have exhausted you!), there is still a countless number of ways of spending your time. Singapore is not so large that it is difficult to get from one place to another, so sightseeing is a relatively straightforward operation. For a good view of Oriental life you can take a walk through Chinatown and become acquainted with its customs and colourful shops. Be a native and visit Trengganu Street, where fresh flowers, local fruits and dried foods adorn the sidewalk stalls.

Singapore's historical heritage is a source of much interest, and around the island you can find various landmarks which owe their presence to the country's development over the last 100 years. A bronze statue of Sir Stamford Raffles can be seen in front of Victoria Theatre, and again on the bank of Singapore River. The latter is a copy, erected where Raffles is first believed to have stepped ashore in 1819, when he selected the island as a British maritime base. The National Museum and Art Gallery, which celebrated its centenary in 1987, is worth visiting for its fabulous 380-piece Haw Par Jade collection alone. Also housed in this gracious Victorian building are many historic documents and artefacts which chronicle the lives of some of Singapore's most famous names.

The island abounds in parks, gardens and nature reserves, all of which provide peace and tranquility away from the bustle of the streets. Open-air concerts are held in the wonderfully exotic Botanic Gardens, while birds, butterflies and the occasional monkey provide entertainment at Bukit Timah Nature Reserve. Mandai Orchid Garden is well worth a visit. Here you can see a whole hillside covered with the most exotic blooms, and a Water Garden containing rare tropical plants. And of course the fabulous Tiger Balm Gardens are always there for a few hours sightseeing. Pagodas and parkland reflect a more rural side of Far Eastern life. Tours are run to and around all these places, as well as the other main attractions in Singapore. Your hotel should be able to give you full details of what is going on. Remember also that since Singapore is situated just off the southern extremity of the Malay Peninsula (with a connecting causeway between), it is possible to spend time in Malaysia itself. There are also fifty-seven islets which are included under Singapore's jurisdiction, many of which offer their own highlights and attractions.

Since Singapore does not have distinct wet and dry seasons, the island makes an ideal long-haul holiday spot throughout the year. Most rain falls during the northeast monsoon season, November to January, when showers are usually sudden and heavy. However, even at this time, Singapore is warm, and humidity remains fairly high.

Accommodation: The choice of hotels in Singapore is extensive, especially when you consider the small size of the island. All the international names can be found – Sheraton, Excelsior, Hilton International, Mandarin Oriental, Holiday Inn, Hyatt Regency – as well as an excellent choice of Far Eastern-based companies. Bargain prices are the norm in Singapore, due to over-supply and strong competition. Service remains excellent, however. The Dynasty and Goodwood Park both offer extremely comfortable accommodation, though perhaps the city's finest hotel is the Shangri-La. For real old-fashioned luxury, Raffles is the place to be. This historic landmark has no pretensions about rivalling its modern competitors in size as it has only 127 rooms: however, since its refurbishing it does provide every amenity in an old-world atmosphere that no amount of modern sophistication can recreate. Not for nothing did Somerset Maugham describe Raffles as standing 'for all the fables of the exotic East'. Kipling and Coward both chose to make this their home and workplace when in Singapore.

Almost all hotels have a central location, and prices range from roughly S$50 per night for a standard single room to S$260 for a de luxe double. Due to competition it's often possible to obtain reductions on the usual rates, or get an upgraded room for the price of a standard.

How To Get There: In terms of who to travel with, Asian Affair is *the* main company dealing with Singapore. They offer a variety of Far Eastern tours, covering either Singapore alone, or jointly with Hong Kong, Malaysia and/or Thailand. The choice of holidays is extensive, and virtually every tour includes Singapore at some stage. A typical example of a two-destination trip would be three nights in Singapore, followed by nine nights on the island of Penang, just off the west coast of Malaysia. Alternatively, if you want to travel even further afield, why not enjoy Hong Kong, Bangkok, Hua Hin and Singapore all in the same trip? It should be noted that Asian Affair offer excellent rates on de luxe hotels and, that, as a subsidiary of Singapore International Airlines, they also offer good flight reductions. Independent travel is equally feasible, with a range of seven-night city packages making life a bit easier. The company covers over eighty hotels in twenty destinations, and offers the widest coverage of South-East Asia and the Orient available on the market.

The main airline serving the area is Singapore Airlines; they can arrange your holiday plans as well (see Appendix II).

Further information about Singapore can be obtained from the Singapore Tourist Promotion Board (see Appendix I).

Leningrad

To many people the thought of a trip to Russia might not match up to their idea of a dream holiday. Sub-zero temperatures, fiery Cossack dancers and Chekhovian samovars are perhaps the pictures that spring to mind. But Russia has much more to offer than the stereotypical images with which it has become synonymous, and with the predominant spirit of *glasnost*, first-time visitors to this great continent might be in for one or two surprises. To an extent there is still a feeling that Moscow is the place where it's all happening, but life beyond this political centre goes on, offering as stimulating a holiday as you could enjoy anywhere else in the world.

Leningrad – tourist centre of the European north of the USSR – is situated on the shores of the Gulf of Finland, where the River Neva joins the Baltic Sea. With a population of over five million, Leningrad has grown, since its foundation in 1703, to become Russia's second biggest city in size and economic importance. As the cradle of the Great October Revolution, it is a city packed with cultural and historical interest. Museums, magnificent architecture, memorials and rivers, theatres, restaurants, cinemas and concerts: all of these, and more, make Leningrad one of Russia's most popular cities for tourists. Of particular interest are the 'White Nights' and 'Russian Winter' arts festivals, held in June and December and January respectively. The former, of course, takes its name from the spectacular phenomenon of the silvery twilight which envelops Leningrad at night during June. Both festivals bring more life than usual to the city, allowing you the chance to see some of the best artistic talent Russia has to offer.

Getting around Leningrad is relatively simple (although you'll always be able to make life easier for yourself if you're even vaguely acquainted with a few basics of the Russian language). The Metro system is fairly comprehensive, although trams and buses are more useful around the city. Incidentally, bus and tram tickets are sold at a flat fare of five kopeks (100 kopeks equals one rouble). Plans of the public transport system are available in hotels. Also worth considering are the various river trips, especially those by hydrofoil. These leave from the pier nearest to the Summer Palace gardens and take you to the palace at Petrodvorets and the Peter and Paul fortress.

To really get the feel of Leningrad you're best to explore, as far as possible, on foot. You'll soon notice how much at odds the northern light and landscape are with the European architecture and colours. The combination is unique, lending itself to the undoubted charm of this city. See the parapet statues in the vast Palace Square, destined to stare eternally at the Staff Headquarters opposite. Visit the Alexander Nevsky Monastery where Corinthian columns support the Church of Trinity, and pay your respects to two of the greatest Russians of all time, Tchaikovsky and Dostoyevsky, at the Tikhvian Cemetery. At the Hermitage, guided tours help you find your way around the incredible Royal Art collection – it's easy to get lost in the 400 halls which house a staggering two million works of art. Just outside the city the Petrodvorets, Pushkin and Pavlovst Palace complexes carry a reminder of Nazi occupation during the Leningrad blockade. Looted and burned at the time, these palaces are still being restored today. In the Partridge Room at Petrodvorets, progress is slow: silk which once lined this room is recreated at a rate of only 2.5 cm a day.

After exploring the city, at the end of the day there's the Kirov Ballet. Nijinsky and Nureyev are two names associated with the Kirov that spring to mind, but there's new talent now and the company is as strong as ever. Even if you don't want to spend an evening at the ballet, you could visit the building. It may be smaller than the Moscow Bolshoi, but it's still one of the most significant points on the arts map of Russia.

If there's one thing which Russia is not good for, it's the choice of shops. Nevertheless, Leningrad's main street reveals an interesting cross-section of the Russian way of life. Known as the Nevsky Prospekt, it is to Leningrad what Gorky Street is to Moscow and the Kreshchatik to Kiev. It's the oldest, and one of the most beautiful streets in Leningrad, usually seething with people. Opening off it are squares and gardens which complement buildings such as the Admiralty, Kazan Cathedral and Pushkin Drama Theatre. There's certainly more than a morning's sightseeing, so leave enough time for a leisurely stroll along part of it at least. Nobody's going to blame you if you don't make the whole two miles!

Leningrad, like Moscow, is a year-round destination. It's summers are short, but pleasant and warm, while its winters (November to March) have lots of snow and temperatures well below freezing. Wrap up warm – that means a hat and boots. Thaw and rain combine to make spring very wet underfoot. If there is a single good time to go, then try for June and the 'White Nights' arts festivals. Recent years have seen such a tourist boom though, that December and January are often the only time package deals are still available. By all means travel independently, but be prepared to tackle the service bureau, and the ladies who run it, at your hotel. With a good package tour such problems are avoided as your rep should shoulder the bureaucracy. Dinner will be included and you can pre-book sightseeing trips and evening entertainment.

A trip to Leningrad, independently or otherwise, is certainly worth any minor problems you might encounter along the way. As the 'Venice of the North', Leningrad will certainly live up to its name, and, whatever anyone might say to you, don't be fooled into believing you can't have an exciting holiday in Russia. There's a whole continent there that most of us know very little about.

Accommodation: Centrally-located hotels are lacking in Leningrad. Many hotels are situated some distance from the city centre, although there are a couple more conveniently located. The modern Leningrad Hotel is one, while the other is the Yevropeyskaya, just off Nevsky Prospekt. This is a delightful old building, complete with Art Nouveau interior. Both offer more than adequate facilities, although don't expect absolute five-star-plus service. If you are travelling independently, a double room will cost you roughly £50–100 per night. Prospective travellers should note that with many package deals you often won't be told where you are staying until you actually arrive in Russia.

How To Get There: The main tour operator to Leningrad is Russia's own, Intourist. As well as single-destination trips to Leningrad, they also offer package deals including Moscow and Kiev. Sovereign Cities also run tours to Leningrad and Moscow. Package deals to Russia are most commonly run in the form of two-destination trips to Moscow and Leningrad. From either of the above operators, tours cost roughly from £5–600. Included in this are return flights, rail/flight transfers between cities, twin-bedded room with private facilities, breakfast and detailed excursion meals, excursions, and all airport transfers, charges and porterage.

The main airlines serving Russia are British Airways and Aeroflot.

For further information contact Intourist Moscow Limited and Sovereign Cities at Redwing (see Appendix II).

San Francisco

Situated on the tip of its magnificent Bay, San Francisco is arguably the most beautiful city in the western US. It is also one of the world's most international cities, its population of over 700,000 including large Chinese, Hispanic, Vietnamese and Japanese communities. The city was founded in 1776 by

San Francisco

the Spanish Army and Catholic Church, but was denied its present prosperity until the Gold Rush, just over sixty years later. Its international atmosphere can be partly attributed to those early days, when people of all creeds and colours flocked to San Francisco, either in search of gold, or simply to be part of the development taking place. Over the years the city has been described as 'Baghdad by the Bay', 'the cool grey city of love', and, by the more conservative, as the 'kook capital of the world'. It's the US's most European, 'old-fashioned and civilised' city, and makes a good starting point for a tour, especially of the western US.

San Francisco International Airport lies roughly fifteen miles south of the city. Connecting buses run virtually twenty-four hours a day, and taxis are also available, although they cost considerably more. Once in town, public transport is more than adequate, with a comprehensive bus network as well as the 'Muni' (San Francisco Municipal Railway) reaching all parts of the city. Cable cars do still run in San Francisco, although the service has been cut over the years. Nevertheless, they provide an attraction in themselves, and are an enjoyable, slightly different way of getting around. Ferry boats cruise the Bay, offering an ideal opportunity to view the city from one of its most striking vantage points. Alternatively, if you'd rather walk, downtown streets are laid out in an easy-to-follow grid pattern, so finding your way around doesn't pose a problem.

Whichever way you look in San Francisco, you'll be struck by the beauty of the combination of man-made and natural wonders. Chinatown, Japantown and Little Italy reflect the city's ethnic origins, all offering highlights – museums, cuisine, shops – of their own unique cultures. Chinatown is of particular interest, since it is here that the largest Chinese population out of mainland China can be found. For a taste of the American 'Frisco' though, visit the magnificent Bay area with attractions such as Fisherman's Wharf, the Cannery and Pier 39. Restaurants, fish-markets and sidewalk stalls can be found next door to art galleries and speciality shops. Or why not spend some time at Ghirardelli Square and admire the fantastic views over the Bay? The Square used to be a chocolate factory, but has been converted to a Victorian-style de luxe shopping and restaurant complex. Look out for the Ice-Cream Parlour, forget about the calories, and sample a San Francisco legend in the form of delicious chocolates and ice-cream sundaes!

Outdoor attractions are numerous in San Franciso, the most obvious being Golden Gate Bridge. The adjoining Golden Gate Park is one of America's finest city parks. Lakes, botanical gardens and herds of buffalo in paddock fields can all be seen here, as well as the delightful Japanese Tea Garden. The park is also home to several museums, including the Morrison Planetarium, the Asian Art Museum and the California Academy of Sciences. Like other outdoor places of interest, Golden Gate Park is a popular spot for tourists and San Franciscans alike, the whole year round. With a typical northern Californian climate – warm winters and cool summers – San Francisco's outdoor life can be extremely enjoyable.

Should you prefer to be inside, San Francisco offers a range of museums and galleries that are enough to keep you occupied for several days. The Museum of Modern Art is certainly worth a visit, as is the California Palace of the Legion of Honor, which houses a variety of French art. Also to be noted is the display of coins and other related exhibits at the Old Mint. At night, museums may close, but then comes the chance to enjoy the range of concerts and plays on offer. The San Francisco Symphony Orchestra is deservedly popular, or alternatively, if theatre is your interest, there are usually several major ex-Broadway shows running at selected theatres. Other forms of after-dark entertainment include a wide range of bars and nightclubs, as well as live bands and casinos.

San Francisco has blossomed from a former Spanish settlement into one of the US's greatest cities. Children and adults alike will find much to occupy their time in this city, not to mention the various attractions close by. The northern Californian coastline is considered one of the most beautiful in the world; Yosemite National Park is only a five-hour drive away (not far by American standards), as is Lake Tahoe also. And of course there is the Napa Valley wine country. A couple of days can easily be spent touring the famous Californian vineyards and sampling their excellent produce.

Accommodation: San Francisco offers an extremely varied range of accommodation. Top-ranking hotels in the city are the Westin St Francis (regarded as one of the best in the US), Mark Hopkins Inter-Continental, and Mandarin Oriental. Both the Inter-Continental and Mandarin offer superb views over the Bay, while the Westin's restaurant facilities are exceptionally fine.

Pricewise, guests can expect to pay over $150 for a double room in these first-class hotels.

Slightly cheaper are Sheraton Palace, the Donatello, Holiday Inn and the Huntington. All have fairly central locations, and offer more than adequate accommodation and facilities. Guest houses abound in the city, offering comfort at more modest prices. Of the many, a few worth mentioning are the King George, Pension International, Pension San Francisco and Hotel Essex. You should note that all hotels have an additional charge for the use of in-room telephones. Even if there is no reply to your call, you will still be charged, and quite heavily at that!

If there is one San Franciso hotel which deserves special mention it is the Sherman House. Here you will find all the style and comforts of a château hotel in France, but in a personalised atmosphere more akin to that of a family-run guest house. When you arrive the owners will be there to greet you in person, and to check that all is as it should be in your luxurious room. Four-poster beds, antique escritoires, marble fireplaces and polished black-granite bathrooms are all there for your enjoyment. The building itself is a registered landmark, built in 1876 in Victorian palazzo style. It has been carefully restored, and now stands as one of San Francisco's most prestigious hotels. Such opulence comes at a price though, and guests pay up to $650 a night for a suite.

How To Get There: Main tour operators to San Francisco are Airtours, Bales Tours, Jetsave, Jetset, Kuoni, Sovereign (Redwing) and Speedbird. All offer excellent package deals (see Appendix II).

Main airlines serving San Francisco are Pan Am, British Airways, TWA and Northwest Orient. From Scotland it is possible to fly direct with Thistle Air out of Prestwick.

For further information about San Francisco, contact the United States Travel Information Centre (see Appendix I).

Sydney

The east coast of Australia was first sighted on 20 April 1770 by Captain James Cook from his ship the *Endeavour*. It wasn't until eighteen years later that anybody actually set foot on this ground, when Captain Arthur Philips arrived from England with 1,030 men and women, of whom 736 were convicts. Such was the start of the first white settlement in Australia, and even today visitors can still see the spot where it all began – the Circular Quay area right in the heart of Sydney. Considering 1988 was only the bicentenary of Australia, the rate of growth of this island continent has been quite staggering. From a small handful of early settlers, has grown a population of 3.5 million in Sydney alone. Within that 3.5 million, Italian, Chinese, Jewish and Greek communities all co-exist with native Australians. Where once the simplest of houses stood, there now rise office blocks and apartments, standing tall against the backdrop of a seemingly permanent blue sky. Spanning the harbour, the massive Harbour Bridge – which carries thousands of people each day – overlooks Bennelong Point, site of the spectacular Opera House. This is Sydney in 1991, where just twenty minutes from the town centre you can relax on the beach, surf on the waves and soak up the sun, before returning to the excitement of one of today's most dynamic holiday spots in the world.

Due partly to Australia's recently celebrated birthday, and partly to decreasing flight prices, Sydney is now one of the most popular long-haul holiday destinations, especially for those wanting to combine a visit to the Antipodes with a tour of the Far East. The city is so well equipped for foreign visitors that trying to see everything in what is often a short space of time can be very difficult, if not frustrating. For this reason it is advisable to have a good idea of what you want to do, where you want to go and in which hotel you should stay, before you travel.

Sightseeing around Sydney is simple: taxis are good, if you want someone else to do the work for you, (although the chances of hailing one on the street are often pretty slim); buses run between the central business district and suburban areas, and the red Sydney Explorer bus takes you around twenty of the city's top attractions. Sydney's subway system (electric trains) will drop you off as near to your destination as possible, or if you prefer something slightly more alternative and energetic, why not hire a bicycle for the day? Ferries are the best way to see the harbour at a leisurely pace: sightseers and shoppers alike make good use of the many regular services available. The Sydney Harbour Explorer cruise enables you to step off and rejoin at different points along the way. As well as seeing the Opera House and Pier One – an old shipping terminal redeveloped as an entertainment area, with a market, shops and restaurants – you are given a chance to see The Rocks. This is the area where the first settlers landed, which, from having been a city slum, is now one of the most interesting and attractive areas to visit. Wine bars, trendy boutiques and 'Australiana' shops are just a few of the businesses now flourishing here.

Many of Sydney's points of interest can be reached on foot. While the city's public transport system is more than adequate, walking is probably the most effective way of really getting to know Sydney, and understanding what Australian city life is all about. The Botanic Gardens, Domain Park and the Art Gallery and Museum are all within easy reach of the city centre, as are a host of other galleries and gardens, all filled with features of historical and cultural interest. For a spectacular view of the city, you can ride the elevator up 1,000 feet to the observation deck and revolving restaurants at the top of Sydney Tower. You'll certainly be able to see where you are, as long as you've a head for heights. Or if you prefer sights of a different kind, head for Kings Cross, the 'Soho' of Sydney, where there's always plenty going on.

If you want to leave the city centre behind for a while, Sydney's suburbs offer the perfect diversion for an afternoon's entertainment. In Paddington, Victorian terraced houses complete with ornate wrought-iron balconies make you feel as if you've never left home. Galleries and restaurants vie with pubs and curio shops for your attention. If you're interested in period architecture, then Elizabeth Bay House and Vaucluse House will keep you occupied – both have been lovingly restored to recreate the atmosphere and elegance of days gone by. Or if you just want to relax and enjoy the luxury of being on holiday, grab a towel and head for the beach. It doesn't matter what season it is, there's always a barbie going on somewhere. Beaches are often busy though, as the temperature remains mild throughout the year, without extremes. In high summer – from December to February – the average temperature is around 25°C; in the depths of winter – June to August – it's nearer 16°C.

Since the weather is unlikely to be a determining factor in the time of year you choose to visit Sydney, it's probably worthwhile considering a couple of dates when there's even more going on than usual. January sees the Festival of Sydney, bringing a month of cultural activities, pageants and parades to the city, although do be warned that obtaining tickets at this time of year (especially for anything at the Opera House) will be almost impossible, unless you've booked well in advance. It's best to join a tour which includes tickets, unless you're lucky enough to know someone who can buy tickets locally. The Royal Easter Show – March to April – is Sydney's biggest event, with a ten-day agriculture and horticulture fair, exhibitions, animals and entertainment. If you're a sailing fan, then 26 December is the start of the Sydney to Hobart yacht race, followed on New Year's Day by something completely different, a Highland Gathering. On with the kilt and out with the caber as Oz goes Scottish for a day of games and pipes at Wentworth Park. Finally, Chinese New Year – January to February – is almost as spectacular here as it is in Hong Kong itself. Lion dances abound as the streets of Chinatown surge to the sound of the beating drum.

Sydney is the type of place that you'll want to keep going back to until you've seen and done it all. It's a beautiful city which makes the most of its fabulous bay and waterways. It's also alive twenty-four hours a day, every day of the year, so don't be disappointed if you feel you only scratch the surface of Australian life. Even if you're only there for a couple of days as a stopover point in a wider-reaching itinerary, they will be an exciting and exhilarating forty-eight hours, which will leave you wanting more. At whatever time of year you go, and for however long you stay, you'll certainly feel it's been time well spent.

Accommodation: The choice of accommodation is extremely wide, with first-class prices ranging from roughly A$75–115 for single rooms, A$170–270 for doubles, A$45 for comfortable motels and apartments (twin-sharing is cheaper), and budget-style (although not as plush) upwards of A$20. Of the first-class hotels, three of the most noteworthy are the Regent, Inter-Continental and Hilton. All have central locations, and all have features distinct to them alone. Opened in 1985, the Inter-Continental is probably Sydney's most atmospheric and elegant hotel, although Kables Restaurant at the Regent, or the Marble Bar and San Francisco Grill at the Hilton, merit equal praise and attention. The self-catering Park Apartments and Sheraton Wentworth Hotel both offer more than adequate facilities at slightly lower prices, while Plainsman Motor Inn, Breakers Motel (Bondi Beach) and Manhattan Hotel provide comfortable accommodation at extremely reasonable prices.

How To Get There: Tour operators who specialise in Australia are Australian Pacific Tours, Bales Tours, Cox & Kings, Kuoni, Silk Cut, Speedbird and Thomas Cook (see Appendix II).

The main airlines serving Sydney are British Airways, Cathay Pacific, Qantas and Singapore Airlines.

Further information about Australia can be obtained from the Australian Tourist Commission (see Appendix I).

Vancouver

Of the three main centres in Canada, Vancouver stands apart from Toronto and Montreal in its spectacular setting, and for its sheer entertainment value. British Columbia is one of the most beautiful areas in the world; towering Rocky Mountains, virgin forests and vast expanses of semi-arid sagebrush land cover the 950,000 square miles which make up this province.

In Vancouver, the spirit and beauty of British Columbia come together. Parks and rivers complement buildings and bridges, completing the picture of a city set between Burrard Inlet and the snow-capped coastal mountains of the Rockies. Vancouver enjoys the type of cosmopolitan atmosphere that can be attributed to only the most varied of populations. Chinatown alone is one of the largest Asian quarters in North America, and large German and Ukrainian communities are also scattered throughout the city. It's difficult to believe that in little over a hundred years, Vancouver has grown from a tiny coastal trading community of scarcely 100 households, to a dynamic, international gateway of almost 1.3 million people. Development has not spoilt the city, but rather enhanced it, even to the extent that Gastown, site of Vancouver's first permanent settlement, has now been restored to its original Victorian charm, complete with gaslit, cobblestoned streets.

Testimony to the city's appeal has been chronicled through the years. In 1792 Captain George Vancouver said 'To describe the beauty of this region will on some occasion be a very grateful task to the pen'. Over 100 years later George Bernard Shaw reiterated such sentiment in saying '. . . We shall certainly come to Canada . . . and Vancouver is the pick of Canada'. Another century has passed, and these words still ring true today.

Vancouver International Airport is situated eleven miles southwest of the city on Sea Island, in the area known as Richmond. Buses run frequently into town, and taxis are also available: alternatively, car hire facilities can be found at the airport. Since Vancouver is a relatively easy city in which to drive, hiring a car can be a good idea. This is especially true if you want to roam further than the city boundaries, to explore the Pacific coastline yourself, although coach excursions are always on offer. Getting around town is quick and convenient. The automated Light Rapid Transit underground/overground rail network reaches virtually every part of the city, and extensive bus and taxi services are also available. Visitors should note that bus fares are set at a flat rate, and taxi fares can be extremely expensive over long distances. Vancouver streets are easy to follow, so walking is usually an attractive option. A sea-bus runs between the Harbour and North Vancouver, and a skytrain between the harbour and New Westminster.

Vancouver boasts the largest city park in North America, and any visitor to the city could easily spend a day here. Only ten minutes from downtown Vancouver, Stanley Park is a massive 1,000 acres, filled with woodlands, trails, gardens, picnic sites, seashore and playing fields. Special attractions within the park include miniature train rides, a zoo and children's pet zoo, Vancouver Aquarium and snack bars. Other parks include Queens Park, with a colourful setting of 10,000 plants, the traditional Japanese Garden at Nitobe Memorial Gardens, jungle beasts at Vancouver Game Farm and Fantasy Garden World, whose famed Dutch castle is always popular. One of the best ways to describe Vancouver would in fact be as a city of parks, but since there are so many (115 to be precise), to detail them all would hardly do each justice. These are just a few, so you should look into what the others have to offer and see what suits you best.

If you want to combine museums and parks, the best place to go is Vanier Park. Besides the beautiful parkland itself, visitors can enjoy the display of north-west coastal Indian culture – from the Stone Age to totemic art – at the Centennial Museum, and the stars, light and sound show at the Planetarium next door. Also at Vanier is the Maritime Museum, where you can see the historic schooner St Roch, the first ship to navigate the north-west passage in both directions, and to circumnavigate the continent. For more Indian culture, the Museum of Anthropology at the University of British Columbia contains one of the world's greatest collections of north-west coast Indian arts, including replicas of Haida longhouses. Also at the university is the Fine Arts Gallery which features both modern and traditional art forms. Back in downtown Vancouver the Buschlen Mowatt Gallery – the city's foremost gallery – houses international and contemporary Canadian art, including works by Hockney, Picasso and Frankenthaler.

With so much to occupy you in Vancouver, you might find

yourself with little time left for shopping. However, there are one or two areas which no self-respecting tourist should miss. Gastown is a must if you want to sample the spirit of early early Vancouver, not to mention the shops and boutiques selling everything from leatherwork to antiques. Cafés, restaurants and pubs are always alive, and on Saturdays and Sundays there is an antique market and a flea market. Along at the West end there is Robsonstrasse which, with its international restaurants, boutiques, speciality shops and hotels, is something of a shopper's paradise. The street was originally called Robson Street, but the name was changed in the 1950s when thousands of German immigrants arrived. In the city's east-central area, Chinatown is full of attractions: food markets, restaurants and curiosity shops are all overflowing with wonderful oriental imports.

Vancouver is a popular holiday spot in its own right, although it is also an excellent base for visiting the attractions close by. Granville Island, with its famous public market, is only a short boat trip away, while a fifteen-minute ride from downtown Vancouver brings you to Grouse Mountain, one of Canada's most popular ski areas in the winter. Day-long cruises on board the *Queen of the North* take you through the Inside Passage and some of the world's most beautiful scenery, and of course there's always the Rockies. If you intend to visit the Rockies, the most popular route is via Calgary. Visitors should try to be there for the Calgary Exhibition and Stampede in early July, when everything you ever wanted to be true about the Wild West actually comes to life! July and the summer months can also be a good time to visit Vancouver, although temperatures do get quite hot. Spring tends to be fairly pleasant – warm with cool nights, autumn is a bit colder, and winter brings heavy snowfall. The city's attractions are enjoyable at whatever time though, and visitors are guaranteed an exciting holiday.

Accommodation: Vancouver hotels are very varied and there is always somewhere to suit your taste and budget. In the top price range (C$200–300 for a double room), three of the best are the Mandarin Oriental, Four Seasons Hotel and Pan Pacific Hotel. All three have central locations and excellent facilities. Sport lovers should take note of the extensive range of facilities at the Mandarin, including a health club, squash and racquetball courts, a billiard room and a sauna. Slightly cheaper (C$100–200 for a double room) are Nelson Place Hotel, Bosman's Motor

Hotel, Kingston Hotel and Austin Motor Hotel. Nelson Place is convenient for theatres, while Austin Motor is close to Stanley Park, BC Stadium (home to American football's BC Lions and soccer's Vancouver Whitecaps) and beaches. In the economy range (up to C$100), visitors have a large choice of hotels and guest houses. A few of the best are the YM/YWCA, Woodbine Hotel and Hazelwood Hotel. All are comfortable and clean with good facilities.

How To Get There: At least thirty-eight tour operators organise tours to Canada, of which twenty-seven arrange city stays. Among the best are Bales Tours, Canada Air Holidays, Silk Cut, Speedbird, Thomas Cook, Twickers World and Unijet (see Appendix II).

Main airlines to Vancouver are Air Canada, British Airways, Canadian Airlines International and Wardair.

Further information can be obtained from Tourism British Columbia (see Appendix I).

Classic Grand Tours

What exactly is a Classic Grand Tour, and what is it that transforms an ordinary holiday tour into one which can be called 'classic'? These are questions that have been given serious consideration in compiling this section, which have demanded some sort of adopted criteria by which the chosen holidays have been judged.

Two of the main factors relevant in deciding which countries or regions should (or shouldn't) be, included, are the comfort of the holiday, and whether it represents good value for money, not only in itself but also in the context of the travel market in general. The places chosen have, over the years, either earned a reputation as traditional holiday spots, or have almost become revered because they are areas of outstanding natural beauty. Indeed, in many instances, they are a combination of both. With their towering mountains and turbulent rivers, the Canadian Rockies, for example, will never cease to impress visitors. Or the Aeolian Islands, an area virtually untouched by tourism, and which offers visitors peace and tranquility in its secluded bays and beaches.

A strong sense of historical relevance is another feature common to many of these classic holidays. Certain themes are given particular emphasis if the area in question is renowned for specific historical and cultural elements. For instance, a trip to the US's Deep South would hardly be complete without a tour of its many points of musical interest. And if you're visiting Tuscany, then the magnificent cultural heritage so special to towns such as Florence and Siena will probably take up much of your time. What makes these trips outstanding though, is the style in which it is possible to experience them. Comfort and quality are the main hallmarks of a classic tour, and as such, any traveller can be assured of more than just an 'average' holiday.

It has been suggested that these are the type of tours that 'you would like to send your mother on'! While, in all probability, everybody's mother *would* enjoy these holidays, their appeal is much wider. There are few of us who would pass up the chance of spending a week in the châteaux of the Loire, and few who would turn down the superb cuisine and elegance of Britain's country house hotels. These are just some of the holidays with lasting appeal which have been deemed worthy of the name 'classic'.

The Canadian Rockies

Towering mountains, tree-covered hills, rivers and waterfalls: these are some of the natural wonders which hold tourists in awe worldwide. Who could fail to be impressed by Austria's dense, green hills, or northern Scotland's turbulent rivers? How many people would pass up the chance to witness the breathtaking beauty of snow-capped Kilimanjaro? Yet in Canada, all these sights, and more, are found together; and the wonderful thing is that you need not travel all over the country to see them. With their National Parks, grizzly bears, forests and lakes, the Canadian Rockies in western Canada are one of the most incredible areas of outstanding natural beauty in the world. Spread between British Columbia and Alberta, they offer visitors to Canada the prospect of a holiday packed with beauty, wilderness and excitement, combined with such a diversity of sights and scenes that you might be crossing between countries rather than provinces.

Situated on the west coast of British Columbia, Vancouver makes a good starting point for a tour of the Rockies and surrounding area (see Cities section). Known as the 'Gateway to the Pacific', the city is a multi-ethnic, multi-cultured haven of shops, parks, museums and galleries, offering more than enough attractions to fill your time. From Vancouver, the choice is yours as to where to go next.

One idea is to head eastwards towards Banff, stopping off along the way. It won't be long before you realise that you really are in 'the Land of National Parks', since these are dotted all over the country. Mount Revelstoke makes a good stopover point, offering plenty of outdoor pursuits, as well as some glorious scenery. Meadows of wildflowers border 1,000-year-old cedars and quiet lakes, while all around, the Rockies stand tall against the sky. An alternative stopover is Glacier National Park; the park's name sums up its scenery, created over the years by long winters, heavy snowfalls and thundering avalanches. Ice-covered peaks, sheer mountain walls and narrow, spruce-covered valleys are thrown together in a splendid panorama. Don't forget your camera!

Arriving in Banff you are just into Alberta, and at the heart of the Rockies. Settlement of this area goes back almost 11,000 years, although its National Park wasn't created until 1885, following the discovery of hot springs at the foot of Sulphur Mountain. Some 1,300 km of trails criss-cross their way around the park, and activities such as mountain-climbing, ski-touring, cross-country skiing, horse-riding, fishing and boating are all on offer. If you prefer something slightly less energetic, why not visit Bankhead, an old mining town, where displays and talks bring this ghost-town to life? Banff itself offers entertainment, with a range of shops, accommodation and restaurants. If you're there in the summer, you'll also be able to enjoy the Summer Arts Festival which is giving the town increasing recognition as an important cultural centre.

Heading northwards from Banff you come to Jasper National Park. From here you can cut across towards the west coast, passing Mount Robson – the highest peak in the Canadian Rockies – to Prince George. This town, a major logging centre, is situated at the tip of British Columbia's 'Caribou Region', and from here you have easy access to the Yellowhead Highway, which takes you westward via Vanderhoof and Smithers to Prince Rupert, on the west coast. The journey between Prince George and Smithers shows some of Canada's most barren and rugged terrain, while the final leg to Prince Rupert takes you through the beautiful Skeena River Valley. Look out for Ksan, an authentically reconstructed Gitksan Indian village where you can learn about the heritage of the northwest coast Indians and watch the Inuit craftsmen at work.

If you want to make this a round trip, the next stage is to return to Vancouver. Head directly south down the roads and you'll eventually get there, or alternatively, you could sail down the coast. Follow the famous 'Inside Passage' and, after a full day watching the magnificent British Columbian coastline, you'll reach Vancouver Island. This island is home to Victoria, British Columbia's capital, and its renowned Butchart Gardens. Here you will also find the Pacific Rim National Park, so called because of its miles of beach along the west coast. If you're there in summer you might catch sight of sea-lions, or even a grey whale feeding off the shoreline.

These are just a small handful of the highlights in and around the Canadian Rockies. If you'd prefer to see more of Canada's towns, two of the best ones to visit are Calgary and Kamloops. Calgary is situated to the south-west of Banff, so can easily be combined if you're visiting the National Park. Try to make it there in the first half of July for its famous Stampede, the world's largest rodeo, when bareback riding, bull riding, steer wrestling and chuckwagon racing are just a few of the Wild West attractions put on for your entertainment. Further to the west, and not too far from Vancouver, lies Kamloops. The town is surrounded by rugged cattle ranching country, and is certainly worth stopping off at, even if you don't stay there.

How to get there: Independent travel in Canada can be extremely rewarding. However, due to the immense variety and choice of places and sights, it can also be somewhat bewildering. Visiting the country with an organised tour is often the best idea, especially given the extremely wide range of holidays now available, particularly around the Rockies. Many companies deal with western Canada, for example Canada Air Holidays and Speedbird, who offer a range of tours within this area, but some of the most thorough coverage is given by Thomas Cook. Their numerous tours include more traditional journeys such as 'From the Rockies to the Pacific', the 'Trans-Canadian Railway', and the 'Canadian Pioneer', which covers British Columbia and Alberta, but also take you to Montreal, Toronto and Ottawa. Coeur D'Alene and a journey through the two-million-acre Lola National Forest are included in 'The Western Wilderness' tour, which reaches further north, to Edmonton, than many other trips. 'Canadian Rockies and the Cariboos' finds you exploring a selection of places further inland than you might otherwise reach, with the added bonus of three days spent touring the area by helicopter. On all of these holidays you are accompanied by an official guide, and service tends to be of a more personalised nature. Prices range from £1,300–£1,500, for ten to seventeen days, which includes return flights from this country.

Further information can be obtained from Thomas Cook (see Appendix II). Information about Canada in general is available from the Canadian Tourist Board (see Appendix I).

New England in the Fall

Autumn is not a time of year often associated with taking a holiday, since in many parts of the world it is that halfway point between the end of one tourist season and the beginning of the next. Summer is over and the ski-slope snows of winter are, as yet, flakes on the horizon. But in New England – the US's most British corner – autumn (or fall, as it's otherwise known) brings a vivid natural beauty, the like of which is difficult to find anywhere else in the world. If you're interested in visiting New England, then autumn is *the* time of year to be there, when the forests of the Adirondacks in Vermont and New Hampshire set the countryside ablaze in a mass of crimson, copper and gold, and the coming gloom of winter is easily forgotten.

For any tour of New England the most obvious starting point is New York, although some may prefer to begin further south in Washington. Despite the many attractions that New York offers, it might be included on your itinerary almost incidentally, simply because it is a convenient starting point rather than a central concern on your overall tour. Nevertheless, few visitors would pass up the chance of exploring at least some of this city before heading north into the heart of New England. Time will probably not be on your side in New York, so the best idea is to try and be selective about what you want to see, and where you want to go. From New York you could either head straight north, remaining inland, or alternatively, follow the coastline up towards Boston. Mystic Seaport might be your first stop on the coast, where tall ships, historic houses, and sea shanties are all to be enjoyed. The folk museum chronicles former whaling days and gives visitors a glimpse of the type of nautical history that has contributed so much to this part of the US. Newport, with its harbour, shops and boutiques lies slightly further north, and here you can take a trip to Hammersmith Farm, where Jacqueline Kennedy Onassis spent her childhood. Heading north, you'll pass along 10 Mile Drive, where you can see exclusive high society homes. Another place of interest before Boston is Plymouth, America's hometown, where the Pilgrims first stepped ashore in 1620. *Mayflower II* is here, as well as Plymouth Plantation, an open-air museum depicting the lives of the seventeenth-century pilgrims.

Boston, New England's capital, is clustered around its harbour, and stands as one of the US's most historically significant cities. In the eighteenth century, inhabitants of this area fought against British rule to gain their independence, and today the city is full of restored features from the days of colonialism and revolution. Built on a small peninsula, Boston is a particularly attractive city, and an easy touring place for visitors; simple to explore by foot, rather than relying on public transport. The Freedom

170 Classic Grand Tours

Trail is one of the best walks through the city, marked by a red line on the pavement along a one-and-a-half-mile route. For what is a relatively small American city, Boston is packed with enough features of interest to keep any visitor occupied. If you're not pushed for time, then Greater Boston – covering 1,050 square miles – is also filled with an abundance of attractions!

North of Boston lies the Maine Coast and York Harbour, as well as the US's oldest fishing port, Gloucester, and the distinctly named Kennebunkport. Heading inland from here you travel through the wooded Maine countryside – spectacular in the fall – to North Conway. This mountain area has some magnificent scenery, which can be seen to full advantage from points such as Franconia Notch and the Old Man of the Mountain rock-sculpture, slightly to the east. If you take the new scenic route, the Kancamagus Trail, through the White Mountains of New Hampshire, you'll reach Stow, 'Ski Capital of the East'. Lake Placid and Lake Champlain are both near here, giving access to the Cascade Lakes region and the heart of the Adirondack Mountains. The changing colours of the deciduous forests which cover this area are quite stunning, and certainly show New England at its best.

Other places of interest include picture-book towns such as Camden, north of Gloucester, and Acadia National Park. Mount Washington, New England's highest peak, is situated in the northern region of the White Mountains, not too far away from Quechee Gorge, Vermont's 'Little Grand Canyon'. Farm villages, cheese factories, cider mills and maple-sugar plants can all be found just to the north of Stowe, while witch country can be seen in real life in the coastal town of Salem, between Gloucester and Boston.

New England offers visitors many more sights and attractions than the few highlights mentioned here. It's one of the US's most scenic and beautiful areas, filled with a diverse and fascinating mixture of old and new. Nowhere in the US will you find a people more proud of their heritage, and this is reflected in the care taken to preserve traditions, customs and buildings which have survived during the past two centuries. This is where America was born, and this is where you'll find the roots out of which a massive continent has grown.

How To Get There: Of the various companies running tours to New England, some of the most comprehensive coverage is offered by Thomas Cook. As well as their Autumn and Grand Autumn Tours, they also offer 'Summer in New England' and 'New England to the Great Lakes' trips. Prices start at roughly £1,200 for twelve days, all-inclusive except for meals – check when booking.

If you don't mind driving yourself, Poundstretcher offer a 'Complete New England tour' as part of their pre-planned fly-drive programme. Prices start at roughly £1,000 for a two-week package, and this includes return flights, a hire-car for two weeks, and accommodation (see Appendix II).

Further details can be obtained from Thomas Cook (see Appendix II) or alternatively, contact the United States Travel Information Centre (see Appendix I).

Art Towns of Tuscany

Florence, Pisa, Siena, and Grosseto: the country is Italy, the region, Tuscany. Dante, Benvenuto Cellini, Botticelli, Leonardo da Vinci, Michelangelo and Raphael: just a few of the names associated with this fabulously rich area. Rich in art, literature and music; stunningly beautiful landscapes and architectural splendours. Tuscany's history dates back to 351 BC, when Etruria, the land of the Etruscans and an area embracing modern Tuscany, was annexed by Rome. Later, in AD 774 the region became a frontier district of Charlemagne's empire, ruled by the counts of Lucca. Such a varied history presents today's visitor to Tuscany with a problem. Where do you start? The wealth of culture is so immense that to cover it all would take years. The answer is to be selective in what you see and do, and if you're left wanting more (as you inevitably will be), return when you can, and as often as possible. You'll never need to repeat yourself, and there will always be something new to experience.

It could be argued that every town, city, village or hamlet in Tuscany is an 'art town'. Wherever you go you'll come across works of art and architecture that, through the years, have become part of one of the largest cultural legacies in the world. The leaning tower in Pisa; Michelangelo's David at the Accademia in Florence; Franciscan and Dominican churches in Siena, the Roman amphitheatre at Fiesole – the list is endless. There are numerous theme packages to Tuscany, all of which attempt to cover as much as possible in the time available. One of the best of these is organised by Prospect Music and Art. Prospect's coverage of Tuscany is fairly comprehensive, with a range of tours covering most of the region. On all tours, guests are accompanied by one of the company's experienced tour leaders – art historians and archaeologists – whose contribution is usually invaluable. As well as its emphasis on art and music, Prospect provides a personal flavour, with tour groups seldom exceeding twenty people.

Florence is featured as a single destination holiday, with eight days dedicated to the treasures of this beautiful city. The departure point is Heathrow, and arrival in Pisa is followed by rail transfer to Florence. Tours are organised every day, but three afternoons are left free for you to follow your own pursuits. Highlights of this holiday are numerous, such as a morning in the Uffizi, one of, if not *the* world's greatest art gallery; a visit to Michelangelo's Medici mausoleum and Laurentian library; a tour of the Bargello, Italy's most important museum of Renaissance sculpture; and a morning spent at Palazzo Vecchio, the seat of Florentine government for seven hundred years. In addition, there's also an excursion to Siena, home of Duccio, the Lorenzetti brothers and Simone Martini. The trip as a whole can be summed up as 'From Renaissance to Baroque'. Your accommodation consists of a four-star hotel in the very heart of Renaissance Florence. Restoration of Hotel Brunelleschi has provided guests with every modern comfort, while retaining all the architectural characteristics of the Renaissance period.

Prospect Music and Art also offers Siena as a single destination holiday, in which you can enjoy six days exploring this medieval town and the surrounding Tuscan hills. Accommodation is provided at the Hotel Garden, which offers superb views of the town and surrounding countryside. Visits are arranged to Siena cathedral (building work began in 1150 but didn't finish until two centuries later); the Pinacoteca, which houses a magnificent collection of Sienese paintings from the twelfth to seventeenth centuries, and Palazzo Pubblico, symbol of Sienese prominence in the Middle Ages. One of the delights of this trip is that, even though only six days long, there is still time for four excursions, as well as two free afternoons. Monteriggioni, a typical Tuscan walled hill-town, fills one afternoon, and tours are also organised to San Gimignano, Pienza, and Montalcino. On your final day, time is also spent in Volterra, before continuing to Pisa and the return flight to London. Prospect's efficiency in planning

Art Towns of Tuscany

your days strikes an extremely good balance between organised tours and free time. The risk of suffering from the clichéd, but true, architectural and cultural indigestion, is consequently minimised.

If you prefer a wider-ranging itinerary and want to travel a bit further, the 'Romanesque to Renaissance' tour will provide you with exactly that. This tour takes in the best of Tuscany, concentrating on the area to the west and south of Florence. Four nights are spent in Lucca and three in Siena, at the Hotel Celide and Hotel Garden respectively. Tours and excursions are intermingled with free afternoons and rail trips, covering a total of nine different towns. From Lucca, trips are made to Pisa, Pistoia, San Gimignano, and Monteriggioni, and from Siena you visit Pienza, Prato and San Pietro. The range of artistic works seen over the eight days is impressive, too comprehensive to be detailed here. Highlights come in the form of an afternoon at the cathedral and other splendid buildings on the 'Campo dei Miracoli' in Pisa; the silver altar and a della Robbia frieze in Pistoia; frescoes by the 'trecento' Sienese masters Ghirlandaio and Benozzo Gozzoli, and the National Gallery in Siena. And of course the towns provide an attraction in themselves, each with its own distinct charm and grace. Pienza especially is worth the visit; it is a masterpiece of Renaissance town planning.

These are just three of the tours to Italy by Prospect, although they are the three main ones which deal with Tuscany. If you want to explore Italy further there are other tours which, between them, cover virtually the whole of the country. Prices for the Tuscany tours range from £600–760 per person, depending on your choice of holiday and the time of year at which you travel. Prospective travellers should note that tours are only run on certain dates, so it's best to check what's available, and when. The price covers virtually everything that you might need, including return flights and accommodation, as well as details such as taxes, visa fees, and entrance to galleries and museums. Breakfast is included, and other meals where indicated. During the tour, your guide will also give an illustrated lecture, usually with slides. If you are contemplating a trip with Prospect, you should also consider their 'Study Days', run in London on certain Saturdays, which cover a variety of topics in relation to their holidays.

Independent travel to Tuscany is an equally feasible option, although it requires considerably more pre-organisation on the part of the traveller. If you do want to travel independently, one of the best companies to contact is Abercrombie and Kent, who are well acquainted with Tuscany and will be able to help you decide on itineraries and hotels. Alternatively, comprehensive package deals are available from Serenissima Travel Ltd, and Fine Art Courses Ltd. The latter offer excellent deals as part of their Italian Palaces and Gardens brochure.

Further details about Prospect's tours are available from Prospect Music and Art Ltd (see Appendix II for details).

The Deep South: USA

Pageants and parades, colourful floats, big bass drums and jazz, where every day is Mardi Gras: America's Deep South is a land of music, and the heart of the US's musical heritage. Satchmo's New Orleans, Country and Western in Nashville, and Rock'n' Roll in Memphis, home of Elvis Presley and his legendary Graceland. But music is not the only history that has been made here. The American Civil War has also left its mark on the South, and features such as preserved plantation homes provide interesting sightseeing. This area is not without beautiful scenery either; the Blue Ridge and Smoky Mountains, and the golden beaches of Virginia and the Carolinas are worth seeing. This is the South as it has always been imagined, and visitors today won't be disappointed.

Considering the southern states are so (relatively) close to the tourist areas of Florida, they receive comparatively little attention from British holiday-makers. This is a shame, as they have much to offer visitors, be they interested in music or not. New Orleans – down Louisiana way – is one of the best-known towns of the South, and a place where anybody on any budget can have a great time. Known to generations as 'Crescent City', and more recently as the 'Big Easy', New Orleans is an amazing mixture of cultures from all over the world, influenced predominantly by its Gallic-Hispanic and Caribbean heritage. In the 250 or so years since the town was founded, it has become famous for, amongst other things, Mardi Gras celebrations and cuisine, and its Vieux Carré (French Quarter). The latter is one of *the* places to visit in New Orleans, comparable to New York's Greenwich Village and Soho, or the old Latin Quarter and Montmartre in Paris. Although the alleys and side-streets are somewhat grubby, you can't help feeling that a cleaner image would detract from the area's appeal. Nightlife in the French Quarter centres around Bourbon Street, and is certainly worth experiencing.

The Deep South: USA 175

New Orleans is a city packed with features of interest. If you can make it there for Mardi Gras – Shrove Tuesday, forty days before Easter – all the better. Parades usually begin about two weeks in advance, or on Shrove Tuesday itself. The Jazz and Heritage Festival is held in the last week in April and the first week in May, and is world-famous for Louisiana food and music: jazz, folk, gospel and popular. In late June and July there are two relatively new festivals: la Fête and the New Orleans Food Festival. La Fête offers special events in the French market, a fireworks display on the river on 4 July, and festivities on Bastille Day, 14 July, while if you're at the Food Festival you can sample excellent Louisiana food, prepared by the best Creole and Cajun chefs.

From New Orleans, you have a wide choice of places to visit. You could head eastwards, along the Gulf of Mexico towards Pensacola (if so, try and stop off at Biloxi, a typical Southern town in a picture-book setting), or there's always Houston or Dallas to the west. A popular alternative is to head north, to Memphis and Nashville. Memphis has long been known as home to the 'Blues', and as such, offers visitors an impressive range of 'Blues Clubs' for evening entertainment. Tupelo, Elvis Presley's birthplace, is not far away, and Kentucky Lake – well known for its wildlife – is also close by. A bit further up the road and you find Mammoth Cave National Park. Here you can see an amazing cave system, the largest in the world, created by an underground river running through limestone rock.

Nashville is the home of many of America's Country and Western stars, as well as the Grand Ole Opry, the famous showcase of 'classic' country music performed in the Grand Ole Opry House. The capital of Tennessee, Nashville is rated among the top ten holiday spots in the US. The town's history stretches back to 1779, when Colonel James Robertson led a small band of North Carolinians across the Cumberland River to found Fort Nashborough at Cedar Bluffs, on Christmas Day. This name was changed to today's Nashville in 1784, and the town was chosen as the state capital in 1843. Today, you can see a replica of the fort on the waterfront, just a few hundred yards from the original site.

Nashville's population now stands around the half-million mark, and the town's area has grown from its original one-acre site to over 500 square miles, encompassing all of Davidson County. Downtown Nashville has recently undergone a 'revitalising programme', and has become the main area for leisure-time activities, especially in the evening. Try and make it to Riverfront Park, an open-air music theatre, and also include historic Second Avenue on your tour if you can. The Avenue is situated in the Warehouse district, and has been renovated into smart shops, restaurants and offices. It's worth a trip for the district itself, which is filled with wonderful nineteenth-century Victorian buildings. Music Row is another place to get to. Here you'll find nearly every major record label (along 16th Avenue, South), as well as the Country Music Hall of Fame. Music Row is the headquarters of Nashville's music industry.

Chattanooga, also in Tennessee, is within easy touring distance from Nashville, and could be the next point on your itinerary. The town is known as the 'scenic centre of the South', and you'll soon understand why when you visit. Ruby Falls rates among the world's most spectacular underground scenes, while the gardens and rock formations on Lookout Mountain are really quite superb. If you're there on a clear day you should be able to see five states from the mountain. Here you can also see the site of the Civil War 'Battle above the Clouds', and of course there's always the famous Chattanooga Choo-Choo, now housed in the converted old station.

Another option from Nashville is to head eastwards towards Cherokee. On your way you can stop off at Great Smokey Mountain, the most visited of all America's National Parks, before continuing to Cherokee, where you can experience life in a forgotten era at Cherokee Indian Reservation. Alternatively, you might consider going further north from Nashville, towards Lexington. If you make a slight detour you can visit Dollywood, home of the Parton family, not far from Gatlinburg. There you'll find a theme park, and, not surprisingly, plenty of musical entertainment.

Lexington is actually across the border in Kentucky, where the style of music changes from Country to Bluegrass. White-fenced horse farms, just like the movies, are one of the main sights here, so to really feel the spirit of the state, why not spend some time at Kentucky Horse Park? Entertainment includes a hay-ride, the museum of the horse, and in the evening, good old hip-slapping fun at a square dance.

These are just a few suggestions for how you might spend your time in the Deep South. Other places you might visit are Montgomery, Atlanta, Natchez – where you'll find the US's longest national park – and Charleston (Charles II's town).

How To Get There: There is a range of companies who organize tours to this part of the US, all of whom give fairly comprehensive coverage. However, if music is what you are especially interested in, one of the best trips is run by Orientours, as part of their Classic Tours programme. Their 'Classic Tour of American Music' covers most of the places mentioned here, and they will also tailor a holiday for you, should you wish to travel independently. Prices for American Music range from roughly £950–1,050, including return flights from London. The tour is also accompanied by a guide.

Other companies who cover this area, although not with the specialist emphasis on music, are Thomas Cook and Speedbird. If you don't mind driving yourself, Poundstretcher also offer a good deal as part of their Pre-Planned Fly Drive brochure.

Further information is available from Orientours London Ltd (see Appendix II).

Further information about the US, and the Deep South in particular, can be obtained from the United States Travel Information Centre (see Appendix I). Alternatively, you could contact Travel South USA, an organisation which deals specifically with the Southern States. (See Appendix II).

British Country House Hotels

From the Scottish Highlands to the south coast, scattered across the countryside and hidden away in quiet corners, are a selection of country homes and manor houses, which open their doors to the public and invite you to indulge in an *Upstairs Downstairs* existence, with the emphasis on enjoying the luxuries of 'Upstairs' living. Britain has always been proud of its heritage, and after a visit to one of its country house hotels, you'll understand why. In direct opposition to many of today's hotels, these establishments offer their guests only the genuine article; reproduction furniture and plastic imitations are simply not the done thing! These are the castles and great country seats that have turned to hotelling to keep alive financially. Most of these hotels stand in their own extensive and beautiful grounds, and are run by staff for whom nothing is too much trouble. Bedrooms are generally immaculate, antique-filled public rooms are majestically grand, and elegance is the order of the day. The incredible thing is that most of us are only half-an-hour's drive away from such an experience, but often don't realise it. Although the locations of the hotels mentioned here might not suit everyone, these are just a small selection of the very best of Britain's country house hotels.

The area around Fort William in the north of Scotland contains some of Britain's most dramatic scenery. What better way to visit it, or to start any tour of the country for that matter, than staying at a multi-award-winning hotel? The Airds Hotel lies roughly twenty-five miles from both Oban and Fort William, overlooking Loch Linnhe and the Morvern mountain range. The building dates back over 250 years, and is open from mid-March to mid-November. Fifteen bedrooms, all with private facilities, provide guests with comfortable, if not ostentatious, accommodation, as do the three large public rooms. If you're here in the summer you can spend many a pleasant evening in the attractive sun lounge, watching the glorious sunsets fade into darkness. From the dining room the view is equally stunning: a marvellous accompaniment to the traditional Scottish food for which Airds' restaurant is justifiably renowned. Prime cuts of local meat, salmon caught in the surrounding waters, and vegetables grown in the kitchen garden. The hotel's location is also a bonus, allowing guests easy access to a variety of historical attractions; Argyllshire, Glencoe, Castle Stalker and the Isle of Mull are all within reach.

Travel down from Fort William, past Perth and Gleneagles, and you come to Dunblane. This town lies about five miles from Stirling, with its famous castle, and seven miles from Bannockburn, where Robert the Bruce defeated Edward II in 1314, ridding Scotland of English rule. Cromlix House is situated just outside Dunblane in the grounds of a spectacular 5,000-acre estate. Fourteen bedrooms including eight suites, all complete with period-style furnishings, offer excellent accommodation in an atmosphere of real Victorian grace. Of the several public rooms, the library is especially charming, while the dining room offers superb views across the lawns and gardens – a perfect setting in which to enjoy the beautifully presented, first-class cuisine. Cromlix is open all year round, and is fully occupied for much of the time, so advance booking is essential. Tennis, riding, hill-walking, bird-watching, shooting (both clay and live game by prior arrangement) and fishing are all on offer. Within day-touring distance are attractions such as Loch Lomond, Blair Castle, and the cities of Edinburgh and Glasgow.

Continue south from Dunblane, across the border into England, to Yorkshire, home of the spectacular dales. Middlethorpe Hall, open all year round, is a late seventeenth-century manor house, overlooking York racecourse. It was rescued from complete dereliction in 1980 by Historic House Hotels, and has since been restored to its former opulence and luxury. Uniformed doormen greet you on your arrival, welcoming you to the twenty-six-acre estate which constitutes Middlethorpe. Inside, crystal chandeliers and oil portraits, more commonly associated with stately homes than hotels, make you feel as if you're staying somewhere really unique. In the evening, cocktails in the drawing room precede a standard of cuisine that is amongst the finest in northern England. Middlethorpe's thirty-one bedrooms are spread between the main house, adjacent eighteenth-century stable courtyard and beautifully restored Gardener's Cottage. Colour television, direct-dial telephones and private facilities are common to all rooms, complementing the outstanding furnishings. As if the house and gardens aren't enough to keep you occupied, attractions close by are also numerous. Castle Howard of *Brideshead Revisited* fame is not far away, and neither are Beningbrough Hall, a National Trust property, or Fountains Abbey, one of the most important medieval abbeys in Europe.

Warwickshire is one of England's most attractive counties, filled with old-world Cotswold villages – many complete with stocks on the village green – quaint houses, and narrow canals. Oxfordshire and Cambridgeshire are both nearby, providing even more of the same gentle countryside. Just outside Stratford-upon-Avon stands Ettington Park, a large mansion surrounded by forty acres of grand estate. Incredible as it may seem, Ettington is still in the same ownership as it was at the time of the Domesday Book. Although the present house doesn't date back that far – most of it is nineteenth-century – its Gothic-style architecture shows influences of earlier manors on this site.

Inside, original antiques, fine oil paintings, and intricately carved wooden fireplaces can be found throughout all the rooms. Nine suites are included among the forty-nine bedrooms, all of which have private facilities, colour television and telephone. Downstairs, the public lounge rivals any original Edwardian ballroom in both size and luxury, while the dining room's 1740 rococo ceiling reminds you of the type of craftsmanship sadly missing in many of today's interiors. Cuisine is first class, and the menu comprises one of the finest of any British country house hotel.

Outdoor activities are too numerous to list: suffice it to say that a wide range of sports, games and hobbies are available.

The superb leisure complex also offers a heated indoor swimming pool, sauna, whirlpool spa bath and solarium. Attractions close by include everything that Stratford has to offer: theatre, Shakespeare's birthplace, Anne Hathaway's cottage, Warwick and its castle, and the towns of Oxford and Banbury.

There are a number of country house hotels in the London area, but none so fine as Berkshire's Cliveden. Set in 375 acres of gardens and parkland, and dating originally to 1666, Cliveden is the only stately home in England which is now a hotel. It was built by the second Duke of Buckingham and has been home to (amongst others) George III's father, Frederick, Prince of Wales – from 1739 to 1751 – as well as the first Duke of Westminster. In 1906 it was received as a wedding present by Nancy Astor from her father-in-law. Regular guests at Cliveden have included Churchill, Kipling, Lawrence of Arabia and Bernard Shaw.

The immense range of antiques, tapestry wall-hangings and valuable paintings in the house is impressive. All of Cliveden's twenty-five bedrooms are enormous, and all have their own grand, private bathrooms. Public rooms are equally extensive, and include an excellent library, a marvellous Adam-style morning room (previously Nancy Astor's writing room) and the outstanding, small French dining room, complete with intricate gold leaf in the ceiling pattern. The main dining room, which offers a superb view towards the River Thames, serves classical cuisine with a strong British influence.

Leisure facilities are extensive at Cliveden, with squash, tennis and fishing included amongst the most popular pastimes. There is an outdoor heated swimming pool in the walled garden, and riding, boating and golf can all be arranged locally. Nearby attractions include Windsor Castle, Ascot, Newbury and Henley regatta. Cliveden is open throughout the year.

Such is the style and atmosphere of Britain's leading country house hotels. There are many others besides those mentioned here, all of which are deserving of attention. Prices for the above hotels, for dinner with wine, bed and breakfast for two, start at around £150, rising according to your choice of accommodation. Prospective visitors should consider the choice of seasonal breaks available, when reductions are often on offer.

Further information can be obtained from the hotels themselves (see Appendix III).

If you would like further information about country house hotels in general, one of the most comprehensive guides is *The*

Best of British Country House Hotels and Restaurants by Katie Wood, published by Fontana Paperbacks.

Italian Lakes

Mention Italy and most people think of the architectural wonders of places such as Florence and Rome, magnificent artwork in Siena, and the waterways of Venice. Such impressions are perfectly justified, but this is a country where natural beauty is often forgotten in the enthusiastic response to its huge legacy of man-made treasures. Northern Italy, while being home to much of the country's industry, also offers visitors a chance to enjoy the healthy air of the lower Alps and the Dolomites. And there is water too; just as much as you'll find in Venice, if not more, in the beautiful lakes which have an almost Mediterranean feel to them. Garda, Como, and Maggiore are the three main lakes, and all provide their own particular attractions in the towns and villages which skirt the edges. Visiting just one of these lakes reveals a rural side of Italy that many people only ever glimpse in their hurry to reach the well-known cities.

Lake Como is the smallest of the three lakes, and is situated south of the Swiss border, directly north of Milan. Surrounded by hills and mountains, the valley setting of Lake Como is quite spectacular. Bellagio, on the tip of the V-shaped Bellagio Peninsula, makes an ideal base for visitors, since from here the other lake-side towns are within easy reach, either by road or boat. In spite of its popularity, Bellagio has retained its character and charm, most obviously in its cobbled streets, winding alleys, squares and old churches. If you climb the hills behind the town, there are wonderful views towards the snow-capped Alps, as well as enough mountain trails to keep even the most energetic walker happy. Bellagio's town centre is a relatively quiet place since there is very little traffic, so exploring the streets and shops is a delightfully hassle-free experience.

The town of Como itself, an ancient silk-producing city on the southern tip of the lake, is full of typically beautiful Italian architecture. At Piazza del Duomo you can see the wonderful Pretorian Palace which dates from 1215, and nearby there's the Renaissance Gothic Duomo dating from 1396.

From Como you can take a water bus up the lake which stops at all the villages along the way. On the western shore of the lake you'll find the popular resorts of Cadenabbia and Tremezzo, and from both there are superb views across to the Bellagio Peninsula. Historic luxury villas and bright gardens are the main hallmarks of these towns. The most famous of these is Villa Carlotta, on the edge of Tremezzo. Here there is a fine collection of sculptures and paintings, as well as stunning gardens full of azaleas. Slightly north of Cadenabbia is the town of Menaggio, from where you can take a boat across to the east side of the lake and the villages of Varenna and Lecco.

Lake Maggiore, Italy's second largest lake, lies to the west of Lake Como and stretches right across the Swiss border into the Alps. Baveno and Stresa on the western side of the lake are the two most popular villages on Maggiore, although Pallanza also makes a good base. The Borromean Islands in the middle of the lake can be seen from all three towns, and from both Baveno and Stresa there are good views of Pallanza. Baveno is a fairly small town, but full of activity. Queen Victoria and Winston Churchill both spent holidays here, although the town has seen many changes since their day. Beside the parish church, you can almost feel the town's history seeping through the stonework of the centuries-old buildings. There are plenty of shops and bars in Baveno, as well as a weekly market to explore. If you're there in July or August you'll also be able to enjoy occasional open-air concerts.

Stresa is possibly the most lively resort on Maggiore's western shore. Its narrow streets are crowded with colourful craft shops and cafés full of local delights, and all surrounded by wonderful eighteenth-century architecture. Exotic shrubs and plants thrive in Stresa's mild climate and can be seen at their best in the gardens of Villa Pallavicino. Or alternatively you could visit Isola Madre, the largest of the Borromean Islands, which is almost entirely occupied by botanical gardens, complete with white peacocks, pheasant and wild parrots. If you enjoy combining horticulture with walking, the botanical gardens of Villa Taranto in Pallanza are said to have over 20,000 different species of plants and flowers, planted around 7 km of paths. From Stresa it's easy to reach Gignese for a game of golf, or there's always the hydrofoil up the lake to the Swiss resorts of Locarno and Ascona. Monte Mottarone is a short ride by cable car, from where there are superb views of Maggiore, mountains and the Lombardy Plain towards Milan. If you can make it to Stresa at the beginning of September, you'll be able to enjoy this town's International Music Festival.

Heading towards the east coast of Italy, and Venice, you'll reach Lake Garda, the largest of the Italian lakes. From Sirmione at the southern tip to Riva in the north, Lake Garda stretches roughly thirty miles, encompassing a diverse range of towns and scenery. Vineyards, and groves of orange, lemon and olive trees are predominant in the south, giving way to majestic fjord-like terrain as you head north in the direction of Austria. It is in fact the north that attracts most of Garda's visitors, to the main towns of Limone on the west coast, Riva on the northern tip, and Malcesine on the east. Limone takes its name from its historical lemon gardens, which flourish in the Mediterranean climate. The town is built into the cliffs, and has a maze of pedestrian-only streets to keep you occupied. Evening entertainment can be found down at the water's edge, where bars and cafés provide an enchanting way of spending the after-dark hours. A wide range of watersports is on offer at Limone, as well as walking, swimming and boat hire during the day.

Riva is possibly the most celebrated of all the Italian lake resorts, so it's not surprising to find ancient and historical buildings complemented by modern hotels. More shops and cafés can be found in Riva, concentrated mostly around the twelfth-century 'La Rocca' fortress and 'Apponale' clock tower. Traffic is banned from much of the centre, leaving it a relatively quiet place – apart from the people! The surrounding mountains contain some excellent walks, allowing you to experience thoroughly the beauty of the Trentino area. If you have time, try to make it to the stunning Varone Falls, although be prepared for cooler temperatures, regardless of how warm it is in Riva itself.

In Malcesine you can follow up Riva's fortress with a thirteenth-century castle, rising above the town on a sheer rock face. If heights are your forte, you'll certainly enjoy the cable-car ride up Monte Baldo, from where the views are quite spectacular. At the top the many varieties of wild flowers confirm this area's title as the 'Botanic Garden of Italy'. Back on the ground – or rather in the water – windsurfing, water-skiing and boating are all available. And of course, the lakeside cafés are there to serve as much tea and coffee as you wish.

These are the lakes most commonly frequented by visitors to the north of Italy, but they are not the only ones. Lake Orta and Lake Iseo are both as attractive as their larger counterparts. If you're looking for complete tranquillity, and peaceful, civilised isolation, then Pettenasco along the eastern shore of Lake Orta could be just the place. There is a good selection of hotels in all the resorts mentioned, able to accommodate anybody on virtually any budget, for however long or short a time as you wish. Even if you just fancy a short break, the lakes' accessible position in the north of Italy means that they can be reached in a relatively short travelling time, even if you're not flying. And of course, if you've got more time to play with, there are also the delights of Milan, Verona and Venice to be enjoyed, all of which are close enough to be reached fairly easily.

How To Get There: There are various companies offering trips to the Italian Lakes, either to one by itself, or to a combination of two. Intasun's Lakes and Mountains brochure covers all three lakes, with prices starting at around £300 per person for seven nights, including half-board and return flights. Similar offers are available from both Inghams and Crystal Holidays. Alternatively, Quo Vadis have an excellent deal in their Special Breaks brochure, for four nights in Stresa, on Lake Maggiore, in a first-class hotel. Prices start at around £300, although cheaper deals are available if you want to take advantage of their fly-drive programme. Further information is available from Quo Vadis (see Appendix II for tour operators).

See Appendix I to contact the Italian Tourist Office.

Châteaux of the Loire

The diversity of France's scenery and culture always impresses its visitors. From Paris in the north, right down to the glitz of the Riviera in the south, this is the land of cheese and wine picnics, high fashion and lazy summer days. Every year, thousands of visitors flock to Paris, yet surprisingly few take the time to explore in any depth one of the more rural areas of France, only a few hours away from the capital. Val de Loire – the Loire Valley – is France's pastoral haven, full of magnificent buildings, steeped in history, and more or less one continuous vineyard! There are many châteaux in the Loire Valley, and a large number have now opened their doors to the public as luxurious hotels. Even those which have managed to remain in private hands are also frequently open to the public. The best are situated between Angers and Blois – a distance of roughly eighty miles – so all you really have to decide is which is the one for you.

Akin to a holiday in one of Britain's country house hotels, time spent in a French château is time for spoiling yourself

Châteaux of the Loire

and indulging in the elegance of your surroundings. Travelling from Paris, one of the first château hotels you come across in the Loire Valley, is Château d'Esclimont. Built in 1548, this château is surrounded by magnificent park and woodland, not to mention the traditional moat, still protecting the building itself. The words of François de la Rochefoucault, 'C'est mon plaisir', can be seen inscribed in the stone over the entrance of the castle, and after just a single night spent here you will understand why that phrase still rings true today. Public rooms rival those of the most exclusive establishments in France, and the fifty-three bedrooms are fully equipped with everything you could wish for: all have private facilities, telephone, colour television and a minibar. (Not all the bedrooms are in the castle itself: some are in the three adjoining pavilions.) Apart from the acres of ground to explore, there is also a swimming pool and tennis court, both of which are invaluable for working off extra pounds, easily put on in one of the hotel's four restaurants. Château d'Esclimont is located at Saint Symphorien, not far from Château de Chambord, the hunting lodge of Francis I. Chambord, which is open for public viewing, is one of the most impressive châteaux in the whole of the valley.

Continue south and into the western part of the Loire, and you'll reach Chênehutte. Here, a former Benedictine priory has been converted into Hôtel le Prieure. Beautiful views over the Loire can be enjoyed from almost every one of the hotel's thirty-three bedrooms, all of which have private facilities and direct-dial telephones. In the restaurant, both à la carte and table d'hôte meals are available. For the more energetic there is a heated swimming pool and tennis court, but if you prefer something slightly more sedate you can always putt away the hours on the mini-golf course.

If you're interested in trying something a bit different from cosseted luxury, but wish to remain in traditional surroundings, head for Fontevraud-l'Abbaye, where you'll find Prieure Saint Lazare. The historical surroundings of the royal abbey of Fontevraud offer visitors peace and tranquility in what is best described as a monastic atmosphere. The abbey dates back to the eleventh century and is still complete with cloisters and gardens. There is a total of sixty-four rooms in this 'hotel', and while they are hardly opulent or luxurious, they have been modernised to a more-than-adequate standard of accommodation, all with private facilities and telephone. The old refectory of the abbey has been converted into the present dining room, where you can enjoy traditional French dishes.

From Fontevraud it is only a short distance to the town of Tours, a good place for a day's sightseeing. In the town's old quarter you can explore the churches and gardens, and there is also a former Bishop's Palace, which now houses the Musée des Beaux Arts. Tours is also a convenient place to stop off if you want to head further south to Saumur and Angers. There are impressive castles perched above both of these towns; the first overlooks the Loire, and the second, the Maine.

Excursions from Chissay are numerous, including the wonderful Château de Chenonceau close by. The town of Vouvray, where you can try some of the local Touraine wine, is within easy touring distance, as is Anjou à Gennes. Here you can see caves which were literally dug out of the rocks to serve as homes in prehistoric times.

This is in fact a remarkable feature of another Loire hotel, the Hôtel les Hautes Roches. Situated near Vouvray, right on the bank of the Loire River, the main part of the hotel is an elegant eighteenth-century building, housing the reception and lounge, some bedrooms, and a renowned restaurant. It is the other bedrooms, though, which are such an interesting feature. Rather than build modern extensions on to the side or back of the hotel, and risk spoiling its charm, further accommodation has been created by burrowing into the hill behind. The soft tufa rock made this a relatively easy process, and now guests can enjoy a really alternative type of bedroom, but still complete with private facilities, telephone and television.

This is just a small selection of some of the château hotels in the Loire, all of which are of interest to visitors. This really is a beautiful area of France, quite different in character, and refreshingly peaceful in comparison with other French holiday spots.

How To Get There: From Britain the Loire is a relatively easy area to reach, as well as being an excellent location from which to continue travels further afield in France. Road and rail links are efficient, and Paris, with its two airports, is only a few hours away.

By far the most comprehensive and interesting tour available to this region is that offered by the Fine Art Tour specialist, Inscape.

Their Châteaux of the Loire tour is an eight-day air-based trip round the very best of the castles and hotels. For around £880, the holiday offers return London-Paris flights; transfers from Paris to Seillac, where the tour is based, with accommodation in the sumptuous estate grounds (complete with swimming pool and tennis courts) of Domaine de Seillac, where guests have their own cottages. Also included is half-board (and the cuisine is first class); daily coach excursions to the châteaux you are touring with your informed expert guide, all entrance fees, tuition, study packs and tips.

A maximum of twenty people are on the tour, and rather than 'blitzing' round ten castles a day, and having only a couple of photos to recall the place, the tour sensibly takes the approach that a few sites, well seen, are better. Between one and three hours is therefore spent at each château, and by the end of the tour each guest has a good idea of the historical development of the Loire château from its medieval origins to its glorious era in the sixteenth and seventeenth centuries.

The route followed includes the most outstanding châteaux, including Azay-le-Rideau, Chenonceau and Chambord. There is a free morning in Blois and a visit to a vineyard, and the timing of the trip to mid-May ensures you miss the worst of the crowds.

Further information is available from Inscape Fine Art Tours (see Appendix II) and the French Government Tourist Office (see Appendix I).

Aeolian Islands

Just to the north of Sicily, lying virtually unnoticed by all but their inhabitants, and unmarked on most maps, are the Aeolian Islands, one of the most remarkable archipelagos in the world. This group of seven islands is one of the best-kept secrets of today's travel market. Their name derives, supposedly, from the Greek God of Wind, Aeolus, who lived on Vulcano, one of the two remaining active volcanic islands. All seven are volcanic (Salina is composed of six volcanoes) but only from Vulcano and Stromboli can steaming vapours and deep, ominous rumblings still be observed and heard.

Lipari, the capital of the Aeolian Islands, is the largest, with an area of thirteen square miles, while Panarea is the smallest and prettiest – at only 1.3 square miles it's hardly surprising that it can't be found on the map! All the islands are inhabited, with the exception of Alicudi and Filcudi. Stromboli actually has a population of about 700, which is quite amazing considering it also has volcanic activity every hour. This display of magnificent, natural fireworks is compulsive viewing for the few tourists who visit these islands.

Unless you're looking for complete isolation, Lipari is the best island to take as your base: it has three or four first-class hotels as well as a wide range of self-catering accommodation. Lipari's population extends to all of 10,000, and the people are as friendly as you could wish for. From Lipari you have various options as to how you fill your time. You could head straight for the other islands to explore their concealed coves and inlets, or alternatively, you could familiarise yourself with the traditions and customs which are so much a part of Aeolian history on Lipari itself. The boat trip around Lipari lets you appreciate just how small the island actually is, as well as showing you the fabulous scenery: horse-shoe bays, steep cliffs, black-hole caves and delightful beaches are all framed between the blue of sky and ocean. The town of Lipari, situated on the east side, is the most important centre on the island. Dominated by the sixteenth-century acropolis (called the Castle), this feature rises majestically from the rocks and can be seen from every angle. Archeological findings have revealed that the Castle was once the centre of Neolithic, Iron, Bronze and Hellenic Age populations. Other places of interest on the island include an eleventh-century cathedral, rebuilt in the Baroque age but retaining some of the original features, and the Aeolian Museum, where exhibits from over 1,300 tombs can be seen. The tombs were recovered during excavations of the classic Necropolis, and the oldest date back to the sixth century AD.

Once you've found your way around Lipari, choose another island, hop on a boat, and see what else this secluded hideaway has to offer. One of the delights of coming here is that, from whichever island you are on, all the others are visible. Vulcano is the nearest to Lipari, and is popular for its therapeutic hot water sea-bed springs and natural mud-baths. While there you can climb to the crater of its volcano – an impressive sight in itself – and admire the view from the top. Although the volcano still steams away quietly, the last eruptive activity was in 1890. Like many Aeolian beaches, Vulcano's consist of black sand, and are not exactly ideal for sun-bathing.

Viewed from a distance, Stromboli is one of the most striking islands. Rising out of the Tyrrhenian Sea, its deep green slopes stand out against the blue sky. Along the eastern side, small white houses provide relief from the bold colours behind. Excursions on Stromboli include a visit to the local observatory (a good vantage point for seeing night-time eruptions), and a trip to the crater. Visitors are advised to take the organised tour to the crater, rather than going independently. From Stromboli you can take a trip to Strombolicchio, a forty-three-metre-high rock, a mile out into the sea. In 1927 steps to the top of the rock were completed, as well as an extensive terrace, dominated by a lighthouse.

Salina offers you the chance to relax (even more!) and enjoy a glass of local wine. This island is the largest producer of wine in the archipelago, and is renowned for the white 'malvasia'. While on Salina there is an excursion to the sanctuary of the Madonna del Terzito. The sanctuary dates back to 1630 and, since then, has been the goal of frequent pilgrimages. From Salina it's easy to reach the most remote islands of Filicudi and Alicudi, both uninhabited. Turtles, sponges, seahorses and flying fish can be seen in abundance in the surrounding seas, and in early summer you're likely to spot swordfish. The Grotto of Bue Marino makes an interesting excursion from Filicudi. Its pointed arch entrance leaves you wondering what you'll find inside, and gives no indication of how far back it stretches into the recesses of the rock.

If you want to find a beach where you can laze in the sun, head for Panarea. Stroll along the clifftops, covered in wild flowers in spring, sample some of the local seafood, choose your spot and wander down to the yellow-sand beach. Life on this small island is idyllic (there aren't even any cars) although in Aeolian high season (August) it can be rather too popular with the Italians. However, if there is any one place in the world you can guarantee peace, quiet, and a taste of the old Mediterranean, that place is the Aeolian Islands.

Accommodation: On Lipari accommodation is relatively varied, given the size of the island. Hotel Carasco is situated outside Lipari itself, but in one of the most beautiful bays on the island. Telephones, air-conditioning and private facilities are standard features in all rooms, most of which have balconies. Hotel Villa Meligunis provides guests with large, airy public rooms, and there are bars, televisions, telephones and air-conditioning in each bedroom. Dating back 700 years, the building has been restored to offer first-class accommodation. If you favour self-catering, there are a variety of lets available, sleeping from three to six people.

How To Get There: Holidays to the Aeolian Islands are organised by a specialist company called Italia nel Mondo. Return flight prices, to either Catania or Palermo on Sicily, cost from £140–240, depending on when you travel. From Sicily, coach or rail transfers are organized to Milazzo, from where it takes less than an hour by hydrofoil or boat to reach Lipari (check if transfers are included when booking). Hotel accommodation on Lipari is cheap, ranging from £10 per night, bed and breakfast, to £24 per night, half-board, based on twin-sharing. If you'd like to combine Sicily and the Aeolian Islands, Italia nel Mondo offer their Grand Tour, focusing on art and archaeology. The tour concentrates mainly on Sicily, but also takes you to Lipari.

Further details are available from Italia nel Mondo Travel Services Ltd (see Appendix II).

Amalfi Coast

From Naples to Sicily, the attractions of southern Italy are many, not least the wonderful coastline around Amalfi. This is an area which has always been popular with the British for winter holidays – nearby Sorrento in particular – due to its pleasant low-season climate. In summer the coast is visited by people from all over the world, most of whom congregate in the town of Amalfi itself. Despite its popularity, though, Amalfi, and the rest of the towns along this stretch of coast, have not suffered the type of intense and ugly commercialisation that has struck so many other resorts. True, up-dated facilities and new hotels have arrived, and yet the charm of the coastal villages is still alive, and life goes on at the relaxed pace so typical of much of Italy. Fishing is one of the area's main industries and also provides a popular pastime among visitors. The scenery is magnificent, complete with clear-blue waters and a backdrop of steep hills. Houses sit tentatively on the rocks overhead, surrounded by terraces of citrus trees. And if you want to really get away from it all, there are countless inlets and coves, far from the busier village beaches.

There are roughly a dozen towns scattered along the Bay of Salerno, from Positano at the western end, to Vietri S. Mare in the east. White stone buildings form one of the most striking common features of these towns: another feature is the incline of the hills down to the sea. Heading eastwards from Naples, Positano and Praiano are the first towns you come across. Positano was supposedly founded by the inhabitants of Paestum, slightly to the north, when they sought shelter from Saracen pirates. Built on the site of a tenth-century Benedictine abbey, the town was fortified after being plundered by the Pisans in 1268. Today it is a quiet fishing village – although its income is boosted considerably by tourism – apparently spurred into action only by rivalry with its neighbouring Praiano over fishing. So strong is the competition between these two towns that they have developed their own 'rules' concerning the surrounding waters. These stipulate a series of nautical manoeuvres, which must be carried out within a certain time around a shoal of fish, if the catch is to be deemed fairly 'won'!

Praiano's beach, and Marina di Praia, at the end of the Valley of Praia, offer good bathing in spectacular settings. If you enjoy the quiet life, this is one of the towns where you'll come across fewer tourists. Locals are friendly and there's plenty of opportunity for relaxation. If you want an interesting excursion, there's always 'la Porta' grotto near Positano, where traces of early civilisations have been found.

Further along the coast, past Conca dei Marini and Grotto dello Smeraldo (the Emerald grotto, so called because of the colourful play of light filtered through water), lies the town of Amalfi, cradled in one of the coast's many bays. Houses are piled up the side of the Lattari Mountains, narrowing the mouth of Valle dei Mulini (Valley of the Mills), which ends here at the sea. Amalfi was founded in the fourth century AD by Roman citizens who were on their way to Constantinople, and who were shipwrecked on the Tyrrhenian coast. Its history encompasses a series of civil battles, leading to its establishment as a Free Republic, which lasted until 1137, when attacks by the Pisans destroyed its military and commercial power. Since then, Amalfi has never really regained its former political status, but has flourished as a popular Italian tourist centre.

There is a definite eastern influence in Amalfi, attributable partially to a Greek population who used the area for growing flax, wheat, fruit and olives. Such commodities are still grown, although production has been threatened throughout history by freak storms which have hit this part of the coast. The worst storms are recorded as having occurred in 1013 and 1343, when most of the town was destroyed, but visitors today have little cause to worry about not getting the sort of beautiful weather usually associated with Amalfi. One unfortunate side-effect of such storms has been the gradual erosion of Amalfi's beach, which today is considerably smaller than it once was. With the rest of the coast to choose from however, this is hardly a problem.

Amalfi's history is chronicled throughout the town by the various monuments and statues. Look out for the colourful ceramic panels by Diodora Cossa which represent an 'Historical Synthesis of the Town of Amalfi', and the monument to Flavio Gioia, the inventor of the compass, who was born here. Built in the ninth century, Amalfi's cathedral is architecturally impressive, despite being modified and restored over the centuries some ten times. Today it presents an imposing façade, approached by steep steps leading up to the door, with adjoining graceful cloisters. Also worth exploring is the restored dockyard area, where huge galleys were built during the time of the prosperous Republic. And if you're here at the right time, there's the Regatta of the Ancient Republics, a lively and colourful parade, which takes place every four years on the third Sunday of June. Each year, at the end of June, you can enjoy the fishermen's musical procession in honour of St Andrew, Amalfi's patron saint.

If you continue along the coast, heading into the hills away from the lower road, you'll find the village of Ravello, perched on top of the cliffs. This is a charming town, known, amongst other things, for the inspiration it gave the composer Richard Wagner. Today, at Palazzo Rufolo, concerts of Wagner's music are given on the terrace overlooking the bay. Also worthy of note at the Palazzo are its beautiful gardens. Other sights in the town include the church of Santa Maria, the remains of a twelfth-century castle, and the cathedral, with its wonderful Arab-Byzantine pulpit made in 1722.

Coming back down to the coastal road, Minori is followed by Maiori and Erchie, leading to Cetara. This is one of the most tranquil spots along the coast, frequented mostly by tourists looking for nothing but sun, sand and peace away from the crowds. Cetara itself is fairly quiet: worthy of inspection are St Peter's Church, and a Saracen bell-tower once used as a lookout post by pirates. Cetara curves back into the recesses of the hills, forming one of the most picturesque towns on the whole coast, while Vietri S. Mare is only a short distance away, followed soon after by the larger town of Salerno.

These are the main towns along the coast of Amalfi. Quaint and enchanting are two words which describe them well, although their diversity goes much further. As a holiday in itself, visiting these towns will more than adequately fill your time, although if you're exploring the rest of Italy, the Amalfi Coast forms a perfect respite from the art and architecture of major centres like Venice and Florence.

Accommodation: Hotels in all the towns offer adequate accommodation, although mention should be given to Hotel Cappucini-Convento in Amalfi itself. Dating back to AD 1000, this was once a monastery, but was converted into a hotel at the beginning of the nineteenth century. Set high above Amalfi, overlooking the bay, the hotel has impressive public rooms and traditional bedrooms, as well as superb views.

One of the main and best companies offering holidays in Amalfi is Quo Vadis. Their prices are extremely competitive, especially given the type of personalised service they offer their clients. For around £400 you can enjoy seven nights in one of Amalfi's hotels, and for a little bit more you can stay at the Cappucini-Convento. Included are return flights, half-board accommodation, airport-hotel transfer (and vice-versa), and all local taxes and service charges. Alternatively, Magic of Italy specialise in Italian holidays, offering good deals to Amalfi. Prices start at around £280 for three nights (see Appendix II).

Information about Italy in general is available from the Italian Tourist Office (See Appendix I).

European Battlefield Tours

Scattered across Europe there are beaches, plains and fields with a historical relevance that may not at first sight be evident. However, such areas are as significant to battlefield history as Tuscany is to art. Ypres, the Somme, Normandy, Arnhem, Bastogne – these are the places where men fought and died in the name of freedom, places which will always be found in the history books. One of the most rewarding ways of visiting these areas is by travelling with a company who really know what they're talking about. Major and Mrs Holt's Battlefield Tours is a small company developed by Tonie and Valmai Holt, who have operated these popular tours for the past fifteen years. They have travelled all over the world, covering the battlefields of Tunisia in North Africa, Gallipoli, the Great Sepoy Rebellion in India, and Europe. Their experience has created a holiday company with a difference, which caters for enthusiasts, historians, and anyone who has an interest in seeing the fascinating legacy of the world's most notable battlefield sites.

Looking back to World War One, two of the most significant places were Ypres and the Somme. 'It's a Long Way to Tipperary' is a three-day tour which serves as an introduction to anyone visiting these places for the first time. Following the route of the British Expeditionary Force, your itinerary includes Mont Cassel, Poperinghe, Ypres, Passchendaele, Vimy Ridge and the Somme. The trip covers features such as the headquarters of General John French (Earl of Ypres) and Marshal Ferdinand Foch, St George's Memorial Church at Ypres, preserved Canadian and German trenches at Vimy Ridge, and the Fortress of Thiepval which now stands as a huge memorial to those who died. At Passchendaele there is a detailed tour of the battle area, and you are given a chance to see the sprawling German cemetery at Langemarck. If this is an area of particular interest to you, there is an alternative three-day tour which concentrates solely on 'Wipers' and Passchendaele, looking closely at the Immortal Salient, a small section of Belgian soil which the British Expeditionary Force clung to for four years, but at the cost of almost a million casualties.

An introduction to World War Two is the basic idea behind the 'D-Day: the Longest Day' tour. The four-day itinerary covers from Pegasus Bridge, near Caen, to St Mere Eglise. Following the tracks of the 'Tommies' and 'Joes', you can trace the progress of the strongest invasion armada ever launched, that of the 1st American and 2nd British Armies, which fought against Hitler's 'Fortress Europe' on 6 June 1944. Eisenhower and Montgomery, Rommel and von Rundstedt are among the names which crop up during the tour, and you are able to consider at first hand the role each played. Also to be seen is the steeple from which an American paratrooper hung, the cliffs at Omaha, and the Utah, Gold, Juno and Sword beaches.

A tour with a slightly different emphasis is 'Oh What a Literary War', which is usually accompanied by a guest speaker. This tour takes you away from the front-lines, to see behind-the-scenes rest areas where men such as Wilfred Owen and Siegfried Sassoon wrote much of their poetry. Where appropriate, the graves of these, and other celebrated writers, are visited, and your attention is focussed on poets, prose writers and musicians of the First World War. Starting off in Ypres Salient, the tour takes you south through Loos and Ors, to the Somme. Here you have a two-night stay before returning to Calais via the site of the base hospitals, near the Bull Ring of Etaples, where Vera Brittain served. Your hotel at the Somme is the historic Hotel Postillon in Amiens. Other features of interest on this tour include the Menen Gate Last Post Ceremony, Butterworth Trench, and a torchlight expedition to Devonshire Cemetery in the Somme. Prospective travellers should note that this is described as a 'participation tour', and guests are expected to bring their favourite pieces – music or poetry – on which it is hoped they will present a short, ten-minute, talk.

Belgium and Luxembourg are the settings for Battlefield Tours' 'Battle of the Bulge/Maginot Line'. This is an area through which Adolf Hitler twice tried to force his troops, first in 1940 when Rommel tried to outflank the Maginot Line, and again in 1944 when Von Rundstedt's forces tried to split the tiring British and American armies. Liège, Trois Ponts, Bastogne, the city of Luxembourg, Patton's grave, and Hackenberg Fortification are all included among a wide variety of sights on this five-day trip. Time is left free for shopping – or whatever else you wish to do – and much of the travelling is done through the beautiful valleys and vineyards of the Moselle district. One of the highlights of the trip is the visit to Hackenberg Fort, the world's largest underground fort. Here you can ride on the fort's underground train through cavernous tunnels that have recently been opened, take a trip around its unusual museum, and see the gun turrets rising out of the ground. All in all, there is a lot packed in to your five days.

These are only a small handful of Major and Mrs Holt's Battlefield Tours – not forgetting those that take you further afield to places such as Turkey, or the trail of the American Civil War. Holland (notably Arnhem) is also featured among their European options, as well as a range of trips covering France, Belgium and Italy. Although some tours are more specialised than others, this adds to the enjoyment of discovering new places and learning a bit of history along the way. Different tours are run at different times of the year, some with several departures and others with only one or two. For the European options, prices range from £200–800 per person, based on twin accommodation with private facilities, and include high-standard hotel half-board, often wine with dinner (but do check whether dinner is included every day), all detailed excursions and entrance fees to museums and sites, guides/special guests, commentaries, tour kit (maps, passenger list, etc.), films and interviews where detailed, transfers on the same coach throughout the trip, and air travel/cross-channel return fares.

Further information is available from Major and Mrs Holt's Tours Ltd (see Appendix II).

American Civil War Battlefield Tours

People usually visit the US to experience an up-to-the-minute lifestyle in the 'new' world, but the States have a long and colourful history, largely unknown to most Europeans. The beautiful Southern states have a strong identity of their own, much of which was forged by a common experience of the American Civil War – the most significant war in US history, in which more Americans were killed than in the First and Second World Wars together. This vast campaign waged for four years in the 1860s across the beautiful countryside of the 'Old South', up and down the mighty Mississippi River, in the gentle plantation landscape of Virginia, and into Scarlet O'Hara's beloved Atlanta. Although the Confederates were eventually vanquished, their legend still lives on and draws the people of the South together even today. 'The Old South was ploughed under. But the ashes are still warm' said playwright Henry Miller. A number of tour operators now run exciting trips throughout the South where you can see its great cities, combining the modern US with the unique historical heritage of the area, all threaded together with a common theme: the American Civil War.

The greatest battles of the war took place near the two capitals, Richmond and Washington DC, barely 100 miles apart. Richmond, Virginia was the Confederate capital and at the very heart of the revolt. Confederate president Jefferson Davis's own White House has been lovingly restored and now contains a huge collection of Confederate memorabilia. Richmond's graceful Capitol Building is a creation of the earlier revolutionary, Thomas Jefferson, Virginia's favourite son. Mr Jefferson's elegant domed home, Monticello, lies sixty miles to the west in Charlottesville, near the spectacular Blue Ridge Mountains and Shenandoah Valley, where the legendary Confederate, General Thomas 'Stonewall' Jackson, lived up to his name.

The Northern capital, Washington, DC, was under constant

threat from the Southern armies. It's a showpiece city, with a plethora of enormous white classical buildings. Here you can see the original White House, where Abraham Lincoln orchestrated the Northern victory. Lincoln didn't have long to savour his victory as he was mortally wounded by a Southern actor, John Wilkes Booth, while attending a play at Ford's Theater a mere five days after the end of the war. The theatre itself is as it was on Lincoln's final and fateful evening, and now houses a Lincoln Museum. Washington's appeal is not confined to the past: the most visited museum in the country is in fact the magnificent Smithsonian Air and Space Museum.

Harpers Ferry, West Virginia, has a dramatic setting on a peninsula jutting out into the Shenandoah and Potomac Rivers – Thomas Jefferson said it was worth crossing the Atlantic just to see the view. Much of Harpers Ferry has changed very little since it was thrust into the spotlight by John Brown's 1859 raid to free slaves, which set the wheel in motion for the eventual bloody conflict. The countryside is dotted with battlefield parks, as at Manassas, Virginia, where the war's first battle went the way of the South. The most impressive battlefield park is located in Gettysburg, Pennsylvania, where the South's greatest general, Robert E. Lee, made a desperate bid by invading the North, culminating in the largest battle of the war, which lasted three days. Lee's defeat signalled the Confederacy's 'high tide' and the beginning of the end. Since nearly all of Gettysburg is an open air museum, you get a strong feeling of the momentous events which went on around you. In nearby Lancaster County, the Amish people live their lives in a simple, traditional eighteenth-century German manner. Visiting this area is like being in a time warp. Petersburg Battlefield in Virginia saw the South's last stand, ending in Lee's surrender to General Ulysses S. Grant at the Appomattox Court House in 1865.

The war in the west centred on control of the Mississippi River, which passes through exotic New Orleans, Louisiana, home of rag-time jazz, cajun and creole cooking, and paddle steamers. Natchez, Mississippi, has preserved its elegant ante-bellum mansions and clapboard architecture prevalent when cotton was king – a lifestyle shattered by the civil war. Vicksburg sits on a bend of the river and is surrounded by a vast Military Park commemorating the great siege which took place there. The slow pace of life in Lynchburg, Tennessee, might be explained by the presence of the Jack Daniels Distillery where you can discover how sour-mash whiskey gets its distinctive kick.

After the North's success in the west, General Sherman's armies pushed east to the very heart of the Confederacy. The battle for Atlanta is recreated in a massive 3D show at the Cyclorama in Atlanta. Today the city is a thoroughly modern, international location – the flagship of the 'new South'. Martin Luther King's battle to guarantee human rights – won a century before by Lincoln and his armies – is enshrined in the Martin Luther King Centre. Sherman's highly destructive 'March to the Sea' from Atlanta to Savannah assured his title as the most unpopular man in Georgia, even to this day! Fortunately Savannah itself was not destroyed and is still a gracious and charming garden city. Hundreds of elegant eighteenth and nineteenth-century buildings are laid out in squares amongst the azaleas and dogwood. Stone Mountain is a massive 400-foot granite cliff face upon which are carved in bass relief the three giants (literally) of the Confederacy, Lee, Davis and Jackson – Lee is nine storeys high!

Charleston, South Carolina, was the 'seedbed of Confederacy' and it was here that it all began in 1861 when Fort Sumter was attacked in Charleston Harbour. You can visit the fort on boat tours. The city boasts beautiful cobbled streets and historic buildings.

How To Get There: A number of tour operators offer trips to the South with a central theme of the war between the states. Major and Mrs Holt's Battlefield Tours specialise in running trips to major battlefields throughout the world. The 'US Civil War: Eastern Campaign' tour visits the many battlefields around Washington, Richmond and Gettysburg. Twelve days, including flights, costs around £1,299. Classic Tours' 'Atlanta to the Sea' is a twelve-day journey between Atlanta and Washington, DC, also visiting the holiday resort of Hilton Head, South Carolina, for £950. The Battle for the Missippi is an eleven-day tour visiting New Orleans, the Deep South and ending in Atlanta, for £950. Thomas Cook in conjunction with Voyages Jules Verne offer a tremendous seventeen-day tour – 'The Confederate Trail from New Orleans' – which combines the major sights of all three previously mentioned tours in a historic journey through New Orleans, Atlanta, Richmond and Washington, DC (£1470).

Further information is available from the United States Travel Information Centre or Travel South USA (See Appendix II).

Adventure Holidays

From earliest times, man has had the urge to explore. Those who discovered new continents, countries and species, in their search for honour, glory and adventure, became popular folk heroes.

Then came the late twentieth century: the world shrank to the size of a global village, and suddenly everyone was hopping onto planes and jetting abroad in their search for sun, sea and sand. But like the waves that flowed and ebbed inexorably on countless package holiday beaches, the tide of human holiday-makers eventually peaked and started to decline. Today, although such holidays still comprise a large part of the overall travel sector, tame sun-seeking trips to foreign parts are no longer as popular as they once were. The intelligent holiday-maker of the 1990s is an altogether more sophisticated and discerning animal. He or she is in search of an entirely different experience, hoping to capture some of the excitement of the 'real' travel of former times, but in a safe and controlled fashion, as part of a small and like-minded group, and often within a challenging physical and personal environment. Thus has the great adventure holiday boom sprung forth.

The gap between rough and unpredictable independent travel on the one hand, and mollycoddled, sedentary and anonymous cheap package holidays on the other, has finally been bridged. Nowadays, it's quite possible to buy an 'off the shelf' trip which combines all the ingredients that go to make an adventure holiday: isolated surroundings, challenge, excitement, rugged scenery and a sense of achievement. Never before has it been possible to enjoy such a wide selection from within such a broad spectrum of adventure theme holidays. From 'soft' trips – such as lodge-based 'comfort' safaris – to 'hard' trips – like dog-sledding expeditions to the Arctic – packaged adventure holidays are enjoying enormous and increasing popularity today.

Especially popular are safari-based trips on which you can see Africa's wilderness and wildlife on foot, horseback, by off-road vehicle, train or even hot-air balloon. Whether you opt to sleep under canvas or thatch, the choice of tour operator is yours. If your taste for adventure lies in cooler climes however, then the range of Arctic trips available is wider today than ever before.

202 Adventure Holidays

All right, so you may not be the first person ever to set foot on a particular area, or observe a certain species. But to you – the adventurer – each new experience will be a personal 'first', and the likelihood is that each adventure holiday you make will leave you with a host of abiding memories and the probability of making enduring friendships.

Japan

When Rudyard Kipling said 'East is east, and west is west, and never the twain shall meet', he had not experienced modern Japan, where the traditional mystic East has crashed into the glitz and technology of the West to form a dynamic and exciting new economic superpower. One minute you can be in the frenetic atmosphere of downtown Tokyo, and the next, turn the corner and face a simple and serene wooden shrine. The Japanese see no paradox here, and even the most Westernised businessman will travel back to the village of his ancestors to pay his respects during the Festival of the Dead. The peaceful world of Buddhist temples, cherry blossoms, and the tea ceremony lives on in apparent harmony with great neon forests and 'bullet' trains, making Japan quite unlike anywhere else in the world.

Japan is a country of lofty mountains and exotic islands, with the largest, Honshu, providing many of the most captivating sites. Tokyo, obliterated by fire bombs in 1945, has arisen, phoenix-like, spreading across the Kanto Plain in the shadow of the perfect Mt Fuji to become the hub of Japan's modern life. Despite this, in the very centre of Tokyo, overlooked by the glass and steel of a business district lies the Imperial Palace (recently valued at the equivalent of the entire state of California) surrounded by thick woods and enclosed by a moat and stately gateways. The Meiji Shrine is another island of tranquillity in an ocean of frenzy, set in a large wooded park with a gate of 1700-year-old cypress trees. The other Tokyo comprises a vibrant modern city, especially around the Ginza, the famous shopping area, where you will find an amazing array of stores, and, when night falls, explosions of colour from brilliant moving neon signs as intense as the nightlife. Elegantly painted pagodas and geisha houses vie with the modern delights of Tokyo for your undivided attention.

Near Tokyo are the extremes of both man-made and natural beauty. The ancient city of Kamakura cannot be missed on any itinerary. Surrounded by mountains and a bay, its vermillion shrines and Zen temples are set amongst cedars and azaleas and the atmosphere is the very essence of peace. Mt Fuji's flawless cone dominates the entire area and has gained great spiritual importance. Hikone also provides natural splendour with wonderful mountains, virgin forests, and hot bubbling springs. The wilderness around Nikko is special, where the indigo-blue Lake Chuzenji flows over a spectacular 350-foot waterfall. In Nikko itself stands the towering red and gold Toshogu Shrine where during the spring festival a thousand men parade in the colourful traditional costume of their ancient samurai forebears.

The modern spectacle of Tokyo contrasts with the immense sense of history which pervades the ancient capital of Nara, which is a virtual outdoor museum and seemingly little changed since Buddhism first flourished here in the eighth century. The incredible Todaiji Temple, the haunt of saffron-robed monks, houses an enormous bronze statue of the Buddha (the Daibatsu) fifty-three feet high and weighing 452 tons. The massive structure in which it is housed is the largest wooden building in the world, and outside the temple's gates 1000 tame deer roam free. Nearby Kyoto has kept its traditional face and developed a modern side. It was an imperial capital for over 1000 years and is thus dotted with innumerable shrines, temples, and tranquil landscape gardens, as well as sumptuous palaces; it is a place not to be missed.

Further west on Honshu is the city of Hiroshima, modern, of course, and a historic legacy of the first wartime atomic bomb. Its Peace Park, which lies at the very centre of where the explosion occurred, has a museum which will leave you with abiding and thought-provoking impressions of the apocalypse.

The Inland Sea between the islands of Honshu, Shikoku, and Kyushu is a world of its own, with hundreds of fascinating islands to explore. Japan's other islands house many treasures. Kyushu has smoking, cloud-wreathed volcanoes, boiling mud ponds, and grand pagoda castles. The northern island of Hokkaido is Japan's last frontier, with primeval forests, mountains and lakes. The islands around Okinawa, between Japan and China, are sub-tropical with the most un-Japanese landscape of beautiful beaches and spectacular coral reefs.

Japan's railway system is one of the best in the world, with its famous 'bullet train' – Shinkansen. A Japan rail pass is a good way to see the country, but must be bought before entering Japan from the Japan Travel Bureau or Japanese Airlines (JAL). It costs about £120 for seven days and is valid on some buses and ferries. Driving is not recommended in Japan as the roads are overcrowded and few signs are in English. It is possible to travel independently, but the language problem and the cost can be large barriers. Accommodation is readily available, ranging from de luxe and business Western-style hotels to Japanese-style inns (Ryokan) and guest houses (Minshuku), where you can save money and get a good feel for Japanese life.

How To Get There: Travelling to Japan with a tour will make things easier and may actually save you money, and with more than thirty UK operators offering trips, there is no shortage of choice. The Japan Travel Bureau (JTB) offers a wide range of opportunities: the 'Shogun' escorted tour contrasts modern Tokyo with the riches of Kamakura and Kyoto and the natural beauty of Hikone and Kyushu. Fifteen days including all travel and half-board accommodation in a shared double-room costs around £2,150 per person. The JTB also offers independent travel options with a return flight and five nights in either Tokyo, Osaka, Kyoto, Hiroshima or Kobe for £987 per person. The 'Freedom of Japan' package gives true travel independence as it provides a return ticket, a Japan rail pass, and hotel coupons for eleven days at a cost of £1,227. JAL offer escorted tours, such as 'Romantic Japan' which journeys to Tokyo, Hikone, Kyoto and Okinawa. Fifteen days half-board in a shared double room, including all travel, costs £1,700. They also offer tours while in Japan, side trips, Japanese-style inn packages, and even Zen meditation and ceramics study programmes in Kyoto. Kuoni offer an escorted tour to Tokyo, Kyoto, Nara, Hong Kong and Bangkok, sixteen days on half-board including all travel for £1,600. Speedbird's 'Images of Japan' travels to Tokyo, Kyoto, Hiroshima and the beautiful Inland Sea. Thirteen days, half-board, travel-inclusive, costs £2,100. Other experienced operators to Japan are Bales Tours, Jetset, Keith Prowse and Travel 2.

For the independent traveller, JAL fly regularly to Tokyo and Osaka from London but fares can be high, up to £2,000 for a return ticket, so check in the newspaper for discounted flights. JAL and a number of small companies offer a good internal air service and there are ferries between Japan, China and South Korea.

China

China is an entire world within one country. The traditional Chinese view of their country is not only as the world's centre, but also the entirety of the civilised world. Their word for China, *zhonghua*, means the 'Middle Kingdom'. It is certainly a vast country, ranging from mountains, deserts, plateaux, and river valleys to sub-tropical jungles. The *Han* Chinese make up almost all of the population but live on only 40 per cent of the land. The remaining 60 per cent is populated with a myriad of colourful and exotic peoples, including the Muslim Uyghurs, Tibetans, Manchurians, and Mongolians. China's ancient culture continued to flourish while others – Greece, Rome, and Persia – fell by the wayside. The Party leadership now relies on this same culture and historical legacy to bring in much-needed foreign capital. The threat of over-commercialisation was recognised by the early twentieth-century writer Lu Xun who remarked 'It's not whether to preserve our tradition, but whether our tradition can preserve us'. But the raising of the 'Bamboo Curtain', its creation of special economic zones, and its own brand of *perestroika* have all shown that the rest of the world matters to China. While the tragedies of Tiananmen Square demonstrate that things do not always change quickly, China still retains a fascinating culture, albeit one sometimes difficult to understand.

Beijing, in the northeast, is the capital and in all senses but geographical the centre and heart of China. It is laid out in three rectangles, the inner sanctum being the magnificent Forbidden City, and therefore the centre of their world. Once forbidden to all but the Emperor, his eunuchs and entourage, the imposingly walled and moated Forbidden City covers 250 breathtaking acres with six elegant palaces and fabulous gardens of cypress and pines, and is no longer forbidden to you or anyone. Recognising the significance of the area to all Chinese, the new Communist government placed its showpiece, the huge, modern Tiananmen Square (Square of Heavenly Peace) next to the Forbidden City. Unfortunately as recent events have shown, it has not lived up to its name. The splendid Temple of Heaven is a beautifully painted three-tiered pagoda with panoramic views. Near to Beijing is the tremendous Great Wall, a truly epic achievement, which you can now experience by helicopter. The Wall snakes up and down, over hills, plains and desolate deserts for many thousands of miles, skirting the Mongolian border.

The ancient walled city of Xi'an in central China has been the capital of eleven dynasties, including the first, founded by the powerful Qin Shi Huang. In Xi'an you can see one of the world's great archaeological finds, the unbelievable Terracotta Legions of the first emperor's tomb. At least 7,500 full-size and intricately created warriors, all individuals, have stood guard over the tomb for twenty-two centuries, and incredibly the actual burial chamber still lies unexcavated.

Beautiful Suzhou in the east has been little affected by China's modernisation. It is a refined city of canals and graceful gardens. Linked to Suzhou by the ancient Great Canal is Hangzhou, where you will find fine silks and the captivating and peaceful West Lake, surrounded by weeping willows and colourful temples: 'In Heaven there is Paradise. On Earth, Hangzhou and Suzhou' says an ancient proverb.

The north is known for culture and architecture; the south for spectacular scenery. The mountains of Guilin, in the south, are renowned for their beauty. A cruise on the Li River reveals unbelievable misty limestone hills which rise vertically for hundreds of feet from the river banks, flanked by bamboo glades and rice fields. Fishermen in sampans use tamed cormorants and lanterns to fish at dawn. An ancient poem describes these hills as 'jade hairpins'. This is the China of dream holidays; an experience you will never forget.

The crowded British Colony of Hong Kong, the base for many tours, is an enclave of capitalism in an ocean of communism, with its glass and steel modern high-rise buildings squeezed between the mountains and the sea. Hong Kong's smaller twin, the Portuguese colony of Macau, is a relaxed area with a curious Chinese/Mediterranean atmosphere. Another region not Communist-controlled is the island trade centre of Taiwan, where many magnificent treasures from the Forbidden City were taken when the Nationalist government fled there in 1949.

The ancient Silk Road connected China with the great empires of India and Byzantium. It winds through the bleak deserts and emerald green oases of western China and once carried silk and jade to the west, while Buddhism, Islam, Christianity and Marco Polo came to China. It passes the fascinating Islamic, almost Near Eastern, cities of Kashgar, Ürümqi, and Turfan around the desolate Taklamakan Desert, past the curious 'singing' sand mountains and spectacular Buddhist caves of Dunhuang of Gansu Province, and the towering White Pagoda Mountain of Lanzhou, through to Xi'an.

This overview barely scratches the surface of China. You can also experience the vast grasslands of Inner Mongolia, the Stone Forest near Kunming, the 127 miles of the stunning Yangtze River, the Ice Festival of the Old Russian city of Harbin, the soaring skyscrapers of Shanghai, the world-famous cuisine of Canton, the amazing 100,000 images of the Buddha in the Longmen Caves in the old imperial capital of Luoyang, the explosive (literally) Chinese New Year, and the great mountains and exotic culture of Tibet (see separate section on Tibet).

How To Get There: Air travel to China is usually to the international airports of Beijing, Guangzhou (Canton), Shanghai and Hong Kong. Pearl Cruises operate numerous luxury cruises, but if you're more adventurous you will probably want to travel on the Trans-Siberian Railway between Moscow and Beijing. Inside China air, road, rail and river routes are extensive. Hotels are usually prearranged and designated for foreigners. They lack atmosphere and are invariably modern. The official Luxingshe travel agency organises most tours and provides guides. Independent travel can be difficult simply because of the problems of language and cultural differences, but at least sixty-seven tour operators include China on their lists.

Thomas Cook in conjunction with Voyages Jules Verne offers a vast range of fascinating China tours. Their 'China the Beautiful' tour covers many of its most picturesque areas, including Hong Kong, Guilin, Suzhou, Beijing, Xi'an, and cruises along the Yangtze River and Grand Canal: twenty-three days, £1985. 'On the Tracks of Marco Polo' you can trace the Silk Road by train through Paris, Istanbul, Samarkand, Ürümqi, Turfan, Lanzhou, Xi'an, and Hong Kong (see pp. 22–6 for details). Their 'Beijing and Moscow' tour offers an inexpensive alternative with six days in Beijing and one day in Moscow for £500 per person. The China Travel Service, an official agency, provides an extensive programme of tours including the 'China Selection' visiting Hong Kong and Guilin (for 3 days, £871). On Speedbird's China Horizons with Japan extension you can voyage to the two giants of the Far East (18 days, £2700). Other experienced operators to China include Abercrombie & Kent,

Bales, Far East Travel, Redwing, Silk Cut and Twickers World (see Appendix II).

Mexico

Mexico is the fusion of two great empires, the Aztec and the Spanish. The ancient glories and traditions of the awe-inspiring pre-Columbian civilisations have continued on throughout the Spanish colonisation, and today still survive just below the veneer of European culture. Mexico's cultural debt to Spain is strong both through religion and language, but the endurance of Aztec culture can be seen in things as basic as the Mexican flag (depicting an Aztec legend), the diet, and even the name Mexico (the most powerful Aztec group). Added to this blend is the influence of her giant neighbour, the economic empire of the US, which led the nineteenth-century dictator Porfirio Diaz to lament 'Poor Mexico, so far from God, and so close to the United States'. Attempts to shake off ancient and colonial vestiges and drag Mexico into the modern world have left a unique mosaic of both the old and new worlds.

Mexico is about a quarter the size of the US and encompasses desolate deserts in the north, volcanoes of the central plateau, and lowland jungle in the south, with over half of the country lying above 3,000 feet. The bulk of its people live in the centre near Mexico City. Over half of the population is of mixed race (*mestizo*), 16 per cent are of European descent, and over a quarter are still pure Indian, often divorced from mainstream life and still speaking ancient languages.

The capital, Mexico City, is a vast and rapidly growing metropolis built on the site of the Aztec island capital of Tenochtitlan. It lies in central Mexico at 7,460 feet, beneath the imposing snow-capped volcanoes Iztaccihuatl and Popocatepetl. Currently containing a quarter of Mexico's population, it could soon be the largest city in the world. It is a microcosm of diverse Mexican culture, most evident at La Plaza de las Tres Culturas where a modern glass and marble skyscraper towers over a Spanish Franciscan church which was built on top of an Aztec temple. The city's centre is the enormous Zocalo Square, flanked by the National Palace, built by the conquistador Cortés on the ruins of the palace of the final Aztec king, Moctezuma II. Aztec remains, such as the giant Templo Mayor, continue to be unearthed as the city expands; the greatest repository of these treasures is the spectacular National Museum of Anthropology in Chapultepec Park. Mexico City's colonial past is evident in broad avenues, beautiful parks, and churches such as the pilgrimage centre of La Basilica de la Nuestra Senora De Guadalupe. It is also a modern smog-filled city, and an exciting place, if sometimes overwhelming.

Taxco, 100 miles south of Mexico City, had no connecting road until 1930 and has thus kept its refined colonial atmosphere, built on the fortunes of silver mining. Its white stucco houses with red-tiled roofs, and its narrow cobbled streets will survive, since the entire town has been declared a national monument. Also near the capital is Teotihuacan, the most important and impressive archaeological site in the country. The Causeway of the Dead runs through a colossal ancient city of stepped pyramids, including a temple to the plumed serpent god Quetzalcoatl. The creators of this vast complex are still shrouded in mystery. Teotihuacan humbled even the later Aztecs who called it the 'City of the Gods'; it is a place not to be missed. Tula is a charming colonial town, but nearby, four huge and sinister monolithic statues of volcanic rock, the Atlantes, gaze down from the summit of a pyramid.

Northern Mexico is mostly plateaus and deserts, best viewed from the Copper Canyon Railway which winds through fantastic mountains and the 12,000-foot Urique River Canyon.

Monte Alban in the south is a striking Zapotec (pre-Aztec) complex at 6,500 feet which overlooks the twenty-seven spires, gardens and cloisters of the peaceful city of Oaxaca. The beautiful holy Mayan city of Palenque, engulfed by jungle since the tenth century, is only starting to be revealed. Its palace and stepped Temple of Inscriptions lie in a small clearing in the Chiapas jungle, a small indication of the heights Mayan culture reached before its mysterious collapse.

The Yucatan Peninsula juts into the Caribbean and was the centre of Mayan civilisation; many still speak Mayan here. Merida, the 'White City', has tree-shaded boulevards and whitewashed mansions. In the Yucatan jungle lie the fragments of astounding lost Mayan cities, such as Chichen Itza, with its Pyramid of Kukulkan (Mayan for Quetzalcoatl) and observatory (where astronomy reached a very sophisticated level), and Uxmal with its rounded Pyramid of the Magician.

Graham Greene described these temples as 'enormous tombstones of history'.

Beach resorts have boomed in the last decade. Acapulco on the Pacific coast is a jet-setter's paradise with more than twenty beaches spread around a bay, where one can see the death-defying Quebrada cliff divers. Mazatlan is famous for its deep-sea fishing but has also developed as a beach and water-sports centre. Puerto Vallarta is set in lush tropical mountains with luxury hotels and beautiful beaches. On the Caribbean coast in the Yucatan is Cancun, which was a small island fishing village just ten years ago, but whose thin stretches of powdery white sand have become world-famous.

How To Get There: Air travel to Mexico is simple as eight major airlines fly from London to Mexico City, including Pan Am, KLM, Air France and Iberia. Cruise ships use Acapulco, Puerto Vallarta and Mazatlan as major ports of call. Internal air travel on Aeromexico and Mexicana is regular and widespread. Train and bus networks are also extensive. The relative ease of internal travel makes going independently a viable option. This is especially true as accommodation ranges greatly depending on your needs, from simple guest houses to elegant hotels. Tourism has been growing rapidly as people realise the fact that North America means more than the US and Canada. Over sixty UK companies now offer packages to Mexico.

Kuoni's impressive Colonial Cities tour visits the best of the ornate remains of Spanish colonialism including Taxco, and finishes with four nights in Acapulco; fifteen days on half-board cost £900 per person including flights. Steamond, a specialist operator, offers the 'Sun and Ruins' tour, journeying to Mexico City, Oaxaca, the ruins of Monte Alban, Palenque, Chichen Itza, and Uxmal, and then to the sun of Cancun; seventeen days costs £1,700 for travel and accommodation. Thomson's 'Mexican Encounter' gives you a brief affordable taste of Mexico through Mexico City, Taxco, and Acapulco; seven days' travel and accommodation for £600. Journey Latin America offers a more personal tour, such as the 'Quetzal' which visits the major Mayan sites in the Yucatan and Guatemala via Belize; twenty-eight days, land travel and accommodation only, costs £500; air travel to Guatemala can also be arranged. Other experienced tour operators to Mexico are Bales Tours, Exodus, Explore, Hayes & Jarvis,

Speedbird, Thomas Cook, Voyages Jules Verne and Wexas (see Appendix II).

Eastern Europe

In the past the socialist countries of Eastern Europe have not been the first choice for holiday destinations because they seemed somewhat grey and uninspiring, but the amazing recent developments in this fascinating region have finally exploded this myth. The six 'Iron Curtain' countries – Czechoslovakia, Bulgaria, Romania, Hungary, Poland, East Germany (now part of the Federal Republic) – seem well on the way to democracy, and they and the two socialist independents of Yugoslavia and Albania are no longer seen as a homogeneous 'bloc' but rather an intriguing mix of cultures at the crossroads of Europe. An amazing variety of cultures and landscapes is found squeezed between western Europe and the USSR and Asia, including the Westernized alpine region of Slovenia in Yugoslavia, the historic castles of Bohemia in Czechoslovakia, and the golden beaches of Bulgaria's Black Sea Coast. With the continuing liberalisations, Eastern Europe will rival any area in the world as an enchanting and fascinating place to visit.

Slovenia in northwest Yugoslavia is an affluent and advanced region, where picturesque villages, imposing castles, and beautiful lakes adorn the magnificent Julian Alps and whose western atmosphere reflects Austria's long influence. The peaceful, glacial Lake Bled, surrounded by the towering Julian Alps and forest, encircles a small island upon which sits a fairy-tale red-steepled church. Every Sunday you can see churchgoers rowing out to this island, singing hymns as they go. An ancient grey castle sits perched high on a cliff top, dominating the whole island and looking down on elegant and grand hotels at the Lake's edge. Scenic and peaceful Lake Bohinji lies under Yugoslavia's highest mountain, the soaring Mt Triglav, home of the mystic gods of the ancient Slovenes. There is excellent skiing at the World Cup venue Kranjska Gora, amidst scenic mountain woodlands, though without the cost of western European resorts. Ljubliana, the Slovene capital, is a lively cultural centre with an historic Old Town of medieval streets and Baroque churches, overlooked by an ancient castle. Folklore bursts into the forefront once a year with a colourful traditional wedding festival held each June. Near Ljubliana are the spectacular Postojna Caves with huge caverns, underground lakes and rivers, and fantastic panoramas of stalagmite 'cities'. Ptuj in north-east Slovenia is an old city with Roman, medieval, and Baroque buildings. Slovenia is also home to the beautiful Adriatic beach resorts of Portoroz and the crumbling Venetian splendour of Piran.

Bohemia in western Czechoslovakia is a captivating historic region of spectacular palaces, spas, castles and mountains, crowned by Prague (the 'Paris of the East'), a beautiful and cultured city. Prague's five 'towns' (districts) are crowded around the Vltava river, which is spanned by thirteen ancient bridges. This majestic city is a subtle blend of Romanesque, Gothic, Renaissance and ornate Baroque styles, which bursts into life during the world-famous Spring Music Festival. The Old Town is a maze of medieval streets and painted façades, and the Lesser Town contains an amazing collection of Baroque churches. Dark spires of the intricate Gothic bulk of St Vitus Cathedral rise over Prague Castle in the old imperial area of Hradcany. Goethe described Prague as a 'jewel in the country's crown of stone'. It is ringed with solitary castles nestling on wooded hills, most notably the impressive 600-year-old fortress of Karlstejn and the round towers of the Renaissance palace Konopiste.

Western Bohemia's elegant spas lie in a beautiful forest setting and have long been a favourite of the European élite, including Beethoven, Edward VII and even Karl Marx. Karlsbad's twelve springs are surrounded by refined white colonnades and parks, and the spas of Marienbad and Fratisky also share this graceful atmosphere. The lofty ridges of the Giant Mountains dominate northeast Bohemia, and give rise to the historic River Elbe.

On Bulgaria's Black Sea Coast, thickly wooded mountains meet golden beaches, river estuaries and historic towns, making this location an attractive alternative to a beach holiday. Drouzhba is the oldest and most luxurious Black Sea resort, having grown up around the sumptuous Grand Varna Hotel. The coastline is dotted with sheltered beaches and inlets. Albena is a new resort squeezed between forested mountains and the sea. Its five-mile beach has good facilities for all water-sports. Near the large family resort of Sunny Beach is the ancient museum town of Nessebur occupying a small peninsula. This 3000-year-old city was once a Greek trading centre, which later boomed between the eleventh and fourteenth centuries and now has forty-one beautifully sculpted churches. Its winding cobbled streets are lined with traditional wooden houses. Bulgaria's biggest port, Varna, still retains some of its Roman and Byzantine glory in its extraordinary baths. Near Varna you find the only petrified forest in Europe, where hundreds of natural columns of calcified sandstone rise from a small desert. Burgas, the Black Sea's second largest city, has long thin beaches of black sand.

How To Get There: Yugotours offer many trips to Slovenia; a week in Bled, Bohinji, Kranjska Gora, or Portoroz costs between £182–500 per person for travel and half-board accommodation. Or you can take two-centre holidays to Slovenia and either ancient Dubrovnik, Montenegro or the beautiful Adriatic Islands. The Lakes and Mountains Tour journeys through the Slovenian Alps and Ljubljana, visits nearby Italy and Austria, and ends with a week on the sun-drenched Adriatic coast; eight days, £450. The Grand Tour of Western Yugoslavia combines the Slovenian mountains with the coast and ancient cities of Split and Dubrovnik; fourteen days, £520.

Čedok, the official Czechoslovak tourist agency, runs many tours to Bohemia including the 'Bohemian Castles Tour' which traces the rich architectural history of the region; eight days, including travel and half-board accommodation, costs £300 per person, and the 'Bohemian Rhapsody' which journeys to the elegant spas of western Bohemia costs £300 for eight days.

Balkan Holidays' 'Discover Bulgaria Tour' takes fourteen days for £350 per person all-inclusive and their 'Best of Bulgaria Tour' is thirteen days for £400; these combining the sunny Black Sea coast with a week in Bulgaria's historic mountainous inland, spending two nights in Istanbul.

Other Eastern European countries also house some fascinating sights. Transylvania in Romania is a dramatic and atmospheric mountain region rich in folklore and mystery, home to Vlad 'the Impaler', inspiration for Bram Stoker's famous Count Dracula. Romanian Holidays do the Dracula Tour and Black Sea Coast, fifteen days on full board for £300. The historic Danube in Hungary flows past the graceful city of Budapest, a treasure trove of beautiful Gothic architecture and graceful cobbled streets. Serenissima's 'Spring on the Danube' is a seven-day tour on full-board for £900. Poland's historic city of Cracow has retained its medieval atmosphere and Warsaw has recreated its Gothic splendour after the ravages of the Second World War. Polorbis's 'Panorama of Poland' is a fourteen-day tour on half-board for £575. With the spectacular breaching of the Berlin Wall, Eastern Germany and particularly East Berlin has become a vibrant and exciting place to visit. Eastern Germany's pride lies in its great cultural centres at Leipzig and Dresden, the latter a splendid fairy-tale city rising above the Elbe. Berolina's 'Highlights Tour' takes eleven days, is full-board and costs £359. The rarely-visited, isolated country of Albania is an exotic mix of Greek, Roman and Turkish cultures and relics. Voyages Jules Verne's 'Classical Tour of Albania' is an eight-day trip on full-board for £279 per person (see Appendix II for details).

Venezuela

Venezuela has long been overshadowed by the marvels of Brazil and Peru as a destination for the adventurous traveller. But undeservedly so, for Venezuela offers a microcosm of all the exciting attractions of South America. Here the lofty Andes, lush rainforest, and blue Caribbean all meet, giving you an unparalleled variety of beautiful landscapes in one country. Venezuela is bisected by the mighty Orinoco river and is dotted with waterfalls, including the world's largest, which plummets over a half a mile from a jungle mountain described in Conan Doyle's isolated *Lost World*. Venezuela is also a country of fascinating people, from Indians living in houses raised on stilts, to the ancestors of Spanish colonialists, African slaves, and German immigrants, creating a singularly rich and colourful culture.

The capital, Caracas, lies in a long narrow valley ten miles from the Caribbean coast. It was founded by the Spanish, and has since become a bustling modern city controlling Venezuela's vast oil reserves. Pockets of the old town remain within this rapidly growing metropolis. It is also the home of numerous monuments honouring the 'Liberator' Simon Bolivar, who, in the early nineteenth century, lit the flame of revolution in South America against Spain which led to the eventual independence of an entire continent. When you climb the tree-covered Mount Avila which towers over the city, you can see an amazing panorama of modern Caracas on one side and the turquoise Caribbean on the other.

At 2,800 beautiful miles, Venezuela has the longest Caribbean coastline of any country, with palm beaches, spectacular coral reefs, and splendid, peaceful islands, many inhabited only by flamingos. One of the most enchanting islands is Margarita, where you will find unspoilt beaches and sleepy fishing villages, with jungle-clad mountains rising above. Facilities are excellent for all activities from scuba-diving to fishing, and yet the prices are considerably lower than some better-known Caribbean resorts.

The northwest combines many different landscapes and lifestyles, including the huge flat grasslands and swamps of the Llanos, where cowboys herd cattle and go to rodeos as if they were in Texas. Rising above the flat plains is the northern branch of the Andes, the massive snow-capped mountains of the Cordillera de la Merida, which dominate the beautiful colonial university town of Merida. An amazing cable-car ride (the world's longest and highest) takes you to over 15,000 feet where you're surrounded by incredible green and white peaks and the vast green expanse of the Llanos. Maracaibo, Venezuela's second city, is bordered by a huge lake of the same name and an oil-laden desert, bursting into life during La Chinita Festival in November when the city stays awake for days on end. To the north live the Goaro Indians, whose life has changed surprisingly little since Europeans first came here in 1499, and whose stilt houses above the Lake Maracaibo inspired the name 'Little Venice' – Venezuela.

The southern half of the country is composed largely of lush jungle, great rivers, and highlands. You can travel up the huge, slow-moving Orinoco river which is fed from the highlands in the west and flows right the way across the country, past the colonial and modern city of Ciudad Bolivar (formerly Angostura of the bitters fame), before ending in a huge delta in the east. To the south lie the wilds of the Guayana Highlands, covered with jungle, laden with gold, diamonds and oil, carved by rivers and waterfalls, and populated by nomadic Indians and fantastic animals. The two main bases for exploration are Ciudad Guayana where the Orinoco and Caroni rivers blend (also where the world's largest oil reserves may lie) and Canaima, which sits on a lagoon and is surrounded by rainforest and waterfalls. The breathtaking Angel Falls, which plunge over 3,000 feet off Auyan Tepuy before falling to earth as fine spray, were described by Sir Walter Raleigh as a 'mountain of crystal'. The most amazing feature of these highlands are enormous flat-topped mountains, flanked by mile-high sheer cliffs and clouds, called tepuyes, where Indians believed the gods lived. These isolated fantastic plateaux were shaped by ancient oceans and provided the inspiration for Conan Doyle's *Lost World* of primeval jungle and dinosaurs, something not difficult to believe in this otherworldly landscape.

How To Get There: Viasa is the national airline of Venezuela, and along with British Airways, it provides direct services between

London and Caracas, with a return flight costing in the region of £450. Many cruise lines stop along the beautiful Caribbean coastline or go up the Orinoco, including Ocean Cruise Lines. Internal travel by air on either of the two domestic airlines, Aeropostal or Avensa, is the best way to get around as the most expensive internal flight costs no more than about £15. There is only one train line, in the north, and bus travel is also quite limited, although roads between the cities are good. Accommodation is generally good, with excellent international hotels in Caracas (some say the lowest-priced city for visitors in the world) and smaller, cheaper hotels elsewhere. Independent travel in northern Venezuela is possible, but is obviously much more difficult in the dense southern jungles. Tourism is beginning to grow but is still far from reaching saturation point.

About thirty-five UK operators currently organise trips to Venezuela. Through Kuoni you can book the Ocean Cruise Lines' 'Grenadines and Orinoco River Cruise' which journeys to some of the most exclusive Caribbean islands as well as cruising up the Orinoco to Ciudad Guayana, with an excursion to Canaima, plus a free week in Barbados; a seven-day cruise with double berth, and seven days in Barbados, including all travel and accommodation for £1,200 per person. Venezuelan Tours are a small specialist company that will tailor-make a holiday for you, based on your wishes and wallet, and can vary trips from three days, including Caracas, Canaima and the Angel Falls for about £630, to a £2,000 extravaganza all over the country. Voyages Jules Verne's 'Two Great Rivers' is a fascinating river and sea journey up the Amazon and Orinoco; seventeen days, all-inclusive for £3,500. Silk Cut's 'Venezuela, Ecuador, and Peru' combines the jungles of Venezuela, colonial splendour of Ecuador, and magnificent Inca ruins of Peru; twenty-two days, in double rooms, including travel and half-board accommodation for £2,100 per person. Bales visits the modern cities of Caracas and Maracaibo, as well as Caribbean beaches and lush jungles; eighteen days, £1,300. Exodus has an excellent trip which includes a river expedition up the Orinoco delta to the base of Angel Falls; sixteen days, £1,400. Other experienced operators to Venezuela are Ilkeston, Journey Latin America, Explore and Twickers World (see Appendix II).

Indonesia

The Indonesian national motto, 'Bhineka Tunggal Ika', means

'Unity in Diversity' – a very apt statement for a country which comprises over 13,000 islands stretching between the Indian and Pacific Oceans. Inhabiting this varied archipelago is the world's fifth largest population; an amalgamation of over 300 ethnic groups with different languages, customs and religions. These islands have been controlled for a time by Hindu, Buddhist and Muslim invaders, as well as Dutch colonialists, who prospered from trading the island's great spice wealth. Although Indonesia's relics reflect this amazing diversity, its natural attractions vie with its historical remains, for the islands boast hundreds of volcanoes, rainforests, and some of the world's most beautiful beaches.

Java is a densely populated island of ancient culture and modern government. Java's cultural heart, Yogyakarta, is dominated by a lofty and active volcano. The city's centre is the ornate small walled city of the Sultan's Palace (*Kraton*). Yogyakarta is home to dramatic traditional Shadow Plays (*wayang*) which enact entire ancient legends accompanied by a unique Gamelan orchestra. Nearby is Prambanan, the largest Hindu temple complex in Java, where 244 temples to the Indian gods Shiva, Brahma and Vishnu were constructed over a thousand years ago. The lavishly carved spire of the tremendous Shiva Temple rises 150 feet over this beautifully restored relic. A mere twenty-five miles from Prambanan is the largest Buddhist sanctuary in the world, Borobudur, underlining the unparalleled diversity of religions and cultures which typify Indonesia. The massive 650-foot square base of this mighty pyramid rests on a small hill, above which is a mountain of stone rising in tiers, with hundreds of serene Buddhas and over three miles of amazing relief carvings showing life in Java over 1000 years ago. The capital, Jakarta, is a bustling, modern city, whose Old Quarter reflects the grandeur of Dutch colonialism, as well as other influences, seen in the enormous Istiqlal Mosque and ancient exhibits of the Central Museum. Sumatra is a huge island of spectacular volcanoes and unexplored rainforests, populated by many peoples still observing ancient traditional ways of life. The Karo Highlands is home to the fiercely independent Karo Batak people who have succeeded to a large degree in isolating themselves from the outside world and retaining their own language and unique raised 'horned roof' houses. Nearby is the enormous Lake Toba, a huge volcanic crater now filled with water. The Lake is surrounded by high mountains and rimmed by a precipitous crater ridge and beaches. It encircles the island of Samosir, which is the centre of the Toba

Batak culture, and is a relaxed and scenic island of rice paddies, fascinating Batak architecture, and haunting carved sarcophagi. Sumatra is home to numerous wildlife reserves, where you can see tigers, elephants, rhinos, and orang-utan, 'man of the forest', at the amazing Bukit Lawang Sanctuary.

The paradise island of Bali is known worldwide for its splendid beaches, dramatic volcanoes, friendly people, and its own special potpourri of Hindu culture. For years Westerners visiting Bali have stayed for ever to immerse themselves in its unforgettable atmosphere. Ubud is Bali's artistic capital which blends a mixture of Western expatriate art and local crafts. It is also home to some of Bali's most skilled dancers, who perform the thrilling Monkey Dance (*Kechak*) in rich costumes and carved masks. Nearby is the huge Goa Gajah (Elephant Cave) with its spectacular carved entrance. Well worth a visit is the huge barren outer crater of Mount Batur from which rises a stunning volcanic inner cone. Beach resorts dot the coast, especially in the south. These include Sanur Beach and Kuta, and the more relaxed resorts of the north and east, such as Candi Desa, whose beautiful white sandy beach lies in the shadow of palm trees beneath Bali's holy volcano, the soaring Gunung Agung. Far up on its lava-covered slopes lie the thirty temples of Besakih, Bali's 'Mother Temple'. Here, as at Bali's other 20,000 or so temples, colourful and joyous festivals often take place. Other places well worth a visit include the ancient walled village of Tenganan, home of Bali's original inhabitants (the *Bali Aga*); the amazing Water Palace of Tirtagangga; the black sandy beach and colourful coral reef of Anturan; the breathtaking Sea Temple of Tanah Lot, and the beautiful turtle island of Serangan. Bali is a truly magical 'Island of the Gods'.

Java, Sumatra and Bali are the most often visited of Indonesia's islands, but there are many other intriguing places to visit, including the unspoilt scenery of Lombok, claimed to be as Bali was twenty-five years ago. The Toraja of Sulawesi are a secluded people whose beautifully ornamented houses and spectacular cliff-face graves are amazing. Kalimantan on the jungle-clad island of Borneo is a region of great natural splendour and exotic animals. Irian Jaya is the Indonesian half of the remote island of New Guinea, much of it still unexplored and home to peoples largely unaware of the outside world. Other engaging islands include the tiny Komodo with its famous dragon and the spectacular volcanic island of Flores.

How To Get There: Over fifty operators offer tours to Indonesia, including Grass Roots Travel who specialise in tours to the most fascinating of Indonesia's islands. The 'Islands of Indonesia Tour' does just this by journeying to its largest island, Sumatra, its most populous island, Java, and its best-known tourist island, Bali; twenty-two days in a shared double, including travel and half-board accommodation for £1,650 per person. Kuoni offers a peaceful seven-day Bali beach holiday for £740 (meals not included). Society Expeditions, in association with Twickers World, offers the 'Project Secret Islands East of Bali II' cruise to Bali, Komodo, Flores and to the island of Biak off Irian Jaya; nineteen days on full board from £3,805. Bales Tours offer a nineteen-day tour through Sumatra, Java, and Bali, and on to the remote lands of the Toraja in Sulawesi for £1,750 including travel and half-board accommodation. Hayes & Jarvis's 'Indonesia Experience' also visits Sumatra, Java, and Bali, as well as Lombok; twenty days, £1,900. Other experienced operators to Indonesia are Abercrombie and Kent, China Travel Service, Explore, Silk Cut, Tradewinds and Travel 2.

The national airline is Garuda Indonesia, and the Dutch airline KLM also has regular flights to Indonesia. Many cruises berth in Indonesia, including Pearl Cruises. The internal air system is extensive, with Garuda offering a 'Visit Indonesia Pass' for between two and thirty-five cities. Railroads are only found on Sumatra, Madura, and most extensively Java, and there are buses between major cities. Accommodation ranges from grand international hotels to beach cottages and inexpensive small hotels. Independent travel is an option as there is a well worn tourist trail in Bali and much of Java, and prices are low once you get to Indonesia, but of course tours take away many of the problems that independent travellers experience.

The USSR

The USSR spreads out across vast steppes and towering mountains to encompass a unique kaleidoscope of lands and cultures, from the sophisticated Baltic Republics and deserts of central Asia to the frozen forests of Siberia. The amazing variety of landscapes and architecture is enough to attract anyone, but the greatest natural resource of the country is its people. An unparalleled diversity of peoples with different languages, religions and cultures populate this huge land. Russians make up half of the population, the rest comprising a blend of Lithuanians, Islamic Azerbaijanis, Georgians, Uzbeks, Eskimos and many more. For a long time these people have not been accessible to Westerners, but the thaw in East–West relations under Mr Gorbachev has led to a great increase in cultural exchanges and tourism.

Winston Churchill's view of Russia and the Russians as a 'riddle wrapped in a mystery inside an enigma' has long characterised the Western misapprehension of the Soviet people, but this is now being broken down through changes brought about by *glasnost*. A pioneer in this area is Goodwill Holidays with their 'Meet the Russians' programme. It was founded to promote international understanding across political boundaries and now offers many inexpensive and all-inclusive holidays throughout this giant country. These holidays allow you not only to see the sights, but also to 'meet the people', in their own homes or at work, be they university lecturers, factory workers, or doctors. This provides you with a fascinating insight into one of the most important and influential countries in the world. You will not find the people grey or reticent, but very friendly and eager to talk, to learn from you as you learn from them. Goodwill can arrange special interest tours for you to meet specific groups of people. Despite the name, you will meet not only Russians but many of the other colourful peoples found throughout this fascinating country.

The capital and heart of the country, Moscow is an exciting cosmopolitan city of museums and world-famous theatres, the starting point for Goodwill's 'Art and Architecture' Tour. Moscow is an intriguing mix of the old and new, soaring skyscrapers rubbing shoulders with exotic onion-domed churches. This is most evident at Moscow's best-known landmark, the Kremlin, whose thick red walls and large towers not only encompass the leadership of the modern USSR, but also beautiful fifteenth and sixteenth-century palaces, three extravagant cathedrals, and the golden-domed belfry built by Ivan the Great. Across the wide cobbled Red Square are the nine magnificent multi-coloured domes of St Basil's Cathedral, contrasting with the sombre red and black modern stone cube of Lenin's Mausoleum.

The tour's next stop is the elegant cultural city of Leningrad, built by the Westernised Tsar Peter the Great in the early eighteenth century, and the cradle of the 1917 October Revolution. Its many islands are linked by over 300 bridges, which, with its Italian-influenced Russian classical architecture, has earned it the name 'Venice of the North'. Its highlight is the amazing Hermitage Museum, set in the enormous yet graceful Winter Palace, rivalling the Louvre with an incredible collection of international art works from all eras. Interspersed with these impressive sights are down to earth encounters with local people. The tour is seven-days, all-inclusive at £532 per person.

The scenic Trans-Caucasian Republics of Armenia and Georgia can be experienced in Goodwill's 'Life in the USSR Tour'. Georgia's stunning capital, Tbilisi, is set amongst the Suran Mountains. The captivating Old Town is an island of ancient and medieval buildings within a sea of classical and Renaissance architecture. Yerevan, the Armenian capital, lies in a beautiful valley, from where you can see the twin peaks of Mount Ararat, where Noah's Ark is supposed to have come to rest. The city is almost 2,800 years old and has many beautiful historic buildings constructed of multicoloured volcanic rock. Intermixed with all this culture and history is the opportunity to discuss life in the modern day Soviet Union. This is a fourteen-day tour, all-inclusive, for £649 per person.

You can experience the vastness of Siberia's 'sleeping land' of taiga forest, lakes, and rivers in the 'Life in the USSR Siberian Tour' and meet its people. Travel from Moscow is on the famous Trans-Siberian Railway to Irkutsk, a traditional trade centre with China and Mongolia and a patchwork of European, Russian, and Mongolian buildings. Nearby is the dazzling Lake Baikal, the world's deepest, surrounded by seemingly endless forest. Sitting on the edge of an enormous forest, the town of Bratsk has grown around an enormous hydro-electric power station. This magnificent journey finishes back in Moscow; it is a fourteen-day tour, all-inclusive for £698 per person.

The USSR's truly exotic face is exposed in the 'Peace and Friendship Tour' to Central Asia. Setting off from Leningrad, the tour travels to Tashkent, the capital of Uzbekistan, which was destroyed by an earthquake in 1966 and is now completely rebuilt. Dushanbe, a modern garden city and the capital of Tadzhikistan, is towered over by the Hussar Mountains. Flanked by desert, and in complete contrast, is the ancient and fabled city of Samarkand. Once conquered by Alexander the Great and Genghis Khan, this magnificent place flourished in the fourteenth century under Tamerlane. It is undoubtedly an eastern Islamic city, punctuated by wonderful mosques, blue domes, and the strikingly coloured inlaid stone of the massive Ulugbeg Observatory. Samarkand remains one of the great historical cities of the world. The 'Peace and Friendship Tour' takes fifteen-days, is all-inclusive and costs £554 per person.

At least fifty-four companies operate more traditional tours, including the official agency Intourist, which offers extensive tours, such as the Black Sea, seven days at £500 per person for travel and half-board accommodation; the famous Trans-Siberian Express, fourteen days, £800, and historic cities in 'The Golden Ring of Ancient Russia', seven days, £500. Page & Moy, a specialist operator, offers 'Moscow Weekends' for as low as £289 per person for travel and half-board accommodation and its 'Grand Russian Tour' travels to the cultural centres of Moscow and Leningrad, the wilds of Siberia, and the independently-minded Baltic republics, seventeen days, £1,000. Voyages Jules Verne's 'Baltic Capitals' visits the sophisticated Baltic republics, seventeen days for £1,600 all-inclusive. Other experienced operators are Serenissima, Thomson, and Wexas (see Appendix II).

Flights are usually on Aeroflot to Moscow or Leningrad. The Soviet shipping line, CTC Lines, offers many inexpensive cruises. The USSR's railway network is extensive, and includes the exciting Trans-Siberian Railway through Siberia to Mongolia, China, and Japan (via a ferry). Intourist offers motoring holidays in European USSR and the Trans-Caucasus. Most tourist hotels are modern and isolated from the local people, but Trade Union Hotels (used by Goodwill Holidays) are also used by Soviets. Independent travel is rarely possible because accommodation must be arranged beforehand and only a few train lines are open to foreigners, but tours need not be expensive.

Bhutan

Sandwiched between the great cultural powers of Tibet and India, Bhutan has long isolated itself from the outside world and is even now only changing slowly. Buddhism (the Drukpa Kagupa sect) still infuses Bhutanese society and even gave rise to their name for Bhutan, *Druk Yul*, meaning Land of the Thunder Dragon. It has remained largely untouched by the 'progress' of its neighbours and, in many ways, retains an ancient way of life. Bhutan's spiritual home is Tibet, whence came its religion (Lama Buddhism) and language. It has avoided the corruption of an invading Chinese army (unlike Tibet) and a tourist army (unlike Nepal). The introduction of tourism in 1974 was one element in a slow and limited modernisation programme carried out by the King, the Precious Ruler of the Dragon People, Jigme Singye Wangchuk who said 'We want to move forward, but only when we are prepared. We have time to go slowly'. Bhutan – for long a secret and unvisited place – is thus today one of the most exclusive and fascinating countries in the world.

It is about the size of Switzerland, but has three distinct climates, with lush tropical foothills and jungles in the south, the frozen great Himalayas in the north, and, in the centre, temperate valleys where most of its 1.3 million people live. In these secret valleys, brilliant splashes of colour from rhododendrons contrast with the blue-green of pine and fir trees. The hills are dotted with a few thick-set lavishly carved and painted wooden houses, terraced paddy fields, fluttering Buddhist prayer flags, and impossibly placed temples. Most towns are in such valleys, and are dominated by massive whitewashed fortress-monasteries, called *dzongs*, where the prayers of Buddhist monks continue side by side with local government.

Thimphu, the capital, lies in the west at 8,000 feet, in a long narrow valley, surrounded dramatically on all sides by high pine-clad hills. It is more of a town than a capital city, its colourful traditional houses painted with dragons, tigers, and yaks. Thimphu is towered over by the massive turrets and beautifully gilded roofs of the enormous Tashichho Dzong, around which the town has flourished. In the evening the unearthly sound of hundreds of red-robed monks' prayers fills the air. The dzong bursts into life each year when the Thimphu Tsechu festival is held in its courtyards. Brightly dressed dancers recount ancient traditional Buddhist tales with leaps and bounds while cunning clowns vie to parody their every move. The Handicraft Emporium is the best place for you to purchase beautifully hand-woven and carved crafts, as they are not easily available elsewhere.

Paro Valley west of Thimphu is where all flights land. Also near here landed the bringer of Buddhism to Bhutan, the revered Guru Rimpoche, although legend recounts that he flew on a tiger's back. In honour of this, the Taktsang Monastery (Tiger's Nest) was built, lying precipitously on the edge of a sheer 3,000-foot cliff, its serene temples and reclining Buddhas accessible to you and pilgrims alike via a winding ascent by foot or horse. The Paro Valley is one of the most graceful in Bhutan, and was once the centre of trade with Tibet. Here you will also find the Paro watchtower where the National Museum of Bhutan is housed, and where once a year the biggest and most flamboyant festival in Bhutan, the historic Paro Tsechu, takes place.

The main land route from India enters the forbidden kingdom of Bhutan from the southwest at the small gateway town of Phuntsoling. Bhutanese stamps are very intricate and highly prized (one stamp was in fact a tiny record which played the National Anthem!) and since the Philatelic Office of Bhutan is centred here this is the best place to buy them. Phuntsoling also has Bhutan's one and only department store.

The ancient capital, Punakha, lies a short distance northeast of Thimphu. The huge Punakha Dzong, summer residence of the King, sprawls haphazardly for, in common with all dzongs, it was built without either plans or nails. Inside its numerous fascinating courtyards are many ancient temples, including the Machhin Lhakhang, which contains the remains of Ngawang Namgyal, a rebel Tibetan warrior-priest who forged Bhutan into one nation in the seventeenth century. Also in the Punakha Valley is the 10,218-foot high Dochu La Pass, where you can view a majestic panorama of the eastern Himalayas.

Tongsa, in central Bhutan, is the impressive ancestral home of the royal family. The Tongsa Dzong, which once controlled the flow of trade between east and west Bhutan, is perched precariously on a ridge overlooking an enormous river valley, which is carpeted with vines and flowers as far as the eye can see.

Bhutan boasts 320 varieties of exotic birds, while the tropical southern jungles contain tigers, elephants, golden langur monkeys, and buffalo. The lush central valleys support black bear, wild boar, and pheasants, and the frozen wastes of the northern Himalayas are home to the rare snow leopard, blue sheep, and yaks. If you decide to visit the Manas Game Sanctuary in the southeast you will need a special permit to see the best of Bhutan's tropical fauna.

Tourism in Bhutan is limited, both by the government and the lack of facilities and is mostly restricted to the west, where Thimphu, Paro, and Phuntsoling all contain modern hotels; guest houses can be used elsewhere. The centre and the east are slowly being opened up for trekking holidays. Independent travel is virtually impossible and is discouraged by the Bhutanese Tourist Corporation who levy a daily tourist tax of about £70 for those not in a group (unless you happen to be official guests of the royal family!). There is no railway network but fairly good paved roads serve many locations.

How To Get There: Among the few specialist tour operators going there, Bales Tours offer an excellent package taking in Bhutan, Sikkim, and India, including the major sites of Phuntsoling, Paro, Taktsang, and Thimphu. The trip takes fifteen days, using a shared double room and travel and half-board accommodation are included in the price of about £2,000 per person. Bhutan Travel, an official agency, operates many tours, including an eight-day trip taking in many of the amazing highlights of Bhutan for between £885 and £1,330 depending on the season, prices from India, Thailand, or Nepal. Exodus offers a fascinating eighteen-day trip combining visits to dzongs in the Paro Valley with nine days spent trekking along the mountainous Tibetan border for £2,200; and a package consisting of a nature trek in the spring, north of the rarely visited central Bumthang Valley, led by animal and botanical specialists; twenty-three days in all, seven of which are spent trekking, £2,790. Thomas Cook offer a package taking in the wonders of Nepal, Tibet, India, and China as well as Bhutan in twenty-six days, £2,995. Abercrombie and Kent, Serenissima, and Wexas also provide tours to Bhutan.

Both British Airways and Air India fly to Calcutta, and from there the national airline, Druk Air, flies on to Paro. You can enter Bhutan by road from India at Phuntsoling.

India

India has a history which stretches back over 5,000 years. Not for nothing was it known as the 'Jewel in the Crown' of the British Empire, for India boasts an extraordinary richness of culture, scenery and resources unrivalled anywhere else in the world. Many aspects of that richness, and the special relationship which India enjoyed with Britain, still remain today. But when you first arrive, be prepared to face an intensity of contrasts which is quite unnerving to start with: ugliness vies with beauty, repression with privilege, materialism with spirituality. Neither films nor brochures prepare you fully for the shock of India's enormous diversity of customs, creeds and caste. After a while though, chances are that you'll start to fall under its magic spell. Look for the beauty of India and you'll find it – plenty of it – from dramatic Himalayan peaks to dusty Rajasthani deserts;

from gaudy flower garlands to pungent fragrant incense; Moghul temples to Empire monuments. And on a personal level, vignettes of India's romance glimpsed on your travels will remain forged in your mind as lifelong memories. As Rudyard Kipling remarked, 'Some people say that there is no romance in India. Those people are wrong. Our lives hold quite as much romance as is good for us. Sometimes more.'

As the usual airport for arriving visitors, Delhi is your obvious starting point. Combined with nearby Agra and Jaipur, Delhi forms a corner of the so-called 'Golden Triangle' which contains some of India's most famous sights. Delhi itself is but one of India's many mind-warping contrasts. The country's capital, New Delhi, displays a civilised array of government buildings, wide avenues and cool, manicured parks. By contrast, Old Delhi's turmoil of narrow streets, with its thronging crowds of human and vehicular traffic, seems like a different planet. And yet Old Delhi perhaps captures the spirit of the 'real' India far better than its genteel, cleaner, neighbouring district. For while you are likely to stay in one of the hotels of New Delhi, the old city contains many places of interest to lure you in and enchant you. Places such as the Red Fort – the ultimate symbol of Moghul power and elegance. Outside stand impassive red sandstone walls: inside, cool marble halls and exquisite gardens. Don't miss the *son et lumière* held here every evening. Also not to be missed is the Jami Masjid or 'great mosque' – India's largest. Its vast but serene courtyard contrasts with the chaotic cacophany of Chandi Chowk, bustling marketplace of the old city.

The architect of New Delhi, Sir Edwin Lutyens, described his work as 'Western architecture with an Oriental Motif'. The buildings certainly bear all the hallmarks of British Empire grandeur. Best examples are the ceremonial Parliament Buildings, Viceroy's House and the National Museum of Art and Sculpture. A note of caution, however: exploring Delhi thoroughly is a gargantuan task. Especially if it's your first visit, keep moderation in mind, and save some of the sights until your next visit: the remainder of India's Golden Triangle has much else to offer you.

Around 120 miles southeast of Delhi lies Agra, home of the most beautiful building in India – many would say the world – the Taj Mahal. It epitomises the 'Jewel in the Crown', standing as a serene and eloquent seventeenth-century testimony to the power of love. The story is told that while the then Emperor, Arjuman Banu, was away fighting a war, his wife died suddenly. On hearing the news the Emperor became stricken with grief and vowed to build her a memorial more beautiful than anything the world had ever seen. It took an army of workers and nearly eighteen years to achieve what many would regard as the epitome of Indian architectural perfection. When the Emperor himself died, his son ordered a new tomb to be built beside the old one, but this time in darker marble. Thus was the immortality of the Emperor and his loved one assured. In sunshine, the Taj Mahal is exquisite: by moonlight or the setting sun, it is awe-inspiring. Only one word of warning however: trying to avoid the pushy rickshaw drivers and guides who continually tout for your custom can be more than a little irksome: patience is a necessity as well as a virtue.

To the east of Agra and at the very heart of Rajasthan lies the famous 'pink city' of Jaipur. This region is the 'country of Kings': land of legends, music and culture. Jaipur's colour and vividness is reflected in its people's costumes – the men often wear pink or yellow turbans: the women are frequently covered in traditional jewellery literally from head to toe. Seen in the reflected light of dusk or dawn, the rose-pink stones of Jaipur's walls have an almost ethereal quality. Its wide streets set it apart from those of most historical cities in India. Not to be missed are the City Palace (a mixture of Mogul and Rajasthan architectural styles), the Palace of the Winds (where harems would watch the world from a cleverly designed façade while remaining invisible themselves), and the Mantar Observatory (complete with astronomical instruments).

Seven miles north of Jaipur is Amber, once the capital of Rajasthan. Amber boasts a complex of fortresses, palaces, temples and pavilions all in a striking setting above a lake. As an alternative to driving there you could try taking one of the elephant rides.

Accommodation: As far as accommodation is concerned, there's a very wide choice in most centres, from a basic double room for under £5 per night, to international-style hotels with air-conditioning and swimming pools at £30 plus. Some of these hotels are former Maharajan palaces and exude an opulent (though sometimes rather faded) historic grandeur. Food is, surprisingly, not of a very high standard in India. The old adage that the best curries in the world are found in Bradford *is* true! Stick to vegetarian dishes on your travels if you want to avoid the worst excesses of 'Delhi belly', and only drink bottled water bought from a reputable source.

How To Get There: If you intend to spend a lot of time and little money in India then going independently is likely to be your preferred option. However, inclusive tours take a lot of the hassle out of travelling, particularly the time spent queuing for tickets, and the nuisance of avoiding advances from unsolicited touts. Amongst the large number of tour operators offering trips to India, we would recommend Pleasureseekers, who provide chauffeur-driven cars for travel within the country. Their 'Unknown Rajasthan' tour of fifteen days duration can be combined with Nepal, Goa or selected itineraries and costs £620, land travel only. Their fourteen-day 'Lost Cities of Rajasthan' tour for around the same price takes in no fewer than eight cities within the region. Pleasureseekers offer the added attraction of providing a service for the independent traveller to India, offering permutations and combinations of travel options within the country. You choose where and when you want to go and they organise the programme: ask for details of their Indian Gateway service. Other operators to consider are Cox & Kings, Hayes & Jarvis and Bales Tours, all of whom offer both specific Rajasthan trips and more general tours of India.

The low cost of living in India means that on a tight budget both you and your rupees can go far. A number of airlines fly to India. Principal carriers are Air India and British Airways. Travelling independently does necessitate a certain attitude of mind, however. Be prepared to bargain before taking up one of the many offers of transport with which you will be inundated. Cheap rickshaws (cycle and auto) abound in the major towns and cities, alongside old-fashioned, metered taxis. There are no self-drive car hire facilities in India but hiring a chauffeur-driven car is often a pleasure, and an inexpensive one at that. Buses tend to be overcrowded and pretty uncomfortable. Rail travel – one of the best legacies of the British Empire – is very much a part of experiencing the country. Don't be in a hurry though, and for long-distance travel take the 'express' or 'superfast express' trains. You can choose from first-class air-conditioned luxury through a spectrum of (dis)comfort to second-class unreserved benches and worse. It's worth paying a local travel agent to obtain your tickets since queueing can often take hours. Fares range from £1–10 per 100 miles. A good investment is the Indiarail pass which gives you unlimited rail travel options of between seven and ninety days. Not much cheaper than buying tickets, but you save in queuing time. Domestic air travel is by Air India but it's often difficult to arrange tickets.

Peru

Today the descendants of the Incas live in crude shanty towns encircling Spanish-built cities, but their empire once rivalled even that of Rome. Peru was the cradle of the once great Inca civilisation (Empire of the sun-god), whose spark was astonishingly snuffed out by only a few hundred Spanish adventurers in the sixteenth century. The Incas and their predecessors left behind fantastic reminders of their achievements, scattered throughout the barren deserts of the west, towering mountains of the centre, and lush Amazonian jungles of the east. Massive fortresses and intricately carved temples dot the landscape, reminding one that it remains the home of this mysterious people, whose identity, despite defeat many centuries ago, still seems to dominate Peru, just as the amazing hidden mountain-top of Machu Picchu dominates its magnificent landscape. This great legacy, combined with its natural diverse beauty, makes Peru the most enchanting country in South America.

The capital, Lima, is a Spanish city founded by the conquistador Francisco Pizarro in a river valley in western Peru. The Spanish also left their legacy, from bullfights to ornate Baroque churches: in the cathedral you can still see Pizarro's mummified body. Among Lima's other attractions are its splendid museums, chronicling the wonders of Peru's ancient civilisations. Lima is a bustling modern city and the hub of modern Peru, but to experience the lands of the Incas you must move inland to the mountains.

The coastal deserts contain many of Peru's ancient mysteries, including the baffling Nasca lines, in the south. These are enormous designs etched on the desert floor to create huge pictures of a monkey, condor, spider, and others. They can only be viewed from the air so their purpose is still unknown (some say it was to contact ancient astronauts!), though you can fly over them to view the splendid artistry and organisation needed to create these enigmatic images. Arequipa is dramatically situated on a high desert plateau, dominated by the beautiful snow-capped volcano, El Misti, from which clouds of sulphur arise ominously. It is a beautiful colonial city built entirely of shining white volcanic stone; its cobbled streets, white buildings, and fantastic Baroque cathedral remind you more of Andalusia than South America. To the north lies the ancient clay city of Chan-Chan, whose beautifully carved walls, though falling to ruin now, once encompassed the capital of the Chimu culture and the largest mud-brick city in the world.

An exciting introduction to the soaring Andes is El Tren de la Sierra, a fascinating and evocative train journey from the desert coast of Lima through breathtaking valleys to the mountains and the very heart of the Inca lands. At 11,500 feet lies the centre of the Inca world, the ancient capital and holy city of Cuzco, from where the Incas ruled an empire that stretched through a large portion of western South America. Cuzco is still an Inca city underneath (literally), as Spanish buildings were erected directly on top of the original massive foundations. The mountain slopes around Cuzco are filled with llamas and alpacas wandering through the ruins of Inca shrines. One mile above the city rests the imposing Sacsahuaman Fortress, built with megalithic carved boulders fitted together expertly without mortar. Once a year the fortress explodes with life and colour as the Quechua Indians (the Incas) turn back the clock four centuries in the Inti Raymi festival, with hundreds of Inca warriors dressing in rich, intricate costumes to pay homage to their sun-god.

Cuzco is the gateway to the hidden wonders of Machu Picchu, forgotten even by the Incas until rediscovered by the American explorer Hiram Bingham in 1911. Perched on top of the Andes, this amazing city – described as 'a landscape built by Titans in a fit of sheer megalomania' – must be seen to be believed. Flanked by jungle-clad peaks, the ruins of carved temples and houses perch up in the clouds exuding an otherworldly quality. The Chilean poet Pablo Neruda called Machu Picchu 'a glacier for the multitudes, breakwater in the Andes'. It is doubtless one of the world's wonders and will be a highlight of your trip to Peru.

To the south lies Lake Titicaca, one of the highest lakes in the world at 12,000 feet, where the bizarre Uro Indians make their homes on floating reed islands (modernisation for them has meant a floating school house and football pitch!). On the lake's shore lies Puno, the centre of colourful Peruvian folklore, where you can buy beautiful alpaca textiles.

In complete contrast to the mountain culture of western Peru, the east is covered with the vast jungles of the Amazon River

Basin. Iquitos, the base for Amazon river trips, is surrounded by lush tropical rain forest filled with amazing wildlife, including pumas, anacondas, and 4,000 varieties of birds. From here you can take a memorable river trip through the dense emerald-green jungle to visit primitive Indian villages, and absorb the spirit of the Amazonian forest.

How To Get There: Many airlines connect London with Lima, including Viasa, Varig, Air France, Lufthansa and KLM, with an apex return ticket costing about £750. International cruises stop at Callao (the port for Lima), such as Paquet Cruises, who offer an eighteen-day Chile-Ecuador-Peru cruise for about £3,000 per person including flights. Aeroperu and Faucett Airlines provide a good internal service and offer air passes for unlimited travel. Train journeys in Peru take you through some spectacular scenery, especially the line from Lima to Huancayo and from Arequipa to Puno, with a steamer connection across Lake Titicaca to Bolivia. Bus travel is cheap and the routes extensive. Accommodation can be cheap but varies wildly, from international-standard hotels in Lima to basic hotels in other areas, where government-run hotel *Turistas* or *pensiones* are often the best value. Independent travel is becoming more common as the tourist industry expands, but most people still go with tours, and at least forty-five UK operators journey to Peru.

Journey Latin America, a small personal company, offers the 'Pelicanito', a fifteen-day journey to Lima, El Tren de la Sierra, Arequipa, Lake Titicaca, Cuzco, and Machu Picchu for £1,300 per person for travel and accommodation. Explorandes are a Peru-based company offering a wide variety of tours in Peru, including a trek along the Inca Trail and the 'Andes and Desert Expedition' which visits the Inca highlands, spectacular sand dunes, and Chan-Chan, eleven days, including land travel only and half-board accommodation, for approximately £750. Both Hayes & Jarvis's 'Peru Highlights', eighteen days land travel and half-board accommodation for £1,600, and Thomas Cook's 'Lost World of the Incas', nineteen days, land travel and half-board accommodation for £1,950, explore the best of Peru, including Machu Picchu, the Nasca lines, and Lake Titicaca. Twickers World offers a trip contrasting the sights of the Andes with the lush Amazonian jungle, seventeen days land travel and half-board accommodation for £1,721. Voyages Jules Verne's Grand Tour of South America visits Ecuador, Bolivia, Argentina and Brazil, as well as Peru in a twenty-four-day trip for £2,400. Other experienced operators are Bales Tours, Exodus, Serenissima, Speedbird, and Wexas (see Appendix II).

Arctic Lands

Greenland and Iceland: two Arctic lands conjuring up images of snowy wilderness and extreme cold. Preconceptions can often deceive however. Iceland only just clips the Arctic Circle at its northernmost point, and much of Greenland lies south of it. Today you don't have to stay in an igloo, nor travel by husky-drawn sledge, nor even live on a diet of whalemeat. Eric the Red heroics can be dismissed when considering these modern-day countries: discomfort is not a necessity for those travelling here. Hotels have replaced igloos; vehicles and snow-mobiles are widespread, and food – especially seafood – is varied and often delicious. The two things that have changed very little over the ages are those which will always attract the visitor: the wildlife and the landscapes. If you're an adventurous spirit who longs for a chance to leave the crowds and noise behind, a tour to Iceland and Greenland offers the opportunity to experience a fresh, invigorating and unconventional holiday, with spectacular, unspoilt scenery, undisturbed wildlife and plenty of room to breathe the crystal-clear Arctic air.

Greenland is the biggest island in the world. Much of it is covered by ice – up to two miles thick in places. This vast white icecap slopes down to the coast where it lurches forward, 'calving' off to form spectacular shoals of icebergs. As they say in Greenland 'At rejse er at leve' – 'To travel is to live' – and in the Arctic, travelling overland often means travelling over snow. The few roads that do exist are confined to the coastal towns, and of course there are no railways. So one of the necessities (and also one of the highlights) of a Greenland trip is the experience of dog-sledding. What could beat this for a sense of freedom in the fresh Arctic summer air: sliding along over a giant snowy playground with the warm sun shining down at midday (or at midnight) from a cloudless blue sky?

One of Greenland's paradoxes is the presence of some fifty or so natural warm springs. These provide pool-sized baths in which you can laze with family and friends, while contemplating icebergs drifting slowly by in nearby fjords. So don't forget to wear your swimming trunks under your down jacket! If you visit during the autumn or winter months, one of the highlights is the unforgettable sight of the northern lights, banding and veiling eerily across the night sky. The other main highlight of a tour to Greenland is of course the flora and fauna. Reindeer are plentiful, arctic hare and fox are ubiquitous, and bird life is seasonally abundant. The determined can even catch a glimpse of polar bears and the rare musk oxen.

Iceland has been dubbed the land of ice and fire: the paradox of glaciers and icebergs existing alongside volcanoes, hot thermal springs and geysers, is even more pronounced here than in Greenland. Icelanders are well aware of this resource: the country's power is all derived from geothermal energy. Well worth visiting is the Great Geyser in Haukadalur which periodically ejects a dramatic waterspout eighty metres high. And there are more hot springs in Iceland than any other country in the world. With its abundance of rivers, waterfalls, lakes, glaciers and icecaps, Iceland's stunning natural scenic beauty and remoteness offer visitors the prospect of a unique and unforgettable holiday. Try to make time to see the wildlife, particularly the birds. Ornithologists will find Iceland a delight: Some seventy-two species nest regularly and over 240 different visiting species have been recorded. Geologists too, will love this young country and the fascination of watching solid rock actually being formed from molten larva. This is a place where one can actually see, smell, taste, touch and hear the power of nature.

Even without the problems of Greenland's location, a country thirteen times the size of the British Isles, yet with a population of only 53,000, can't be expected to boast a sophisticated tourist industry. Nevertheless, tourism has developed to the extent of there being a fairly wide range of hotel-based holidays, particularly in the southern tip of the island. Some operators offer tours to the east and west coasts as well. But true adventure-seekers will be more interested in the range of 'explorer'-type holidays available which are basically as hard as you want them to be. However, if you're not prepared to 'rough it', it's best to avoid these. Such trips vary from tent-based hikes where you carry all supplies and equipment, to exclusive husky sledge tours, to canoe expeditions of twenty days or more where 'participants must be in excellent physical condition'.

Although the choice of comfortable hotels is greater in Iceland than in Greenland there are no five-star international hotels. Even those deemed to be Iceland's best are fairly basic by European standards. Idiosyncrasies – such as only having sulphur water in which to bathe – combined with the very limited variety of shops, make Iceland (as Greenland) a destination for those looking for the 'great outdoors' experience rather than a luxury holiday. Many of the organised holidays are of a specialised nature, for example walking tours, horse treks, boat cruises or flights. You can choose from a range of classical saga, bird-watching, natural history or photographic adventures. Again, these can be as challenging as you want to make them: even the most experienced hiker can find much that is new, unexpected and exhilarating.

How To Get There: Twickers World is recommended for its wide choice of tours to both countries. With seven Iceland options and three Greenland tours, you can select from a range of either multi-activity explorer, horse-trekking or dog-sledding trips. Prices range from £676 for a guest house-based eight-day trip to southern Iceland, to £2,385 for a twelve-day dog-sledding trip to Greenland. For connoisseur walkers, Dick Phillips' trips to Iceland are good value. Erskine Expeditions offer six expeditionary type trips to Greenland. Other specialists are Arctic Experience (see Appendix II for details).

Although Greenland has scope for the independent traveller, Iceland is considerably more 'user-friendly'. Remember that both countries are very expensive by UK standards and inclusive tours will generally offer far more competitive prices than those which the independent traveller can obtain. Icelandair operate flights to both Greenland and Iceland and Scandinavian Airline System (SAS) fly to Greenland. If you have only a short time in Iceland fly-and-drive holidays are an ideal way to see the country: all but the interior highland tracks are passable with a normal saloon. Iceland bus passes offer unlimited travel within their duration – an ideal economical way of getting about. 'Fly as you please' and 'air rover' air tickets allow you to travel economically on domestic Iceland flights.

Although Greenland has a score or so of basic hotels which cater for tourists, if you're going independently we advise you strongly to book your accommodation before flying. Contact Tusarliivik, the Greenland Homerule Authorities – Information and Tourism (see Appendix I for details).

A full range of overnight accommodation is available in Iceland, from simple campsites and youth hostels, to farmhouses, and, at the top end of the scale, first-class hotels (though basic by five-star standards). Again, if you are going on your own it's important to book your flight and accommodation ahead, since demand tends to outstrip supply. The experienced hiker in southern Greenland can stay in hostels, or in mountain huts which generally lie close to local farmhouses. These huts cost around Dkr (Danish Krona) 50 per night and are open mid-June to early September. You can also hire a dog team plus driver during the season, February to May. One company, DVL Travel (Danish Youth Hostel Travel Bureau), will give advice and make preliminary arrangements for you (see Appendix II).

For further detailed information consult the tourist boards: the Danish Tourist Board and the Iceland Tourist Information Bureau (see Appendix I for details).

Tibet

Tibet is vast and mountainous, a misty, mysterious and in many ways misunderstood country. Trying to get to grips with the scale of Tibetan geography is like handling an articulated truck after being used to a mini: its sheer size – some seven times that of France – defeats the imagination. Lying at an average altitude of 16,000 feet, it's the highest country on earth, aptly dubbed the 'Roof of the World', isolated as it is from the rest of humanity by gargantuan mountain ranges: the Himalayas to the south, the Kunlan to the north.

Strictly speaking, Tibet comprises two regions, the Tibetan Autonomous Region (TAR), twice the size of France, which forms part of the much larger historical, ethnic Tibet. After occupation by the People's Republic of China in 1951 Tibet was allowed to run its internal affairs by the Chinese, although major differences in language, culture and tradition were continual points of friction between the two countries. Not until the Cultural Revolution in 1976 could the 'Forbidden Land' start to return slowly to its former ways, and in 1979 the door opened a crack to allow Western visitors their first glimpse of Lhasa, fabled city and residence of the Dalai Lama.

Tibet's very remoteness has always attracted restless travellers in search of adventure. If you fall into this category, a trip here would have been virtually unthinkable only ten years ago. But by capitalising on Tibet's fascination to the outside world, the Chinese Government has boosted tourism slowly but surely to the extent that several thousand Westerners took advantage of visiting the country last year. If you value isolation, mountain wilderness, a certain amount of hardship, and a sprinkling of Buddhist tradition, then Tibet is the place for you. Perhaps its fascination will eventually become tarnished by tourist developments. Even if it's not destined to become a mainstream holiday destination, and despite its inbuilt resistance to change, Tibet *is* changing inexorably: the sooner you experience its mystery and intrigue, the closer to the 'real' Tibet you will have come.

On the itinerary of virtually all travellers here is its capital, Lhasa, which, in an almost medieval atmosphere, boasts a plethora of spectacular monasteries and palaces set against a backdrop of stark and treeless mountains. Most notable of its buildings is the magnificent Potala Palace, former residence of the Dalai Llama, which many consider to be one of the most beautiful buildings in the world. You will more probably be struck by its aura of authority however, with its five gilded pavilions standing tall and imposing (and somewhat forbidding) on their dominating hilltop setting. Within, the thousand darkened halls containing altars, statues and frescoes lit by flickering and acrid lamps, leave you with a mysterious and lasting impression. Tibet's most revered temple is Jokhang Monastery, home to large numbers of devout Buddhist pilgrims, dressed humbly in their saffron robes. Drepung Monastery (another of Lhasa's many) is vast – reputedly the largest monastery in the world – and definitely worth seeing. The Norbulingka Jewel Park, former summer palace of the Dalai Llama, and the Sera Monastery, should not be missed. One word of warning however: especially if you have arrived by air, take time to acclimatise to Lhasa's high and rarefied atmosphere, which at 13,000 feet can leave you breathless to start with. Your biggest problem in Tibet is likely to be acclimatising to the elevation; altitude sickness can develop slowly and complete adaptation can take several weeks.

Other cities which you may wish to visit are Gyantse, manageably small and largely unchanged, which contains the spectacular white and gold Kumbum Monastery; and Shigatse which boasts the fifteenth-century Tashilunpo Monastery, once the seat of the Panchen Llamas and ranked amongst the most important of Tibet's monasteries.

Apart from its historical and religious interest, the quality which draws visitors to Tibet is its often windswept but always dramatic scenery. You will inevitably find travelling within the country difficult: four-wheel drive capability is essential. Above all, Tibet is a destination suited for those happy to 'rough it', since luxury will definitely not be a feature of your holiday: Lhasa, Shigatse and Tsetang are the only places in which there is anything resembling Western-style accommodation. Independent travel within Tibet is possible, but only recommended for seasoned travellers. Public transport is very limited, and such bus services as do exist, while cheap, are uncomfortable, unreliable and slow. You can however hire four-wheel-drive vehicles, with driver, in Lhasa. Tibetan or Chinese-style guest houses will charge you less than £1 for a bed; further afield, truckstops cater for the independent traveller.

While not permitted officially, trekking is still possible in the country and there are a number of favourite places for those considering an energetic hiking holiday amidst the yaks and nomads. Mount Kailash in the south-west corner of Tibet is regarded by Buddhists as the 'navel of the universe' thus arguably qualifying as the ultimate destination if you're into the gentle art of navel gazing. Circuiting the mountain is an old Buddhist tradition – pious monks will perform this exercise twenty-one times in their lifetime – and demands a certain fitness in tackling an 18,000-foot pass. If you're going to do some trekking don't be fooled into thinking that Tibet's climate is always cold; while nights can be chilly, during the day it's often quite hot, and there is very little rain for most of the year.

If you can make your trip coincide with one of the many religious festivals which occur throughout the year, you will be assured of an unforgettable experience. The most important of these are the Monlam, or Prayer festival, and the Sakadawa festival. Because of the fluctuating Tibetan lunar calendar, the dates of these events change from year to year.

How To Get There: For the independent traveller, flying into the country via Hong Kong or Chendu (in China) is easy but expensive. Given all the constraints of independent travel within Tibet; however, organised trips have much to commend them. From among the limited number of tour operators offering trips to the country, we would recommend Voyages Jules Verne, whose twenty-six-day 'Mountain Peoples of the Himalayas and the Tibetan Plateau' offers an extremely comprehensive itinerary which includes Lhasa, Gyantse and Central Tibet (along with much else) for £2,995. Their £1,395 'Journey to Lhasa' comprises a seventeen-day package, of which half the time is spent in Tibet.

Both trips are fully inclusive of airfare, full-board and lodging. Exodus provide a twenty-seven day strenuous walking tour to Kailish and Manasrowar for £2,390 and a thirty-one-day trekking and exploration tour of the forests of south-eastern Tibet for £2,590, each including flight and food. Other names to consider include Sherpa Expeditions, Bales Tours and Abercrombie and Kent (see Appendix II for details).

For more information about the country in general contact the Office of Tibet (see Appendix I for details).

Morocco

Morocco is the closest country to Britain that can be regarded as truly exotic. Its historic trading importance as the merchant crossroads for Africa, Arabia and Europe still lingers today in an extraordinary and stimulating array of cultural and artistic contrasts.

Of all Moroccan cities, Marrakesh stimulates the senses like no other. Once the capital of an empire which stretched from Toledo to Senegal, its gardens are still supplied with water from eleventh-century underground channels. Entering Marrakesh has been described as switching from a black-and-white television to a full technicolour movie. The vivid colours of this dusty, pinky-red city, with its jewel-like Moorish palaces and temples set against a backdrop of palm trees and azure skies, leaves a lasting impression. It's difficult not to be overwhelmed by all that's going on around, as you witness a kaleidoscope of humanity in its various forms and guises: story-tellers, snake-charmers and belly-dancers vie for your attention alongside fortune-tellers, faith-healers and street-corner dentists.

The main hives of activity are centred on the rather inappropriately named *Djemaâ el-Fna* or Assembly of the Dead, and the medina, with its myriad of souks or markets. Edith Wharton's *In Morocco* – written in 1920 – still rings true today: '. . . from all these hundreds of unknown and unknowable people, bound together by secret affinities, or intriguing against each other with secret hate, there emanated an atmosphere of mystery and menace more stifling than the smell of camels and spices and black bodies and smoking fry which hangs like a fog under the close roofing of the souks.' Atmosphere apart however, the raw humanity of the place is definitely not for the faint-hearted: if the sight of drug peddlers, lepers, and young children with outstretched hands upsets you, then avoid it. But if you want to experience the look, feel and smell of a real Arabian city, you won't be disappointed by Marrakesh.

When you decide to get away from the hustle and bustle of the souks, and the constant demands on your attention and wallet, then go (if possible at sunset) for a walk in the Menara Gardens. The mélange of palaces such as the Bahia or the el-Badi, as well as the famous Saadien Tombs, all testify to the affluence and opulence of successive Moroccan dynasties. Superb artistic detail can be admired in the splendid Berber carpets, Essaouriran pottery and Saadien woodcarving in the Museum of Moroccan Art, which is housed within the Dar Si Said Palace. If experiencing palatial (literally) surroundings is a priority, then book in at the Hotel La Mamounia, former haunt of Winston Churchill. La Mamounia, which some regard as the finest hotel in the world, combines exquisite colonial surroundings with excellent leisure facilities. In addition to its swimming pool and tennis courts, the hotel can make arrangements for you to go horse-riding or even skiing.

Sadly, Marrakesh is becoming somewhat over-commercialised and despite the frequent cries of 'hashish, hashish' it's not the refuge of dreamers and drop-outs that it used to be. Westernisation is starting to make an impact, and jeans and T-shirts can be seen replacing traditional veils and *djellabas*. Acquiring a reliable and reasonably priced guide (don't pay more than 50 dirham for a day) is sometimes a good way of seeing the more authentic parts of the city. Haggling is a way of life in Morocco and if you don't want to be ripped off in a major way, be prepared to learn and practice the art, even when you see *prix fixe* signs.

Edith Wharton wrote: 'The souks of Marrakesh seem, more than any others, the central organ of a native life that extends far beyond the city walls into secret clefts of the mountains and far-off oases where plots are hatched . . .' Those secret clefts beyond the towering red minaret of Koutoubia lie within the atmospheric – almost stage-set – snow-capped mountains of the High Atlas. These rise majestically out of the dry Saharan plain, their coolness and airiness coming as something of a release after the dust and claustrophobia of the city. Sharing a taxi is a good – though less comfortable than it sounds – way of reaching the Atlas, or if you're on a tighter budget there are buses which leave from Marrakesh. In both cases, be prepared to share with improbable numbers of passengers, animal as well as human.

At 13,833 feet, Mount Toubkal is the highest mountain in northern Africa and the showpiece of the Atlas, although if you're reasonably fit and prepared to make the non-technical two-day ascent, it's quite possible to climb it yourself. If skiing is your priority, Morocco's most famous resort is on the slopes of Mount Oukaimeden. Also well worth visiting are the Cascades of Setti-Fatma in the Ourika Valley, or the tiny mountain villages of Imlil, Toufliht or Taddert.

Once your stomach has settled itself to Moroccan cuisine – typically a rich and often spicy couscous with mint tea as an accompaniment – you will probably enjoy the food, although mains water (which is heavily chlorinated) can cause stomach upsets and is not recommended. Pre-departure you should obtain cholera and typhoid inoculations. Avoid swimming and paddling in fresh water, since bilharzia is present. Medical advice is available in all main centres, but rural health care can be rudimentary.

How To Get There: Travelling independently to Morocco is not necessarily cheaper than taking an organised tour, although the flexibility it affords is sometimes an advantage if you're the sort who likes to travel on as the mood takes you. Royal Air Maroc operates flights to a number of Moroccan cities, including Marrakesh: the airport is only four miles from the city. The railway south from Tangier terminates at Marrakesh, and there is a good (on the whole) road network as well. There is quite a wide choice of hotels in most sizeable centres and self-catering accommodation is available in Marrakesh as well. If you prefer camping, there are also established campsites with good facilities in many parts of the country.

Of the tour operators travelling to Morocco, amongst the best is the specialist company Moroccan Sun. Other operators which include Morocco among their destination portfolio include Kuoni and Cox & Kings. For Atlas-lovers, Twickers World, Sherpa Expeditions and Exodus Expeditions offer a variety of inexpensively priced walking trips which demand varying degrees of fitness.

For further advice contact the Moroccan National Tourist Office (see Appendix I for details).

Kashmir

Think of an exotic holiday location and, for many people, Kashmir will spring to mind. Its beautiful lakes, set against a dramatic backdrop of tree- and snow-covered mountains, provide an almost theatrical setting, while its clear blue skies and ethereal air refresh your body and stimulate your senses. Combine all this with a slice of history – a stay in one of the colonial-style houseboats for which Kashmir is famous – and you have the perfect recipe for a relaxing but invigorating holiday.

Although Kashmir is actually a state within northern India, its Himalayan altitudes and forested landscapes make it a far cry, both scenically and geographically, from the dry and dusty plains often brought to mind in images of India. It is this unique quality which gave rise to Kashmir's famous legacy of houseboat holidays. During the days of the Raj, when hard-pressed builders of the British Empire asked the maharajas of Kashmir permission to build houses as places of retreat from the oppressive plains summers, they were refused. Undaunted and ever-resourceful, the British officers took to the lakes instead. They ordered intricately carved and ornately decorated floating homes to be constructed from Kashmir cedar, to accommodate British families in gracious and civilised style.

The British were not the first to discover Kashmir's delights, however. The Moguls themselves aptly christened Kashmir 'Paradise': they too escaped the hot Indian plains during summer, and travelled to Srinagar in the heart of the Kashmir valley. It was here that they laid out Srinagar's many formal waterfront gardens, with great care and skill. Today, this place still retains its peculiar beauty and fascination. Its waterways, its tranquil lakes – such as Dal and Nagin with their houseboats – its blossoming gardens, not to mention its numerous activities, in the form of watersports, trekking and camping, make it a memorable holiday destination for lotus-eaters of every persuasion.

The two main locations for houseboats are Nagin – a ten-minute bus ride from Srinagar – and Dal, which is closer but more popular. Kashmir's houseboats themselves vary enormously, and as such it's as well to check in advance what's in store for you. Some of the elaborate cedarwood boats amount to floating palaces: up to 100-feet long, complete with Kashmir carpets and chandeliers, capturing something of the ambience of the Raj era. Others are smaller, less elaborate and less well equipped. Most have from three to six bedrooms, almost all have their own 'houseboy', and you may have a resident cook or at least a cook-boat moored nearby. When you arrive at your lake, a traditional canopied *shikara* or Indian gondola takes you to your appointed houseboat. These *shikaras* rejoice in some splendid names: *Happy Life*, *Flying Prince*, *Kilroy*, and even *Shark* (not necessarily a reference to its owners' financial persuasions!).

Within a few days, when you've absorbed something of Kashmir's restful and unique mood, you'll be ready to try one of the many activities available either locally or further afield. Srinagar itself has a strong Moslem culture. Alongside the narrow streets of its old town, venerable stallholders, often puffing on their hooka pipes, will sell you carpets, silks, spices or woolstuffs. Srinagar's network of canals and wooden bridges make fascinating exploring, as do its superb lakeside gardens, such as the Garden of Bliss or the Garden of Love. Other local excursions include *shikara* trips to floating bazaars or through nearby bird sanctuaries. If you're feeling energetic you could consider a walking trip to the ancient Kingdom of Ladakh or 'Little Tibet', as it's known, which lies some 300 km east of Srinagar. This 'antique land' is a stronghold of Buddhist life and culture. In the summer you can spend time exploring some of its monasteries, villages and trails set amidst spectacular mountain scenery, though for much of the year the whole region lies under snow. This is, *par excellence*, the place within India for adventure travel fanatics, though its combination of burning hot days and bitterly cold nights (not to mention high altitudes and demanding walking) requires considerable adaptability and an enthusiasm for the active life.

Three hours west of Srinagar, a magnificent bus journey takes you to Gulmarg – rated as one of the most outstanding hill resorts in the world. By spring and summer an enchanting valley adorned with meadows full of wild flowers, it is transformed in winter to become the country's premier winter sports resort, with excellent snow conditions from December through to April. Exciting downhill runs and beautiful crosscountry trails through forests, compete with the growing sport of heli-skiing, described as the most exciting development to hit the Himalaya since snow was invented! There is no single best time of the year to visit Kashmir, although spring and summer are good for houseboat sojourns. The bus trip from Jammu (the nearest railhead) to Srinagar costs from 50–100 rupees. Local transport is readily available in the form of taxis, coaches and rickshaws, not forgetting *shikaras*. Finding places to eat in Srinagar is not a problem and there are a number of bars within the city. You can hire trekking equipment from the Department of Tourism, Tourist Reception Centre, Shervani Road, and selected Tourist Offices in the state.

How To Get There: A large number of tour operators include Kashmir – often in association with other parts of India – in their brochure. Abercrombie & Kent offer a number of permutations and combinations, matching houseboat retreats with trips to Ladakh, Gulmarg and elsewhere. Their eleven-day 'Kashmir Escape' includes seven days in and around Srinagar for an inclusive price of around £1,000. Trekking and *shikara* 'staying on' extras are available at between £200–400 extra. Cox & Kings offer a sixteen-day Kashmir trip called 'Gardens of Pleasure' which includes Srinagar, Gulmarg and Leh, as well as stopovers in Delhi. The tariff of £1,500 includes accommodation, full-board and flights. Wexas (a travel club catering for 'unpackaged' travellers) offers a similar trip and at a similar price. They also offer a twenty-four-day trekking expedition which comprises two moderate treks of a week each in Kashmir and Ladakh, as well as a houseboat stay. The all-inclusive price starts at around £1,400. Also for the energetic, Twickers World offer an excellent twenty-four-day hiking/houseboat trip to Kashmir for around £1,500, all-inclusive.

Indian Airlines has flights connecting Srinagar to Delhi and Bombay, which themselves are nine hours' flying time from the UK. Independent travel is an option for those with time to spare: fixing accommodation and transport can sometimes be rather time-consuming, however.

Further information about Kashmir can be obtained from the Government of India Tourist Board (see Appendix I for details).

Northern Canada

Canada's vast and beautiful wilderness is more like a continent than a country. It encompasses six time zones and an area forty-one times the size of the UK, yet it has a population only half that of Britain's. For the visitor to Canada it is the untrammelled landscapes, boundless vistas and serene tranquillity which leave a lasting impression. Certainly Canada's larger cities – Quebec, Vancouver, Toronto, Winnipeg, Montreal, Ottawa – are cosmopolitan and dynamic centres of population. But the 'real'

Canada exists beyond the city limits, in the million lakes, immense forests and uncounted rivers of its great outdoors. This landscape has remained essentially unchanged since the days of fur traders, trappers and explorers, and nowhere more so than the north. Here, in Yukon and Northwest Territories, you can still travel a thousand miles in one direction and never once encounter a road. This is northern Canada – the great outdoors experience.

To best appreciate the wild side of Canada you need to have a smattering (or more) of pioneering spirit. Stay away if you're in love with luxury: these areas are not for the conventional holiday-maker, but if you're prepared to put up with some discomfort, the rewards and memories will last a lifetime. Once experienced, the Canadian wilderness remains with you: it haunts your memory and calls you back time and time again. To best experience this matchless land you need to use the time-honoured methods of travel used by the Indians and Inuits: kayaking, canoeing, trekking and horse riding. The legacy of adventure, typified by such explorers as Sir Alexander Mackenzie and Isabella Bird, is very much alive and kicking in the cultural makeup of Canadians today. As a visitor to Canada, you're spoilt for choice from the bewildering array of activity and adventure holidays available. Whether your interest is hiking or back-packing, sailing or windsurfing, kayaking or white-water rafting, the list of possible holidays, packaged or independent, is endless. Your only constraints are energy, time and imagination!

Nowhere is the wilderness experience more exciting than 'up north'. The way of life in the Northwest Territories and Yukon have remained little changed over generations: two-thirds of the population of Northwest Territories are ethnic groups, many of whom still pursue their traditions of hunting and trapping in order to make a living. This is the most sparsely populated part of Canada, with a population measured in only tens of thousands – many square miles to the person. The list of attractions here is a synthesis of all that makes adventure travel so special – varied and abundant wildlife, unparalleled scenery, personal challenge, Indian and Inuit history, a visual paradise for photographers – the list goes on and on.

In the heady days of the 1890s, the fever which attracted people 'up north' was gold. At the height of its boom days, Dawson City's population rose to over 30,000. Although gold is still part of Yukon's economy, the population of Dawson

City is well under 1,000 today. Though the immensity of Yukon and Northwest Territories still bears the imprint of gold miners, the greatest impression is made by its original inhabitants – the wildlife. Bears, moose, caribou, whales, seals and eagles are an ageless and essential component of the scenery.

How To Get There: Independent travel to and within northern Canada is certainly possible. The country is readily accessible from the UK, the flight taking from seven hours (east coast) to over nine hours (west coast). Among the airlines flying to Canada are British Airways, Air Canada and Wardair. Once you get there, transport both by air and on the few roads that exist is generally available, but this area is not to be trifled with and those who travel independently must be aware of the risks that their isolation can bring them.

Today over thirty tour operators offer package trips to Canada. Most of these options are essentially 'on the beaten track' experiences. It's easy to feel at home in a country where the British form the largest single ethnic group – approximately 40 per cent of the total population in fact. One company which specialises in reaching the parts of Canada which many others ignore is called Accessible Isolation Holidays. As its name suggests, Accessible Isolation Holidays aims to provide holidays in remote and untouched areas, while still remaining accessible to the outside world, should the need arise. Their dossier includes a plethora of trips intended for individuals and groups alike, and virtually their only requirement is that you arrive healthy and with an eager spirit of adventure.

Their trips to Northwest Territories include a number of treks (all prices exclude flights from the UK with Air Canada): 'Ellesmere Top of the World', a sixteen-day trip for £2,277 in the world's most northerly National Park; 'Subarctic Mosaic Trek', seven days for £585, within the World Heritage Site of the Wood Buffalo National Park, river rafting included; 'Mackenzie Mountain Trail', eight-days for £835 along the Nahanni Range of the Mackenzie Mountains; 'Best of Canadian Arctic', nine days for £827, within the Auyuittuq National Park. For the more energetic, white-water rafting, mountain biking, sailing and canoeing trips are all on offer in Northwest Territories. Every tour is led by expert guides and instructors who remain in radio contact with the operator at all times. Each guide is also coached in the art of producing excellent cuisine under sometimes difficult circumstances. If you prefer four-walled accommodation, then seven days in the Nahanni Mountain lodge – where the only 'locals' you'll encounter are dall sheep, moose, caribou and perhaps black bear, not to mention the bird life – are bound to appeal. You're flown in by plane, explained the ropes, then left alone, except for your radio link to the outside world.

Accessible Isolation Holidays trips to the Yukon include a number of rafting, canoeing and hiking trips, the latter including a Grizzly bear observation trek. Prices vary from £840 for eleven days, to £1,900 for thirteen days, excluding Air Canada flight. At the Ruby Range lodge – accessible only by float plane – activities include guided hiking, canoeing, exploring by boat, and fishing. Seven days, excluding flights, costs £779 (see Appendix II for details).

Summers in northern Canada are warm and dry. July temperatures can exceed 80°F, and constant daylight can also take some getting used to. Further information on climate, and other aspects of Canada's great outdoors, can be obtained from the Canadian Tourist Board (see Appendix I for details).

Safari in Kenya

Kenya has been called 'the whole of Africa in one country' and 'the land of infinite contrasts'. After all, what other country can boast glacial ice, a sandy coastline, arid deserts, sweeping savannas, large lakes, rainforests – even an inland sea? Certainly the diversity of scenery in this 'land like no other' is memorable. But perhaps the best description you can apply to Kenya is the 'land of safari'. A large area – over ten per cent – is set aside solely for the protection of wildlife. There are some thirty-seven National Parks and Reserves: household names like *Tsavo, Masai Mara, Aberdares* and *Mount Kenya*. These are great tracts of wilderness devoted to the preservation of flora and fauna – undoubtedly Kenya's greatest attraction. Isak Dinesen, writing under her *nom de plume* of Karen Blixen, remarked 'There is something about safari life that makes you forget all your sorrows and feel the whole time as if you had drunk half a bottle of champagne, bubbling over with heartfelt gratitude for being alive'. That message is as true today as it was in her time.

On any safari, your arrival is likely to be in Nairobi, Kenya's capital, although a handful of airlines fly into Mombasa on the coast (ideal if you want to combine beach and safari). From

Nairobi you have access to the rest of the country, although how you continue depends on whether you travel independently or with a tour. Independent travel has much to be said for it, allowing for greatest flexibility of both time and itinerary. Going with a tour, however, can be just as rewarding, and, usually, more hassle-free, since Kenyan officialdom can sometimes be difficult to overcome quickly.

Whichever way you travel, a good idea is to incorporate a wide range of countryside into your safari. This allows greatest potential for game viewing. Your first move might be to head north towards the Aberdare mountains, and Aberdare National Park. This is the location for the famous Treetops (access via the delightful Outspan Hotel), where Princess Elizabeth became Queen, and also for Treetops' newer equivalent, The Ark. Access to The Ark is by the Aberdare Country Club, a splendid colonial hotel with views over the mountains. The Ark itself is a unique Lodge in the heart of the Aberdares, built in the shape of Noah's boat, and situated at possibly the largest salt-lick in this part of the country. Here there are regular sightings of rhino, elephant, buffalo, and bushbuck, to name but a few, as well as the occasional leopard. The Ark is also one of the most likely places to see the rare and elusive Bongo, a large, bright chestnut antelope, although it has to be said that sightings are not frequent.

From The Ark it is only a few hours drive to Samburu National Park, further to the north. Driving through this semi-arid land, you are likely to see a wide variety of game. If you want to make your visit really special, then accommodation at Larsens Camp is recommended. This is a tented camp on the banks of the Ewaso Nyiro River. From the comfort of your luxury tents (complete with bathroom, electricity and all mod. cons.) you can watch the crocodiles in the river, or the elephants crossing further downstream.

If you don't mind a slightly longer drive (about five hours), Lake Baringo in the west provides an ideal break in the middle of any safari. Another colonial haunt, the Lake Baringo Club looks onto the lake, and offers guests the chance to relax, while also observing the great numbers of birds nesting in this area. Roughly 450 species are estimated to be in evidence here, including everything from the common weavers and superb starlings, to fish-eagles and the brightly coloured lilac-breasted roller. Another bonus is the number of hippos found in the lake. Usually seen – not to mention heard – through the day, at night these creatures seem to delight in thrilling guests by grazing on the hotel lawns.

Not far from Lake Baringo is Lake Nakuru. This is where the flamingos are customarily found – an estimated 1.5 million of them. The sight they present is literally straight out of the movies; a carpet of pink against the backdrop of green hills and blue water. Before heading for Nakuru it's worth checking out the flamingo situation, since during years when there has been above average rainfall, they sometimes can be found at Lake Bogoria close by, where the water level remains lower. Lake Bogoria is worth a visit anyway, simply for the sight of the hot springs gushing their vapours and boiling water up out of the ground. A modern Dante's inferno, the springs provide a constant source of challenge to campers who try to wash their pots here, but usually find the water far too hot!

Back at Lake Nakuru there is another National Park, excellent for viewing some of the smaller mammals usually overshadowed by the 'Big Five' (elephant, lion, rhino, leopard, and buffalo). A wide selection of bats can be found, as well as monkeys, baboons, jackals, bat-eared foxes, genet cats, and Rothschild's Giraffe. Accommodation is provided in the nearby town of Nakuru, or if you prefer to be 'on the spot', Lion Hill Camp is available in the park. The view from here, high on the hillside, is quite stunning.

No visit to Kenya would be complete without a visit to the Masai Mara. Even the light aircraft flight from Nairobi to the Mara is worth a journey in itself. To the south-west of the capital, meeting the border of Tanzania, this really is the type of land *Out of Africa* has shown us. The superb scenery is quite breathtaking – there is nothing quite like the dark afternoon clouds gathering on the horizon, contrasting with the rich gold of the plains. This picture is only completed, of course, by the full complement of elephant, giraffe, buffalo, zebra and, if you're there at the time of the migration (August/September), row upon row of wildebeest stretching as far as the eye (and very often the binoculars also) can see. Visitors to the Mara can drive for hours on end without ever coming across another vehicle, in a land peopled only by animals. Prides of lion are prevalent, and if you're lucky, you may even catch the females out looking for dinner. It may sound gruesome, but few sights are as captivating as a lioness stalking her prey.

While at the Mara, guests have the chance to enjoy what might be not only the highlight of their holiday, but also of a lifetime.

Mara Balloon Safaris offer a unique opportunity to 'ride the winds' at sunrise, over the Masai Mara, in the world's largest hot-air balloons. Lift-off is at 6.00 a.m. and the cost is roughly £150, but despite the early start – or indeed, because of it – and the extra money, this is an experience which you'll never forget. Drifting over the plains you can literally pick the fruits off the top of the trees, all the time gazing down on whatever animals happen to pass by. After about an hour touchdown finds you toasting in the morning with a glass of pink champagne (out of silver goblets, no less), before tucking into a hearty breakfast cooked on the balloon burners. There is nothing quite like it.

Accommodation in the Masai Mara comes in a variety of forms. As well as lodges with exotic names such as Keekorok and Kichwa Tembo, you will also find one of the true colonial-style camps remaining in Kenya. Governors' Camp is situated right on the Mara River and offers more than adequate accommodation in luxury tents (the bathrooms even have a bidet). The superb cuisine – barbecues at lunch and four-course dinners – are enjoyed either on the lawns or in the grand marquee dining room, while drinks are served in the thatched bar. One of the delights about Governors' is that the camp is not cut off from the park by fences or boundaries. Animals are free to come and go as they please, although Masai guards are always there to ensure your safety. Many a visitor has had to leave their lunch-table early due to an over-eager elephant heading their way!

Such is the Kenyan world of safari. There are few people who visit this land without vowing to return. From the bustle of Nairobi and five-star establishments such as the famed Norfolk or the Nairobi Safari Park Hotel (recently completed, this is probably the most exotic hotel to be found in Africa), to the down-to-earth dust and magical insight into raw nature, this is a land which creeps under the skin unnoticed, but leaves you wondering how you ever survived without visiting before.

Of the many companies which organise tours to Kenya, one in particular deserves mention for their excellent specialised and escorted tours. Grass Roots is a fairly young company, although its directors have been travelling to Kenya for the past thirteen years. Some tours are personally escorted by the directors, whose specialist knowledge in mammals, birds and geology fulfils even the most inquisitive minds. The 'Connoisseurs' Safari covers all places mentioned above, although alternative tours to places such as Tanzania, and even Rwanda to see the gorillas, are available throughout the year. Grass Roots are also accustomed to organising independent travel throughout Africa, and what they can't tell you isn't worth knowing. It's this sort of company who really allow safaris to be considered as 'Classic Tours'. Prices range from roughly £1,000 to £2,300. This includes return flight, full board accommodation on safari, bed and breakfast in Nairobi, all transfers, a guaranteed window seat in your safari vehicle, all game park fees, and the important, but hopefully not essential, flying doctor service. Further details are available from Grass Roots Travel Ltd (see Appendix II).

Other reliable companies travelling to Kenya and who can be found through local travel agencies are Abercrombie & Kent, Kuoni and Guerba Expeditions.

If you want to travel independently, but with the aid of a driver, one of the best companies to contact is United Touring Company (UTC) (see Appendix II).

Safari in Zimbabwe

Zimbabwe is an old country yet a young nation, home to both amazing natural phenomena and to landscapes which resemble early English watercolours; one of the last remaining areas of unspoiled Africa – in short, a country like no other. Its mountainous eastern highlands contrast with the remote bush country of the Zambezi river valley, and although it lies within the tropics, Zimbabwe's climate is moderated by altitude, so temperate conditions prevail all year round except for the Zambezi valley. With its unspoilt qualities, marvellous climate and abundant wildlife, Zimbabwe forms an African heartland destination of beauty, excitement and space: this is the 'real' Africa, the ideal place for your off-the-beaten-track safari experience.

Most famous of its attractions, and one of the seven wonders of the world, is the Victoria Falls. Livingstone – the first white man to set eyes on this spectacle – described 'scenes so lovely they must have been gazed upon by angels in flight'. Certainly, the sight of a million gallons of water a minute plunging 400 feet into a chasm below and churning up a cloud of spray which gives it the local name of *Mosi-oa-Tunya* (smoke that thunders), is unforgettable. Lush tropical rainforest flourishes unexpectedly in the humid atmosphere alongside the gorge. For the adventure seeker, white-water rafting trips and kayaking expeditions can be taken below the falls: less energetic but equally memorable are the fifteen-minute 'Flight of the Angels' by light aircraft and the 'Sunset Cruise' on the Zambezi above the falls.

Downstream from its frenzied journey over the Victoria Falls, the mighty Zambezi glides into Lake Kariba – at 5,000 square miles one of the largest man-made lakes in the world. Here thrives a rich variety of birds, mainly waterfowl; storks, herons and waders, not to mention the elusive lily trotter. With its scattering of islands and fringe of forests, Lake Kariba is a paradise for game-watchers and bird-watchers alike. To reach it you simply take one of Air Zimbabwe's daily flights, followed by a boat or light aircraft trip to a lodge or camp.

Continuing through a series of gorges, the Zambezi flows into the Mana Pools National Park in northern Zimbabwe. This park varies from woodland along the valley, to grassy mountainous escarpments above, while lush mahogany woodland and grassland vegetation cover the floodplain. Mana Pools is an ornithologist's paradise, as well as being home to some of the world's last remaining black rhino. Accommodation here includes camps at Ruckomechi and Chickwenya.

Matusadona National Park, a beautiful wilderness area stretching from Lake Kariba to Zimbabwe's interior, supports a rich and varied flora and fauna, including large concentrations of elephant, buffalo, hippo and impala, not to mention many species of birds. The relatively inaccessible Bumi River forms its eastern boundary, while the Sanyati Gorge borders the park on its western side. Matusadona Park can be visited throughout the year, with accommodation in Bumi Hills, Tiger Bay, Fothergill Island or Spurwing Island.

Situated in southwest Zimbabwe, on the border with Botswana, Hwange is Zimbabwe's largest National Park at over 9,000 square miles of bush, forests and plains. Its numerous artificial water holes support plentiful herds of elephant (estimated at 20,000 – as many as in the whole of Kenya), buffalo, sable and, of course, carnivorous predators. This is one of the few parks in Africa where the rhino exists in appreciable numbers. In all, over 100 species of mammal and over 400 species of bird have been recorded within its boundaries. Around two hours from Harare, Hwange Safari Lodge (which overlooks a water hole) and Sikumi Tree Lodge both offer good accommodation.

The mysterious Great Zimbabwe Ruins are a series of thirteenth-century artefacts shrouded in mystery and intrigue, and testifying to a highly ordered and civilised past society. Of great rarity, these ruins cover an area of some 720 hectares, and contain the largest single ancient structure in sub-Saharan Africa – the Great Enclosure – which is eleven metres high and 243 metres in girth. Excursions to Great Zimbabwe Ruins can be arranged using Air Zimbabwe's scheduled service on Mondays and Thursdays.

Founded in 1890, the capital of Zimbabwe – Harare – is a small city of wide and clean streets, shady suburban avenues, bustling commercial activity and friendly inhabitants. It boasts a modern museum, an art gallery, Botanical Gardens, the Robert McIlwaine Recreation Park with a lake and game enclosures, as well as excellent restaurants, nightclubs, casinos and hotels.

Certain periods of the year are better than others for visiting Zimbabwe. The dry winter season spans April to October, and this is the best period since the grasses are low and game-viewing is easier. Temperatures are rather higher during September and October, and the rainy season is from November to March. Some areas become inaccessible during the wet season although when the rains do fall it's usually in short refreshing bouts, with bright blue skies following shortly afterwards.

How To Get There: Independent travel to Zimbabwe is an option for the traveller with time to organise his or her holiday. On the whole, making your own arrangements is not too difficult, although these are unlikely to work out any cheaper than an organised tour. Zimbabwe's infrastructure is good (for Africa), with excellent roads, and reasonably priced car hire. Accommodation ranges from luxury hotels in the major cities (not forgetting the colonial Victoria Falls Hotel), and luxury safari lodges such as Bumi Hills, to tree lodges like Sikumi, or rustic island lodges like Fothergill, in Kariba. Air Zimbabwe and British Airways are amongst the major airlines flying to the country. An apex British Airways return fare, London to Harare, costs around £770 for the direct ten-hour flight. Cheaper flights (from Air Portugal for example) are available but these involve several stopovers. Air Zimbabwe has good domestic links between the major towns and cities and these are inexpensive; Harare to Victoria Falls costs £80 return.

There are a large number of tour operators offering trips to Zimbabwe. Among them, recommended operators include Abercrombie & Kent, Grass Roots, EcoSafaris, Twickers World and Guerba Expeditions. At the luxury end of the market, Abercrombie & Kent offer a comprehensive range of tailor-made trips such as 'Zambezi Wildlife', 'Zimbabwe and Botswana *à la carte*', 'classic camping safaris' and 'adventure safaris'. These modular, seven to seventeen-day trips cost up to £2,500 including full-board, accommodation and flights. Grass Roots also offer up-market packages or independent travel to Zimbabwe, with prices starting at £2,100. For a more economical trip to Zimbabwe, you could consider Twickers World, whose nineteen-day Zimbabwe wildlife and bird safari offers a wide-ranging game/bird-watching trip for around £1,500, including full-board, accommodation, lodging and flights. An active, three-week tour of Zimbabwe and Zambia with Guerba Expeditions costs as little as £655, excluding flights; while EcoSafaris offer a variety of reasonably-priced safaris, canoeing or bird-watching tours to Zimbabwe.

Further information is available from the Zimbabwe Tourist Office (see Appendix I for details).

Safari in Botswana

Time moves slowly in Botswana. If you're looking for a wilderness experience with a distinctive pioneering flavour then this is the place for you: some of Botswana's neighbours have lost this atmosphere in the name of 'progress'. Undoubtedly Botswana's greatest asset is its fauna: almost a quarter of its area is devoted to wildlife conservation. Some of southern Africa's largest herds congregate in unfenced reserves here, whilst the bird life is amongst the best anywhere in the 'dark' continent. Botswana is a landlocked country of unrivalled contrasts and endless horizons. The vast and virtually waterless Kalahari desert – made popular by Laurens van der Post – covers two-thirds of the land surface. Yet the Okavango, the world's largest inland delta, covers an area the size of Northern Ireland. This contrast is one of the delights of a Botswana holiday, for no visit is complete until you experience the lure of both desert and delta. Combine the large wildlife population with Botswana's very sparse human population – under two persons per square kilometre – and you have the perfect recipe for an unforgettable wilderness experience. As Ernest Hemingway wrote: 'We had not left it yet, but when I would wake in the night I would lie listening, homesick for it already'.

For a country the size of France, one of the problems confronting the visitor is devoting sufficient time to experience all the attractions. Foremost among the highlights is the Okavango Delta. This is Africa's 'last Eden' and the heart of Botswana's life support system. Rain which falls on the Angolan highlands 1,000 km away gradually swells the Okavango river, reaching the Delta some six months later, paradoxically just as the winter season is underway. As the delta level rises, channels form and spread, providing a life-sustaining source of water for the abundant surrounding wildlife. The best way to experience the flavour of Okavango's beauty and tranquillity is to be punted along in almost complete silence in a *makoro* or dug-out canoe: the best time to visit is between May and June.

The Moremi Wildlife Reserve which covers an area of 3,000 square km, extends into the delta and includes Chief's Island – only reachable by air or boat. Moremi is thought to be the first example in which an African people – in this case the Batawana – set aside part of their land expressly to be protected for ever. The reserve displays a wide variety of habitats: swamps, floodplains, reedbeds, mopane woodland and savanna. It qualifies as one of the most beautiful reserves in Africa with an extraordinary range and quantity of species too numerous to mention here.

Also among the finest game reserves in Africa is Chobe National Park which borders Moremi Wildlife Reserve. Stretching along the Chobe River and taking in most of Botswana's northern boundary, Chobe National Park is well known for its enormous elephant population (said to number 40,000): several hundred can be seen in one day. Bird life is also abundant on the flood plains and along the banks of the river.

Although not actually in Botswana, Victoria Falls deserves a mention being only 90 km from Chobi across the Zimbabwe border. The 'Vic' Falls or *Mosi-oa-Tunya* (smoke that thunders) is an unforgettable sight – one of the world's natural wonders; twice as high as Niagara and half as wide again. The sight of the mighty Zambezi thundering into the gorge below is astonishing. Don't miss it, and don't forget an umbrella either!

If you have time on your Botswana trip after seeing all of the above, try to visit the salt pans of Makgadikgadi and Nxai – difficult to pronounce and not particularly easy to reach either. For much of the year these are expanses of bare salt stretching as far as the eye can see. But after the summer rains, huge herds of wildebeest, zebra and gemsbok congregate here. Stay away if luxury is important to you: these pans can only be reached by four-wheel-drive vehicles and there is no permanent accommodation, only seasonal tented camps.

Accommodation: During your trip to Botswana, you'll find its remoteness both an attraction and a drawback. For example, rough-terrain safari vehicles are essential for visiting all the game reserves. However, despite this isolation, rough and ready accommodation is by no means an essential part of your safari experience here. The largest hotels in or near Gaborone and Francistown are of a reasonable standard: most others have fairly basic amenities. The standard of lodges, camps and services is often very good and some lodges even boast luxury chalets, swimming pools and gourmet meals as the norm. But if you're the type who prefers to sleep under canvas or even under the stars, plenty of camps offer basic accommodation, right down to those consisting only of an ablution block. The sites at Chobe and the Okavango are worth considering. The Botswana Division of Tourism provides a publication 'Where to Stay in Botswana' giving details of prices and facilities (see Appendix I for address).

How To Get There: The remoteness factor will probably point you towards choosing a packaged safari in Botswana. We recommend Twickers World, whose rugged fourteen-day 'Botswana Explorer' takes in the best of the country. Among the other tour operators offering Botswana deals, Guerba Expeditions offers a three-week game-viewing trip which takes in the northern Kalahari, Okavango, Chobe and Victoria Falls, all for £640, flights not included. Abercrombie and Kent boast a range of high-quality driving and flying safaris, with prices ranging from £1,800–2,800. Grass Roots offer a 13-day safari covering both Zimbabwe and Botswana. All inclusive prices start at £2,100.

For all but the most die-hard do-it-yourselfer, Botswana is probably best appreciated on an organised tour. However, if you do decide to travel independently, British Airways operate flights to Gaborone. Although it is possible to hire a four-wheel-drive vehicle when you arrive, at rates similar or slightly higher than in the UK, the organisation and standard of many organised tours is such that you will probably see more wildlife in a shorter time and without the worries of vehicle breakdowns, by travelling 'packaged'.

Safari in Zambia

Zambia is a wild and vast, landlocked plateau which some people call 'the oldest country in the world'. With its prolific and abundant wildlife, Zambia qualifies as one of Africa's best game-viewing countries, and nineteen sites (some nine per cent of the country) have National Park status. Safari trips are extremely rewarding, especially for those who want to take a 'walk on the wild side' (that is, a safari on foot). Its bird life, plentiful and varied, is depicted in the Zambian national symbol, a fish eagle. However, it it not only the wildlife which brings visitors to Zambia: magnificent scenery is also a major attraction. In the south, peaceful man-made Lake Kariba stretches into the distance, while further upstream the mighty Zambezi creates a thundering roar and cloud of spray as it forms Africa's greatest natural wonder – the Victoria Falls.

Luangwa Valley is part of the Great Africa Rift System. In Zambia it contains five National Parks, each centred on the Luangwa river, a major tributary of the vast Zambezi. Zambia's strict policy of conservation is helping to maintain the extraordinary richness of wildlife interest within this area. North and South Luangwa and Kafue National Parks are amongst the largest and best-known in all Africa; for sheer size, unrivalled in the whole continent. Dissected by the Luangwa river, South Luangwa holds one of the greatest concentrations of animals and birds of any National Park in the world. Its clear river lagoons support plentiful hippopotamuses, while the plains are home to vast herds of elephant, antelope, giraffe and zebra. Leopards and other carnivores abound here, and countless numbers of birds can be seen. As in the rest of Zambia, safaris in South Luangwa usually take place during the dry winter months, from June to November. North Luangwa is similarly impressive, its species list including some lesser-known animals such as puku, roan antelope and hartebeest.

Less than an hour's flying time from Zambia's capital, Lusaka, lies the vast National Park of Kafue, equal in area to the whole of Wales. All the well-known plains-dwelling game congregates within this park and you stand a good chance of seeing some of the 600 or so species of birds recorded here, especially along

Safari in Zambia

the flood plains and banks of the River Kafue. Notable among Kafue's wildlife are the black rhinos although these tend to be somewhat solitary and secretive. The showpiece of this park is the lechwe, a small antelope all but exterminated by previous poaching.

Despite its small size, Lochinvar National Park boasts an extraordinary variety of bird life, and is readily accessible from Lusaka. Further north lies Sumba National Park, an undisturbed wilderness bordering Lake Tanganyika. Guided walks, night game-viewing drives and night boat-rides are all available, while Lake Tanganyika is an angler's dream, supporting over 200 different species of fish. During the dry season, September to November, large herds of elephant congregate along the lake shore. You can fly to Sumbu from Lusaka, changing aircraft at Ndola.

The one sight not to be missed by visitors to Zambia is the famous Victoria Falls, one of the great natural wonders of the world. From March to May, when the Zambezi is in full flood, more than one million gallons of water surge over the falls each minute. Especially beautiful by moonlight (its lunar rainbow is an unforgettable sight) the spectacle is best viewed from the aptly-named Knife Edge bridge, not far from the settlement of Livingstone (named after the famous Scottish explorer). However, you'll need an umbrella if you want to avoid getting soaked. There are several Zambia Airways flights to Livingstone each week, departing from Lusaka International Airport. Alternatively you can hire a car in the capital and drive the five-hour journey to the Falls. For the energetically inclined, rafting safaris are available between June and November. Lasting anything up to a week, these trips take you from the base of Victoria Falls to Lake Kariba, a distance of eighty miles. Negotiating the 200 rapids found in-between is an exhilarating – if sometimes nerve-racking – experience. In quieter moments you can catch sight of hippo, crocodile and other wildlife.

Accommodation: Within the country accommodation varies from luxury hotels in the capital, such as the five-star Inter-Continental and Pamodzi, to park lodges and chalets (some very comfortable indeed) to canvas, permanent or temporary, camps. On the whole there are plenty of hotels within the main towns, but accommodation both here and within the National Parks is often in high demand and it's best to book beforehand, if you're travelling independently. These lodges are owned by a number of different organisations whose addresses are available from the Zambia National Tourist Board (see Appendix I).

How To Get There: Over ten airlines serve Lusaka International Airport, which lies some fifteen miles outside the city, and there are several tour and ground operators based in Lusaka and the principal centres of population.

It is possible to travel within Zambia independently, but the logistics of organising accommodation, travel and meals are often complicated. For these reasons I would recommend that you choose one of the several tour operators which offer Zambia within their portfolio. Having a common border with Zimbabwe and easy access to Botswana, Zambia is often combined with these countries to offer broader-based safari trips. One of the most experienced operators, and in my opinion the best for Zambia, is EcoSafaris who offer a choice of three seventeen-day trips; a Luangwa safari, a Zambia general interest and wildlife safari, and a David Livingstone safari. In 1991, EcoSafaris are running a special wildlife and conservation tour led by Sybil Sassoon, which visits the Luangwa Valley, Kansanka National Park and Victoria Falls. Parts of this trip are away from the usual tourist circuits and opportunities are available to meet conservationists working in the field. Tours such as this which are associated with the Kansanka Trust, include rare chances to study and enjoy some of Zambia's most untrammelled wilderness areas. Their boast is 'We don't only touch the wild: we help you become part of it'. EcoSafari's tours cost between £1,675 to Luangwa and £1,925 for the David Livingstone tour, including flight, accommodation and full board. Exodus, whose sixteen-day Luangwa 'ultimate safari on foot in untamed Africa' costs £1,690 including flights, board and accommodation. Abercrombie and Kent offer a ten-day Luangwa safari 'Zambia Adventure' for upwards of £1,430, fully inclusive. This trip includes a choice of three camps at which to stay (see Appendix II for details of tour operators).

Great Events

The full spectacle of a 'great event' cannot be conveyed by the media; some world events have to be experienced to be believed. These occasions can be carnivals, theatrical productions or religious festivals, which often provide the annual cultural climax for their host town or country. It is the chance to capture the atmosphere at first hand that attracts people to events such as Oberammergau's ten-yearly Passion Play, Rio's Carnival and the annual International Arts Festival in Edinburgh. All of these occasions draw huge crowds from all over the world, and transform totally the cities in which they are held.

Great events must be one of the best ways to experience a country's traditional culture. Songkran (or New Year) in Thailand is an unforgettable experience partly because of its tradition, which reaches far back into Thai history and which has remained largely unchanged for hundreds of years. When you visit Thailand at this festival you find yourself drawn into the Thai lifestyle, and this experience undoubtedly provides a highlight of your holiday. Similarly, the magnificent pomp and splendour of religious ceremonial occasions such as St James's Day in Santiago de Compostela, or the Holy Blood Procession in Bruges, are inspiring and these beautiful cities provide a truly memorable setting.

One must make allowances for the unique nature of this type of holiday: thousands of people converging on one place for a single event create certain problems. Accommodation becomes limited, and often more expensive than usual. However, there are so many different packages now available with reputable tour operators that, given enough forethought, many of these difficulties will be removed by early booking both for tickets and accommodation. You can be assured that these drawbacks will be more than compensated for by a cultural and sensual experience likely to remain with you for a very long time indeed.

Carnival in Rio

Rio de Janeiro's Carnival is the world's largest and most spectacular party. Four days of parades, pageants, and costume balls, all accompanied by the distinctive rhythm of the samba, create an unforgettable atmosphere. Throughout the day the city is a colourful whirl of music and dancing, and the festivities continue long into the brightly-lit night. The streets are decorated with coloured lights and streamers, and impromptu bands play from temporary bandstands erected on street corners.

In Brazil, Rio is knows as *Cidade Maravilhosa*, or 'marvellous city', and this, if anything, is an understatement. Overlooked by the enormous twelve-foot-high Statue of Christ on the summit of the Corcovado Mountain, Rio de Janeiro is one of the largest cities in South America. The capital of Brazil until 1960, Rio remains the country's cultural centre, and its pleasant climate makes it a popular choice for holiday visitors. It provides a breathtaking setting for the Carnival festivities. Its long stretches of palm-lined sandy beaches and lush green mountainsides alongside colonial architecture and modern skyscrapers, combine to create a unique landscape of striking and exotic contrasts.

The Carnival officially takes place on the five days that precede Ash Wednesday, but preparations get under way as early as November, when costumes and floats are planned, and contestants for the many samba competitions start practising their steps. Samba is the central and unique element of the Rio Carnival. The city's social clubs each sponsor an Escola de Samba (samba school) – a huge group of singers, dancers and musicians who compete with the other samba schools in the giant parade of the Escolas on Carnival Sunday. This is a highly competitive event lasting from 8 p.m. on Sunday to midday on Monday, and hundreds of thousands of onlookers cheer the clubs on as they dance along the Rua Marques de Sapucai. Since a single school can have between 2,000 and 3,000 participants, one begins to appreciate the massive scale of this famous festival.

Costumes make a major contribution to the carnival scene. Many are so exotic that they take months to create, with huge spangled and feathered head-dresses that are almost as tall as their recipients' heads. At the other extreme are costumes which are little more than a strategically arranged string of beads! Not only are these outfits displayed on the streets, however; another important feature of Carnival week is the series of fabulous costume balls held in nightclubs, hotels and club ballrooms. If you want to attend one of these grand balls, you must wear formal dress, or go in costume. Elaborate silk gowns and powdered wigs are the norm!

Of course, amidst all the fun and festivity, there are the usual disadvantages of visiting a city at its busiest. It is vital to book accommodation well in advance, and rates are increased at this time of year. The Carnival, which can take place at any time between the first week in February and the end of March, is right in the middle of Brazil's hottest season when temperatures can reach a sweltering 104°F in the shade. Since Carnival week is a national holiday many shops and restaurants are closed from the Saturday. Those that stay open are inevitably crowded.

Carnival activity is not simply confined to Rio itself. Visitors who manage to tear themselves away from the fascination of the city will see the 'electric trios' of Salvador, and many variations on the samba, such as the frevo, maracatu and caboclinhos, performed in small clubs all over Brazil.

How To Get There: There is a wide choice of options open to both the independent and package traveller. A number of tour operators specialising in long-distance world travel actually offer Carnival packages, thus taking the trouble out of organising accommodation and tickets for the events.

For the independent traveller, Rio has its own international airport, and there are passenger cruises from Europe run by Lamport and Holt lines which call at its port. It is possible to drive or take a bus to Brazil from the US, but the volatile political situation in Central America can often disrupt travel routes considerably.

Carnival starting dates until the year 2000 are set out below.

1991 – February	9th	1996 – February	17th
1992 – February	29th	1997 – February	8th
1993 – February	20th	1998 – February	21st
1994 – February	12th	1999 – February	13th
1995 – February	25th	2000 – February	4th

The one drawback of choosing to visit Rio at Carnival time is that accommodation prices are raised to include 'a Carnival supplement' of anything up to £200 per room per night! These price increases are a result of the overwhelming demand for accommodation during the Carnival period.

British Airways' Speedbird programme offers an excellent Rio trip: they combine Rio with Angra dos Reis; offer the Carnival, and offer Rio as part of their 'Brazilian Cocktail' tour, which is one of the most exciting South American packages on the market, combining Rio with Manaus, Brasilia, Salvador and Iguacu. Twelve days cost from £1720, using British Airways and Varig scheduled flights and first-class hotels.

Kuoni offer a choice of three hotels in Rio, and prices start at £742 for five nights in February, including flights; supplements of between £72 and £210 per night apply during Carnival week. Kuoni also offer an advance ticket service, whereby you can book seats and excursions for an approximate charge of US$110. They stipulate that they have no control over location, price or quality of the seats, and that tickets may be cheaper if purchased in Rio, but these disadvantages must be weighed against the possibility of not getting tickets at all. Thomas Cook, Hayes & Jarvis, Silk Cut and Redwing are also worth consulting.

If you wish to combine a stay in Rio with a more extensive exploration of Brazil, you can take advantage of the Brazil airpass which costs US$330 and allows twenty-one days of unlimited travel between all cities served by the airlines Cruzeiro, Transbrasil, Varig or Vasp.

For further information the Brazilian Tourist Information Department can be contacted at the Brazilian Embassy (see Appendix I).

Bangkok at Songkran

In Sanskrit Songkran means 'to pass into', and as such is an appropriate name for the festival celebrating the coming of the old Thai New Year on 13 April. This tradition, the liveliest and most colourful of all Thailand's many religious festivals, is rooted in centuries of South-East Asian culture and is not only observed in Thailand but also in Kampuchea, Laos and Myanma (Burma).

Although the gradual Westernisation of Thailand has meant that these days New Year is celebrated on 1 January in common with Western countries, the Songkran festival still has a great religious and traditional significance for the Thai people. Celebrations last for three days, and an overabundance of water and beautiful women are the impressions most likely to remain with a visitor to Thailand at this exciting time.

Water has always played a particular role in Thai culture and is commonly used both to signify respect for elders, and

Bangkok at Songkran

spiritual cleansing. During the Songkran, images of the Buddha are bathed with perfumed water, and young people perform a ritual hand-washing of their elders and parents. This is done as a mark of respect and the young people take this opportunity to ask forgiveness for any wrongs during the previous year. In ancient days, the elders were actually given a bath and a new set of clothes by the young. These days the custom is for a water and flour mixture to be smeared on the face and body. Visitors are not exempt, so don't go out in your best clothes!

The day before Songkran is a public spring-cleaning day, when all Thai housewives give their homes a thorough cleaning. This custom has a religious significance: old and useless objects must be thrown away or else they are considered to bring bad luck upon the unhappy owner.

Over 90 per cent of Thai people are Buddhists, but their form of this religion differs in many respects from 'pure' Buddhism. Thai religion contains elements of Hindu, fairy tales and animalism, with shrines to animals and mythical figures, as well as to Buddha. A large element of superstition is displayed in many of the traditional Songkran customs, such as the releasing of live birds and fish. Thais believe that this act of kindness earns them great spiritual merit, although the ritual does have a practical origin, dating back to the days when the central plains of Thailand were periodically flooded during the rainy season. Once the water level dropped, baby fish were left stranded in pools, far from the rivers. Farmers caught these fish, kept them until Songkran Day and then released them into the canals, by which act they not only gained merit but also preserved their staple diet. Nowadays, however, birds and fish are purchased in the markets. In Paklat, near Bangkok, a procession of beautiful girls carry fish bowls to the nearby river where the fish are then released. This is a popular tourist attraction, as well as drawing crowds of young local men!

Thai women, many of whom are exquisitely beautiful, also feature predominantly in the Songkran celebrations in Chiang Mai, in the north of Thailand. Here a huge afternoon procession is the highlight of the day's festivities, which culminates in the choosing of a Songkran Queen. Chiang Mai's celebrations are renowned for their gaiety, and visitors must expect a crowded town and a certain amount of drenching, but throughout the country people cease all work for three days and perform their own unique games, songs and dances.

Since Songkran is a religious festival it is not surprising that every Thai visits his temple, or *wat*, during these three days in order to bring food to the monks, for whom Songkran is also a time of feasting and celebration. Another, though more serious, Songkran custom is a memorial ceremony to the dead, performed by monks wherever bones or ashes of the dead have been deposited. In some places, villagers bring bones of their dead to the *wat* to be blessed.

How To Get There: For the independent traveller, more than thirty-five airlines use Bangkok's Don Muang airport every week, and this recently-renovated airport is one of the most pleasant in Asia. Thailand can also be reached by train with relative ease, since there is a direct rail route between Singapore in Malaysia, and Bangkok. The scenery on this route is quite spectacular.

Bangkok now boasts over 20,000 hotel rooms, spanning the entire rage of the price market. Due to this recent increase in accommodation there has been a certain amount of price-cutting and it is often possible to get excellent bargain deals. All but the most basic hotels are air-conditioned and extras such as swimming pools, bars and nightclubs can be found in many middle-to-upper range ones. Most hotels operate on an accommodation-only basis.

Many dozens of tour operators now offer package deals to Thailand all year round. Kuoni is considered a bit of a specialist in Thailand and it is certainly one of the companies who operate inexpensive charter flights to keep the costs down. Those wishing to visit Thailand during the Songkran festival are advised to book especially early, since Bangkok is particularly busy, as is Chiang Mai.

Seven nights in Bangkok with one of the major tour operators including Kuoni, Hayes & Jarvis and Speedbird will cost from £499–808, staying in de luxe accommodation and including return flight. For a single night's accommodation in a moderate or inexpensively priced hotel, you are likely to pay between £10–50.

For further information about Thailand, contact the Tourism Authority of Thailand (see Appendix I for details).

The Holy Blood Procession in Bruges

One of the most prosperous European trading ports in the Middle Ages, Bruges is now a peaceful, quaintly cobbled city in the north of Belgium. The network of picturesque canals encircling the city has earned it the name 'the Venice of the north'. Bruges is a city with a long history, and the annual procession of the Holy Blood on Ascension Day is one of the attractions which brings many visitors here to participate in a week of festivity.

The story of the Holy Blood begins with the Crusades in 1145, when a large European army marched to the aid of the King of Jerusalem, whose Holy Land had been invaded by the Saracens. In the ensuing fierce battles, the bravery of one man, Thierry d'Alsace, Count of Flanders, became legendary. As a reward for his great courage, the victorious King Baudouin of Jerusalem entrusted Thierry with a phial containing a portion of holy blood, kept in Jerusalem and reputed to be the blood collected from Christ's wounds by Joseph of Arimathea, and Nicodemus. Having decided to take the relic to Bruges, the Flemish Count commissioned the Abbot of St Bertin to carry it to the city, rather than risk taking it there himself. This the faithful Abbot did, and, on Thierry's return in 1149, the blood was placed in the Basilica of the Holy Blood, built in its honour. Thierry's homecoming was a time of great celebration for the people of Flanders, and they lined the flower-strewn streets, waving banners representing the trades of the city. All the city dignitaries turned out to congratulate the heroic Count who had brought such a great honour to their city.

The celebrations in honour of Thierry and the Holy Blood are a tradition that has been preserved in Bruges, and the Holy Blood Procession is an elaborate affair. Visitors come from all over the world to experience Bruges at its liveliest. Amidst the pealing of every church bell in the city, the normally quiet streets throng with people as the relic of the Holy Blood, an ornately carved gold casket, is carried by church dignitaries from the chapel in the Basilica to the Cathedral of the Holy Saviour, where high Mass is then celebrated. The procession that follows the casket-bearers is a spectacular re-enactment of the story of the Holy Blood, including scenes portraying key biblical stories and figures.

The first part of the procession begins with Adam and Eve and tells of the Fall of man. Cain and Abel, Abraham, Moses, Joseph, Jacob and David, all make their appearance, leading us to the announcement by the shepherds of the birth of the Messiah. The second part of the procession retraces with tremendous realism the principal events in the life of Christ, culminating with His crucifixion, where the Holy Blood is said to have been collected. The story of the Abbot's journey to Bruges with the phial is next told, followed by the triumphant return of Thierry d'Alsace and his greeting by civic and religious dignitaries.

The procession having returned to its starting point in Burg Square, the Bishop of Bruges then lifts the relic of the Holy Blood and blesses the crowd. This then is the unforgettable spectacle which attracts so many to Bruges – a wonderful combination of pomp, spectacle and religious solemnity which makes this event unique.

How To Get There: There is no airport at Bruges, so travel by air is to Brussels (fifty-five minutes from London) and then by road or rail to Bruges (approximately one hour). As Bruges is near the north coast, many visitors choose to travel by sea from Dover or Folkestone, and P&O, North Sea Ferries and Sally Line all operate daily sailings. Dover to Ostend takes approximately three hours forty-five minutes by ferry, and one hour forty minutes by jetfoil. There are many tour operators and local coach companies who offer packages to Bruges, of which the Belgian Travel Service offers a package best suited to visiting this particular event. Caprice Holidays Ltd, Hoseasons Holidays Abroad, Sally Tours, Osprey Holidays, Time Off, Intasun City Breaks, Inntravel and Swan Hellenic are also recommended for their Bruges packages.

Belgium has excellent road and rail networks, and Belgian Railways offer a 50 per cent reduction to all travellers going to Bruges for the Holy Blood Procession. This reduction can be obtained at any Belgian station on journeys of over 40 km.

Belgium boasts a large range of hotels ranging from luxury international class to family pensions and inns. The Belgian Tourist Board operates a grading system, whereby approved hotels may display a shield, indicating that they conform to the official standards set by Belgian law to guarantee certain standards of quality.

A typical four-day package by sea and coach will cost between £135–165 (travel only). Prices for travel by air are similar.

Tickets for grandstand and bench seats at the procession may be reserved in advance from 1 February. These cost 250BF and 200BF.

The Belgian National Tourist Office has details of all packages to Bruges, and a list of graded hotels. Tickets for the procession can be obtained from the tourist office in Bruges (see Appendix I for details).

St James's Day in Santiago de Compostela

Santiago de Compostela, situated on Spain's north-west coast in the region of Galicia, is considered to be the holiest city in Spain. The site of the shrine to Spain's patron saint, St James (Santo Iago), Santiago became second only to Jerusalem and Rome as a place of pilgrimage following its consecration in the Middle Ages. Today it still thrives as a religious centre, but its historic atmosphere combined with the beauty of the surrounding Galician countryside makes Santiago a popular choice throughout the year for the more discerning visitor, who wishes to discover the other side of Spain. If you want to see this peaceful ancient city come to life with all the zest of one of Europe's most important and colourful fiestas, come during the St James' Day celebrations. A holy year is declared when St James' Day, 25 July, falls on a Sunday, but whatever the year the festivities of the week following the 25th attract visitors from all over the world, who come not simply for the 'fiesta experience' but also to experience the city as it must have been when crowded with bands of pilgrims in the Middle Ages.

The eve of St James' Day, 24 July, sees the first of the events that are to last for a full week. A mock burning of the twelfth-century cathedral, said to have been built over the tomb of St James and now housing his casket of ashes, takes place at night, accompanied by an elaborate firework display on the Plaza del Obradoiro. High Mass is celebrated in the cathedral on 25 July, which is also the Galician National Day, and a famous feature of this service is the lighting of the *botafumeiro* (literally, 'smoke barrel'), an enormous silver incensory which is hauled to the roof and then swung, smoking and steaming, in a wide arc across the cathedral and over the heads of the congregation. Another custom involving the cathedral takes place at the beginning of a holy year, when a sealed seventeenth-century door, known as the holy door, is opened. This door remains open for the duration of the year. The next holy year is in 1993 and the door will be opened on 31 December 1992.

Many choose to visit Santiago de Compostela at this time as the culmination of a modern pilgrimage across the north of Spain from France. The Camino de Santiago, or Way of St

James as it is known, is the route followed at one time by two million medieval pilgrims a year, and it traverses some of the most beautiful countryside in Spain. The ancient route was lined with monasteries, chapels and hospices and many of these still survive today. Beginning at Canfranc in Navarre, pilgrims stopped at Pamplona, Santo Domingo de la Calzada, Logrono, Burgos, Leon, Astorga and Santiago de Compostela, where they assembled in the vast Plaza del Obradoiro to pay homage at the shrine of St James. Modern-day pilgrims visiting Santiago during the St James' Day celebrations experience the town thronging with people, much as it would have been in the Middle Ages. If a peaceful exploration of the labyrinth of narrow passages and historic sites is more to your taste, then this is not the time for you to visit! Santiago is also a university city, and at night the centre comes to life as the young Spanish students enjoy themselves.

How To Get There: There are only two companies operating package deals by air to Santiago de Compostela. Iberia, Spain's national carrier, offers various tour options which combine a visit to Santiago with other historic cities in northern Spain and Portugal. Lanzarote Villas is the only other company operating from the UK. Brochures for both companies may be obtained from most travel agents. For the independent traveller flight-only deals are available from Iberia and Ecuador Travel. A return flight during the main season will cost £187 return, and off-peak drops to about £108.

SSS International is a Spanish coach company operating services twice and three times a week from London direct to Santiago. The best sea crossing is from Portsmouth to Santander. For those with their own transport and two or three weeks to spare, the Camino Santiago is a recommended route.

Santiago is full of hotels ranging from the luxury Hotel de los Reyes Catolicos (a sixteenth-century pilgrim's hospice) to the small Hotel Suso in the Rua del Vilar, highly popular with genuine pilgrims on 25 July. With the exception of the Reyes Catolicos, most of the larger hotels are on the outskirts or in the modern part of the city. It is possible to find more modest accommodation in the centre, however, but be prepared for noisy nights during festival time. All accommodation may be booked in advance from the UK, and those choosing to go to

Santiago for St James' Day are strongly advised to book well in advance.

Accommodation prices are on a par with the rest of Europe, with two people paying between 3,250–14,000 pesestas for a double room. One person occupying a double room pays 80 per cent of the full price, and all guests are required to pay a further 6–12 per cent in IVA tax.

Although public transport in Spain is considerably cheaper than elsewhere in Europe, many people prefer the flexibility of the hire-car option, and this can be arranged before leaving the UK. Atesa Car Hire and Dial Spania both offer competitive rates: £90–110 for a week's rental, depending on car size.

For further information contact the Spanish National Tourist Office (see Appendix I for details).

Oberammergau Passion Play

Every ten years thousands of people flock from all over the world to a small scenic village in Bavaria. They come to see the world-famous Passion Play which has been performed once every decade since the mid-seventeenth century.

The play is a completely unique and unforgettable theatrical experience. Dating back to 1632, the Passion Play arose out of a pact made with God by the elders of Oberammergau. Devastated by the plague that was sweeping across Europe and already mourning the loss of a fifth of the village's population, the elders vowed to God that, if He should spare the rest of the villagers, they would undertake to re-enact the 'Passion of Christ' as a mark of their thankfulness. Their prayers were answered and not one more villager succumbed to the fatal disease. In return, Oberammergau has faithfully kept its word and thirty-six epic productions of the play have taken place since, the latest in 1990.

The play is performed in a huge open-air theatre which seats 5,000 and the cast of 1,500 consists entirely of the villagers of Oberammergau. The 600 actors taking speaking parts must all have been born in Oberammergau, and the roles of Mary and the other female characters are traditionally taken by unmarried women. Many of the roles have been handed down in the same family through countless generations. Depicting the suffering, crucifixion and resurrection of Christ, performances last for six hours, with a three-hour lunch break to allow the actors a well-deserved rest and the audience to stretch their legs. The grand scale of the production incorporates the use of children and animals, bringing vividly to life the biblical stories. Between the months of May and September approximately 400,000 visitors will attend what is surely one of the most spectacular events in the world religious calendar.

Oberammergau itself, set in a peaceful Alpine valley twenty miles south of Munich and not far from the Austrian border, is a beautiful place. Surrounded by mountain peaks, the village is an ideal base for a walking holiday, and its central location makes it easily accessible from Austria, Italy and the north of Germany. The Passion Play is not the only claim to fame of this remarkable village. Oberammergau is also renowned for its wood-carvings, and many of the village houses are decorated with these. Few visitors can resist their appeal as souvenirs. Even outside the Passion Play period, this is a destination worth visiting. Freelance accommodation can be easily found, and a marvellous, family-run Gasthof, with excellent cuisine and a warm welcome is the Zur Rose. Contact the West German Tourist Board for details (see Appendix I). The town has a bustling nightlife, especially during the play season, and there are opportunities to experience a typical Bavarian folk evening during the week in the town hall.

It must be added that the town is crammed to the seams during the play season. Accommodation is very scarce, and restaurants extraordinarily crowded – the only way of making sure of either of these necessities is to travel with a reputable tour company, and book well ahead.

How To Get There: A number of tour operators make special arrangements for a play year in addition to their normal itinerary. Orientours, a specialist company with over thirty years' experience in organising pilgrimage tours to the Holy Land, offer a wide range of holiday ideas to bring the lands of the Bible to life. They are arguably the most experienced operator in this field. As well as touring Greece in the steps of St Paul, visiting Turkey to see the Seven Churches of Asia, or admiring the great cathedrals of France, Orientours arrange a special tour programme in a Passion Play year, providing the best and most extensive range of tour itineraries based around a visit to Oberammergau. Their programme for the 1990 play included six different tours, by either coach or air, which combined a night in Oberammergau with sight-seeing in Italy, Bavaria, the Tyrol and Seefeld. Tickets and seating arrangements for the play were all organised for you, and Orientours also welcome group bookings to the Passion Play. They offer group-leader concessions and three itineraries designed exclusively for groups.

Wallace Arnold and Overland have joined together to produce a variety of coach tours, taking in, of course, the Passion Play. You can choose between a short six-day break or a full-length fifteen-day holiday. Inghams also offer a package whereby guests who are including the event in one of Inghams' many holiday combinations in Austria may book tickets for the play, and Thomas Cook arrange a programme of tours based around the Passion Play.

Since the Passion Play only occurs once every ten years, it is impossible to give an accurate idea of tour prices. With the above-mentioned companies, the tour price usually includes air and coach travel, entrance fees to listed sights, all accommodation and a first-class ticket to the play.

Accommodation in Oberammergau is usually in private homes, since hotel space is extremely limited at this time. Homes offering to take visitors must fulfil the exacting standards set by the Passion Play Committee.

For further information, contact the West German Tourist Board (see Appendix I). Brochures for the above companies may be obtained from most travel agents, or by contacting the companies direct (see Appendix II for details).

The Edinburgh International Festival

Edinburgh, Scotland's historic capital and one of the most beautiful cities in the world, plays host each summer to millions of visitors who come especially to participate in its internationally-renowned festival. Since the festival tradition first began in 1946 Edinburgh has maintained its well-earned reputation as organiser of the most prestigious Arts festival in the world, providing a rare chance for people to experience something from every spectrum of the arts world.

Edinburgh provides the ideal setting for such an illustrious array of artistic and cultural events. Described by Robert Louis Stevenson as 'a place where it seems to me, looking back, it must always be autumn and generally Sunday', Edinburgh's most distinct atmosphere is one of genteel elegance. It's a comparatively small city, bordered by the magnificent scenery of the Firth of Forth and centred on its old town and imposing Castle. Edinburgh Castle, perched high on a rocky crag overlooking the city's main shopping street, is the city's most famous sight, along with the Walter Scott Monument, Royal Mile and Palace of Holyroodhouse. Visitors to the city will be impressed by the spacious elegance of wide Georgian avenues and crescents of the new town, and intrigued by the maze of steep, narrow 'wynds' that thread throughout the picturesque medieval old town, crammed with tiny shops and historic pubs.

A relatively quiet city for eleven months of the year, Edinburgh suddenly becomes a bustling cosmopolitan centre during the last two weeks of August and first week of September, when the festival comes to town. All the major venues in the city play host to theatre and dance companies, orchestras, chamber groups and soloists from home and overseas. A theme is chosen each year, and over the last few years Italian, Spanish and French themes have reflected a national emphasis. Art exhibitions play an important part in the festival programme, and these range in style from traditional to the more avant-garde. The festival has an artistic significance that cannot be underestimated: many new works have been commissioned especially for performing at this event (T.S. Eliot's *The Cocktail Party* being a famous example). However, one festival event that changes little from year to year is the traditional Military Tattoo, performed nightly in the most spectacular venue of all, the Castle itself. Displays of military marching bands from all over the world, as well as the famous kilted Scottish pipe bands, are the main features of the Tattoo, but the image which stays longest in one's memory is that of the lone piper standing on the floodlit castle battlements, creating a magical atmosphere as he pipes a solitary farewell to end the performance.

Of course, it must not be forgotten that there are two sides to the Edinburgh Festival. As well as the 'official' festival with its big names and large-scale events, there is also the more informal Fringe Festival. The Fringe is distinctive as an arena for new talent and amateur entertainers, with a predominance of student drama and street theatre. In recent years the standard of many Fringe events has been such that the gap between the two halves of the festival is becoming increasingly less distinct. Every available venue in Edinburgh is used for recitals, exhibitions, concerts and poetry readings. Competition for audiences is fierce, considering the number and variety of attractions on offer, and the publicity stunts to advertise individual shows are often as entertaining as the shows themselves! Festivities carry on into the wee small hours, and a city which is normally asleep by midnight finds its streets still thronged with people at 3 a.m.

Other specialist events running in conjunction with the International Arts Festival are festivals of films, books and jazz, all of which are of a high standard and which attract enthusiasts from all over the world.

How To Get There: Situated just one hour beyond Scotland's Border country and only an hour by air from London, Edinburgh is easily accessible. Its airport is located eight miles from the city centre, and operates direct flights to major European cities, as well as connections to other British airports. Edinburgh is two hours' drive from Prestwick, Scotland's transatlantic airport on the west coast; and a forty-five-minute rail journey from Glasgow Airport (domestic and some European flights).

London-bound trains leave hourly from Edinburgh's Waverley Station and there is also a regular coach service from many parts of the British Isles.

Accommodation fills up particularly quickly at festival time, but the Tourist Office claims to be able to fit everyone in. Early application is advised, however. Edinburgh has a wide range of hotels and guest houses and details of these can be found in the Tourist Accommodation Register produced each year and available from the Tourist Office.

Accommodation also varies greatly in price. You can pay from £12–38 per person per night in a bed and breakfast, to £150 per night in one of the city's de luxe hotels. Booking ahead is essential.

The festival Programme is published in early May, and the Fringe Programme is available at the end of June. Tickets for all events are available from festival and Fringe box offices.

Entrance fees and ticket prices for festival and Fringe events vary enormously, from expensive for big names to free for some events. An average festival ticket will cost around £8 while a Fringe show is around £4.

The festival and Fringe box offices are the best places to

contact for information about individual events (see Appendix II, under Edinburgh). Edinburgh City Tourist Information is extremely helpful and it runs an accommodation booking service, as well as providing information about the city in general (see Appendix I).

Activity Holidays

For many people a holiday needs to be more than just a week in the sun doing nothing. You've been on beach holidays; fine for a few days, then boredom sets in. Something more exciting is needed: new challenges, the chance to improve at a sport or hobby, an opportunity to meet different people with common interests – all of these are valid reasons why so many are turning to activity holidays.

In the past, activity holidays tended to appeal largely to young singles with only their own interests to consider. To a certain extent this still applies today. Scuba-diving, high-altitude hiking, and overland four-wheel drive trips are not for the unfit, families, or lovers of luxury. Increasingly, however, tour operators are realising the need to provide 'soft' adventure, and activity holidays which cater for families with a range of pursuits on offer to suit differing ages and tastes. Thus you'll find golfing holidays which also offer gourmet cookery courses and health centres, to appeal to non-golfing partners. And certain holiday villages and resorts like Club Med provide all-day supervision for children, while parents can indulge in sporting pursuits.

Nevertheless, specific activity holidays are still tremendously popular and the range of pursuits on offer is vast. Now you can choose between hot-air ballooning in France, skiing in Colorado, trekking through Nepal, or any of the other exciting holidays that we think are amongst the best in the world.

By Steam across Southern Africa

Spending a fortnight travelling across Zimbabwe and into Zambia on working steam trains is an activity holiday with a difference both for dedicated railway enthusiasts and for those fascinated by the bygone days of steam. The chance to combine an unusual hobby with two weeks of unrivalled scenery, including the Victoria Falls and Hwange National Game Park, is a unique one offered by a company called To Europe – For Steam (TEFS).

Created in 1968 when scheduled standard gauge steam services on British Railways ceased, TEFS aims to enable steam railway enthusiasts to enjoy their hobby by taking them to countries where large and small steam locomotives continue in every-day service. Over the last twenty-one years they have pioneered tours in Jordan, Syria, the Sudan, Vietnam and China, and claim to have brought steam back to the state railways in several countries. The steam tour of southern Africa, known as the 'Zimzam Steam Safari', was first offered in August 1985 and was a huge success. Nothing on the same scale had ever before been attempted in Africa, but the project was greeted enthusiastically by the Zimbabwean authorities, especially by National Railways of Zimbabwe, whose eager co-operation ensured access to many sites of railway interest such as the Bulawayo Diesel and Steam Depots and the Zeco Steam Loco Repair Shops.

Regulars on TEFS tours are an international brigade, coming from all over Europe to share their interest in steam railways.

The Zimzam Tour: The steam two-week safari runs at least once a year (further tours are dependent on customer demand), in late July. It begins in Bulawayo, after a short domestic flight from Harare, and a long-haul from Gatwick, and the first two days are spent in a hotel to acclimatise and to visit a few tourist and railway sites of interest. There is also the chance to see a number of Zimbabwe's most famous sights, and the option of a picnic trip into the Matopos Hills National Park for some game-watching is offered the first day.

Early-morning starts seem to be a feature of TEFS tours, with breakfast at 6.30 a.m. to allow the fullest possible use of each day and to utilise the splendid early-morning light for photography. You leave the hotel early on the third morning to board the Garratt steam train that pulls you across Zimbabwe and into Zambia. Plenty of opportunities for photography are provided, with frequent scheduled photostops *en route*. Guests are also allowed onto the footplate of the locomotives for short stints so that you can get a good close-up view of the workings of a steam train. The tour provides numerous opportunities for railway enthusiasts to enjoy their hobby: the itinerary includes unusual activities such as an evening barbecue in a locomotive depot, a spectacular sunset often providing a dramatic backdrop.

Natural rather than mechanical sights are next on the agenda with a two-day stop in the Hwange National Game Park, one of Africa's largest wildlife reserves. At extra cost guests can opt to spend these next two nights at the Hwange Safari Lodge instead of on board the train, but everyone gets the chance to go on a dawn or dusk game drive. During your stay in the Game Park, a full day's game drive is offered as an alternative to chasing trains in a hire car or a day's train photography from the stationary Garratt.

The spectacular Victoria Falls are the steam train's next destination, and an optional 'Flight of the Angels' plane trip over the falls ensures a unique view of one of the world's greatest natural phenomena. The final leg of the journey takes the train over the bridge across the falls gorge and into Zambia, and the evening is pleasantly whiled away with a Zambezi river cruise and displays of African dancing. The tour then returns to Bulawayo where you have a day free for last-minute shopping or a visit to a lion and bird park.

If enough people are interested, TEFS will organise an extension to the steam safari which leaves the railways behind and goes on to Harare, from where coach trips such as the 'Great Zimbabwe', will be arranged.

Accommodation: Aboard the train sleeping cars are four-berth and fairly large, but passengers are requested to deposit their suitcase in the baggage van, keeping only a travel bag with necessities and a change of clothing in the cabins. However, the only two nights that you will actually spend aboard the train are whilst it is stationary at Dete during the Hwange section of the tour. You could be disturbed by passing trains during the night, but then again elephants are known to come right up to the windows of the Safari Lodge, so it's six of one and half a dozen of the other! During the day guests are arranged four to a cabin, which provides the ideal opportunity to make friends with your fellow steam enthusiasts. Meals are taken in the twin dining car (with bar), which is not air-conditioned, but is placed at the rear of the train to avoid coal smuts landing in your soup.

During your fortnight you stay in two of Africa's finest hotels. The first, the Zimbabwe Sun Hotel in Bulawayo, is a fairly old three-star hotel and all rooms have bath/shower and toilet *en suite*. The Victoria Falls Hotel is the scenic setting for the second stopover. Again, this is a very traditional hotel with first-class facilities and stunning views of the falls from the breakfast terrace. Those opting to leave the train for two nights in the Hwange National Game Park will stay at the Hwange Safari Lodge, which is a splendid modern two-storey hotel, with a game-viewing bar in a tree overlooking a waterhole.

How To Get There: Return flight from London Gatwick is included in the price of £2000 for the fortnight. All hotel accommodation is also included, although the two nights at Hwange Safari Lodge are at extra cost. The Victoria Falls 'Flight of the Angels' plane trip is also extra, at a cost of about £25.

TEFS produce a monthly newsletter which gives details of all proposed tours in advance of advertisements, and provides information on steam activity in many countries. A year's subscription costs £6 plus twelve stamped self-addressed foolscap envelopes. Over the next couple of years, TEFS's extensive tour programme includes steam tours in China, North Korea, Vietnam, Sudan, the USA and Australia (see Appendix II for details).

Golfing in France

For many, playing a round of golf is the ideal way to unwind after a stressful week in the office. Combine this with the outstanding scenery of northern France, the Algarve or the Canary Islands (not to mention the challenges presented by some of the world's greatest championship courses) and you begin to see why this particular activity holiday is every golfer's dream.

A golfing holiday is ideal both for singles and groups of golfers, particularly since you are surrounded by other holiday-makers who share your interest in the sport. Amateur competitions and tournaments help to foster a friendly rivalry between guests, and the lively nightlife of many resorts encourages friendships off the fairway as well as on.

However, for many couples and families, interests other than golf need to be catered for in a holiday. It is in this area that Par-Tee Tours specialize, with their 'Golfing Gourmet Weekends', 'Gourmet Cookery Courses' and thalassotherapy centres, designed especially to suit both the golfer and non-golfer alike.

Many years of experience in organising golf holidays have made Par-Tee the leading specialist in this area. Their managing director is a county golfer herself, and is well-qualified to understand the highly individual needs of the golfer and to design an all-round holiday which takes these needs into account.

Par-Tee Tours offer a comprehensive range of golfing holidays in Brittany, and also in Biarritz in south-west France. They can actually personalise the service to offer individually-designed holidays, business conferences and company golf days. Golf courses in Brittany include two championship courses, one of which was designed by Peter Allis and Dave Thomas, and another which has a green in the middle of a lake! All courses have weekend competitions in which Par-Tee guests are welcome to participate. With some holidays the golf itself is included in the price, and where this is not the case, reduced green fees are obtainable with a Par-Tee Tours discount card.

The unique feature of Par-Tee Tours' holiday selection is, however, their 'Golfing Gourmet Weekends'. These are five-day breaks which combine luxurious accommodation, sporting pleasure and gastronomic excellence to provide the ultimate in golfing holidays. Stay in a twelfth-century château and enjoy the delights of gourmet food cooked by a chef whose gastronomic talents are famed throughout France. What's more, if the culinary arts are more to your taste than golf, Par-Tee offer a cookery course, where, for a small supplement, you can spend three days under the instruction of the chef himself, with copies of the recipes to take home at the end.

If some members of the family prefer to get in shape in a more leisurely manner while the others walk the fairways, Par-Tee even offer a golfing break at a health and thalassotherapy centre in the south-west of Brittany, where you can enjoy rest, relaxation, good food and gentle exercise whilst being pampered by the friendly staff. Thalassotherapy is the use of new physiotherapy methods and natural remedies including the application of warm sea water, mud and algae, to relieve tension and arthritis. Gymnastics, aerobics, massage, sauna, and a heated indoor sea-water swimming pool are also available.

Accommodation is in hotels selected for their particularly high standards. The most spectacular are ancient châteaux, set in extensive and picturesque grounds and offering gourmet evening meals for those whose appetite has been whetted by a day on the golf course or even the beach. Some hotels are situated actually on the golf courses themselves, whilst others are a few minutes drive away in the heart of picturesque Breton towns and villages. There are also self-catering apartments on offer.

Since Par-Tee Tours deal directly with the client and thereby avoid paying an agency commission, they are able to offer extremely good rates. For a week at a hotel in July/August on a bed and breakfast basis, their prices begin at around £170, including ferry (based on four people sharing a car) and go up to about £370. The fly/drive option costs from £450–700 for six nights. Dinner, bed and breakfast is only offered at certain hotels, costing around £600 for a week. The gourmet breaks are priced from £242–388 for five days and the cookery courses cost around £350 for the same length of time.

Other recommended companies offering 'the ultimate golfing holiday' are Sovereign Golf and Longshot Golf Holidays. Both offer a wide range of both winter and summer golfing breaks throughout the world. Both companies have designed comprehensive golfing programmes for all standards of player, and a variety of friendly holiday tournaments to give you a chance to put your skills to the test. Sovereign have recently upgraded their programme, with the emphasis being placed on special needs of golfers, even down to such small details as their new offer of free hire of a four-door car instead of a two-door, to make handling of unwieldy sets of clubs as easy as possible. Longshot offer four nights at £260, which includes a return ferry crossing, bed and breakfast and one green fee per night. These, though, don't have the personal touch of Par-Tee Tours, nor the flexibility of arrangements which are possible through a small specialist operator. (See Appendix II for addresses).

Outdoor Canada

The region of Quebec is as different from English-speaking Canada as the Shetland Isles from southern England. The language, people, culture and cuisine all show their definite French origins, and it's in the setting of this eastern province that one of the world's very best holiday resorts can be found. Grayrocks is a one-and-a-half hour drive from Montreal (a seven-hour flight from London). Few resorts offer enough after a few days to keep you on site, but here every member of the family, from young to old, active or indolent, is completely taken care of, all in a wonderful setting of lakes and mountains. Outdoor Canada conjures up images of long walks, watersports, skiing in winter, golf and tennis in summer, the 'great outdoors'. This is what you'll find in this place.

Spend a few days first in the city – the contrast is all the sweeter afterwards. Montreal is no bland, smog-ridden North American city though. This is one of the most interesting and historic of this continent's metropoli. Fabulous museums; galleries; shopping malls; old (for North America, very old – seventeenth-century!) buildings, and a historic city centre, combine with some excellent hotels and restaurants (Montreal is regarded as the gourmet capital of Canada), and three to four days pass quickly. The St Lawrence river and the many green spaces make this a pleasant city, even for a stay with children. Drive up the Laurentian Highway, past the mountains of the same name. Grayrocks is in the northern end of this region. Thomas Cook feature Grayrocks as part of their extensive Canadian programme. Using Air Canada, they offer a week-long package, commencing on a Monday and including six nights accommodation. Golf packages, making extensive use of their eighteen-hole, par seventy-two course, are also offered.

Set in two thousand acres and bordering the Regional Park of Mont Tremblant and some of Quebec's finest forested valleys, the resort borders Lac Ouimet. Families are extremely well catered for: children under six years of age can share their parents' room at no extra charge; they also have a free, fully supervised activities programme from 9 a.m.–9 p.m. and even babies are catered for in a daycare centre for a small extra charge. While the little ones are enjoying their treasure hunts, hayrides and beach activities, mum and dad can get stuck into some serious unwinding on the tennis courts, golf course, on the windsurfers, dinghies, yachts, pedaloes, or kayaks. The watersports are all free for unlimited use. For an extra charge (average prices) you can take out mountain bikes; go horse-riding; take tennis lessons in the tennis school from professionals (the tennis school is the main reason in the summer why this is one of the Canadians' favourite summer resorts – it is rated one of the best in North America); or you can take up golf, or improve your game under the golf pro's eye. The Spa fitness centre is also free to guests, as is nightly entertainment.

In the winter, the tennis is replaced by skiing, and the sea plane, which you can hire for a reasonable £40 for five for half an hour in the summer, takes off its water skis and puts on its snow ones, as you land on the frozen-over river. The Grayrocks Snow Eagle Ski School (rated number three in North America) draws people from all over Canada and the USA. This is *the* place to learn skiing, with special covered tow-bars, and 65 instructors at your command, the slopes are perfectly shaped for your first tumbles. More experienced skiers will enjoy skiing in the Regional Park next to the resort. Snow is guaranteed, with the snow-making facilities there adding to the natural stuff.

Accommodation is offered in various options: the de luxe hotel has apartments and rooms, and then there are condominiums across the lake. Prices by British standards are very reasonable. The all-inclusive package which offers three full meals a day is excellent value, as the food here is first class. The service, in common with all Quebec, is slow, but when it comes, it's been worth waiting for! The French-style cuisine is of the standard of a first-class restaurant at home. Not that you'll want to leave the resort, but if you want a change of scenery, two excellent Relais et Châteaux hotels with excellent dining rooms within forty-five minutes are La Sapinière in Val David (tel. 819 322 2020), and L'Eau à la Bouche in St Adèle (tel. 514 229 4151).

Don't forget the French phrasebook. Even if your school French isn't too bad, the French Canadian accent will throw you!

Air Canada offer a 30-day advance purchase return fare from between £320 and £400. Grayrocks prices vary according to the type of package and season. For example, two adults sharing a one-bedroom apartment on the vacation week package will pay £250 to £320 for six nights. A two-bedroom apartment shared by four people costs between £180 and £230. On a golf package, two people sharing a one-bedroom apartment will pay between £330 and £430. Full board supplements on the vacation and golf week packages cost £214 (adult) and £143 (child under twelve).

For further information: obtain the Canada brochure from Thomas Cook Far Away Holidays (see Appendix II for details).

Club Med – Activity Holidays Par Excellence

For the ultimate all-round activity holiday, Club Med is ideal. Established forty years ago, Club Med aims to provide the holiday-maker with everything needed for the perfect holiday, all in one location. With 100 resorts, known as 'villages', worldwide, and offering almost every activity under the sun, Club Med caters for all tastes: there's scuba-diving, sailing, snorkelling, tennis, golf, cycling, summer skiing and windsurfing, to name but a few.

The emphasis is definitely on having fun in an informal, friendly atmosphere. Club Med welcomes singles, couples, groups and families, providing for the latter separate children's clubs at many villages, where daytime care and supervision is given for children between the ages of four months and twelve years. Qualified instructors look after the children between 8.30 a.m. and 9 p.m., instructing the older ones in a multitude of sports and leisure activities. Over and above the usual Club Med facilities, a Cadet Club for twelve- and thirteen-year-olds and a Juniors' Club for teenagers of fourteen and fifteen offer tournaments, picnics, discussions and guided tours of the area.

Each resort is organised village-style, and accommodation is in luxury hotels (at the top of the range), bungalows or Polynesian straw huts, depending on the location. Restaurants, bars and boutiques are part of each complex and equipment and instruction for a huge variety of sports and activities is provided on site, generally without extra charge. On the whole, once you have paid your all-inclusive price, only your drinks from the bar are extras.

As well as the usual popular Mediterranean holiday spots such as Spain, France, Italy and Greece, Club Med villages are also found in almost 40 countries: Israel, Egypt, the Bahamas, Florida, Switzerland and Thailand are a few examples of the exotic and varied locations on offer. Each village is designed to blend in with the architectural style of its country. Tours and excursions are organised from the village, giving you a chance to explore the surrounding country and see some famous sights, like the pyramids, Acapulco, or Disneyworld.

Club Med is also renowned for the extremely high standard of its cuisine. No matter where your resort is, the chef is sure to be French, bringing that traditional touch of Gallic excellence to every meal, whether it is a buffet or a four-course dinner. Seating is traditionally at tables of eight in the main restaurant, so that making friends comes naturally, but in the second restaurant – the typique (i.e. local style) – the tables are for six, four and two. The restaurants themselves are always situated in prime locations, sheltered by palm trees or overlooking the sea.

The choice of activities on offer at Club Med villages is superb. Most villages have numerous tennis courts, many of which are floodlit. At least thirty villages are equipped for golf practice, and, for more experienced players, there are often courses situated just next door to the village. Almost every resort has its own swimming pool – some even have two!

For the more adventurous, Club Med offers great opportunities to have a go at more unusual sports, such as archery, pétanque and snorkelling. First-class equipment is provided for every sport on offer, as is qualified instruction where necessary. Whether you want an intensive training course in one particular sport, or perhaps just a more relaxed sampling of something new, Club

Med provides it all. And with a range of tropical beaches to sun yourself on, who could blame you for choosing not to do anything at all?

One of the major attractions of Club Med for a family holiday is the variety of entertainment on offer for children: a daily baby club takes care of Club Med's youngest visitors (four months plus), where qualified staff and nurses will play with the children and make sure that they also rest. Mums and dads have a chance to join in at dinnertime in the baby restaurant. All facilities and utensils necessary for baby care are available for guests' use.

Children aged two and three are welcomed at the P'tit Club, where days are spent on the beach or by the swimming pool, and the highlight of the week is the show staged by the kids for their parents.

The Mini Club and the Kids' Club cater for children between four and eleven years, and offer the chance to learn a new sport or handicraft. Kids are supervised from 9 a.m. till 9 p.m. Older children will find the Cadet Club and Junior Club right up their street – in fact, there's literally something for everyone.

Some resorts don't have every club. The US Sandpiper resort offers the most for children and has the added bonus of being situated near Disney World.

Accommodation: Accommodation varies from the height of luxury to pretty basic. Top of the range are hotels like the ten-storey luxury hotel in St George's Cove, Bermuda, and the French country chateau at St-Aubin-sur-Gaillon. Club Med is best known, however, for its more typical 'bungalow villages', where small lodgings in detached, semi-detached or maisonette style are scattered around landscaped gardens or on the beach. All bungalows have their own private bathroom or shower facilities.

If you really want holiday accommodation with a difference, where atmosphere rather than luxury is what counts, then try one of the eleven Polynesian-style 'straw hut villages'. These are a nostalgic reminder of the very beginnings of Club Med, located actually on the beach and made of woven bamboo with a thatched straw roof. Furnishings are basic in the extreme – a single room containing twin-beds and hanging space for clothing – and washing facilities are communal. The huts do not have electricity.

How to get there: Club Med offers inclusive packages consisting of flight and accommodation. Flights are with over forty major airlines and can be taken either from London or Paris. Travelling by train from Paris to certain resorts is a second option offered as a package deal. Transfers to and from Club Med villages are included in all package deals from London and Paris.

For those who prefer to travel independently this is also possible, although the travel insurance included in the cost of the holiday does not cover you for independent travel arrangements.

Prices vary enormously depending on distance of location and scale of resort. The more accessible European villages mostly range from £250–650 for seven nights at the height of the summer season. However, if the more exotic destinations are your choice, prices begin at around £800 per week and can go as high as £1,650. Your holiday cost includes return flight and transfers; seven or fourteen nights accommodation; full-board (including wine with meals); all sports activities unless otherwise specified (using first-class equipment and with qualified instruction); all other Club Med leisure activities and entertainment and holiday insurance.

For further information, see the Club Med brochure, available from travel agents, or direct from Club Med (see Appendix II for details).

Flotilla Sailing in the Aegean

Yachting in the azure seas of the Aegean, an activity traditionally enjoyed only by the rich jet-set, is now, more than ever, within the financial reach of less wealthy holiday-makers. The increasing popularity of sailing holidays came with the advent of flotilla sailing – a totally unique form of boat holiday.

The word 'flotilla' means 'small fleet', and up to a dozen yachts sail together, under the discreet overall supervision of a lead boat on which there is a qualified crew comprising skipper, engineer and hostess. Each day's route is planned by the skipper and a late-afternoon rendezvous is arranged at a specific port or harbour, but it is entirely up to you how you make your way there and what you do on the way. As well as the various tasks to be done aboard ship, such as cooking, cleaning and crewing, there is plenty of time to anchor for a cooling swim or sunbathe on a deserted beach. You could try your hand at snorkelling or windsurfing with the equipment usually provided on the yachts.

At night there is the opportunity to explore tiny harbour villages, untainted as yet by Mediterranean commercialism, and share an evening of local culture in a taverna with the rest of the flotilla.

The combination of freedom with the security of qualified leadership makes flotilla sailing an ideal holiday for people with an interest in exploring the largely unspoilt Aegean coast at a leisurely pace but who have insufficient funds either to own or charter a crewed yacht, or who lack the nautical experience necessary for individual yacht hire.

Most flotilla companies require that at least one person on board 'knows the ropes' before embarking. Some companies offer weekend primer courses on the English coast for those who need to brush up on their practical know-how. However, even the most inexperienced sailors can enjoy the delights of an off-shore vacation by opting for the 'mix'n match' option, where beginners and the more advanced share a yacht, giving an opportunity to form friendships which can last for years.

The Greek and Turkish seas are the most popular locations in the world for flotilla sailing, as weather and sea conditions are perfect for all levels of sailing experience or ability. With negligible tides and currents, cloudless blue skies and near-constant sunshine, you're unlikely to have to worry about anything worse than sunburn!

Provided that you enjoy sailing, a boat holiday such as this is suited to all ages and all types. Groups, families, couples and singles can all be accommodated on a variety of different-sized boats. Flotilla sailing really does provide the ideal way to enjoy a relaxing, leisurely vacation in the sun, as well as experiencing the extra excitement and challenge of an activity holiday.

How To Get There: Of the few companies who operate flotilla sailing holidays, Sunsail International and the Yacht Cruising Association are leading the market. Sunsail in particular offers a wide range of sailing holidays, catering for all levels of experience (although complete novices are recommended to take a basic sailing course at the Emsworth Sailing School in the south of England prior to attempting any flotilla holiday other than the 'mix'n match' option stated above). Guidelines are given in their comprehensive brochure as to the level of aptitude needed for the various types of boat. Their five flotilla fleets cover most of the Aegean coasts of both Greece and southern Turkey, as well as elsewhere in the Mediterranean. Most holidays are for two-week periods, although demand has recently led them to offer one-week breaks as well.

Prices, which include a return flight from London Gatwick, vary enormously according to season, location and type of yacht and cruise. Two weeks in late July and early August (the height of the season) on a two-man yacht ranges from £750–1,000 per person, whilst in early June prices are around £200 less. However, the more people sharing a yacht, the lower the price, and prices for a four-man yacht in high season stand at between £200–400 lower than those quoted above. For those preferring to make their own way to their chosen flotilla base, Sunsail offer a reduction of £50 per person on all departure dates except 17 July to 27 August when the reduction is £100.

For those who would prefer to be based on shore, but who wish to try out various different watersports or to get a taste of flotilla sailing by opting for a one-day cruise only, Sunsail have devised a separate programme entitled 'Sunsail Clubs'. Six clubs in Greece and Turkey offer a vast variety of watersports, and sailing tuition is available at extra cost. Alternatively, you can combine a week ashore with a week's cruise with a flotilla. The many options offered by this company make it easy to find something to suit almost every individual preference – ideal for families or larger groups.

If an active sailing holiday sounds too much like hard work but a vacation afloat still appeals, then perhaps a luxurious cruise aboard a private yacht is more to your taste. Abercrombie and Kent offer four, seven and eleven-day cruises around the south-western coast of Turkey, with all-inclusive prices starting at £911.

If you want to venture further than the Aegean for your sailing holiday then perhaps a felucca sailtrek down the Nile could be just what you are looking for. Transglobal, a company which specializes in finding new and exciting ways of travelling across the more exotic parts of the world, have developed this unusual style of sailing holiday, whereby you sail at a leisurely pace down the Nile between Aswan and Luxor, powered only by the wind. Feluccas are traditional Nile sailboats whose design has remained unchanged for centuries, and they are very distinctive with their tall white sails. A crew of two Egyptian sailors do all the work for you, leaving you free to soak up the sun or make several sightseeing stops. Between five and ten passengers are carried on each boat, and at night you sleep under the stars on a cushion-covered deck. Transglobal offer fifteen-day sailtreks from £500–600, including flights.

For further information and brochures, Sunsail International and other companies mentioned above may also be contacted direct (see Appendix II for addresses).

Walking the Austrian Alps

Lush green valleys dotted with wooden chalets; rolling meadows where the only sound is the melodic jingle of cow bells, and majestic snow-capped mountains providing a breathtaking backdrop to this rural idyll. Austria is a walker's paradise. Miles of signposted paths and trails meander across the Alpine countryside, and an extensive network of funiculars, gondolas and chairlifts provide easy access to the higher slopes. The walkable area is, in fact, so vast that even in mid-summer you can get away from it all and find yourself alone in a sunny mountain pasture. Lower down, mountain huts and cafés provide an opportunity for welcome rest and refreshment.

Austrian folk are renowned for the warmth of their hospitality, and this reputation is well-deserved. Many people offer bed and breakfast accommodation within their picturesque chalets and farmhouses, which are invariably well-kept with intricately carved wooden balconies and roof edges, and window boxes brimming over with a profusion of brightly-coloured flowers.

The Tyrol region, stretching west from the Swiss border, and the Salzkammergut – the Austrian Lake District – are the best areas for a walking holiday, with many resorts geared specifically towards catering for this type of visitor. Seefeld, Kitzbuhel and Soll are three of the most popular Tyrolean resorts, whilst Zell am See and Fuschl attract many holiday-makers to the Salzkammergut, in the heart of which lies that famous musical city, Salzburg, home both to Mozart and *The Sound of Music*.

Seefeld is a a large resort situated nearly 4,000 feet up on a wide plateau, fourteen miles north of Innsbruck. Despite its size and reputation as a busy tourist centre, Seefeld has retained its Tyrolean atmosphere and is an excellent base from which to explore the miles of signposted trails, criss-crossing the forests and meadows of the Inn Valley. You can ascend the Gschwandkopf and Rosshutte peaks by cable-car or mountain railway and try a few more testing hikes to nearby peaks.

Kitzbuhel and Soll are both familiar names to Ski Sunday fans, to whom their reputation as superb winter ski resorts is well-known. Yet both towns are equally popular with summer visitors, especially walkers, for whom the extensive network of chair-lifts and cable-cars ensures that many delightful days can be spent hiking across the mountain tops and enjoying the best of the Austrian scenery.

Fuschl is a beautiful village nestling amidst mountains on the shores of Lake Fuschl, in the heart of the Salzkammergut. Here the weather is generally good (on average 5°F warmer than Britain), the air invigorating and the scenery spectacular – in short, it is perfect walking country. With over sixty miles of waymarked trails, and numerous other activities on offer, you certainly won't run out of things to do. Zell am See, between the Tyrol and the Salzkammergut, possesses all of the most attractive features of this lovely area. Nearby is the spectacular Grossglockner mountain pass while surrounding the Zellersee are the majestic mountains of the Hohe Tauern range. The Schmittenhohe is the most popular peak with walkers, and with a cable-car and several scenic restaurants it's easy to see why.

Whichever resort or area you choose and whatever level of walking ability or fitness you possess, Austria everywhere offers an immense variety of simple paths, waymarked nature trails, gentle lakeside walks and more strenuous mountain hikes. Local tourist offices and many individual hotels arrange guided walks, where experienced, qualified local guides lead parties of tourists into areas that they might not otherwise have explored. These are available free of charge to visitors on production of their Austrian Visitor's Card – a card which is legally required to be given to all visitors on registering with their hotel within twenty-four hours of arrival, and which entitles them to various concessions in and around the resort. On such organised walks you have the opportunity to win walking badges, certificates or medals, of which the 'Austrian Hiking Boot' is the highest accolade. For the more independent walker, good walking maps are available from most tourist offices and the staff are usually extremely helpful, giving advice as to the best routes for different abilities and the average time taken to cover them. For all walkers, whether independent or part of a group, sensible footwear and clothing at all times are essential.

Accommodation: Accommodation is available in hotels, guest houses and pensions, as well as in private houses and farms. A good alternative to hotel accommodation is a self-catering apartment within a hotel, combining the freedom of one's own facilities with the convenience of restaurants on site, and maid service if you want it. The Parkhotel Elizabeth at Zell am See is a good example. Demand for these Aparthotels is high, so book ahead. There are also over 400 caravan and camping sites in Austria. A list of all registered accommodation is available from the Austrian National Tourist Office in London (see Appendix I for details).

How To Get There: Many different package holidays to Austria are offered by both major tour operators and smaller, lesser-known companies. A popular option is the two-centre holiday which allows you to combine a week in the hills with a few days in a city such as Vienna, Innsbruck or Salzburg. For a more flexible holiday the fly-drive idea is a good one, and many companies offer a 'go-as-you-please' programme, whereby you decide your own itinerary as you go along, booking each hotel from the one before. Austrian Holidays (in particular), Inghams, Thomson, Austro Tours and GTF Tours are all recommended operators.

Typical package deals for a week's holiday including flight range from £200–400 in Seefeld, Kitzbuhel and Soll. Fuschl and Zell am See vary from £272–432. These prices are for July and August.

Independent travel to and within Austria is easily arranged. Vienna, Graz, Innsbruck, Klagenfurt, Linz and Salzburg all have international airports, and flight times from London are between two and three and a half hours. Those taking a car will find the Dover–Ostend ferry is the quickest and most practical route, and from Ostend to the Tyrol is about a day's drive. Otherwise there are car hire firms with offices in most cities, and a British driving licence is generally recognised in Austria.

Return flights to Austria on scheduled British Airways and Austrian Airline services cost from £115–190 depending on destination, with Salzburg and Innsbruck being the cheapest. Car hire starts at around £130 for a week's rental of a small car, excluding collision damage waiver or deposit. A go-as-you-please package, including accommodation and car rental for a minimum of seven days and a maximum of one month, costs from £360–430, based on two people sharing a car.

Brochures for the above companies may be obtained from

most travel agents, or direct from the companies themselves (see Appendix II for addresses).

Trail Blazing in the Wild West

Mention the Wild West and one immediately conjures up images of cowboys and Indians, saloons and ranches, canyons and corrals. Keen to establish a sense of history, many Americans view with nostalgia the days of the early pioneers, who blazed a trail on horseback across the mid-West wilderness with their families and possessions following behind in covered wagon trains. But those days of adventure are not so firmly in the past as one might perhaps imagine.

American Pioneers and American Connections are two small companies which offer you a chance to step back in time and discover America the way that the pioneers did – on the move. Whether it's the Rockies on horseback, the Grand Canyon from a river raft, or Arizona in a covered wagon, this is the ideal opportunity to experience the awe-inspiring natural beauty of this rugged country.

The part played by wagon trains in the struggle to conquer the West is legendary. What better way, then, to relive history than by travelling though the wildernesses of Utah and Wyoming as part of such a train? Trek along unused trails in the foothills of the Rockies and the Redrock countryside near the Grand Canyon in authentic replicas of original white canvas-covered wagons, pulled by gentle teams of horses and driven by local ranchers. During the day there is the opportunity to ride alongside the train or to go on a guided trailride into the surrounding countryside. At night the wagons form a circle and you can choose to sleep in the wagon or a tent, or simply out in the open, under the stars. The food is cowboy-style around the campfire, and often accompanied by a song or a story.

If the cowboy life itself is more your style, then perhaps you would prefer to explore America on horseback. There are a number of genuine cowboys (and girls) who offer private saddle treks. Using their own extensive knowledge of areas such as Yellowstone National Park, they take groups of adventurous riders off the beaten track and into seemingly unexplored rocky wildernesses. A night under canvas accompanied by the distant sounds of wild animals, and viewing a sunrise over snow-capped mountains are both unforgettable experiences. So is the rare chance to meet Americans who know these wild areas like the back of their hands and who take immense pleasure in being able to show it to others. Some experience in the saddle is recommended, and a couple of days of aching limbs is an occupational hazard suffered by most, but more than compensated for by the precious opportunity to get away from it all.

For those who prefer the relative luxury of a home base, American Pioneers' Triangle C Ranch is an ideal place from which to blaze a few trails. Set in the heart of Wind River Valley amidst the pine-covered mountains of the Shoshone National Forest, sixty miles east of Yellowstone, the ranch accommodates between twenty and twenty-five guests at a time in an atmosphere redolent of the old West. You can spend your days riding the trails or enjoying rodeo games. A basic orientation programme at the beginning of your stay ensures that even those with no experience in the saddle can take full advantage of the excellent riding facilities. A day trip to Yellowstone, an overnight cowboy-style trip into the wilderness, white-water rafting and fishing are some of the activities also on offer.

The canyons of Colorado are some of America's most famous and spectacular natural sights, covering so vast an area that few visitors see more than a glimpse of their full splendour. For a holiday characterised by sheer excitement in an extraordinary setting there can be few experiences to equal that of a white-water rafting trip down the Colorado River or through the Canyonlands National Park. The sense of achievement felt after shooting rapids in the heart of red rock canyons that soar 2,000 feet above you is incredible. Tag-A-Long Tours of Utah offer trips from two to six days, with the longer ones combining a raft trip with plane and jeep rides to give an all-round view of the canyons. Moki Mak also operate fifteen-day raft trips through the Grand Canyon, using eighteen-foot oar-powered rafts which carry four to six passengers plus qualified boatmen.

All of the options mentioned above are offered as packages excluding travel to and from the US. All of these holidays may be included as part of a longer stay in the US. Wagons West, Moki Mak and Triangle Ranch are all subsidiaries of American Pioneers. They also offer a car rental service and traditional Wild West-style accommodation in Wyoming and Utah National Parks. Tag-A-Long Tours is operated by American Connections. Starting points for these expeditions are Moab, Utah and Grand Junction, Colorado. American Connections also offer Texan ranch holidays, with flights to the US included in the package and a full programme of cowboy-style activities. Children are also catered for. All of these holidays can be booked through UK agents.

There are still genuine cowboys who offer themselves as guides for the independent holiday-maker who wishes to explore off the beaten track in the National Parklands, but these can only be arranged once in America and many are only advertised locally or even simply by word of mouth.

In Utah the covered wagon trains operate in April, May, September and October only. In Wyoming the season runs from June to August. The cost per adult is $540. Moki Mak raft trips run during the months of May through to October and the cost per adult is $1,545. Tag-A-Long Tours operate during the same period and their expeditions cost $285, $565 and $895 for the two, four and six-day trips respectively. There are also supplementary charges of around $25 each for both tent and sleeping bag hire.

Seven nights at Triangle C Ranch will cost approximately $500 per person and this includes meals and riding. The ranch is open during June, July and August. Accommodation at other ranches and cabins is around $60–70 per night.

Brochures may be obtained by writing direct to American Connections and American Pioneers at Travel Pioneers Group (see Appendix II for details).

Camel Safaris

For many people an ideal holiday is one which allows them to become more than mere spectators of the life and culture of the country that they are visiting. Opportunities to meet local people, eat traditional food and participate in native customs are eagerly seized, and often provide the highlight of a holiday. What better way, then, to explore a tiny part of the vast Indian Thar desert than by using the mode of transport favoured by local travellers, and only experienced by most Westerners vicariously, through the cinema screen?

Camel safaris are a new and unusual holiday idea which provide the adventurous visitor with a means of experiencing native life, both in the typically nomadic form of transport, and in the small tribal villages visited. Three-day treks, such as the ones offered from imaginative tour operator Transglobal, into the northern Indian desert, enable you to see a side of India that is usually neglected by mainstream tour operators, who focus on the large tourist cities of Delhi, Agra and others. This safari is unusual in providing visitors with a chance to combine a conventional tour of such famous sights as the Taj Mahal and the Amber Fort at Jaipur, with an outdoor adventure that takes you right off the beaten track.

Beginning in the ancient city of Jaisalmer, this particular trek takes you into the heart of the Thar desert in Rajasthan, visiting settlements of nomadic and pastoral tribes whose very isolation from the usual tourist route has left them largely untouched by modern civilisation. Photographic opportunities on a trip of this kind are endless, with the camels themselves providing an atmospheric feature that makes a popular talking-point with people back home.

The camels used on such treks generally carry two people – an experienced local Indian 'driver' and one passenger – so that the responsibility for looking after the camel is not one which holiday-makers themselves have to face. Also, it means that just about anyone is able to participate in these treks, where the only art you have to master is that of staying in the saddle. A camel cart accompanies the party at all times, and those wishing a rest from the saddle may ride in this at any time. The Indian guides also plan and direct the route taken by safari, and they are a mine of information about local life and the surrounding countryside, adding greatly to the interest of your experience. They are also responsible for setting up camp each night and preparing the meals, which, with the exception of tea breaks, are all traditional fare. The tea breaks themselves are extremely reminiscent of colonial days since the tea is served in china cups and presented on silver trays!

Camel riding is an amazing experience, although it can be slightly uncomfortable at first for those unused to days in the saddle. These are proud and stately creatures and their strength and resilience makes them ideal desert creatures. The country through which you travel is also remarkable. The daily prospect of endless sand, broken only by small clumps of dried scrub grass and the occasional settlement, gives the traveller a unique sense of remoteness, and a chance to get away from it all that is welcome after the noise and bustle of India's major cities.

Transglobal also offer other camel treks as part of longer tours. For example, you can go by camel into the Sinai desert for an overnight trip that is led by local Bedouin people. Or there is another excursion into the Wadi Rum desert in Jordan, the setting for the famous film, *Lawrence of Arabia*. Another option is a camel trek to St Simeon's Monastery at Aswan. This trip leads across the golden sands of Aswan's west bank from the Aga Khan's Mausoleum to the Monastery and on to the Tombs of the Nobles, all of which are essential sights for the visitor to Egypt. Transglobal also offer trips that use other modes of animal transport, such as an exploration of Nepal's Chitwan National Park by elephant, a donkey trek to the Valley of the Kings, Luxor, and horse-riding by the Pyramids at Giza.

Transglobal offer 'land only' packages that begin and end in the country of travel, as well as packages which include a pre-arranged flight. The former are useful particularly if you are planning a longer period of travel and wish to include a trek as part of a wider itinerary. For most, however, the conventional flight-inclusive package will be the most attractive.

The Thar desert camel safari is part of a trek called the 'Rajasthan Safari' which lasts twenty-two days, whilst the Jordan trek is called 'Beyond the King's Highway' and lasts only eight days. The trek into the Sinai forms part of the itinerary of the 'Sinai Insight' trip, again lasting eight days, and which cannot be taken on its own, but which must be combined with one of Transglobal's other programmes in Egypt, Israel and/or Jordan.

The trips involving other animals all form optional parts of different tour itineraries, all of which can be found in this company's brochure.

The 'Rajasthan Safari' costs from £500-550 for the land-only package, and around £990 including Egypt Air flights to and from London. There is also a tour supplement of £95 payable to the tour leader. 'Beyond the King's Highway' costs around £300, land-only, and from £510-540 with flights. Air travel is by Royal Jordanian Airlines. The 'Sinai Insight' tour costs just under £200 land-only.

For further information contact Transglobal (see Appendix II for details).

Himalayan Trekking in Nepal

Nepal has the distinction of being the only Hindu kingdom in the world. Bordered by China to the north and India to the west, south and east, most of the country lies on the southern slope of the great Himalayan range, extending downwards from the highest peaks of this most majestic of mountain ranges, through hill country to the upper edge of the Ganges Plain. The lower Himalayas traverse the central region, and it is here that eight of the highest peaks in the world are found, including Mount Everest.

These snow-capped giants attract the more intrepid traveller to what is still a fairly isolated and primitive country. Some come simply to admire the spectacular peaks from the relative comfort of the fascinating capital city, Kathmandu, but the only way to really appreciate their grandeur is to see them close to. Since motorable roads are few in Nepal, a trek is the only way to do this, and a number of companies now offer a range of trekking holidays which take you right into the heart of this beautiful land.

Treks follow local paths and trails and pass through many of the tiny mountain villages that are scattered along the route. Here is the perfect opportunity to meet the Nepalese people in their own homes – a rare glimpse into a vastly different way of life. The treks are led by groups of local Sherpa mountain guides who, as well as supervising the practical operation of the trek, are eager to share their knowledge of this fascinating kingdom with interested tourists. Although the countryside is rugged, a lifetime of mountain experience enables Sherpas to lead treks in perfect safety and their contribution to the broadening of your cultural (not to mention physical!) horizons is immeasurable.

The choice of treks is such that almost anyone who wants to can go. A sense of adventure is essential, as is a certain level of fitness and a readiness to live under fairly basic conditions. All your luggage and equipment is carried by porters and pack animals, leaving you to walk at your own individual pace. Five or six hours' walking is the daily average, and there are opportunities for rest days along the way. Organised treks vary in length from three to eight days, or longer if you organise your own. Accommodation on treks is under canvas, and tents are set up and taken down each day by the guides and porters. The food is traditional but pretty basic, and again prepared by the Sherpa team.

The trekking season is generally from September to May, but the best periods are October to December and March to April. The weather is usually pleasant, with maximum temperatures of around 30°C in May and June. A day's trek in the sun at high altitudes brings with it the inevitable risk of sunburn, so trekkers are advised to be well prepared for this possibility. Summer and monsoon seasons are from June to October, whilst in the winter temperatures fall below freezing with a high level of snowfall in the mountains.

You can combine a trekking holiday with other activities. Since flights to Nepal arrive in Kathmandu, it makes sense to spend a couple of days exploring this fascinating city. In the centre is Dhurbar Square where there is an amazing array of Buddhist and Hindu temples. These have a variety of functions; as well as places of worship, they are used by the local people as market stalls by day and animal shelters by night. There is also the house of the living goddess, where a young girl lives in total seclusion from the age of six to puberty. Pokhara, in the centre of Nepal, is the starting point for many treks, and further south the Trisuli river is the location for river-rafting trips. Three days of exhilarating white-water brings you to the beautiful Royal Chitwan National Park, the ideal place to spend a couple of days on safari with the chance of sighting the famous Bengal tiger in its natural habitat.

Accommodation: Accommodation is improving in Kathmandu with the opening of a number of international-class hotels, but these are particularly busy during the spring and autumn, and it is advisable to book well in advance. Alternatively, there are several lodges or hostels located in the old part of the town in the streets around the Dhurbar Square and in the Thamel district. There are also comfortable hotels in Pokhara and the Chitwan National Park.

How To Get There: While there is good selection of trekking packages on offer, it is also possible to travel independently and to make your own trek arrangements on arrival in Nepal. All trekkers, whether on a day trek or a longer trip, must be accompanied by local guides, and these can be contacted through local agents in Kathmandu. Trekking permits are necessary for travel beyond Kathmandu or Pokhara, and these are issued by the Central Immigration Office.

You can either fly direct to Kathmandu or go via Delhi. Air India, British Airways and KLM are the three recommended airlines offering flights from London to Delhi at least three times a week. A British Airways return flight starts at £430. Royal Nepal Airlines operate daily flights between Delhi and Kathmandu, at £150 return. Emirates and Biman airlines operate direct flights from London to Kathmandu, with routing via Dubai and Dhaka respectively at a cost of just under £500 return.

The organised package option covers a wide range of different types and lengths of treks. For those wanting to avoid the more commercial treks offered by larger companies as part of a tour, the best selection is offered by Sherpa Expeditions in their 'Escape Routes' brochure. Travel to Nepal is excluded from their arrangements, allowing for greater individual flexibility. The longest of their treks is entitled 'Grand Himalayan Adventure' and lasts twenty-six days, taking in two eight-day treks, four days' rafting and a two-day safari. The treks are in the Annapurnas and the high Khumbu region, home of Everest. This programme can also be broken down into each of its individual elements or a combination of any of them to suit individual needs and preferences. All treks are graded from A to C, with A being the easiest and enjoyable by anyone who leads a reasonably active life, and C applying to longer treks at higher altitudes. Other companies offering similar programmes are ExplorAsia, Exodus and Himalayan Kingdoms Ltd. Bales also offer two genuine 'grass-roots' treks, operated by a local agent Yeti Travels. With this company transport from Britain is included in the package, as is accommodation prior to the trek, and there is the added element of a few days in Delhi at the end. The treks themselves last five and seven days in the Annapurna range. Pleasure Seekers is an up-market company also offering a genuine trekking experience, and including the Trisuli river trip and Chitwan safari in their 'Discover Nepal' package. They also offer a range of trek/river/safari combinations.

Perhaps the most luxurious but least adventurous of all the options is the one offered by a number of companies, including Pickfords Travel, Speedbird, Silk Cut and Pleasure Seekers. These packages are ideal for those who wish to explore the Nepalese countryside but prefer to return to a hotel base each night. Short, three-day treks are offered as an option by some companies, as part of a larger-scale tour of Nepal and India.

Sherpa Expeditions' longest trek, the Grand Himalayan Adventure, costs £895 excluding travel to Nepal, whilst the shorter sixteen-day Himalayan Explorer is priced at £525.

Prices for the more luxurious tours, which include Nepal in a wider itinerary, begin at around £1,100.

Brochures for the companies mentioned above can be obtained from most travel agents, or direct (see Appendix II for addresses).

For further information try the Royal Nepalese Embassy (see Appendix I for details).

Diving in the Great Barrier Reef

The Great Barrier Reef is one of the most extraordinary natural sights in the world. Lying between fifteen and 150 miles off the coastline of Australia's north-eastern province of Queensland, the coral reef stretches for 1,250 miles, enclosing a vast lagoon in which are scattered countless tiny islands and coral cays. Apart from magical scenery and tropical weather – tourist attractions in their own right – it is the world under the water that is attracting increasing numbers of adventurous holiday-makers from all over the world, keen to don snorkelling mask or scuba gear to explore beneath the azure waters.

Situated in one of the remotest parts of the world, the Great Barrier Reef was first noted by Captain James Cook in 1770, and the awe which it inspired then can still be experienced over 200 years later. 'A reef such as is here spoke of is scarcely known in Europe. It is a wall of coral rock rising almost perpendicular out of the unfathomable ocean', noted Cook in his journal, and it is only in the last decade that the reef has really become accessible to anyone other than local fishermen and naturalists.

The entire area is now protected by the Great Barrier Reef Marine Park Authority, and some of the larger islands have been developed into flourishing international resorts. More secluded accommodation is also available on some of the smaller islands, and the reef is now well served with both sea and air links to the mainland.

Snorkelling and diving are the most popular activities in this Down-Under paradise, being the ideal way to get really close to the spectacular underwater coral gardens and to view the multitudes of fish of every conceivable colour and shape. The reef is also an ideal place to go in for a bit of big-game fishing – broadbill swordfish, marlin and tuna are all present in abundance. With the added challenge of a potential shark catch, it is not surprising that one British company – Abercrombie and Kent – have organised a unique 'World of Fishing' package to Lizard Island, one of the finest islands on the Great Barrier Reef. For the less amphibious visitor there are glass-bottomed boats and viewing submarines to help you uncover the mysteries of the coral lagoon without wetting even your toes.

Spend a fortnight on the reef itself or take two or three day-trips from a mainland base such as the popular beach resorts of Cairns and Townsville – the choice is yours. There are eighteen islands with accommodation for overnight guests within the boundaries of the Great Barrier Reef Marine Park. Lizard Island is the most northern of these and is renowned as a centre for marlin fishing. It is also the favourite for diving and snorkelling. Daily glass-bottomed boat trips give visitors a tantalising glimpse of the coral world, whilst divers and snorkellers can take a powerboat trip to the outer reef or to selected sites around the island. Dunk Island, further south and only three miles off shore, is an extremely popular holiday island, whilst the nearby Bedarra Island offers a total contrast, with only two resorts, each accommodating sixteen people.

How To Get There: Whilst several companies offer a few nights at either an island or a mainland resort on the Barrier Reef as part of a larger tour of Australia, the only one offering a package deal specifically to an island in the reef chain is Thomson. However, independent travel is easy to arrange, with Qantas flying several times a week from London. Tradewinds offer an extensive selection of low-cost air travel arrangements to Australia, and they also provide details of local travel options, these being rail, coach and air passes which can be purchased in the UK. Australian Airlines and Ansett both offer overseas visitors a thirty per cent discount on internal flights of more than 1,000 km. Tickets must be purchased before leaving the UK.

Transport to the islands is either a short flight by helicopter or amphibious seaplane, or a longer boat trip. These run regularly, although not daily. The main carriers are Air Queensland, Trans-Australia Airlines and Air Whitsunday.

A return flight to Brisbane or Sydney – the two major cities on the eastern seaboard – costs from £750–1,000, without stopovers, depending on the time of year. (Australia's seasons are opposite to Britain's, with the summer high season peaking in December and lowest fares in July and August). Tradewinds Faraway Holidays offer a selection of itineraries with two-, three- and four-night stopovers in places such as Bali, Singapore or Bangkok. Prices range from £802–1,062 in low season, or from £935–1,185 in the high season.

If booked prior to arrival in Australia, internal travel is an excellent bargain. An internal flight from Brisbane to Cairns costs £77, and Sydney to Cairns is £96. Flights to Townsville are exactly £10 less.

Thomson offer twelve days on Hamilton Island from £1,403–1,733, including return flight and two nights' stopover in Singapore. Most companies offering tours of Australia include at least a day on the Barrier Reef in their itinerary. Prices begin at around £1,995. Abercrombie and Kent's 'World of Fishing' package costs £3,704 for seven nights (see Appendix II for addresses).

An American Dream: Skiing in Colorado

The traditionally popular European skiing holiday is beginning to have its drawbacks. Skiers heading abroad in the winter months all too often face long flight delays, long lift queues on overcrowded slopes, the possibility of poor snow conditions and bad weather, and high costs in expensive countries such as France and Austria. Small wonder, then, that British skiers are being gradually lured further west to the American Rockies by the promise of guaranteed snow and great value for money, especially when the pound is strong relative to the dollar.

Colorado is home to such well-known resorts as Aspen and Vail, as well as the attractively-named Beaver Creek, Breckenridge, Snowmass, Copper Mountain and Steamboat Springs. The scope of the skiing here is absolutely staggering, with, for example, a total of 6,192 acres covered by ski runs at Vail. All levels of ability are amply provided for. For beginners, skiing in Europe often means that you are confined to one or two simple slopes in the least scenic part of the skiing area for most of your holiday. Aspen, on the other hand, has an entire mountain dedicated to beginners and practice areas. At the other end of the range advanced skiers will have more than enough of a challenge on their hands with runs that played host to the 1989 World Alpine Ski Championships.

Considering that Vail alone has enough lifts to transport 50,000 skiers per hour, it is hardly surprising that those dreaded queues that can easily waste half your skiing time are virtually unheard of in the resorts of the Rockies. What is more, Vail even has a system of traffic lights strategically placed across the mountain to enable the skier to avoid choosing busy runs.

Accommodation is also a world away from the more functional style of hotel usually found in countries like Italy, Yugoslavia and

Andorra. Self-catering apartments – the most popular type of accommodation – are on a grand scale, with luxurious furnishings (one resort even provides an *en suite* spa bath). A queen-sized double bed per person is the norm! Some resorts such as Aspen have a history behind them – Aspen was a silver boom town in the 1880s – and this is reflected in many of the hotels, which have been beautifully restored to their Victorian origins.

Away from the slopes there's more than enough to do, with a huge variety of restaurants (from McDonalds to de luxe establishments), heated outdoor swimming pools and open-air ice rinks. In fact, there is something to suit all tastes. If you've enough energy left after a hard day on the pistes, you can take a dog-sled or sleigh ride, play a game of indoor tennis, or even go hot-air ballooning. Traditional European *après-ski* beverages of gluhwein and jagertee find American equivalents in the margaritas and Budweisers that are sipped or swigged to a background of live music or cabaret in one of the many bars and nightclubs that provide entertainment into the small hours. Families with young children will find arrangements that are tailor-made to suit their individual needs. At Snowmass, twelve miles away from Aspen, almost all the hotels and lodges lie directly on the slopes, so you can ski in and out with the minimum fuss, and all resorts have children's centres operating with the highest standards of childcare. Whilst parents enjoy the freedom of a day's skiing, the children play in well-equipped playrooms and learn to ski with qualified instructors. Most centres also have a crèche, and babies from the age of two months are welcome. Child reductions on accommodation and ski hire are widely available.

Resorts such as Aspen and Vail have been the traditional preserve of the rich and famous élite of the skiing world, and their high prices and general inaccessibility to a more international market were largely responsible for this. Now, however, major travel operators such as Inghams and Thomson have caught on to the enormous potential of the American ski scene, and British skiers are able to enjoy their hobby in California, Wyoming, Utah, Vermont and even Canada. Prices are surprisingly affordable, especially when the exchange rate is good, although the cost of living in the more sophisticated resorts can be fairly high. However the experience of an American skiing holiday makes it more than worth the extra pennies.

How To Get There: The American Dream is a company which

describes itself as the leading ski operator to the US, and justifiably so. They offer by far the widest range of resorts and holiday itineraries, including the tantalising opportunity to combine a week on the Colorado slopes with a week of Hawaiian sun. They arrange flights from Gatwick, Heathrow and Prestwick to arrive as close to the ski resort as possible, as do the other major tour operators, thus minimising the time spent on internal travel. This means that you can fly direct to Aspen and Steamboat Springs, and to Denver for the resorts of Vail, Beaver Creek, Breckenridge and Copper Mountain with a maximum of two hours' road transfer.

Poundstretcher, a subsidiary of British Airways, also offers ski packages to these resorts, as do American Express and Ski Vacations. Thomson, Inghams, Crystal and Neilson are four of the more widely-known tour operators whose winter brochures also include US resorts (see Appendix II for details).

The skiing season in Colorado begins in November and ends mid-April, and these two months are the cheapest time to go, although Thomson also offer lower prices in January. Prices for a week in a hotel, lodge or apartment on an accommodation-only basis begin at around £450, although you are more likely to pay between £600–700. High season covers the Christmas period and the months of February and March. Lowest prices during this period are around the £530 mark, with average prices of from £800–950.

The cost of lift pass and equipment hire varies between resorts, with Aspen the most expensive and Breckenridge the cheapest. A six-day lift pass at Aspen will cost £92 during the low season and £112 in the high season. Ski hire costs £47 for six days and ski school, four and a half hours a day, amounts to £90.

Dragoman: Overland with a Difference

Africa, Asia, South America – three vast continents which are home to an endless variety of peoples, traditions, cultures and natural wonders, much of it unseen by the average visitor who perhaps never ventures far from major centres of civilisation. There are, however, many people who would like to get as far away as possible from the traditional image of the pandered tourist; for whom it is the rarely-visited heart of these lands that beckons, and contact with the native people that matters.

308 Activity Holidays

It is to these people that a company such as Dragoman Adventure Travel appeals.

Dragoman takes its unusual name from an ancient tradition originating in Africa and the Middle East, whereby local men hired themselves out as guides to early travellers. These men were known as dragomen, and their function was to escort travellers safely overland, arranging accommodation, transport and sightseeing. The areas travelled were often extremely inhospitable: deserts, rainforests and jungles. Their services were so invaluable that even famous explorers such as Livingstone and Stanley employed a dragoman. Although journeying within these continents has improved since Livingstone's day, there are still many difficulties facing even the most indomitable traveller, and dragomen still exist to help Westerners avoid these hazards.

The policy of Dragoman is to provide reasonably-priced trips which are of general interest and which provide an opportunity to explore in some depth the countryside through which you travel. Trips range in length from two to twenty-eight weeks, following routes taken by early traders and travellers. Travel is in specially-designed Mercedes expedition vehicles, which are sturdily built to cope with the sometimes uncompromising terrain, yet which incorporate a high standard of equipment and comfort, ensuring that the ordeal is taken out of overlanding. In fact, what was previously a form of travel to suit only the most hardy and adventurous souls, has now been made available to a much wider clientele. Whilst it cannot be denied that weeks on the road can be fairly arduous and conditions pretty rough at times, anyone aged between eighteen and forty-five, in good health, and with a reasonable level of fitness and determination will find that these difficulties pale into insignificance beside the natural splendours of the countries explored.

Dragoman tours comprise about twenty people, most of whom come as singles, but some also in couples or groups of friends. For the duration of the tour all group members are expected to participate fully in the day-to-day running of the expedition with activities such as setting up camp, cooking and washing. Accommodation is in tents, either in official campsites or on riverbanks, in forest clearings or mission stations. After a few days people often choose to sleep out in the open. Tour itineraries are flexible to allow for particular interests of the group and the vagaries of overland travel (such as digging the vehicle out of mud or constructing makeshift bridges).

It is this unpredictability that constitutes the thrill of a real adventure.

Vehicles are stocked at the beginning of each expedition with staple foods such as rice, pasta, sugar and tea, and this is supplemented with local produce bought *en route*. Cooking is done over open fires or in portable stoves in desert areas. The daily routine varies from day to day. An early start ensures that the most is made of each day, and the time spent on the road is interspersed with frequent stops for sightseeing. The length of each stop depends on what is on offer: visits to museums and archaeological sites, local festivals, river trips, camel rides or treks to really remote areas. In the evening, camp is pitched and after the evening meal the time is spent relaxing around the camp fire or sampling the local nightlife. The average weekly distance covered works out at about 1,000 km in Africa, 1,200 km in South America and 1,600 km in Asia. Two or three days each week are designated as non-travelling days, allowing you a chance to get your bearings and explore a particular area in greater depth.

There are two crew members on all expeditions, both of whom are highly experienced in leading such groups. Dragomen (and dragowomen!) are selected after a long period of training and assessment for their resourcefulness, mechanical expertise and ability to get on with all types of people.

Some Dragoman tours begin in the UK at the port of Felixstowe in East Anglia, whilst others involve flights to and from the start and finish points (which are rarely the same place). The tour prices do not include any connecting flights, since Dragoman travellers come from all over the world. It is possible to join or leave some trips mid-way, but, due to the unpredictability of schedules, exact arrival and departure dates for each of the major stops *en route* cannot be guaranteed.

Prices vary tremendously according to the length of the tour and the area in which it operates. The longest trip – the twenty-nine week 'Afro/Asian Discoverer' – costs from £2,800–3,000, excluding flights to and from Kathmandu and Harare. In contrast, the seven-week 'Inca' expedition in South America costs from £800–900, excluding flights, and the two-week 'Beyond the Pyramids' expedition costs around £260 which excludes a return air fare to Cairo. The only tour which begins and ends in the UK is the 'Middle East & Egyptian Caravan' which lasts eight weeks and costs from £945–1,045. Dragoman also offer treks of varying lengths around India, including an eight-day 'Annapurna' trek into the heart of Nepal for £300–800; a selection of routes through the spectacular game parks of Africa for £600–2,500, and three different tours within South America for £500–2,400.

In addition to the tour price and air fair, Dragoman also charge a separate kitty price which is paid into a central fund at the beginning of the trip and which covers all group expenses. The kitty charge can be anything from £60–550.

In addition to their comprehensive brochure, available direct (see Appendix II for details), there is also a video for hire which describes three of their major expeditions. This is available to prospective travellers on receipt of a £10 refundable deposit. Dragoman also present monthly slide shows at the Tournament Pub on the Old Brompton Road, Central London. These shows are presented by experienced overlanders and, like the video, give a good insight into life on the road.

Appendix I Tourist board addresses and travel details

Country	Voltage	Time difference	UK or central tourist board	Passport/Visa (UK citizens)	Recommended vaccinations
Albania	220V	GMT+1, GMT+2(summer)	Alburist, c/o Regent Holidays (UK) Ltd, 13 Small St, Bristol BS1 1DE (0272) 211711	full passport visa	none
Algeria	127/220V	GMT, GMT+1(summer)	Air Algérie, 10 Baker St, London W1M 1DA (071) 487 5709	full passport no visa	typhoid & polio and malaria
American Samoa	120V	GMT−11	Office of Tourism, Government of American Samoa, PO Box 1147, Pago Pago, AMERICAN SAMOA (010 684) 633 5187/8	full passport no visa	typhoid & polio
Andorra	240V	GMT+2	Sindicat d'Iniciativa de la Valls d'Andorra, 63 Westover Rd, London SW18 2RF (081) 874 4806	visitor's passport no visa	none
Anguilla	110/220V	GMT−4	Anguilla Tourist Office, College House, 29-31 Wrights Lane, London W8 5SH (071) 937 7725	full passport no visa	none

312 Appendix I

Country	Voltage	Time difference	UK or central tourist board	Passport/Visa (UK citizens)	Recommended vaccinations
Antigua & Barbuda	110/220v	GMT−4	Antigua & Barbuda Tourist Office, 15 Thayer St, London W1M 5LD (071) 486 7073	no passport no visa	none
Argentina	220v	GMT−3	Argentine Interests Section, 53 Hans Place, London SW1 (071) 589 3104	full passport no visa	typhoid & polio and malaria
Aruba	115/120v	GMT−4	Aruba Tourism Authority, Emmapark 12, 2595 ET, The Hague, NETHERLANDS (010 31) 070 851181	full passport no visa	none
Australia	220/250v	GMT+8(west) to +11(east)	Australian Tourist Commission, 15 Putney Hill, London SW15 (081) 780 1424	full passport visa	none
New South Wales		GMT+11, GMT+10(summer)	New South Wales Department of Leisure, Sport, & Tourism, New South Wales House, 66 Strand, London WC2N 5LZ (071) 839 6651		

Country	Voltage	Time difference	UK or central tourist board	Passport/Visa (UK citizens)	Recommended vaccinations
Northern Territory		GMT+10.5, GMT+9.5(summer)	Northern Territory Tourist Commission, 4th Floor, 393 Strand, London WC2R 0LT (071) 836 3344		
Queensland		GMT+10	Queensland Tourist and Travel Corporation, Queensland House, 392 Strand, London WC2R 0LZ (071) 836 7242		
South Australia		GMT+10.5, GMT+9.5(summer)	South Australia Department of Tourism, South Australia House, 50 Strand, London WC2N 5LW (071) 930 7471		
Victoria		GMT+10	Victorian Tourist Commission, Victoria House, Melbourne Pl., Strand, London WC2B 4LG (071) 836 2656		
Western Australia		GMT+8	Western Australia Tourism Commission, Western Australia House, 115 Strand, London WC2R 0AJ (071) 240 2881		

Country	Voltage	Time difference	UK or central tourist board	Passport/Visa (UK citizens)	Recommended vaccinations
Austria	220v	GMT+1	Austrian National Tourist Office, 30 Saint George St, London W1R 0AL (071) 629 0461	visitor's passport no visa	none
Azores	220v	GMT−1	Portuguese National Tourist Office, 1/5 New Bond St, London W1Y 0NP (071) 493 3873	visitor's passport no visa	none
Bahamas	120v	GMT−5	Bahamas Tourist Office, 10 Chesterfield St, London W1X 8AH (071) 629 5238	visitor's passport no visa	none
Nassau, Cable Beach & Paradise Island			Nassau, Cable Beach & Paradise Island Promotion Board, 306 Upper Richmond Rd West, East Sheen, London SW14 7JG (081) 878 5569		
Bahrain	120/230v	GMT+3	Bahrain Tourism Company (BTC), PO Box 5831, Manama, STATE OF BAHRAIN (010 973) 530530	full passport no visa	cholera and typhoid & polio

Appendix | 315

Country	Voltage	Time difference	UK or central tourist board	Passport/Visa (UK citizens)	Recommended vaccinations
Bangladesh	220/240v	GMT+6	The Bangladesh Parjatan Corporation, 233 Airport Rd, Teigaon, Dhaka, BANGLADESH (010 880) 2 325155	full passport no visa	cholera, typhoid & polio and malaria
Barbados	110v	GMT−4, GMT−5(summer)	Barbados Board of Tourism, 263 Tottenham Court Road, London W1P 9AA (071) 636 9448/9	full passport no visa	typhoid & polio
Belgium	110/115/220v	GMT+1, GMT+2(summer)	Belgian Tourist Office, Premier House, 2 Gayton Rd, Harrow, Middlesex HA1 2XU (081) 861 3300	visitor's passport no visa	none
Belize	110/220v	GMT−6	Belize High Commission, 200 Sutherland Ave, London W9 1RX (071) 266 3485	full passport no visa	typhoid & polio and malaria
Bermuda	110v	GMT−4	Bermuda Tourism (BCB Ltd), 1 Battersea Church Rd, London, SW11 3LY (071) 734 8813/4	visitor's passport no visa	none

Country	Voltage	Time difference	UK or central tourist board	Passport/Visa (UK citizens)	Recommended vaccinations
Bhutan	220v	GMT+6	UK Tourist Representative, Maggie Payne, Director of Marketing, Adventure Travel, 31 Queensdale Rd, London W11 (071) 603 6650	full passport visa	yellow fever, cholera, typhoid & polio and malaria
Bolivia	110/220v	GMT−4	Bolivian Consulate General, 106 Eaton Square, London SW1W 9AD (071) 235 4448	full passport visa	yellow fever, typhoid & polio and malaria
Botswana	220/240v	GMT+2	Botswana Tourism Development Unit, Private Bag 0047, Gaborone, BOTSWANA (010 267) 3 313314/353024	full passport no visa	cholera, typhoid & polio and malaria
Brazil	110/127/220v	GMT−2 (Fern. Is.) to GMT−5 (Acre)	Brazilian Tourist Department, Brazilian Embassy, 32 Green St, London W1Y 4AT (071) 499 0877	full passport no visa	yellow fever (in the Amazon), cholera and typhoid & polio
British Virgin Islands	110/60v	GMT−4	British Virgin Islands Tourist Board, 26 Hockerill St, Bishop's Stortford, Herfordshire CM23 2DW (0279) 654969	full passport no visa	typhoid & polio

Appendix I | **317**

Country	Voltage	Time difference	UK or central tourist board	Passport/Visa (UK citizens)	Recommended vaccinations
Brunei	230v	GMT+8	Information Bureau Section, Broadcasting and Information Department, Prime Minister's Office, Bandar Seri Begawan 2041, BRUNEI (010 673) 02 40527	full passport no visa	typhoid & polio and malaria
Bulgaria	220v	GMT+2	Bulgarian National Tourist Office, 18 Princes St, London W1R 7RE (071) 499 6988	full passport visa	none
Burma (Myanma)	220/230v	GMT+6.5	Tourist Burma, 77-91 Sule Pagoda Rd, Rangoon, BURMA (010 951) 78376/75328	full passport visa	yellow fever, cholera, typhoid & polio and malaria
Cameroon	110/220v	GMT+1	Tourist Office, Embassy of the Republic of Cameroon, 84 Holland Park, London W11 3SB (071) 727 0771	full passport visa	yellow fever, cholera, typhoid & polio and malaria
Canada	110v	GMT−8(Pacific) to GMT−3.5 (New Foun.)	National Tourist Office of Canada, Canada House, Trafalgar Sq., London SW1Y 5BJ (071) 629 9492	full passport no visa	none

318 Appendix I

Country	Voltage	Time difference	UK or central tourist board	Passport/Visa (UK citizens)	Recommended vaccinations
Alberta		GMT −7, GMT −6(summer)	Alberta Tourism, Alberta House, 1 Mount St, London W1Y 5AA (071) 491 3430		
British Columbia		GMT −8, GMT −7(summer)	Tourism BC, 1 Regent St, London SW1Y 4NS (071) 930 6857		
Nova Scotia		GMT −4, GMT −3(summer)	Nova Scotia Government Office, 14 Pall Mall, London SW1Y 5LU (071) 930 6864		
Ontario		GMT −5, GMT −4(summer)	Ontario Government Office and Tourist Board, 21 Knightsbridge, London SW1X 7LY (071) 245 1222		
Québec		GMT −5, GMT −4(summer)	Québec Government Office of Tourism, 59 Pall Mall, London SW1Y 5JH (071) 930 8314		
Saskatchewan		GMT −6 to GMT −7, GMT −5 to −6(summer)	Saskatchewan Government Office, 16 Berkeley St, London W1X 5AE (071) 629 5834		

Appendix 1

Country	Voltage	Time difference	UK or central tourist board	Passport/Visa (UK citizens)	Recommended vaccinations
Canary Islands	220v	GMT, GMT+1 (summer)	Spain National Tourist Office, 57/58 St James's St, London SW1A 1LD (071) 499 0901	visitor's passport no visa	none
Cape Verde Islands	220v	GMT−1	Embassy of the Republic of Cape Verde, Koninginnegracht, 2514 AK, The Hague, NETHERLANDS (010 31) 70 505950	full passport no visa	yellow fever, typhoid & polio and malaria
Cayman Islands	110v	GMT−5	Cayman Islands Dept of Tourism, Trevor House, 100 Brompton Rd, London SW3 1EX (071) 581 9960	no passport no visa	none
Central African Rep.	220/380v	GMT+1	Office National Centralafricain du Tourisme, BP 655, Bagui, CENTRAL AFRICAN REPUBLIC (010 236) 614566	full passport visa	yellow fever, typhoid & polio and malaria

Country	Voltage	Time difference	UK or central tourist board	Passport/Visa (UK citizens)	Recommended vaccinations
Channel Islands	240v	GMT to GMT+1		visitor's passport no visa	none
Alderney		GMT	States of Alderney Tourism Office, Alderney, CHANNEL ISLANDS (048 182) 2994		
Guernsey		GMT+1	Guernsey Tourist Office, PO Box 23, White Rock, Guernsey, CHANNEL ISLANDS (0481) 26111		
Jersey		GMT, GMT+1 (Mar-Sep)	Jersey Tourism, Weighbridge, St Helier, Jersey, CHANNEL ISLANDS (0534) 78000		
Chile	220v	GMT−3, GMT−4 (Mar-Oct)	Lan Chile, South American Marketing, 199 Victoria St, London SW1E 5NE (071) 233 7288	full passport no visa	typhoid & polio
China (PRC)	220v	GMT+8 (Beijing time for whole country)	China National Tourist Office, 4 Glentworth St, London NW1 5PG (071) 935 9427/9787	full passport visa	yellow fever, cholera, typhoid & polio and malaria

Country	Voltage	Time difference	UK or central tourist board	Passport/Visa (UK citizens)	Recommended vaccinations
Colombia	110/150/220v	GMT − 5	Colombian Consulate, Suite 10, 140 Park Lane, London W1Y 3DF (071) 493 4565	full passport no visa	yellow fever, typhoid & polio and malaria
Congo	220/230v	GMT + 1	Direction Générale du Tourisme, Boîte Postal 456, Brazzaville, CONGO (010 242) 810953	full passport visa	yellow fever, cholera, typhoid & polio and malaria
Cook Islands	230v	GMT − 9.5, GMT − 10 (summer)	Cook Islands Tourist Authority, 433 High Holborn House, 52 High Holborn, London WC1V 6RB (071) 242 3131	full passport no visa	typhoid & polio and malaria
Costa Rica	110/220v	GMT − 6	Instituto Costarricense de Turismo, PO Box 777, Edificio Galerias del Este – Piso 3, Curridabat, San José, COSTA RICA (010 506) 231733	full passport no visa	typhoid & polio and malaria
Côte D'Ivoire (Ivory Coast)	220v	GMT	Embassy of the Republic Côte d'Ivoire, 2 Upper Belgrave St, London SW1X 8BJ (071) 235 6991	full passport no visa	yellow fever, cholera, typhoid & polio and malaria

Country	Voltage	Time difference	UK or central tourist board	Passport/Visa (UK citizens)	Recommended vaccinations
Cuba	110/120v	GMT−6, GMT−5(summer)	Cuban Embassy, 167 High Holborn, London WC1 (071) 240 2488	full passport visa	typhoid & polio
Cyprus, Republic of	240v	GMT+2	Cyprus Tourism Organization, 213 Regent St, London W1R 8DA (071) 734 9822/2593	full passport no visa	none
Czecho-slovakia	220/110v	GMT+1, GMT+2(summer)	Čedok (London) Ltd, 17/18 Old Bond St, London W1X 4RB (071) 629 6058	full passport visa	none
Denmark	220v	GMT+1	Danish Tourist Board, 169/173 Regent St, London W1R 8PY (071) 734 2637	visitor's passport no visa	none
Dominica	240v	GMT−4	Dominica Tourist Office, 1 Collingham Gardens, London SW5 0HW (071) 835 1937	full passport no visa	typhoid & polio
Dominic-an Republic	110v	GMT−4	Dominican Republic Tourist Office Europe, Voelckerstrasse 24, D-6000, Frankfurt/Main, WEST GERMANY (010 49) 69 287551/5970330	full passport no visa	typhoid & polio and malaria

Country	Voltage	Time difference	UK or central tourist board	Passport/Visa (UK citizens)	Recommended vaccinations
Ecuador	110v	GMT −5 (Galapagos −6)	Dirección Nacional de Turismo, Reina Victoria 514 y Roca, PO Box 2454, Quito, ECUADOR (010 593) 239044	full passport no visa	yellow fever, typhoid & polio and malaria
Egypt	220v	GMT +2	Egyptian State Tourist Office, 168 Piccadilly, London W1V 9DE (071) 493 5282	full passport visa	yellow fever, cholera, typhoid & polio and malaria (in rural areas)
El Salvador	110v	GMT −6	Embassy of the Republic of El Salvador, Flat 9, Welbeck House, 62 Welbeck St, London W1M 7HB (071) 486 8182	full passport no visa	typhoid & polio and malaria
Equatorial Guinea	220v	GMT +1	Embassy of the Republic of Equatorial Guinea, 6 Rue Alfred de Vigny, Paris, FRANCE (010 31) 1 4766443	full passport visa	yellow fever, cholera, typhoid & polio and malaria
Ethiopia	220v	GMT +3	Ethiopian Tourist Commission, PO Box 2183, Addis Ababa, ETHIOPIA (010 251) 1 447470	full passport visa	yellow fever, cholera, typhoid & polio and malaria

324 Appendix I

Country	Voltage	Time difference	UK or central tourist board	Passport/Visa (UK citizens)	Recommended vaccinations
Falkland Islands (Malvinas)	240v	GMT −3 to −4	Falkland Islands Tourist Information Service, Falkland House, 14 Broadway, Westminster, London SW1H 0BH (071) 222 2542	full passport no visa	typhoid & polio
Faroe Islands	220v	GMT, GMT+1(summer)	Danish Tourist Board, 169/173 Regent St, London W1R 8PY (071) 734 2637	visitor's passport no visa	none
Fiji	240v	GMT+12	Fiji Visitors Bureau, Suite 433, High Holborn House, 52/54 High Holborn, London WC1V 6RB (071) 242 3131	full passport no visa	typhoid & polio
Finland	220v	GMT+2, GMT+3(summer)	Finnish Tourist Board, 66 Haymarket, London SW1Y 4RF (071) 839 4048	visitor's passport no visa	none
France	220v	GMT+1, GMT+2(summer)	French Government Tourist Office, 178 Piccadilly, London W1V 0AL (071) 491 7622/499 6911	visitor's passport no visa	none

Country	Voltage	Time difference	UK or central tourist board	Passport/Visa (UK citizens)	Recommended vaccinations
French Guiana	110/127/ 220v	GMT−3	French Guiana Tourist Bureau, 12 Rue Aber, 75009 Paris, FRANCE (010 31) 1 42681107	full passport no visa	yellow fever, typhoid & polio and malaria
French Polynesia	220v	GMT−10	French Government Tourist Office, 178 Piccadilly, London W1V 0AL (071) 491 7622/499 6911 Syndicat d'Initiative de la Polynésie Française, Boîte Postale 326, Papeete, TAHITI Office de Promotion et D'Animation Touristiques de Tahiti et Ses Iles, Boîte Postale 65, Fare Manahini, Boulevard Pomare, Papeete, TAHITI	full passport no visa (2 weeks)	typhoid & polio
French West Indies	110/220v	GMT−4	French Government Tourist Office, 178 Piccadilly, London W1V 0AL (071) 491 7622/499 6911	visitor's passport no visa	typhoid & polio
Gabon	220v	GMT+1	Gabonese Embassy, Bureau du Tourisme, 4 Ave., Franklin Roosevelt, 75008 Paris, FRANCE	full passport visa	malaria

Country	Voltage	Time difference	UK or central tourist board	Passport/Visa (UK citizens)	Recommended vaccinations
Gambia	220v	GMT	Gambian National Tourist Office, 57 Kensington Court, London W8 5DG (071) 937 9618/9	full passport no visa	yellow fever, cholera, typhoid & polio and malaria
Germany	220v	GMT+1	German National Tourist Office, 65 Curzon St, London W1Y 7PE (071) 495 3990 Berolina Travel Ltd, 22A Conduit St, London W1R 9TB (071) 629 1664	visitor's passport no visa	none
Ghana	220v	GMT	Ghana High Commission, Information Section, 13 Belgrave Sq., London SW1X 8PR (071) 235 4142	full passport visa	yellow fever, cholera and malaria
Gibraltar	240v	GMT+1, GMT+2 (summer)	Gibraltar Government Tourist Office, 179 Strand, London WC2R 1EH (071) 836 0777/8	visitor's passport no visa	typhoid & polio
Greece	220v	GMT+2	Greek National Tourist Organization, 4 Conduit Street, London W1R 0DJ (071) 734 5997	visitor's passport no visa	none

Country	Voltage	Time difference	UK or central tourist board	Passport/Visa (UK citizens)	Recommended vaccinations
Greenland	220v	GMT−3	Danish Tourist Board, 169/173 Regent St, London W1R 8PY (071) 734 2637 Tusarliivik, Greenland Homerule Authorities, PO Box 1020 DK 3900, Nuuk, GREENLAND	visitor's passport no visa	none
Grenada	220/240v	GMT−4	Grenada National Tourist Office, 1 Collingham Gardens, London SW5 0HW (071) 370 5164/5	no passport no visa	typhoid & polio
Guam	120v	GMT+10	Guam Visitors' Bureau, PO Box 3520, Agana, GUAM	full passport no visa (when flying with most airlines)	none
Guatemala	110v	GMT−6	Guatemala Tourist Commission, 7a Avenida 1-17, Centro Civico, Zona 4, Guatemala City, GUATEMALA (010 502) 311333	full passport visa	typhoid & polio and malaria

Country	Voltage	Time difference	UK or central tourist board	Passport/Visa (UK citizens)	Recommended vaccinations
Guinea Republic	220v	GMT	Office National du Tourisme et de l'Hôtellerie, Boite Postale 1304, Conakry, GUINEA REPUBLIC 44 2606 (operator)	full passport visa	yellow fever, cholera, typhoid & polio and malaria
Guyana	110v	GMT−3	High Commission for the Cooperative Republic of Guyana, 3 Palace Court, Bayswater Rd, London W2 4LP (071) 229 7684	full passport visa	typhoid & polio and malaria
Haiti	110v	GMT−5	Office National du Tourisme d'Haiti, Avenue Marie-Jeanne, Cité de l'Exposition, Port-au-Prince, HAITI (010 509) 2 1729	full passport no visa	typhoid & polio and malaria
Hawaii	120v	GMT−10	Hawaii Visitors' Bureau, 2 Cinnamon Row, Plantation Wharf, York Place, London SW11 3TW (071) 924 3999	full passport no visa (when flying with most airlines)	none

Appendix I | 329

Country	Voltage	Time difference	UK or central tourist board	Passport/Visa (UK citizens)	Recommended vaccinations
Honduras	110/220v	GMT−6	Instituto Hondureño de Turismo, Apartado Postal 154-C, Costado este del Palacio Legislativo, Tegucigalpa, HONDURAS (010 504) 221183	full passport no visa	typhoid & polio and malaria
Hong Kong	220v	GMT+8	Hong Kong Tourist Association, 125 Pall Mall, London SW1Y 5EA (071) 930 4775	full passport no visa	typhoid & polio
Hungary	220v	GMT+1, GMT+2(Apr-Sep)	Danube Travel Agency, 6 Conduit St, London W1R 9TG (071) 493 0263	full passport visa	none
Iceland	220v	GMT	Iceland Tourist Information Bureau, 172 Tottenham Court Rd, 3rd Floor, W1P 9LG (071) 388 5599	visitor's passport no visa	none
India	220v	GMT+5.5	Government of India Tourist Office, 7 Cork St, London W1X 2AB (071) 437 3677/8	full passport visa	yellow fever, cholera, typhoid & polio and malaria

Country	Voltage	Time difference	UK or central tourist board	Passport/Visa (UK citizens)	Recommended vaccinations
Indonesia	110/220v	GMT+7(Java) to GMT+9(Irian)	Embassy of the Republic of Indonesia, 38 Grosvenor Sq., London W1X 9AD (071) 499 7661	full passport no visa	cholera, typhoid & polio and malaria
Ireland	220v	GMT, GMT+1(summer)	Irish Tourist Board (Bord Fáilte), Ireland House, 150/151 New Bond St, London W1Y 0AQ (071) 493 3201	visitor's passport no visa	none
Isle of Man	220v	GMT, GMT+1(summer)	Isle of Man Tourist Board, 13 Victoria St, Douglas, ISLE OF MAN (0624) 74323	no passport no visa	none
Israel	220v	GMT+2	Israel Government Tourist Office, 18 Great Marlborough St, London W1V 1AF (071) 434 3651	full passport no visa	typhoid & polio
Italy	220v	GMT+1, GMT+2(summer)	Italian State Tourist Office, 1 Princes St, London W1R 8AY (071) 408 1254	visitor's passport no visa	none
Jamaica	110v	GMT−5, GMT−4(summer)	Jamaica Tourist Board, 111 Gloucester Place, London W1H 3PH (071) 224 0505	full passport no visa	none

Appendix | 331

Country	Voltage	Time difference	UK or central tourist board	Passport/Visa (UK citizens)	Recommended vaccinations
Japan	100v	GMT+9	Japan National Tourist Organization, 167 Regent St, London W1R 7FD (071) 734 9638	full passport no visa	slight risk of typhoid, polio and rabies in certain areas
Jordan	220v	GMT+2	Jordan Tourist Office, 211 Regent St, London W1R 7DD (071) 437 9465	full passport visa	cholera and typhoid & polio
Kenya	220/240v	GMT+3	Kenya Tourist Office, 25 Brook's Mews, London W1Y 1LG (071) 355 3144	full passport no visa	yellow fever, cholera (coast), typhoid & polio and malaria
Korea, North	110/220v	GMT+9	Regent Holidays (UK) Ltd, 13 Small St, Bristol BS1 1DE (0272) 211711	full passport visa	cholera and typhoid & polio
Korea, South	100/220v	GMT+9	Korea National Tourism Corporation, 2nd Floor, Vogue House, 1 Hanover Sq., London W1R 9RD (071) 408 1591	full passport no visa	cholera, typhoid & polio and malaria
Lebanon	110/220v	GMT+2	Lebanese Tourist and Information Office, 90 Piccadilly, London W1 (071) 409 2031	full passport visa	cholera and typhoid & polio

Country	Voltage	Time difference	UK or central tourist board	Passport/Visa (UK citizens)	Recommended vaccinations
Lesotho	220v	GMT+2	High Commission for the Kingdom of Lesotho, 10 Collingham Road, London SW5 (071) 373 8581	full passport no visa	yellow fever, cholera and typhoid & polio
Libya	150/220v	GMT+2	Department of Tourism and Fairs, PO Box 891, Sharia Omar Mukhtar, Tripoli, LIBYA (010 218) 32255	full passport visa	yellow fever, cholera, typhoid & polio and malaria
Liechtenstein	220v	GMT+1	Swiss National Tourist Office, Swiss Centre, New Coventry St, London W1V 8EE (071) 734 1921	visitor's passport no visa	none
Luxembourg	220v	GMT+1, GMT+2(summer)	Luxembourg National Tourist & Trade Office, 36/37 Piccadilly, London W1V 9PA (071) 434 2800	visitor's passport no visa	none
Macau	110/220v	GMT+8	Macau Tourist Information Bureau, 6 Sherlock Mews, London W1M 3RH (071) 224 3390	full passport no visa	none

Country	Voltage	Time difference	UK or central tourist board	Passport/Visa (UK citizens)	Recommended vaccinations
Madagascar	220v	GMT+3	Consulate of the Democratic Republic of Madagascar, 16 Lanark Mansions, Pennard Rd, London W12 (081) 746 0133	full passport visa	yellow fever, cholera, typhoid & polio and malaria
Madeira	220v	GMT+1, GMT+2(summer)	Portuguese National Tourist Office, 1/5 New Bond St, London W1Y 0NP (071) 493 3873	visitor's passport no visa	none
Malawi	230/240v	GMT+2	Malawi Tourist Office, 33 Grosvenor St, London W1X 0DE (071) 491 4172	full passport no visa	cholera, typhoid & polio and malaria
Malaysia	220v	GMT+7.5 to +8	Tourist Development Corporation of Malaysia, 57 Trafalgar Sq., London WC2N 5DU (071) 930 7932	full passport no visa	cholera, typhoid & polio and malaria
Maldives	220v	GMT+5	Maldive Travel, 3 Esher House, 11 Edith Terrace, London SW10 0TH (071) 352 2246	full passport no visa	yellow fever, cholera, typhoid & polio and malaria

Country	Voltage	Time difference	UK or central tourist board	Passport/Visa (UK citizens)	Recommended vaccinations
Mali	220v	GMT	Société Malienne d'Exploitation des Resources Touristiques (SMERT), Boîte Postale 222, Place de la République, Bamako, MALI 225942 (operator)	full passport visa	yellow fever, cholera, typhoid & polio and malaria
Malta	240v	GMT+1, GMT+2 (summer)	Malta National Tourist Office, College House Suite 207, Wrights Lane, London W8 5SH (071) 323 0506	visitor's passport no visa	none
Mauritania	127/220v	GMT	Société Mauritanienne de Tourisme et d'Hôtellerie, Boîte Postale 552, Nouakchott, MAURITANIA (010 222) 53351	full passport visa	yellow fever, cholera, typhoid & polio and malaria
Mauritius	220/240v	GMT+4, GMT+3 (summer)	Mauritius Government Tourist Office, 49 Conduit St, London W1R 9FB (071) 437 7508	full passport no visa	malaria
Mexico	110v (usually)	GMT−6 (Mex. City) to −8 (Pacific)	Mexico Ministry of Tourism, 1st Floor, 60-61 Trafalgar Square, London WC2N 5DS (071) 734 1058	full passport visa	malaria (in rural areas)

Country	Voltage	Time difference	UK or central tourist board	Passport/Visa (UK citizens)	Recommended vaccinations
Monaco	220v	GMT+1, GMT+2(Apr-Sep)	Monaco Tourist and Convention Office, 50 Upper Brook St, London W1Y 1PG (071) 629 4712	visitor's passport no visa	none
Mongolia	220v	GMT+8	c/o Voyages Jules Verne, 10 Glentworth St, London NW1 (071) 486 8080	full passport visa	typhoid & polio
Morocco	110/220v	GMT, GMT+1(summer)	Morrocan National Tourist Office, 205 Regent St, London W1R 6HB (071) 437 0073	full passport no visa	cholera, typhoid & polio and malaria
Nepal	220v	GMT+5.5	Ministry of Tourism, His Majesty's Government of Nepal, Tripureswar, Kathmandu, NEPAL (010 977) 211293	full passport visa	cholera, typhoid & polio and malaria
Netherlands	220v	GMT+1	Netherlands Board of Tourism, 25-28 Buckingham Gate, London SW1E 6LD (071) 630 0451	visitor's passport no visa	none

Country	Voltage	Time difference	UK or central tourist board	Passport/Visa (UK citizens)	Recommended vaccinations
Netherlands Antilles	110/127v	GMT−4	Netherlands Antilles Organization, Badhuisweg 173-175, 2597JP, The Hague, NETHERLANDS (010 31) 70 512811	visitor's passport visa	typhoid & polio
New Zealand	230v	GMT+13, GMT+12(summer)	New Zealand Tourist & Publicity Office, New Zealand House, 80 Haymarket, London SW1Y 4TQ (071) 930 8422	full passport no visa	none
Nicaragua	110v	GMT−6	Instituto Nicaragüense de Turismo (Inturismo), Apartado 122, Avenida Bolivar Sur, Managua, NICARAGUA (010 505) 25436	full passport no visa	typhoid & polio and malaria
Nigeria	210/250v	GMT+1	Nigeria High Commission, 9 Northumberland Ave, London WC2N 5BX (071) 839 1244	full passport visa	yellow fever, cholera, typhoid & polio and malaria
Norway	220v	GMT+1	Norwegian Tourist Board, Charles House, 5 Lower Regent St, London SW1Y 4LR (071) 839 6255	visitor's passport no visa	none

Country	Voltage	Time difference	UK or central tourist board	Passport/Visa (UK citizens)	Recommended vaccinations
Oman	220/240V	GMT+4	Embassy of the Sultanate of Oman, 44a Montpellier Sq., London SW7 1JJ (071) 584 6782	full passport visa	cholera, typhoid & polio and malaria
Pakistan	220V	GMT+5	Pakistan Tourism Development Corporation, 433 High Holborn House, 52 High Holborn, London WC1V 6RB (071) 242 3131	full passport visa	cholera, typhoid & polio and malaria
Panama	110V	GMT−5	Instituto Panameño de Turismo, Apartado 4421, Centro de Convenciones Atlapa, Via Cincuentenario, Panamá 5, PANAMA (010 507) 26700	full passport no visa	typhoid & polio and malaria (in rural areas)
Papua New Guinea	240V	GMT+10	Papua New Guinea Office of Tourism, PO Box 4144, Embassy Drive, Boroko, PAPUA NEW GUINEA (010 675) 25 6011/1269	full passport visa	yellow fever, cholera, typhoid & polio and malaria

338 Appendix I

Country	Voltage	Time difference	UK or central tourist board	Passport/Visa (UK citizens)	Recommended vaccinations
Paraguay	220v	GMT−4, GMT−3(summer)	Information Service, Embassy of Paraguay, Braemar Lodge, Cornwall Gardens, London SW7 4AQ (071) 937 1253	full passport no visa	typhoid & polio and malaria
Peru	220v	GMT−5	Peruvian Tourist Board, 10 Grosvenor Gardens, London SW1W 0BD (071) 824 8693	full passport no visa	typhoid & polio and malaria
Philippines	220v	GMT+8	Philippine Department of Tourism, 199 Piccadilly, London W1V 9LE (071) 734 6358	full passport no visa (less than 22 days)	cholera, typhoid & polio and malaria
Poland	220v	GMT+1	Polorbis Travel Ltd, 82 Mortimer St, London W1N 7DE (071) 580 8028/637 4971	full passport visa	none
Portugal	220v	GMT, GMT+1(summer)	Portuguese National Tourist Office, 1/5 New Bond St, London W1Y 0NP (071) 493 3873	visitor's passport no visa	none
Puerto Rico	120v	GMT−4	Commonwealth of Puerto Rico Tourism Company, PO Box 15, Coulsdon, Surrey CR3 9UU (081) 651 4740	full passport no visa (when flying with most airlines)	none

Country	Voltage	Time difference	UK or central tourist board	Passport/Visa (UK citizens)	Recommended vaccinations
Romania	220v	GMT+2	Romanian National Tourist Office, 17 Nottingham Place, London W1 (071) 224 3692	full passport visa	none
St Kitts & Nevis	230v	GMT−4	St Kitts & Nevis Tourist Board, 10 Kensington Court, London W8 5DL (071) 376 0881	no passport no visa	typhoid & polio
St Lucia	220v	GMT−4	St Lucia Tourist Board, 10 Kensington Court, London W8 5DL (071) 937 1969	no passport no visa	typhoid & polio
St Vincent & The Grenadines	220/240v	GMT−4	St Vincent & the Grenadines Tourist Office, 10 Kensington Court, London W8 5DL (071) 937 1969	no passport no visa	typhoid & polio
San Marino	125/220v	GMT+1, GMT+2(summer)	Ufficio di Stato per il Turismo, Palazzo del Turismo, 47031, REPUBLICCA DI SAN MARINO (010 549) 992101/5	visitor's passport no visa	none

Country	Voltage	Time difference	UK or central tourist board	Passport/Visa (UK citizens)	Recommended vaccinations
Saudi Arabia	125/235v	GMT+3	Saudi Arabian Information Centre, Cavendish House, 18 Cavendish Sq., London W1M 0AQ (071) 629 8803	full passport visa	typhoid & polio and malaria
Senegal	220v	GMT	Embassy of the Republic of Senegal, 11 Phillimore Gardens, London W8 7QG (071) 937 0925/6	full passport visa	yellow fever, cholera, typhoid & polio and malaria
Seychelles	240v	GMT+4	Seychelles Tourist Office, 2nd Floor, Eros House, 111 Baker St, London W1M 1FE (071) 224 1670	full passport no visa	typhoid & polio
Sierra Leone	230/240v	GMT	Sierra Leone Tourist Office, 33 Portland Pl., London W1N 3AG (071) 636 6483	full passport visa	yellow fever, cholera, typhoid & polio and malaria
Singapore	220/240v	GMT+7.5	Singapore Tourist Promotion Board, 126-130 Regent St, London W1R 5FE (071) 437 0033	full passport no visa	cholera and typhoid & polio
Solomon Islands	240v	GMT+11	Solomon Islands Tourist Authority, PO Box 321, Honiara, SOLOMON ISLANDS (010 677) 22442	full passport no visa	typhoid & polio and malaria

Country	Voltage	Time difference	UK or central tourist board	Passport/Visa (UK citizens)	Recommended vaccinations
South Africa	220/230/250v	GMT+2	South African Tourism Board, Regency House, 1/4 Warwick St, London W1R 5WB (071) 944 6646	full passport no visa	cholera, typhoid & polio and malaria
Spain	220v	GMT+1, GMT+2(summer)	Spain National Tourist Office, 57/58 St James's St, London SW1A 1LD (071) 499 0901 Fax (071) 439 2314	visitor's passport no visa	none
Sri Lanka	230/240v	GMT+5.5	Sri Lanka Tourist Board, London House, 53/54 Haymarket, London SW1Y 4RP (071) 925 0177/321 0034	full passport no visa	typhoid & polio and malaria
Sudan	240v	GMT+2	Public Corporation of Tourism and Hotels, PO Box 7104, Khartoum, SUDAN (010 249) 74053	full passport visa	yellow fever, cholera, typhoid & polio and malaria
Swaziland	220v	GMT+2	Swaziland High Commission, Information Department, 58 Pont St, London SW1X 0AE (071) 581 4976/7/8	full passport no visa	cholera and malaria

Country	Voltage	Time difference	UK or central tourist board	Passport/Visa (UK citizens)	Recommended vaccinations
Sweden	220v	GMT+1	Swedish National Tourist Office, 29-31 Oxford St, London W1 (071) 437 5816	visitor's passport no visa	none
Switzerland	220v	GMT+1	Swiss National Tourist Office, Swiss Centre, New Coventry St, London W1V 8EE (071) 734 1921	visitor's passport no visa	none
Syria	110/220v	GMT+2	Syrian Interests Section, Embassy of the Republic of Lebanon, 8 Belgrave Sq., London SW1X 8PH (071) 245 9012	full passport visa	cholera, typhoid & polio and malaria
Taiwan	110v	GMT+8	Free Chinese Centre, 4th Floor, Dorland House, 14/16 Regent St, London SW1Y 4PH (071) 930 5767/8/9	full passport visa	yellow fever and typhoid & polio
Tanzania	230v	GMT+3	Tanzania Tourist Office, 78-80 Borough High St, London SE1 1LL (071) 407 0566	full passport no visa	yellow fever, cholera, typhoid & polio and malaria

Appendix | 343

Country	Voltage	Time difference	UK or central tourist board	Passport/Visa (UK citizens)	Recommended vaccinations
Thailand	220v	GMT+7	Tourism Authority of Thailand, 49 Albemarle St, London W1X 3FE (071) 499 7679	full passport no visa (15 days)	cholera, typhoid & polio and malaria
Tibet	220v	GMT+8	Office of Tibet, Linburn House, 342 Kilburn High Road, London NW6 2QJ (071) 328 8422	full passport visa	typhoid & polio, cholera, yellow fever, malaria
Tonga	240v	GMT+13	High Commission for the Kingdom of Tonga, 12th Floor, New Zealand House, Haymarket, London SW1Y 4TE (071) 839 3287/8	full passport no visa	typhoid & polio
Trinidad & Tobago	115v	GMT−4	Trinidad & Tobago Tourism Development Authority, 48 Leicester Sq., London WC2H 7QD (071) 930 6566	full passport no visa	typhoid & polio
Tunisia	220v	GMT+1	Tunisian National Tourist Office, 77A Wigmore St, London W1H 9LJ (071) 224 5561	full passport no visa	none

Country	Voltage	Time difference	UK or central tourist board	Passport/Visa (UK citizens)	Recommended vaccinations
Turkey	220v	GMT+2	Turkish Tourism & Information Office, 1st Floor, 170/173 Piccadilly, London W1V 9DD (071) 734 8681/2	visitor's passport no visa	malaria in certain areas
Turks & Caicos	110v	GMT−5, GMT−4 (summer)	Turks & Caicos Tourist Board, 3 Epirus Road, London SW6 7UJ (071) 376 2981	full passport no visa	typhoid & polio
Uganda	240v	GMT+3	High Commission for the Republic of Uganda, Uganda House, 58-59 Trafalgar Sq., London WC2N 5DX (071) 839 5783	full passport no visa	yellow fever, cholera, typhoid & polio and malaria
United Arab Emirates	220/240v	GMT+4	Embassy of the United Arab Emirates, 30 Princes Gate, London SW7 1PT (071) 581 1281	full passport no visa	yellow fever, cholera, typhoid & polio and malaria
United Kingdom	240v	GMT, GMT+1 (Mar-Oct)	British Tourist Authority, 12 Regent St, Piccadilly Circus, London SW1 4PQ (071) 730 3400	visitor's passport no visa	none

Appendix I **345**

Country	Voltage	Time difference	UK or central tourist board	Passport/Visa (UK citizens)	Recommended vaccinations
London			London Tourist Centre, St Paul's Churchyard, London EC4 8BX (071) 606 3030		
			London Tourist Board, 26 Grosvenor Gardens, London SW1W 0DU (071) 730 3488/3450		
Edinburgh			Edinburgh City Tourist Information, 3 Princes Street, Edinburgh EH2 2QP (031) 557 1700		
England			English Tourist Board, 12 Regent St, Piccadilly Circus, London SW1 4PQ (071) 730 3400		
Northern Ireland			Northern Ireland Tourist Board, River House, 48 High St, Belfast BT1 2DS (0232) 231221		
Scotland			Scottish Tourist Board, 23 Ravelston Terrace, Edinburgh EH4 3EU (031) 332 2433		

346 Appendix 1

Country	Voltage	Time difference	UK or central tourist board	Passport/Visa (UK citizens)	Recommended vaccinations
Wales			Welsh Tourist Board, Brunel House, 2 Fitzalan Rd, Cardiff CF2 1UY (0222) 499909		
United States (Mainland)	120v	GMT−5 (NY) to GMT−8 (LA)	United States Travel Information Centre, 22 Sackville St, London W1X 2EA (071) 439 7433	full passport no visa (when flying with most airlines)	none
California		GMT−8, GMT−7(summer)	California Division of Tourism, 2 Cinnamon Row, Plantation Wharf, York Place, London SW11 3TW (071) 978 5262		
Florida		GMT−5, GMT−4(summer)	Florida Division of Tourism, 18/24 Westbourne Grove, London W2 5RH (071) 727 1661		
New York		GMT−5, GMT−4(summer)	State of New York Division of Tourism, 2 Cinnamon Row, Plantation Wharf, York Place, London SW11 3TW (071) 978 5262		

Country	Voltage	Time difference	UK or central tourist board	Passport/Visa (UK citizens)	Recommended vaccinations
Uruguay	220v	GMT−3	230 Park Avenue, New York, NY 10169 USA (212) 949 0577 Dirección Nacional de Turismo, Avenida Agraciada 1409, 4°, 5°, y 6°, Montevideo, URUGUAY (010 598) 904148	full passport no visa	typhoid & polio
US Virgin Islands	120v	GMT−4	United States Virgin Islands, Division of Tourism, 2 Cinnamon Row, Plantation Wharf, York Place, London SW11 3TW (071) 978 5262	full passport no visa (when flying with most airlines)	none
USSR	220v	GMT+3(Moscow) to GMT+13(F.East)	Intourist Moscow Ltd, Intourist House, 219 Marsh Wall, London E14 9FL (071) 538 8600	full passport visa	slight risk of malaria in certain areas
Venezuela	110v	GMT−4	VIASA Airways, 19-20 Grosvenor St, London W1 (071) 629 1223	full passport visa	yellow fever, typhoid & polio, malaria outside urban areas

Country	Voltage	Time difference	UK or central tourist board	Passport/Visa (UK citizens)	Recommended vaccinations
Vietnam	110/220v	GMT+7	TBN World Travel, 7 Palmerston Close, Chester, Cheshire CH1 5DA (0244) 374915	full passport visa	yellow fever, cholera and malaria (in rural areas)
Western Samoa	230v	GMT−11	Western Samoa Visitors Bureau, PO Box 2272, Apia, WESTERN SAMOA (010 685) 20886/20878	full passport no visa	typhoid & polio
Yemen, North	220v	GMT+3	Embassy of the Yemen Arab Republic, 41 South St, London W1Y 5PD (071) 629 9905	full passport visa	cholera, typhoid & polio and malaria
Yemen, South	230v	GMT+3	Embassy of the People's Republic of Yemen, 57 Cromwell Rd, London SW7 2ED (071) 584 6607	full passport visa	cholera, typhoid & polio and malaria
Yugo-slavia	220v	GMT+1, GMT+2(summer)	Yugoslav National Tourist Office, 143 Regent St, London W1R 8AE (071) 734 5243/3969	visitor's passport no visa	none

Country	Voltage	Time difference	UK or central tourist board	Passport/Visa (UK citizens)	Recommended vaccinations
Zaire	220v	GMT +1 (west) to GMT +2 (east)	Zaire Embassy, Tourist Information Department, 30 Rue de Marie de Bourgogne, 1040 Brussels, BELGIUM (010 32) 2 513 6610	full passport visa	yellow fever, cholera, typhoid & polio and malaria
Zambia	220/240v	GMT +2	Zambia National Tourist Board, 2 Palace Gate, Kensington, London W8 5NG (071) 589 6343/6344	full passport no visa	yellow fever, cholera, typhoid & polio and malaria
Zimbabwe	220/240v	GMT +2	Zimbabwe Tourist Office, Colette House, 52-55 Piccadilly, London W1V 9AA (071) 629 3955	full passport no visa	cholera, typhoid & polio and malaria

NB
1) Remember that entry and health requirements change regularly so you should check with the relevant embassy or consulate for up to date information.
2) Many countries require proof of vaccinations, especially if you have passed through an infected area.

VISA AGENCIES
Thames Consular Services, 363 Chiswick High Rd, London W4 4HS (081) 995 2492
The Visa Service, 2 Northdown St, London N1 9BG (071) 833 2709
Visa Shop, 44 Chandos Pl., London WC2 4HS (071) 379 0419/0376 or in the Trailfinders' Travel Shop, 194 Kensington High St, London (071) 938 3848

VACCINATION CENTRES
To find the nearest vaccination centre consult your doctor, travel agent, DHSS, or yellow pages.

Appendix II Tour Operators

Abercrombie and Kent
 Sloane Square House
 Holbein Place
 London SW1W 8NS
 (071) 730 9600

Accessible Isolation Holidays
 Midhurst Walk
 West Street
 Midhurst
 West Sussex
 GU29 9NF
 0730 812535

Airtours plc
 Wavell House
 Helmshore
 Rossendale
 Lancashire
 BB4 4NB
 0706 240033

Air France
 see under French Travel Service

Air India
 172 New Bond Street
 London W1Y 0AY
 (071) 491 7979

American Connections
 95 High Street
 Burnham
 Slough
 Berkshire
 SL1 7JZ
 0345 045904

American Dream, The
 1–4 Station Chambers
 High Street North
 London E6 1JD
 (081) 552 1201

American Express Europe Ltd
 Portland House
 Stag Place
 London
 SW1 5BZ
 (071) 834 5555

American Pioneers
 Travel Pioneers Group
 PO Box 229
 Swindon
 Wiltshire
 SN5 7HJ
 0793 881882

Arctic Experience
 29 Nork Way
 Banstead
 Surrey
 SM7 1PB
 0737 362321

Asian Affair Holidays
 14–18 Heddon Street
 London
 W1R 7LB
 (071) 439 2601

Australian Pacific Tours
 2nd Floor
 William House
 14 Worple Road
 Wimbledon
 London
 SW19 4DD
 (081) 879 7322

Austrian Holidays
 50-51 Conduit Street
 London
 W1R 0NP
 (071) 439 7108

Austro Tours
 5 St Peter's Street
 St Albans
 Hertfordshire
 AL1 3DH
 0727 38191

Bales Tours Ltd
 Bales House
 Barrington Road
 Dorking
 Surrey
 RH4 3EJ
 0306 76881
 Fax 0306 740048

Balkan Holidays Ltd
 Sofia House
 19 Conduit Street
 London
 W1R 9TD
 (071) 493 8612

Belgian Travel Service
 Bridge House
 Ware
 Hertfordshire SG12 9DE
 0920 467345

Bermuda Bermuda
 Regent House
 Bexton Lane
 Knutsford WA16 9AB
 (0565) 53283

Berolina Travel Ltd
 22a Conduit Street
 London
 W1R 9TB
 (071) 629 1664

Bhutan Travel
 Maggie Payne, UK Tourist
 Representative
 Director of Marketing,
 Adventure Travel
 31 Queensdale Road
 London W11
 (071) 603 6650

Bridgewater Boats
 Castle Wharf
 Berkhamsted
 Hertfordshire
 0442 863615

British Airways Holidays
 PO Box 10
 Heathrow Airport
 Hounslow
 Middlesex
 TW6 2JA
 (081) 879 4000

British Travel Service and Paris
  Travel Service
 Bridge House
 Ware
 Hertfordshire
 SG12 9DE
 (0920) 463050 (Reservations)
 (0920) 469755
  (Administration)

Canada Air Holidays and Mason
  International Travel
 50 Sauchiehall Street
 Glasgow
 Scotland G2 3AG
 (041) 332 1511

Canberra Cruises
 see under P&O

Caribbean Connection
 Concord House
 Forest Street
 Chester CH1 1QR
 (0244) 341131

Caribtours
 161 Fulham Road
 London SW3 6SN
 (071) 581 3517

Čedok London Ltd
 17-18 Old Bond Street
 London W1X 4RB
 (071) 629 6058

China Travel Service
24 Cambridge Circus
London WC2 8DH
(071) 836 9911

Classic Orient Tours
Kent House
87 Regent Street
London
WIR 8LS
(071) 434 1551

Club Med Ltd
106 Brompton Road
London SW3 IJJ
(071) 225 1066
(Administration)
(071) 581 1161
(Reservations)

Color Line
Tyne Commission Quay
Albert Edward Dock
North Shields
NE29 6EA
(091) 296 1313

Cox & Kings
St James Court
Buckingham Gate Road
London
SWIE 6AF
(071) 931 9106
Fax (071) 630 6038

Cresta Holidays
32 Victoria Street
Altrincham
Cheshire
WA14 1ET
(0345) 056511

Crystal Holidays
The Courtyard
Arlington Road
Surbiton
Surrey
KT6 6BW
(081) 390 8033

CTC Lines
1 Regent Street
London SWIY 4NN
(071) 930 5833

Cunard
30a Pall Mall
London SWIY 5LS
(071) 930 4321
South Western House
Canute Road
Southampton
SO9 1ZA
(0703) 229933 (Passenger Enquiries)
(0703) 634166 (Bookings)

Dick Phillips
Whitehall House
Nenthead
Alston
Cumbria
CA9 3PS
(0434) 381440

Dragoman Adventure Travel
Camp Green
Kenton Road
Debenham
Suffolk IP14 6LA
(0728) 861133

DVL Travel
Kultorvet 7
Copenhagen K
Denmark
(010) 45 1 132727

Edinburgh Festival
Box Office
21 Market Street
Edinburgh EH1 1BW
(031) 225 5756

Edinburgh Fringe
Box Office
180 High Street
Edinburgh EH1 1QS
(031) 226 5257

EcoSafaris
148 Gloucester Road
London
SW7 4SZ
(071) 370 5032

Ecuador Travel Ltd
37 Great Marlborough Street
London
WIV IHA
(071) 439 7861

Elegant Resorts
Lion House
23 Watergate Row
Chester
CHI 2LE
(0244) 329671

Equity Cruises and Paquet
    Cruises
77–79 Great Eastern Street
London EC2A 3HU
(071) 729 1929

Exodus Expeditions
9 Weir Road
London SW12 OLT
(081) 675 5550

Exotic Islands Holidays
35 High Street
Tring
Hertfordshire
HP23 4AB
(0442) 891551

Explorandes
Avenue Bolognesi 159
Lima 18
Peru
South America
(010) 51 14 469889

ExplorAsia
13 Chapter Street
London
SWIP 4NY
(071) 630 7102

Explore Worldwide Ltd
1 Frederick Street
Aldershot
Hampshire
GUII IBH
(0252) 319448

Far East Travel Centre
3 Lower John Street
London
WIA 4XE
(071) 734 7050

Fine Art Courses Ltd
15 Savile Row
London
WIX IAE
(071) 437 8553

French Travel Service and
    Air France
Geordian House
69 Boston Manor Road
Middlesex
TW8 9JQ
(081) 568 6981

Goodwill Holidays Ltd
Manor Chambers
The Green
School Lane
Welwyn
Hertfordshire
AL6 9EB
(0438) 716421

Goodwood Travel Ltd
Concorde House
Stour Street
Canterbury
CTI 2NZ
(0227) 763336

Grass Roots Travel Ltd
8 Lindsay Road
Hampton Hill
Middlesex
TW12 2DR
(081) 941 5753

GTF Tours
182–186 Kensington Church Street
London
W8 4DP
(071) 229 2474

Guerba Expeditions Ltd
101 Eden Vale Road
Westbury
Wiltshire
BA13 3QX
(0373) 826611

Hawaiian Magic
Gold Medal Travel Group Ltd
Gold Medal House
Metropolitan Drive
Preston New Road
Blackpool
FY3 9LT
(0253) 792200

Hayes & Jarvis Travel Ltd
152 King Street
London
W6 0QU
(081) 748 5050

Hebridean Island Cruises Ltd
Bank Newton
Skipton
North Yorkshire
BD23 3NT
(0756) 748077

Himalayan Kingdoms Ltd
20 The Mall
Clifton
Bristol
BS8 4DR
(0272) 237163

Holiday Islands
125 East Barnet Road
New Barnet
Hertfordshire
EN4 8RF
(081) 441 4064

Hoseasons Holidays
Sunway House
Lowestoft
NR32 3LT
(0502) 500555

Iberia Airlines
29 Glasshouse Street
London W1R 5RG
(071) 437 9822

Icelandair
172 Tottenham Court Road
London W1P 9LG
(071) 388 5599

Ilkeston Consumer Co-op Society Ltd
Travel Department
12 South Street
Ilkeston
Derbyshire
DE7 5SG
(0602) 323686

India Dream Holidays
PO Box 145
5 Denmark Street
London
WC2H 8LP
(071) 836 2059

Inghams Travel
10–18 Putney Hill
London
SW15 6AX
(081) 789 6555

Inn Travel
The Old Station
Helmsley
York YO6 5BZ
(0439) 71111

Inscape Fine Art Tours
Austins Farm, High Street
Stonesfield
Oxon OX7 2PU
(099389) 726

Intasun
PO Box 228
Bromley
Kent
BRI ILA
(0274) 760022

Intourist Moscow Ltd
219 Marsh Wall
Isle of Dogs
London E14 9FJ
(071) 538 8600

Italia nel Mondo Travel Services Ltd
6 Palace Street
London SWIE 5HY
(071) 828 9171

Japanese Airlines (JAL)
JCT International UK Ltd
Hanover Court
5 Hanover Square
London
WIR ODH
(071) 408 1000

Japan Travel Bureau UK Ltd
190 Strand
London WC2R IDT
(071) 836 9367

Jetsave Travel Ltd
Sussex House
London Road
East Grinstead
West Sussex
RH19 ILD
(0342) 312033 (Reservations)
(0342) 328231 (Brochure)
(0342) 327711 (Flight only)

Jetset
Jetset House
74 New Oxford Street
London WCIA IEU
(071) 631 0501

Journey Latin America
16 Devonshire Road
Chiswick
London W4 2HD
(081) 747 3108

Keith Prowse
103 Waterloo Road
London SEI 8UL
(071) 928 1292

Kenya Airtours
see under Airtours plc

Kirker Travel Ltd
3 New Concordia Wharf
Mill Street
London SEI 2BB
(071) 231 3333

Kuoni Travel Ltd
Kuoni House
Dorking
Surrey RH5 4AZ
(0306) 740888

Longshot Golf Holidays
see under Silk Cut Travel

Magic of Italy Ltd
227 Shepherds Bush Road
London W6 7AS
(081) 748 7575 (Reservations)
(081) 748 4999 (Administration)

Magic of the Orient, The
418a London House
26–40 Kensington High Street
London W8 4PF
(071) 937 5885

Major & Mrs Holt's Battlefield Tours
15 Market Street
Sandwich
Kent CT13 9DA
(0304) 612248

Maldive Travel
3 Esher House
11 Edith Terrace
London SW10 0TH
(071) 352 2246/351 9351

Mason International Travel
see under Canada Air Holidays

Meon Villa Holidays
see under Silk Cut Travel

Moroccan Sun
Suite 202, 2nd Floor
Triumph House
189 Regent Street
London W1R 7WB
(071) 437 3968

Neilson Leisure
Arndale House
Otley Road
Headingly
Leeds
LS6 2UU
(0345) 089383

Norwegian Cruise Line
229 Shepherds Bush Road
London
W6 7NL
(071) 408 0046

Ocean Cruise Lines and Pearl Cruises Ltd
10 Frederick Close
Stanhope Place
London W2 2HD
(071) 724 7555

Osprey Holidays Ltd
110b St Stephen Street
Edinburgh EH3 5AQ
(031) 226 2467

Page & Moy Ltd
136–140 London Road
Leicester LE2 1EN
(0533) 542000

Paquet Cruises
see under Equity Cruises

Paris Travel Service Ltd
see British Travel Service

Par-Tee Tours
Fairway House
North Road
Chorleywood
Hertfordshire
WD3 5LE
(0927) 84558

Pearl Cruises Ltd
see under Ocean Cruise Lines

Pickfords Travel
400 Great Cambridge Road
Enfield
Middlesex
EN1 3RZ
(081) 366 1211

Pleasure Seekers Ltd
52 Haymarket
London SW1Y 4RP
(071) 930 3903

P&O and Canberra Cruises
77 New Oxford Street
London WC1A 1PP
(071) 831 1331 (Reservations)
(071) 831 1234 (General Enquiries)

Polorbis Travel Ltd
82 Mortimer Street
Regent Street
London W1N 7DE
(071) 636 2217

Poundstretcher
Atlantic House
Hazelwick Avenue
Three Bridges
Crawley
West Sussex RH10 1NP
(0293) 519233

Prospect Music and Art Ltd
454–458 Chiswick High Road
London W4 5TT
(081) 995 2163/2151/
742 2323

Quo Vadis Ltd
243 Euston Road
London NW1 2BT
(071) 387 6122

Railway Travel and Photography
(RT&P)
Daton House
Park Street
Stafford
ST17 4AL
(0785) 57740
Fax (0785) 57238

Rajasthan Express
Central Reservation Office
36 Chandralok
Janpath
New Delhi – 110 001
India

Redwing Holidays,
Sovereign Golf
Groundstar House
London Road
Crawley
West Sussex
RH10 2TB
(0293) 560777

Romanian Holidays Ltd
54 Pembroke Road
London
W8 6NX
(071) 602 7093

Royal Caribbean Cruises
Bishops Palace House
2a Riverside Walk
Kingston-upon-Thames
KT1 1QN
(081) 541 5044
Fax (081) 546 8803

Royal Viking Line UK Ltd
229-243 Shepherds Bush
Road
London
W6 7NL
(071) 734 0773

Sally Line Ltd
Argyle Centre
York Street
Ramsgate
CT11 9DS
(0843) 595522

Sandals Resorts
161 Fulham Road
London
SW3 6SN
(071) 581 9895

Scottish Highland Railway
Company Ltd
42a Queen Street
Edinburgh
Scotland
EH2 3PS
(031) 220 6441
Fax (031) 220 6422

Select Holidays
ILG Travel Ltd
Centurion House
Bircherley Street
Hertford
SG14 1BH
(0992) 553711

Serenissima Travel Ltd
21 Dorset Square
London
NW1 6QG
(071) 730 9841

Sherpa Expeditions
131a Heston Road
Hounslow
Middlesex
TW5 0RD
(081) 577 2717

Silk Cut Travel, Longshot
  Golf Holidays, Meon Villa
  Holidays
Meon House
College Street
Petersfield
Hampshire
GU32 3JN
(0730) 65211
(0730) 66561 (Longshot)
(0730) 68411 (Meon)

Singapore Airlines
580-586 Chiswick High Road
London W4 5RB
(071) 995 4901

Ski Vacations
30-32 Cross Street
London N1 2BG
(071) 359 3511

Society Expeditions
see under Twickers World

Sovereign
see under Redwing

Sovereign Golf
see under Redwing

Speedbird
  ALTA Holidays Ltd
Pacific House
Hazelwick Avenue
Three Bridges
Crawley
West Sussex
RH10 1NP
(0293) 611444

SSS International
138 Eversholt Street
London NW1 1BL
(071) 388 1732

Steamond Travel
23 Eccleston Street
London SW1 9LX
(071) 730 8640/8646

Sunsail International
The Port House
Port Solent
Portsmouth
Hampshire
PO6 4TH
(0705) 210345

Swan Hellenic
77 New Oxford Street
London WC1A 1PP
(071) 831 1515

TEFS
77 Frederick Street
Loughborough
Leicestershire
LE11 3TL
(0509) 262745

Thomas Cook Group Ltd
PO Box 36
Thorpe Wood
Peterborough
PE3 6SB
(0733) 330111

Thomson Holidays Ltd
Greater London House,
Hampstead Road,
London NW1 7SD
(071) 387 9321

Time Off
2a Chester Close
Chester Street
London SW1X 7BQ
(071) 235 8070

Tradewinds Faraway Holidays
Station House
81–83 Fulham High Street
London SW6 3JP
(071) 731 8000

Transglobal
64 Kenway Road
London SW5 0RD
(071) 244 8571

Appendix III Hotels

British Country House Hotels

Airds Hotel
  Port Appin
  Appin
  Argyll
  Scotland PA38 4DF
  (0631) 73236

Cliveden
  Taplow
  Berkshire SL6 0JF
  (0628) 668561

Cromlix House
  Kinbuck
  Dunblane
  Perthshire
  Scotland FK15 9JT
  (0786) 822125

Ettington Park
  Alderminster
  Near Stratford-upon-Avon
  Warwickshire CV37 8BS
  (0789) 740740

Middlethorpe Hall
  Bishopthorpe Road
  York YO2 1QB
  (0904) 641241

Hotel Groups

Ciga Hotels
  Internation Hotel
    Representatives Ltd
  67–68 Jermyn Street
  London SW1Y 6NY
  (071) 930 4147

Hotels of Distinction
  109 Tottenham Court Road
  London W1P 9HG
  (071) 387 1555

Leading Hotels of the World
  15 New Bridge Street
  London EC4V 6AU
  (071) 583 1712

Mount Charlotte Hotels
  2 The Calls
  Leeds
  LS2 7JU
  (0800) 700 400 (free of charge)

Orient Express Hotels Ltd
  Suite 200
  Hudson's Place
  Victoria Station
  London
  SW1V 1JL
  (071) 834 8122

Prestige Hotels
  21 Blades Court
  Deodar Road
  London
  SW15 2NU
  (081) 877 9500

Sherman House Hotel (San Francisco)
  Contact the US Tourist Board

Trusthouse Forte Hotels
  24–30 New Street
  Aylesbury
  Buckinghamshire
  HP20 2NW
  (081) 567 3444

*Also available from
Mandarin Paperbacks*

ALISON RICE

Travel Tips & Holiday Hints

Small print in English is as small as small print in Arabic, and not quite as pretty. Alison Rice explains the finer points of getting about for today's traveller.

- Don't put your home address on your luggage on the outward journey – it pinpoints an empty house for an eagle-eyed thief

- Self-caterers bound for Yugoslavia should pack a jar of coffee. The local stuff doubles as insect repellent

- If you're taking two bikinis with you, make sure they're the same shape – no funny white bits!

- Buy an insurance policy that has a manned 24-hour telephone number for emergencies

- Use toothpaste as an emergency antiseptic

- Pay as much as possible of the cost of your holiday by credit card. Then you're covered if the tour operator goes bankrupt.

From choosing the right holiday, knowing what to pack, advising on insurance and giving a complete country-by-country breakdown of what to expect around the globe, *Travel Tips* is an invaluable part of your hand luggage.

Alison Rice is a regular columnist for *The Observer* and *Mail On Sunday*, a frequent presenter on local and national radio and a seasoned traveller.

A Selected List of Non-Fiction Available from Mandarin

While every effort is made to keep prices low, it is sometimes necessary to increase prices at short notice. Mandarin Paperbacks reserves the right to show new retail prices on covers which may differ from those previously advertised in the text or elsewhere.

The prices shown below were correct at the time of going to press.

☐	7493 0109 0	**The Warrior Queens**	Antonia Fraser £4.99
☐	7493 0108 2	**Mary Queen of Scots**	Antonia Fraser £5.99
☐	7493 0010 8	**Cromwell**	Antonia Fraser £7.50
☐	7493 0106 6	**The Weaker Vessel**	Antonia Fraser £5.99
☐	7493 0014 0	**The Demon Drink**	Jancis Robinson £4.99
☐	7493 0016 7	**Vietnam – The 10,000 Day War**	Michael Maclear £3.99
☐	7493 0061 2	**Voyager**	Yeager/Rutan £3.99
☐	7493 0113 9	**Peggy Ashcroft**	Michael Billington £3.99
☐	7493 0177 5	**The Troubles**	Mick O'Connor £4.99
☐	7493 0004 3	**South Africa**	Graham Leach £3.99
☐	7493 0254 2	**Families and How to Survive Them**	Creese/Skynner £5.99
☐	7493 0060 4	**The Fashion Conspiracy**	Nicolas Coleridge £3.99
☐	7493 0179 1	**The Tao of Pooh**	Benjamin Hoff £2.99
☐	7493 0000 0	**Moonwalk**	Michael Jackson £2.99

All these books are available at your bookshop or newsagent, or can be ordered direct from the publisher. Just tick the titles you want and fill in the form below.

Mandarin Paperbacks, Cash Sales Department, PO Box 11, Falmouth, Cornwall TR10 9EN.

Please send cheque or postal order, no currency, for purchase price quoted and allow the following for postage and packing:

UK   80p for the first book, 20p for each additional book ordered to a maximum charge of £2.00.

BFPO   80p for the first book, 20p for each additional book.

Overseas   £1.50 for the first book, £1.00 for the second and 30p for each additional book
including Eire thereafter.

NAME (Block letters) ....

ADDRESS ....

....

....